Egg quality – current problems and recent advances

Poultry Science Symposium Number Twenty

Poultry Science Symposium Series

Executive Editor (Volumes 1–18): B. M. Freeman

*Out of print

Volumes 1–18 may be ordered from

Carfax Publishing Company
PO Box 25, Abingdon, Oxfordshire OX14 3UE, England

Volumes 19 and 20 may be ordered from

Butterworths
Borough Green, Sevenoaks, Kent TN15 8PH, England

The cover design shows a mosaic of a cockerel from 1st Century BC (Burrell Collection, Glasgow)

Egg Quality – Current Problems and Recent Advances

Poultry Science Symposium Number Twenty

R. G. Wells
National Institute of Poultry Husbandry, Harper Adams Agricultural College, Newport. Shropshire

and

C. G. Belyavin
Harper Adams Poultry Research Unit, Edgmond, Newport, Shropshire

Butterworths

London Boston Durban Singapore Sydney Toronto Wellington

First published 1987

© **Butterworth & Co. (Publishers) Ltd, 1987**

British Library Cataloguing in Publication Data

Egg quality : current problems and recent
   advances.—(Poultry science symposium
series; no. 20)
1. Eggs—Grading
I. Wells, R.G.   II. Belyavin, C.G.
III. Series
637'.541   SF490.7
ISBN 0–407–00470–X

Library of Congress Cataloging-in-Publication Data

Poultry Science Symposium (20th : 1985 : Harper Adams
   Agricultural College)
   Egg quality—current problems and recent advances.

   (Poultry science symposium ; no. 20)
   Papers from a symposium held at Harper Adams
Agricultural College, Newport, Shropshire, 3–6
September 1985 and organized by the United Kingdom Branch
of the World's Poultry Science Association in
collaboration with Working Group No. 4 of the European
Federation of the Association.
   Bibliography: p.
   Includes index.
   1. Eggs—Quality—Congresses.   I. Wells, R. G.
II. Belyavin, C. G.   III. World's Poultry Science
Association. United Kingdom Branch.   IV. European
Federation of the World Poultry Science Association.
Working Group No. 4.   V. Title.   VI. Series.
SF490.7.P68   1985   637'.5   86–20795
ISBN 0–407–00470–X

Phototypeset by Scribe Design, Gillingham, Kent
Printed and bound in England by Robert Hartnoll (1985) Ltd, Bodmin, Cornwall

Preface

This volume contains the papers of the 20th Poultry Science Symposium which was held at Harper Adams Agricultural College, Newport, Shropshire on 3–6 September 1985. This series of Symposia is now organised by the United Kingdom Branch of the World's Poultry Science Association. The 20th was run in collaboration with Working Group No. 4 of the European Federation of the Association. Members of the Organising Committee are listed below.

The 20th Symposium was on 'Egg quality—current problems and recent advances' and had four main sections. The first was concerned with the nutritive value of eggs and their dietary significance, including a discussion on the cholesterol issue. This was in response to the increasing interest of consumers in the health aspects of their food. The second section provided a review on egg quality assessment, both in commercial practice and in the laboratory. In section three the biological basis of egg quality was analysed with reference to shell formation and pigmentation, yolk lipid composition and albumen structure. Section four comprised a review of recent developments in the control of egg quality through manipulations of the hen's genetic make-up, laying cycle, physical and climatic environment, nutrition and health status. The emphasis in the last three sections was on work undertaken and reported since 1967 when the fourth Symposium in this series covered a similar field of study under the title 'Egg quality—a study of the hen's egg'.

The 17 chapters of this volume have been written by acknowledged experts in their fields, drawn from Belgium, Canada, France, Israel and the Netherlands as well as from the United Kingdom. They should prove to be of great value to anyone involved in the production, marketing or utilisation of eggs.

ORGANISING COMMITTEE
20th Poultry Science Symposium

R.G. Wells (Chairman)
T.E. Whittle (Treasurer)
C.G. Belyavin
D.R. Charles
D.H. Cross
C. Fisher
A. Oosterwoud
H.D. Raine
A.H. Sykes

Acknowledgements

Financial support for this symposium is gratefully acknowledged from:

BEMB Research and Education Trust
British Poultry Science
Eggs Authority
Goldenlay Eggs
Hubbard Poultry UK
ISA Poultry Services
Joice and Hill
MSD Agvet
Poultry International
Ross Breeders
SAPPA Chicks
Shaver Poultry Breeding Farms (UK)
Thames Valley Eggs

Contributors

C.G. Belyavin
Harper Adams Poultry Research Unit, Edgmond, Newport, Shropshire, TF10 8HY, England

K.N. Boorman
University of Nottingham School of Agriculture, Sutton Bonington, Loughborough, Leicestershire, LE12 5RD, England

G. Bulfield
Institute of Animal Physiology and Genetics Research, Edinburgh Research Station, Roslin, Midlothian, EH25 9PS, Scotland

E. Decuypere
Laboratory for Physiology of Domestic Animals, Catholic University of Leuven, Kardinaal Mercierlaan 92, B-3030 Heverlee, Belgium

P. Hunton
The Ontario Egg Producers' Marketing Board, 7195 Millcreek Drive, Mississauga, Ontario L5N 4H1, Canada

S. Hurwitz
Institute of Animal Science, Agricultural Research Organisation, The Volcani Center, PO Box 6, Bet Dagan-50-200, Israel

G. Huyghebaert
Government Agricultural Research Centre, Station for Small Animal Husbandry, Burg. Van Gansberghelaan 92, 9220 Mereobeke, Belgium

J.C. McKay
Institute of Animal Physiology and Genetics Research, Edinburgh Research Station, Roslin, Midlothian, EH25 9PS, Scotland

J.H. Moore
Department of Biochemistry and Physiology, Wye College, University of London, Ashford, Kent TN25 5AH, England

R.C. Noble
The Hannah Research Institute, Ayr, KA6 5HL, Scotland

A. Oosterwoud
Spelderholt Centre for Poultry Research and Extension, 7361 DA Beekbergen, The Netherlands

N.D. Overfield
Ministry of Agriculture, ADAS, Government Buildings, Lawnswood, Leeds, LS16 5PY, England

M. Picard
Station de Recherches Avicoles—INRA, Nouzilly, 37380 Monnaie, France

D.S. Robinson
Procter Department of Food Science, University of Leeds, Leeds, LS2 9JT, England

B. Sauveur
Station de Recherches Avicoles—INRA, Nouzilly, 37380 Monnaie, France

D.H. Shrimpton
Belmington Close, 68 North End, Meldreth, Royston, Hertfordshire, SG8 6NT, England

Sally E. Solomon
Department of Veterinary Anatomy, University of Glasgow Veterinary School, Bearsden Road, Bearsden, Glasgow G61, Scotland

D. Spackman
MAFF Central Veterinary Laboratory, New Haw, Weybridge, Surrey, KT15 3NB, England

S.G. Tullett
The West of Scotland Agricultural College. Auchincruive, Ayr, KA7 4ET, Scotland

H. Tunstall-Pedoe
Cardiovascular Epidemiology Unit, Ninewells Hospital and Medical School, Dundee, DD1 9SY, Scotland

G. Verheyen
Laboratory for Physiology of Domestic Animals, Catholic University of Leuven, Kardinaal Mercierlaan 92, B-3030 Heverlee, Belgium

J. Volynchook
University of Nottingham School of Agriculture, Sutton Bonington, Loughborough, Leicestershire, LE12 5RD, England

K.J. Webb
The Eggs Authority, Union House, Eridge Road, Tunbridge Wells, Kent, TN4 8HF, England

Contents

Opening address

Chapter 1

Egg quality—in production, marketing and consumption

K.J. Webb

I hope you all know a little about our great national game, cricket, because in preparing this opening address I imagined myself to be the 'groundsman' helping to ensure that the 'wicket' is provided for the enjoyment of the professionals who are going to play upon it during the next three days. I am even reminded that three days is often not long enough for the result to be conclusive in cricket. At least on this occasion the weather is not likely to intervene, and it is to be hoped that by the close of this Symposium there will be a 'victory' for one point of view or the other. This will ensure that the poultry industry is offered some very definite guidelines for the re-advancement of the egg component within this immensely important food segment of the farming and retailing sectors of the distribution chain; in line with the rapidly changing interests of the ultimate customer—the consumer.

I intend to divide what I wish to say into three non-technical 'ingredients': the subject matter under review; the present state of the UK industry; and the renewal of consumer faith.

The subject matter under review

First of all what about this undefinitive word 'quality'. Of course all dictionaries do give one definition or another, and the English precis often is shown as 'grade of goodness'. 'Goodness' is said to mean 'excellence', which in turn is explained as *'good in high degree'*, and that phrase could probably be accepted as defining quality. But no matter what words are recorded on the subject I believe that for the uninvolved, that is those who are not actively concerned with an authoritative standard, quality is a matter of personal perception. And what is perception? It is defined as the 'reception of a stimulus through the five senses'. These are, of course, sight, taste and touch (the ones we initiate), and hearing and smell (the ones that force themselves upon us).

In any commercial transaction, which includes the simple purchasing of half a dozen eggs in a grocer's shop or the ordering of egg and chips in a restaurant, the perception of 'value', a kind of sixth sense, has a major influence.

So what does 'value' mean? It is defined as 'intrinsic worth or goodness, and the recognition of such worth or goodness'. Therefore whether the purchaser is seeking quality or value it seems that *'goodness'* is the linking perception and, in the case of eggs, the senses in need of stimulation are those of sight, taste and smell. As quality is often considered to be in conflict with quantity, it is also possible that some of the quantity aspirations of egg producers may well constitute a negative from the quality standpoint, unless quality considerations are always given due priority. It is wise therefore that much of the discussion during this Symposium is likely to be concerned with an understanding of that priority.

When I referred to 'those concerned with an authoritative standard' I had in mind the legislators in particular, those who have given the consumer the delight of choosing between seven sizes of egg rather than the restriction of 'large, medium or small' and who have now introduced the opportunity to choose eggs from the 'perchery'! Any connection between the legislator's perception of quality and that of the ultimate consumer is often difficult to appreciate.

Next I would like to comment on the 'production, marketing and consumption' aspects. And I must admit that here, if I am not very careful, I shall be accused of being authoritative, just like those legislators! After a lifetime in what is often loosely called 'marketing', I have begun to consider myself as something of an expert, and experts are rather inclined to be definitive, as some of you may realise! Marketing is not about 'going to market'; nor is it something that can be added in the warehouse, or the retail outlet, after the goods have been produced; nor is it simply concerned with publicity or selling. Rather it is the thought process and means by which business opportunities are searched for and the appropriate actions then taken to profit from those opportunities by making available the chosen products or services. The interaction and interdependence between production, distribution and retailing activities—and the amount to be allocated to publicity—should always be related to a previously agreed marketing strategy.

The basic role of marketing can be equally applicable to branded or non-branded (often called generic) products and it needs to be understood by producers as much as by the distributors or retailers who are usually much closer to the end customer or consumer. All this may sound very academic but it has to be constantly brought to mind in any discussion remotely connected with the farming industry because farmers, who are so patient during the growing or breeding cycles, tend to snatch at short-term sales opportunities with little or no regard to any longer term marketing strategy. And just imagine how wasteful a very short-term attitude can be to any previously well conceived research programme!

So in all that I say from now onwards please accept that I view marketing not as the link between production and consumption but as the overall influence. Please also accept that I am expressing my own views and not any official guidelines from the UK Eggs Authority.

The present state of the UK industry

It might be somewhat extreme to immediately think of emotive words to describe the present state of the UK egg market so I will content myself with 'temporarily in a state of receding standstill'! Egg consumption in the UK has been on an overall downward trend for some years now, although there have been some signs of a halt to this trend in recent times. I do not intend to burden you with too many statistics. However, just to show that eggs have not been suffering on their own perhaps I should quote a few figures illustrating the weekly consumption for a number of staple foods (*see Table 1.1*).

During this same period fruit, potatoes, poultry and fish have remained quite steady and the only example of a comparable food moving in the other direction is

Table 1.1 Weekly consumption per person of some foods (National Food Survey data)

	1980	1981	1982	1983	1984
Eggs (No.)	3.69	3.68	3.51	3.53	3.21
Sugar (oz)	11.17	11.08	10.31	9.84	9.15
Liquid milk (pt)	4.10	3.94	3.90	3.71	3.53
Butter (oz)	4.05	3.69	3.17	3.27	2.87
Beef and veal (oz)	8.13	6.96	7.06	6.57	6.27
Bacon and ham (oz)	4.20	4.14	3.95	4.02	3.58

1 oz = 28.35 g; 1 pt = 0.5683 l.

fruit juice. Since 1984 there has been a considerable increase in the written and spoken word in favour of the desirability of 'healthy living'. Many so-called 'fads' in eating habits of recent years are becoming fashionable. You no longer have to be a health food fanatic to adopt a 'healthy eating style' hence, for example, the increase in fruit juice consumption. Furthermore, the housewife is looking more and more for products that will cook easily in her microwave, electric grill, or convection oven (and minimise the chore of cleaning cooking utensils). Coincidentally the large family meal is going out of fashion as each individual in the family unit, including mother, 'does their own thing' and eats what they like when they wish.

Quite apart from these rapidly changing in-home eating habits there are equally important changes taking place all the time in the UK retailing of groceries and cooked food. Already in the 1960s and 1970s there was a move away from customer service in the food retailing sector towards the dominance of a few very large and powerful multiple groups who provide in a variety of forms what is called 'one-stop self service'. The 1980s has seen a further concentration of retail power as the leading groups place a greater emphasis on fresh foods, taking business from most fishmongers, many bakers, and some greengrocers and butchers. Now an alternative method of food shopping is developing which features flexible and convenient opening hours, e.g. '7 to 11' or '8 'til late'. The size of these new convenience outlets limits the range of items on offer, and they tend to concentrate on fast turnover or high margin items. These shops are not so likely to feature many fresh foods as they will not be keen to run the risk of wastage. Even the equally newly developing 'bulk food' stores will tend to avoid the 'run of the mill' fresh foods, although the unusual, such as 'free-range' eggs, may coincide with the image these stores desire. The rise in the number of farm shops and roadside stalls selling fresh home-grown produce may well have peaked and there is some talk about farmers and multiple retailers getting together to establish 'farm-fresh' counters in corners of stores. Obviously this would be an opportunity for eggs to be presented 'naturally' and to attract more attention than they sometimes do in their little boxes!

On the confusing question of packaging styles as they currently exist I can do no better than quote Norman Overfield, the ADAS egg quality specialist, who will be speaking later (*see* Chapter 5) and who wrote earlier this year: 'Twenty years ago egg packs were of little significance to the UK egg industry. Keyes trays and pulp packs of basic structure and design were considered adequate as a means of conveying eggs to the customer. However, when the Egg Marketing Board was disbanded and a free market established everyone from the large packers to the small producer/retailer began to experiment with alternative types of pack in order to strive to achieve an advantage. One large packer has claimed that they were obliged to stock over 500 types of pack at any one time! What other product is presented to the buyer in so many different ways? The present disarray reflects a marketing weakness which needs to be sorted out.' I completely support Norman's concern and I even heard a buyer for one of the top three multiples insist that he had only to ask to be offered any packaging style 'his fancy turned to'. Surely there is need for some objective market research, not to find out new ways of being different, but to discover the ultimate pack style that will both protect and present, with allowable compromise between these two requirements.

Now I wish to direct attention for a few moments to the current state of the UK 'eating out' market. Over the period 1975–81 the average number of meals eaten out/person/week showed an 8% increase and, although since then far fewer meals are eaten out at the place of work or in the schools, the commercial fast-food and pub-food sectors have certainly continued to expand. Both these sectors are potentially excellent markets for eggs and egg products. Hence, the Egg Authority's activities currently include a very comprehensive programme of promotion in the catering trade and, in conjunction with Food from Britain, sponsorship of some research into possible increased usage of eggs in added value foodstuffs.

Before leaving this section, I would like to comment on the present 'state of mind' of that 'average' consumer concerning eggs and the egg industry. Remember that 'state of mind' relates to perception, and perception usually derives from matters that can be perceived to be real. The present generation has grown up in the era, uniquely in the UK, of the brown egg. Eggs are always brown and ideally uniformly brown. To my amazement, one day I watched a lady in a supermarket opening her half a dozen box of eggs and taking from a nearby stack of loose eggs two or three eggs she considered to be more uniformly brown than two or three in the box, and swapping them! Has the industry deceived the consuming public into believing that such uniformity is desirable to the point where they actually perceive the brown egg is also more nutritious? Even though in the beginning the industry may have been attracted to the higher price they might achieve for brown eggs, has all the effort to achieve the perfect brown egg been worth it when the end result is to make all eggs look alike? I cannot see the bread industry giving up the sales advantage of allowing the customer choice between white and brown. Another misconception in the minds of many consumers is that the colour of the yolk is an indicator of nutritional value and a growing misconception is that eggs from free-range hens are always fresher. Consumers also believe that eggs sold from Keyes trays are produced under free-range conditions! And that eggs sold in farm shops are from free-range hens! And what they believe about the relative benefits of size of egg does not bear thinking about! And in any case what should they think? It is confusing enough for them to be faced with making the choice from between the four or five sizes often available in the supermarket where over 25% of all eggs are sold.

Then there are the concerns about battery cages and those frightening words cholesterol and salmonella. So a few favourable words about eggs will not be out of place. They have a lot going for them, with the highest quality food protein which, from a Size 3 egg, contributes 11% of the recommended daily amount of protein accompanied by less than 6% of the maximum intake of fat recommended by COMA (1984). The fat itself has proportionally less saturated fatty acids than the maximum desirable as also recommended by COMA (1984). Then there is the comprehensive range of vitamins and minerals. But if I go on I shall be trespassing on the subject of papers to follow.

The renewal of consumer faith

Now to turn to the more positive part of my task—the future needs, including, just possibly, research and development from people like you—based, of course, on a previously agreed marketing strategy!

You may be wondering why I have chosen the heading 'The renewal of consumer faith'—am I some kind of evangelist? Well perhaps I am when it comes to dealing with the practical, everyday needs of the consuming public. The more my mind dwelt on the future of the UK eggs industry, the more I was certain that there could only be any hope of a re-advancement of that industry through determined and cohesive moves to improve the quality of performance throughout the chain of production and distribution. Then there might be a renewal of the faith of the public at large. A faith that has been lost to a considerable extent by all the adverse, and slanted, publicity concerning issues such as animal welfare, and various health scares. The day of judgement is here and urgent steps must be taken if the public is not to drift further away towards other faiths, for instance, in the ever increasing range of 'new' foods. There has to be a cohesive and consistent programme of quality improvement and educational promotion. A wise producer, or product owner, will ask himself, 'How much better can I make it for my customers?', and only then 'How much more profit will it earn me?'. A programme of real quality improvement should have as its aim the increase in 'functional' performance leading to the satisfaction of the consumer.

You may recall that I chose to define quality as *degree of goodness*. I did not state which degree. We all read in product publicity descriptions such as top, best, special, highest, superior, but none of these adjectives have any statutory meaning and really tend to seek out the gullability in the readers. That does not mean that producers should not seek to offer superior performance or value standards, so long as such a description stands for the genuine ability of the product to perform its functions, *as seen by* the consumer.

Although consumers may be accused of making very subjective judgements, their measures of quality do normally emanate from direct experience. When these expectations relate to a product in daily use, such as an egg, they must be given the respect they deserve by any producer wishing to prosper. He or she should not concentrate on the physiology of the bird on the farm, or on productivity improvements, to the exclusion of sufficient concern for quality standards.

This does not mean that if, for instance, 3–4% of the buying public feel that only free range eggs offer the 'degree of goodness' they desire that all egg producers should revamp their system to free range. The other 96% may well be quite content with their perception of 'goodness' and will go on being so provided they obtain that satisfaction consistently. I stress 'consistently' and not 'uniformly' because I believe there is an important point of issue here. If eggs are to be looked upon as a fresh natural food then consistency of performance, within certain laid down parameters, may be much more important as a quality determinant than, for instance, unnatural uniformity of size or colour. I happen to believe that undue attention to uniformity, or sameness, of product has not helped to maintain consumer appeal. Rather it has tended to make eggs look like just another manufactured food item. Often only the picture and the words on the package differentiate one half dozen from another in the next shop. Again I criticise the EEC size grading regulations for adding to this 'manufactured' appearance. Of course, there is a desire for uniformity when it concerns egg shells not cracking in transit or when being boiled, and annoyingly(!) consumers do want shells to crack open easily for cooking. Recently I read that the UK industry loses £12 million a year on eggs that break long before getting anywhere near the frying pan! Consumers also seek consistency, but not necessarily uniformity, in the cooked product and most of all they seek, as the absolute 'degree of goodness', *freshness*—and in technical terms that usually means good albumen quality.

In order for the egg industry to offer consistent freshness, which has to be more important than consistent colour or size, it will probably be necessary to rethink the temperature control measures throughout the production and distribution chain. I realise that some thought is being given to this factor, especially in distribution, with the increasing availability of farm cooled eggs. I have already spoken of the need to settle on the ultimate pack design that will both protect and present. By 'present' I mean attract purchase. Again I am delighted to hear about some very serious efforts in this direction. It is sometimes said that 'eggs are not what they were' and certainly this has to be true in the UK if we think back 50 years. But neither are consumers the same and they may have changed more over the same period. And this change has been accentuated by the arrival on the breakfast or dining table of so many new foods with many varied 'plus' ingredients. Breakfast cereals are fortified with vitamins and minerals and make use of this addition in their very heavy advertising campaigns. Maybe this addition is of no real value but it certainly sounds good and better than anything the egg has had to offer in recent years, with its dependence on colour change. If for purely aesthetic reasons the brown egg is going to remain the panacea in the UK, I would only caution about going too far down the colour grade chart towards the sudden dramatic introduction of the 'black egg'! Then the yolk obviously must appeal aesthetically but is it really known whether the colour should match with the brown of the shell or the white of the albumen! This is not such a light-hearted point as it may sound and maybe it is time that the marketing experts in the industry gave some guidance to the feed compounders.

There certainly seems to me to be a need for several new means of monitoring the key quality control issues. For instance, an objective test for freshness which more closely reflects the flavour experience and which is an improvement on the present Haugh unit test. And how about an improved technique to replace the traditional method of candling, and greater knowledge on what stops a shell forming or being too thin? Many improvements of this kind are needed if the industry is to profit from the increasing interest of consumers in 'healthy eating' and their apparent willingness to pay a little more for the assurance of quality. Notwithstanding the probable continued existence of the welfare issues the 'consistent assurance of quality' is the key to the renewal of consumer faith.

This, plus steps that: (1) present a 'freshness appeal' at the point-of-sale, (2) help housewives feel 'comfortable' in the kitchen with egg cooking, and (3) ensure the availability of quality egg products that will perform for the caterer, are the surest routes to increased consumption, and to the long term profitability of the egg industry.

Reference

COMMITTEE ON MEDICAL ASPECTS OF FOOD POLICY—COMA (1984). *Diet and Cardiovascular Disease*. Department of Health and Social Security, London, HMSO

Part I

Nutritive value of eggs and their dietary significance

Chapter 2

The nutritive value of eggs and their dietary significance

D.H. Shrimpton

Introduction

During the first half of this century, when most of the vitamins were characterised and the naturally occurring amino acids were identified, the hen's egg was recognised as a rich source of nutrients that were essential for maintaining human health. The ways in which these essential nutrients supported life gradually became understood as studies in intermediary metabolism developed and the vision grew that malnutrition could be overcome through application of the newly acquired knowledge.

A treatise published during this period (Pennington *et al.*, 1933) classified eggs as 'protective foods' since they contained nutrients which protected against certain deficiency diseases. However, the authors considered that eggs were of even more importance because, in addition to providing protection, they were 'positive builders of health and well-being'.

In a period of rapid advance in analytical techniques, which made possible an understanding of intermediary metabolism and the identification of the sources in commonly available foods of essential nutrients, it is not surprising that nutritional attitudes of the period were dominated by the need to provide dietary sources of essential amino acids and both fat and water soluble vitamins. It is less easy to understand why the attitude persists today where, for example, the expression 'first and second class protein' remains in use in some quarters whilst others reject the possibility that certain nutrients, though of value in limited quantities, may be harmful when consumed in excess.

For the animal nutritionist, and particularly for the poultry scientist, it comes as a surprise to realise that in debates on human nutrition a balanced diet has, until recently, been concerned with acquiring minimum amounts of each of a number of nutrients with little reference to the balance between them or to the possible consequences of excessive amounts of a few nutrients. However, even today there is relatively little information on the quantitative requirements of mature adult animals who are not lactating or reproducing; and this is the situation of the majority of the human population.

In the sections which follow a brief account will be given of the composition of the egg from a nutritional standpoint. The relevance of these nutrients to the diet of mankind will be reviewed and particular aspects of the composition of the egg will be considered in relation to current hypotheses concerned with diet and health.

Nutrient composition of the egg

A comprehensive and authoritative review of the chemical composition of the hen's egg was published by Brooks and Taylor in 1953 and there has been no need to revise the data quoted by them. Unfortunately the publication is no longer readily available. However, major components of nutritional interest were abstracted, recalculated to an egg weight of 62.5 g, the mid-point of Size 3 eggs, and published by the Eggs Authority (Shrimpton, 1983). This data is reproduced here in *Tables 2.1, 2.2* and *2.3*.

There are small differences in the amounts of certain components reported by different authors and, although these differences are unlikely to be nutritionally significant to a consumer, their origin should be made clear.

First, the absolute amount of the various nutrients present varies with the weight of the whole egg. Secondly, water vapour can pass through the shell at a variety of rates dependent upon the conditions of handling and storage. The changes can be

Table 2.1 The average composition of two-day old hen's eggs calculated for a Size 3 egg weighing 62.5 g

Component	Weight (g)	Proportion of intact egg (%)
White	35.8	57.3
Yolk	19.3	30.9
Shell	7.2	11.5
Loss on separation	0.2	0.3

Brooks and Taylor (1953) data adjusted to the mid-point of Size 3 eggs.

Table 2.2 Major nutritional constituents (in g) in a two-day old hen's egg calculated for a Size 3 egg weighing 62.5 g

Component	Total weight	Nitrogen	Protein	Fat	Dextrose
White	35.8	0.64	4.0	0.010	0.14
Yolk	19.3	0.52	2.6	6.33	0.03

Brooks and Taylor (1953) data adjusted to the mid-point of Size 3 eggs.

Table 2.3 The average fatty acid composition of egg-yolk lipids

Fatty acid	Amount expressed as a % of the total fatty acids	
	Triglycerides	Phospholipids
Saturated:		
C_{14} Myristic	0.7	—
C_{16} Palmitic	25.2	31.8
C_{18} Stearic	7.5	4.1
Unsaturated:		
C_{16} Palmitoleic	3.3	—
C_{18} Oleic	52.4	42.6
C_{18} Linoleic	8.6	8.2
C_{22} Clupanodonic	2.3	13.3
Total saturated	33.4	35.9
Total unsaturated	66.6	64.1

Brooks and Taylor (1953) data.

complex but the net result can be an increase in the weight of the yolk by up to 15%, chiefly from water gained from the white, and a substantial fall in the weight of the white from loss of water to the yolk and through the shell. Lastly, there is inevitably a small loss of constituents when the yolk, white and shell are separated from each other.

Brooks and Taylor (1953) noted the relatively high proportion of cholesterol (2.6–3.4%) in egg yolk and commented on its importance for the nutrition of the developing chick. Indeed it is necessary to keep in mind the fact that the egg is a key part of the life cycle of the bird and that its nutritional value to the human is coincidental. Board (1982) has in particular drawn attention to the biological significance of many aspects of the structure of the hen's egg shell, suggesting that it has been adapted to meet the demands of the environment of the nest cup. Hence changes in composition of the contents resulting from passage through the shell of gases, especially water vapour, need to be taken into account when the manufacturing characteristics of egg yolk and white are being forecast in the commercial preparation of foods.

The contents of vitamins reported by Brooks and Taylor (1953) tend to be low compared with the reports of current analyses, such as those quoted by Paul and Southgate (1978) and this is probably a consequence of the current habit of feeding supplements of vitamins to laying birds. Indeed Brooks and Taylor (1953) indicated the wide range of vitamin A to be expected in yolk, from 200 to 1000 i.u. (equivalent to 60–300 µg retinol) and of vitamin D from 5 to 70 i.u. (equivalent to 0.125–1.75 µg cholecalciferol). The mean values quoted by Paul and Southgate (1978) for vitamins A and D are 400 µg retinol and 5.0 µg cholecalciferol and these increased concentrations are further evidence of the impact of the nutrition of the hen on the nutritive value of her eggs in a human context.

Brooks and Taylor (1953) reported also on the contents of B vitamins and noted the absence of vitamin C. Of particular interest is their summary of the early literature of the century as reviewed by Romanoff and Romanoff (1949) for the content of trace elements in the hen's egg and their data are summarised in *Table 2.4*. Only the mean values of the ranges quoted are given because there is

Table 2.4 Trace elements in the hen's egg (µg/g)

Element	Yolk	White
Aluminium	2.7	0.1
Arsenic	0.2	trace[b]
Boron	trace[b]	1.2
Bromine	7.5	—
Copper	9.2 (3.0)[a]	0.3 (0.5)[a]
Fluorine	4.3	0.2
Iodine	2.7	0.4
Lead	8.1	6.1
Manganese	0.5	trace[b]
Molybdenum	trace[b]	0.1
Silicon	31	21
Strontium	trace[b]	trace[b]
Titanium	0.2	0.1
Vanadium	0.1	0.2
Zinc	45 (36)[a]	0.2 (0.3)[a]

[a]Numbers in brackets are from Paul and Southgate (1978).
[b]Trace = <0.1.
The values listed are the means of the ranges reported by Romanoff and Romanoff (1949) and quoted by Brooks and Taylor (1953).

uncertainty concerning the precision of the values reported due to the analytical techniques used in some instances. Nevertheless the data are of interest, even qualitatively, because of the concern sometimes expressed in relation to the supply of trace elements for the human with the increasing use of refined foods.

Recommended daily intakes of nutrients for the human population of the UK

In the United Kingdom governmental responsibility for recommending nutritional standards for the human population rests with the Department of Health and Social Security (DHSS) and derives from the Committee on Medical Aspects of Food Policy, colloquially referred to as the COMA Committee (DHSS, 1984).

The most recent publication on nutrient allowances (DHSS, 1981a) is a revision of the first report by the DHSS made in 1969 and differs from it mainly in interpretation of the data, the quantities recommended being, for the most part, unaltered.

The recommendations are made on the basis of groups of the population, classification being made by sex, age and activity or, for females, physiological state. The nutrients quoted are: metabolisable energy, protein, three B vitamins (thiamin, riboflavin and nicotinic acid), vitamins A, C and D and calcium and iron. A later report (DHSS, 1984) adds information on total fat and fatty acids and provides qualitative guides on dietary fibre, salt, simple sugars and alcohol. Nevertheless, even the two reports taken together provide a meagre list for comparison with recommended nutrient intakes for poultry. Furthermore, the definitions relating to adequacy are different in the human situation from those most familiar to poultry scientists and those concerned with energy and protein are given below.

Recommended amounts of food energy (DHSS, 1981a)

The basic concept is as follows: 'the average amount of the nutrient which should be provided per head in a group of people if the needs of practically all members of the group are to be met'. Specifically for energy the recommendations are intended to ensure, on average, a balance over a 24 h period for mature adults so that there is no change in body weight over the period. In practice the recommendations are made for each class on the basis of the average requirement of that class. Hence: 'About one half of the individuals in the group would be expected to have intakes less than, and half more than, the recommended amounts; but in both instances the intake should satisfy the requirement of the individuals concerned provided the sharing is in accord with individual needs.'

Recommended amounts of protein (DHSS, 1981a)

The recommended daily amount of protein is equated with the estimated average requirement for the class of individuals and increased by a factor, not quoted, to give a margin of safety. This principle is followed for all nutrients except energy.

Recommended daily amounts (RDA) of nutrients (DHSS, 1981a)

The recommendations for metabolisable energy and for protein are given in *Table 2.5.*

In spite of the limitations imposed on these recommendations by the assumptions made and the paucity of direct experimental data, they represent the best summary available of the average amounts of energy and protein that should be consumed by the population of the UK. However, the recommendations do not in themselves give any guidance on the approach to be made to several fundamental issues. Amongst these are:

(1) Since by definition half the population will receive less than the RDA, what is the point at which a sub-group may be expected to suffer from a nutritional deficiency?
(2) Since by definition half the population will receive more than the RDA, what is the point at which a sub-group may be expected to suffer from malnutrition due to a nutritional imbalance resulting from an excess of one or more nutrients?

Table 2.5 Recommended daily allowances (RDA) of nutrients (DHSS, 1981a) assuming moderate activity commensurate with age

Age (yr)	Metabolisable energy		Protein (g)
	(MJ)	(kcal)	
Male			
3–4	6.5	1560	39
5–6	7.25	1740	43
12–14	11.0	2640	66
15–17	12.0	2880	72
18–34	12	2900	72
35–64	11.5	2750	69
65–74	10.0	2400	60
75+	9.0	2150	54
Female			
3–4	6.25	1500	37
5–6	7.0	1680	42
12–14	9.0	2150	53
15–17	9.0	2150	53
18–54	9.0	2150	54
Pregnancy	10.0	2400	60
Lactation	11.5	2750	69
55–74	8.0	1900	47
75+	7.0	1680	42

Note: Energy allowances are increased by 15–20% for high activity in males and females in the age range 35–54.

Nutritional guidelines

At about the time that RDAs were being revised and republished, nutritionists in the UK independently of the committee structure of the DHSS were considering the implications of epidemiological studies. There have been many since the observations of McCarrison early in the century and all have, in broad terms, compared different environments and within them the style and tradition of eating with health.

The approach is quite different from the laboratory studies. Causality can seldom be demonstrated. There is often debate about the 'most reasonable conclusions' that can be supported from the data. Nevertheless between 1974 and 1983 seven major reports were available in Britain and all shared common ground in relating eating habit with health (DHSS, 1974; Royal College of Physicians of London and British Cardiac Society, 1976; DHSS, 1978; Royal College of Physicians of London, 1981; DHSS, 1981b; World Health Organisation, 1982; Royal College of Physicians of London, 1983). It was the study of these by James and his colleagues which led to the publication of the first complete dietary guidelines for the UK (James, 1983). For the first time an integrated set of proposals was made indicating maxima as well as minima for nutrient intake and including recommendations for minimum intakes of dietary fibre. In introducing the report of James (popularly termed the NACNE Report) Morris, Player and Shrimpton (1983) draw attention to two major theoretical issues with great practical implications which were highlighted in the report and they are quoted here:

'The first is whether in mass diseases with exceedingly high incidence such as dental caries or coronary disease efforts should be made to rectify the manifest relevant dietary defects of the population as a whole, or whether such efforts should be limited to those individuals who can be shown to be at specially high risk. In the Western world opinion is coming to favour the former as a prime basis for public health policy, and to reject the 'selective' approach, among other reasons because it offers too little hope of appreciably reducing population incidence.
    The second is the dilemma that in public education clear and specific, quantitative messages are now manifestly desirable instead of the general admonitions to reduce this, or to increase that, which has so often been ineffectual in the past. However, in the multiple-cause, chronic disease situations that we are concerned with, precise figures derived from population experiments, are often lacking and are unlikely to become available in the foreseeable future. In the figures that it does suggest, the paper seeks to identify the maximum agreement currently achieved by experts in nutritional science and epidemiology, from such experimental data as are available and from the massive other evidence that has accumulated in recent years and is summarised.'

The two paragraphs quoted above illustrate the major difference in conceptual thinking facing the nutritionist when studying humans compared with studies of domestic animals.
    The proposals of James (1983) and his colleagues—the NACNE discussion paper—had far reaching implications and they have been broadly endorsed by the COMA Report (1984) on diet and cardiovascular disease. They form the basis of many District Health Authority policy statements on food and health (e.g. Stockport Health Authority, 1983) and also of corporate (e.g. London Borough Meals Study Group, 1985) and educational (e.g. Kraft, 1985) policies and publications.
    The main recommendations of NACNE (James, 1983) and of COMA (1984) are summarised in *Table 2.6*. In contrast with the earlier recommendations (DHSS, 1981a) summarised in *Table 2.5*, maxima are quoted and dietary fibre is introduced. It should be emphasised that dietary fibre is not synonymous with crude fibre and that whilst there is currently no single definition that is wholly satisfactory, that

Table 2.6 Nutritional guidelines for average daily intakes of nutrients in the UK

		Energy (kcal)	(MJ)	Total fat (g)	Saturated fatty acids (g)	Poly-unsaturated fatty acids (g)	P/S ratio	Dietary fibre (g)	Salt (g)	Alcohol (g)	Sucrose (g)	Protein (g)
Average daily intake (1983)[b]	1980	2850	11.7	128(40.6)[a]	59(18)[a]	14.5(4)[a]	0.24	20	8.12	30(6)[a]		73
	1981	2770	11.6	126(40.9)[a]	49(20)[a]	11.4(4.7)[a]	0.23	20	7.10	—		72
Proposed (1983)[c]	Short term	maintain		115(34)[a]	50(15)[a]	18(5)[a]	0.32	25	7.11	25(5)[a]		maintain
	Long term	maintain		101(30)[a]	34(10)[a]	—	—	30	5.9	20(4)[a]		maintain
Recommended (1984)[d]	Immediate	maintain		77–87(31–35)[a]	37(15)[a]	8.6–16.7 (3.5–6.8)[a]	0.23–0.45	++[e]	+[f]	34		—

[a]Numbers in parentheses represent energy contributed as percentage of total energy.
[b]MAFF (1983).
[c]NACNE (1982).
[d]COMA (1984).
[e]Increase, but not quantified.
[f]Decrease, but not quantified.

used by the Royal College of Physicians of London (1981) is a reasonable description of the meaning of the term. It is:

> 'Dietary fibre is a convenient term for the supporting structures of plant cell walls and the substances intimately associated with them. ..... In general it may be taken to mean the cellulose, non-cellulosic polysaccharides, and other polymers which make up most of the material of the plant cell wall.'

In the guidelines summarised in *Table 2.6* attention is focused on two groups of nutrients: dietary fibre and fats with their component fatty acids. Both are reviewed in the context of maintaining current recommendations for average intakes of energy and protein and assume that increased consumption of complex polysaccharides (dietary fibre) will be achieved by reduction in the consumption of simple polysaccharides, especially sucrose, and fats, especially those rich in saturated fatty acids.

It is against this background that the dietary significance of eggs will be considered in the following sections.

Dietary significance of eggs

The contribution that is traditionally made by eggs to the supply of vitamin D, as cholecalciferol, into the average diet of the UK is well documented and the situation for the supply of this and other nutrients by eggs has changed little since it was recorded in the Report of the Reorganisation Commission for Eggs (1968). However, the argument put forward in this paper depends not upon the supply of essential nutrients, which are not in question for the bulk of the population in the UK, but upon the significance of certain classes of nutrient in relation to trends in patterns of health and diet.

Energy

All nutrients, other than minerals and probably dietary fibre, contribute to metabolisable energy. For the human the following factors from Paul and Southgate (1978) are used: protein, 4 kcal/g; fat, 9 kcal/g; carbohydrate (available, expressed as monosaccharides), 3.75 kcal/g; and alcohol, 7 kcal/g. For practical purposes one may assume that foods provide metabolisable energy in proportion to their analysis as indicated by these conversion factors. Solely from the standpoint of energy, the source is irrelevant and hence there is no unique place for eggs or any other food in this context.

Protein

Provided that the intakes of energy reach those recommended in *Table 2.4* and that 10–11% of this energy is contributed by protein, there is no cause to suppose that any of the essential amino acids will be in short supply. Consequently, given this assumption, and currently in the UK protein accounts for about 11% of the energy supply, there is no need to seek sources of protein that are particularly rich in essential amino acids. There are, of course, for many, non-nutritional reasons for choosing to eat animal proteins, such as pleasure, but in our western society there is no nutritional case for the population as a whole.

Minerals, trace minerals and vitamins

As has already been indicated, eggs are rich sources of all these nutrients, but there is no evidence in the population as a whole of deficiency diseases associated with low levels of any one of these nutrients in the diet. However, there may well be a need to supplement the diets of particular individuals whose patterns of life are different from those of the population as a whole. The two major groups will be those whose total intake of food is low, for example because of age or illness, and those whose activity is very high, for example sportsmen and sportswomen and heavy manual workers.

Dietary fibre

A major challenge to the British diet has been made in the current dietary guidelines (*see Table 2.6*). This is to increase the consumption of dietary fibre by up to 50% from the 1980/81 level of 20 g/d. The egg contains no dietary fibre.

Fats and fatty acids

Tables 2.7 and *2.8* list respectively foods whose fats contain more than 50% of their fatty acids as saturated or mono-unsaturated and those (*Table 2.8*) where more

Table 2.7 Content of saturated and mono-unsaturated fatty acids in foods containing more than 50% of their fat in this form (Paul and Southgate, 1978)

Food	Total fat in 100 g of fresh food (g)	Proportions and amounts of saturated and mono-unsaturated fatty acids	
		% in total fatty acids	Amount in 100 g of fresh food (g)
Butter	82.0	93.0	76.2
Cheese[a]	33.5	93.0	31.2
Chocolate	29.2	93.5	27.3
Herring	18.5	78.1	14.4
Eggs	10.9	85.0	9.3
Duck[b]	9.7	86.1	8.4
Beef[c]	9.1	94.2	8.6
Oatmeal	8.7	57.2	5.0
Lamb[d]	8.1	92.6	7.5
Pork[d]	6.9	90.4	6.2
Bacon[e]	5.2	91.2	4.7
Rabbit	4.0	64.1	2.6
Human milk	4.1	89.5	3.7
Cows' milk	3.8	93.0	3.5
Chicken[f]	3.2	82.7	2.6
Plaice	2.2	61.9	1.4
Turkey[f]	1.1	63.4	0.7
Rice	1.0	56.6	0.6

[a]Cheddar type.
[b]Meat only.
[c]Sirloin, lean only.
[d]Leg, lean only.
[e]Gammon, lean only.
[f]Light meat.

Table 2.8 Content of polyunsaturated fatty acids in foods containing more than 50% of their fat in this form (Paul and Southgate, 1978)

Food	Total fat in 100 g of fresh food (g)	Proportions and amounts of polyunsaturated fatty acids	
		% in total fatty acids	Amount in 100 g of fresh food (g)
Safflower seed oil	99.9	75.5	75.4
Soya bean oil	99.9	57.4	57.3
Sunflower seed oil	99.9	52.3	52.2
Maize oil	99.9	51.6	51.5
Polyunsaturated margarine	81.0	53.7	43.5
Walnuts (without shells)	51.5	71.4	36.8
Wheat bran	5.5	59.4	3.8
Grouse (meat only)	5.3	62.2	3.3
Wholemeal bread	2.7	53.8	1.4
Wholemeal flour	2.0	59.4	1.2
Rye flour	2.0	56.8	1.1
Barley flour	1.7	57.4	1.0
Cod	0.7	56.8	0.4
Mushrooms	0.6	68.6	0.4
Spinach	0.5	74.6	0.4
Baked beans	0.5	63.0	0.3
Green peppers	0.4	68.3	0.3
Turnips	0.3	74.2	0.2
Runner beans	0.2	68.2	0.1
Potatoes	0.1	73.7	trace[a]
Cucumber	0.1	55.3	trace[a]
Apples	trace[a]	64.8	trace[a]

[a]Trace = content less than 0.1 g in 100 g.

than 50% of the fatty acid content is polyunsaturated. Eggs are shown in *Table 2.7* as having a content of saturated and mono-unsaturated fatty acids which is comparable with that of other animal products except for the dairy products and chocolate which are particularly rich in these acids.

Apart from the vegetable oils and some fish, the foods whose fats are rich in polyunsaturated fatty acids are also those which are rich in dietary fibre. However, it is important to notice that although many of these fats have a desirable composition, they are present in the foods in only small amounts.

In *Table 2.9* a summary is presented of the contribution from a Size 3 egg of fatty acids to the recommended daily (24 h) intake as previously discussed. The contributions of total fat at about 8% of the daily allowance, and of saturated and mono-unsaturated fatty acids at about 13% of the allowance, are modest and leave available a substantial margin for the selection of the rest of the food for the day.

However, there is only a relatively small supply of polyunsaturated fatty acids; but this can be rectified by the conventional British habit of eating bread with a fat spread with the egg provided the fat used is a polyunsaturated margarine and the bread is wholemeal. Under these circumstances, using a slice of bread weighing 50 g and 5 g of polyunsaturated margarine, the ratio of polyunsaturated fatty acids to mono-unsaturated and saturated fatty acids changes from 0.16 for the egg alone to 0.48 for the egg consumed with the wholemeal bread and polyunsaturated spread.

Table 2.9 Content of fat[a] and fatty acids[a] in whole eggs in relation to currently recommended daily intakes[b]

Nutrient	Amount in 100 g of egg[c] (g)	Amount in a Size 3 egg of 62.5 g (g)	Recommended daily intake[f] (g)	Contribution from one Size 3 egg to daily intake (%)
Total fat[d]	10.9	6.8	87	7.8
Total fatty acids[e]	9.1	5.7	—	
Saturated and mono-unsaturated fatty acids	7.9	4.9	37	13.2
Polyunsaturated fatty acids	1.2	0.8	16.7	4.8

[a]Paul and Southgate (1978).
[b]COMA (1984).
[c]Calculated from a 'standard' egg composed of 11% shell, 58% white and 31% yolk (Paul and Southgate, 1978).
[d]Fat in most foods is a mixture of triglycerides, phospholipids, sterols and related compounds and the value quoted is for total lipid (Paul and Southgate, 1978).
[e]Conversion factor from total fat to total fatty acids of 0.83 (Posati, Kinsella and Watt, 1975).
[f]Assuming a P/S ratio of 0.45.

Table 2.10 Cholesterol content of foods per 100 g (Paul and Southgate, 1978)

Food	Cholesterol content	
	(mg)	(mmol)
High		
Boiled calf brain	3100	8.02
Boiled lamb brain	2200	5.69
Soft fried herring roe	700	1.81
Whole eggs, poached	480	1.24
Fried lambs' liver	400	1.03
Fried lambs' sweetbread	380	0.98
Stewed pigs' liver	290	0.75
Butter	230	0.59
Medium high		
Roast duck meat	160	0.41
Lobster	150	0.39
Double cream	140	0.36
Stilton cheese	120	0.31
Cooked lamb, lean meat	110	0.28
Cooked pork, lean meat	110	0.28
Boiled chicken, dark meat	110	0.28
Steamed whiting	110	0.28
Medium low		
Steamed plaice	90	0.23
Cooked beef, lean meat	82	0.21
Boiled chicken, light meat	80	0.21
Grilled herring	80	0.21
Lard	70	0.18
Steamed cod	60	0.16
Low		
Human milk, mature	16	0.04
Cows' milk, whole	14	0.04
Cottage cheese	13	0.03
Natural yoghurt, low fat	7	0.02
Cows' milk, skimmed	2	0.01
Vegetable oils	trace	trace

Of course the total fat consumed increases and accounts for nearly 19% of the recommended daily allowance, but it is well balanced.

This example illustrates a major dilemma facing nutrition educationists and the food and agricultural industries. The egg considered as one of the contributors of fat and saturated fatty acids to the diet appears to be undesirable in the context of current thinking. However, considered as a source of all the nutrients it contains, the egg is a comparatively low fat food. Moreover, as part of a conventional diet sensibly selected, it is an excellent contributor to the day's food. Fortunately it is no part of this chapter to resolve the problem of how to educate an entire population to select wisely from a combination of knowledge and self appraisal, but the nutritional problem presented by the egg and its solution is illustrative of the importance of the whole diet and the need to balance individual food items within it. A further point, implied earlier in the chapter but not considered here, is the relation of the intake of energy to the expected expenditure of energy.

Sterols (particularly cholesterol)

In animals and animal products virtually the only sterol present is cholesterol and its content in foods derived from animals is given in *Table 2.10*. The foods are divided into four groups with respect to their content of cholesterol as: high, medium high, medium low and low. Eggs are in the high group.

Diet and health

In the UK there has been a substantial change in the attitude to diet in relation to human health since the publication of the work of James and his colleagues as the NACNE Discussion Paper (1983) and the corroboration of the principles enunciated in it by the subsequent publication of the COMA Report (1984).

Both reviews draw attention to the trend in the average UK diet since 1950 to increase in content of energy and of fat and to decline in content of dietary fibre. These changes, described in detail by Hollingsworth (1983), are summarised in *Table 2.11* from which it can be seen that the climax of the trend was reached in the period 1969–1972.

The significance of these trends in relation to health and especially to cardiovascular disease remains a matter for debate, although the balance of opinion, as distinct from irrefutable proof, is in favour of the approach and changes recommended by the reports of NACNE (1983) and COMA (1984).

Inevitably the question arises as to whether a change in lifestyle will change the probability of developing coronary heart disease and dietary intervention to test, in particular, the fat hypothesis has been attempted on several occasions. One of the most extensive was carried out in the USA by the Multiple Risk Factor Intervention Trial Research Group (1982) and popularly termed the MRFIT trial. The trial studied 12 866 high risk men for coronary heart disease aged 35–57 years and assigned them either to a 'special intervention' programme or to 'usual care' in the community. The groups were followed for seven years and the risk factors declined in both groups but with no statistically significant difference between them. Whilst intervention, including dietary modification to reduce the intake of saturated fats, may or may not have been beneficial, it was certainly not deleterious.

Table 2.11 Total food supplies in the UK, 1952–1982[a]

	1950	1952	1956	1959	1961	1966	1969	1971	1972	1976	1980[b]	1982[b]	Recommended[c]	
P/S ratio	—	—	—	0.17	—	—	0.19	—	0.22	0.20	0.24	0.27	0.45	0.23
Energy (kcal)	2470	3030	3170	—	3150	3160	3110	3080	3070	2920	2850	2800	2500	2500
(MJ)	10.3	12.7	13.3	—	13.2	13.2	13.0	12.9	12.8	12.2	11.9	11.8	10.5	10.5
Protein (g)	78	82	83	—	85	86	86	85	85	83	82	81	69	69
% of energy	12.5	10.8	10.5	—	10.8	10.9	11.0	11.0	11.1	11.4	11.5	11.3	11.0	11.0
Fat (g)	102	124	139	—	140	144	146	144	143	130	128	128	87	77
% of energy	36.8	36.8	39.5	—	40.0	41.0	42.3	42.1	41.9	40.1	40.6	41.1	35.0	31.0
Carbohydrate (g)	315	424	422	—	413	403	389	385	386	378	363	364	333	333
% of energy	50.6	52.4	49.9	—	49.2	47.8	46.9	46.9	47.1	48.5	47.9	47.6	50.0	50.0
Dietary fibre (g)	—	—	22.5	—	21.7	21.2	—	21.2	20.6	19.8	—	19.8	30	30

[a]Quoted in COMA (1984), being derived from the 'Food Consumption Level Estimates' of the Ministry of Agriculture, Fisheries and Food.
[b]Changes in the methods of estimation were made in 1980 and 1982 and also in 1960 and 1974.
[c]From James (1983) and COMA (1984).

Another large scale intervention study, also in the USA, was directed towards lowering the concentration of circulating cholesterol with the expectation of reducing the incidence of coronary heart disease. In this study of the Lipid Research Clinics Program (1984) 3806 middle-aged men were studied. All had been selected because they exhibited hypercholesterolaemia and all were placed on a moderate diet which could be expected to reduce plasma cholesterol. One group was treated with a bile acid sequestrant cholestyramine resin, the other received a placebo and both were studied for 7.4 years.

Whilst the dietary modification had little or no effect, as judged longitudinally, on the incidence of coronary heart disease, the use of the sequestrant resulted in a significant ($P<0.05$) reduction in the risk of coronary heart disease. It was concluded that lowering total plasma cholesterol by lowering the low density lipoprotein cholesterol fraction reduced the incidence of coronary heart disease in high risk men. The trial was not designed to provide information on a normal population but it gave no indication that conventional dietary modifications could be successful in treating such a group. However, whilst it supported the view that high levels of total plasma cholesterol were associated with coronary heart disease it provided no explanation for their origin. Furthermore, the diet common to all participants provided a maximum of 400 mg of cholesterol a day and had a P/S ratio of 0.8, but even so had little effect on the incidence of coronary heart disease even though some lowering, up to 5%, of the total plasma cholesterol was achieved.

Against this background the content of saturated fatty acids and cholesterol in the egg are only disadvantageous with respect to their possible effect on health if the complete diet is comprised of items of food with a similar composition to eggs or indeed if eggs were the sole source of nourishment. However, in a mixed diet of the kind traditionally associated with the UK, it is possible to include eggs without contravening the dietary recommendations of current nutrition and health research workers.

In conclusion it must be emphasised that insofar as dietary significance is concerned, eggs are little different from any other wholesome food, their significance being dependent upon the composition of the total diet and the habits and genetic background of the consumer. Perhaps in this field of activity more than in almost any other it is necessary to keep an open and receptive mind and reject the temptation to pursue to the point of irrationality attractive hypotheses which lack as much in evidence as they possess in charm. More than a century ago Huxley (1881) warned of similar perils in respect of the major biological debate of his day with the words that '.... the scientific spirit is of more value than its products, and irrationally held truths may be more harmful than reasoned errors'.

References

BOARD, R.G. (1982). Properties of avian egg shells and their value. *Biological Reviews*, **57**, 1–28

BROOKS, J. and TAYLOR, D.J. (1953). *Eggs and Egg Products*. Scientific and Technical Surveys, No. 20. The British Food Manufacturing Industries Research Association, Leatherhead, Surrey, UK

COMMITTEE ON MEDICAL ASPECTS OF FOOD POLICY—COMA (1984). *Diet and Cardiovascular Disease*. Department of Health and Social Security, London, HMSO

DHSS (1974). *Diet and Coronary Disease*. Report on Health and Social Subjects, No. 7. London, HMSO

DHSS (1978). *Prevention and Health—Eating for Health*. London, HMSO

DHSS (1981a). *Recommended Daily Amounts of Food Energy and Nutrients for Groups of People in the United Kingdom.* Report on Health and Social Subjects, No. 15. London, HMSO

DHSS (1981b). *Report on Avoiding Heart Attacks.* London, HMSO

DHSS (1984). *Diet and Cardiovascular Disease.* Report on Health and Social Subjects, No. 28. London, HMSO

HOLLINGSWORTH, D.F. (1983). Rationing and economic constraints on food consumption in Britain since the Second World War. *World Review of Nutrition and Dietetics,* **42**, 191–218

HUXLEY, T.H. (1881). *Science and Culture and Other Essays: The Coming of Age of the Origin of Species.* London, Macmillan

JAMES, W.P.T. (1983). 'NACNE', a discussion paper on proposals for nutritional guidelines for health education in Britain. London, Health Education Council

KRAFT (1985). *Tried and Tested.* Cheltenham, The Kraft Kitchen

LIPID RESEARCH CLINICS PROGRAM (1984). The Lipid Research Clinics coronary primary prevention trial results. *Journal of the American Medical Association,* **251**, 351–374

LONDON BOROUGH MEALS STUDY GROUP (1985). London, Wandsworth Borough Council

MAFF (1983). *Food Facts* No. 6, October 20. London, Ministry of Agriculture, Fisheries and Food

MORRIS, J.N., PLAYER, D.A. and SHRIMPTON, D.H. (1983). Preface to 'NACNE', a discussion paper on proposals for nutritional guidelines for health education in Britain. London, Health Education Council

MULTIPLE RISK FACTOR INTERVENTION TRIAL RESEARCH GROUP (1982). Multiple risk factor intervention trial. *Journal of the American Medical Association,* **248**, 1465–1477

PAUL, A.A. and SOUTHGATE, D.A.T. (1978). *McCance and Widdowson's The Composition of Foods.* London, HMSO

PENNINGTON, M.E., PLATT, F.L., SNYDER, C.G. and MANDEVILLE, P. (1933). *Eggs.* Chicago, Progress Publications

POSATI, L.P., KINSELLA, J.E. and WATT, B.K. (1975). Comprehensive evaluation of fatty acids. III. Eggs and egg products. *Journal of the American Dietetic Association,* **67**, 111–115

REORGANISATION COMMISSION FOR EGGS (1968). Report. London, HMSO

ROMANOFF, A.L. and ROMANOFF, A.J. (1949). *The Avian Egg.* New York, Wiley

ROYAL COLLEGE OF PHYSICIANS OF LONDON (1981). *Report on Medical Aspects of Dietary Fibre.*

ROYAL COLLEGE OF PHYICIANS OF LONDON (1983). Obesity. *Journal of the Royal College of Physicians,* **17**, 3–58

ROYAL COLLEGE OF PHYSICIANS OF LONDON AND BRITISH CARDIAC SOCIETY (1976). Prevention of coronary heart disease. *Journal of the Royal College of Physicians,* **10**, 213–275

SHRIMPTON, D.H. (1983). *Eggs, Nutrition and Diet.* The Eggs Authority, Technical Bulletin No. 16, pp. 21–29.

STOCKPORT HEALTH AUTHORITY (1983). *Food and Health Policy.* Stockport, Stockport Health Authority

WORLD HEALTH ORGANISATION (1982). *Prevention of Coronary Heart Disease.* Report of a WHO Expert Committee. Technical Report Series 678. Geneva, WHO

Chapter 3

Biochemical aspects of the relationships between dietary cholesterol, blood cholesterol and ischaemic heart disease

J.H. Moore

Introduction

Intense interest in the metabolism of cholesterol was stimulated by the publication of a number of reports (e.g. Gertler, Garn and Lerman, 1950) indicating that the concentration of cholesterol in the plasma of patients with ischaemic heart disease was greater than that in the plasma of matched control subjects. The presence of cholesterol in atherosclerotic lesions had been long established, and it was shown that this cholesterol was derived from that in the blood plasma. Since cholesterol is usually present in human diets, particularly in those consumed by populations of the Western World, it was natural that questions should be raised concerning the possible relationships between intake of cholesterol from the diet, blood cholesterol levels and ischaemic heart disease. Research scientists have been reluctant to provide answers to such questions simply because the elucidation of the mechanisms of, and factors controlling the metabolism of, cholesterol in mammalian tissues has proved to be an extremely difficult and time consuming task. On the other hand, nutritional and medical evangelists of one persuasion or another have shown no such reluctance, and there can be few topics that have generated such a volume of ill-informed and sensational comment. Far from being the toxic substance that some would have us believe, cholesterol is synthesised *de novo* in most mammalian tissues where it is utilised as an essential structural component of cellular membranes and lipoproteins; it is also the biosynthetic precursor of vitally important compounds such as the bile acids and steroid hormones. Although our knowledge of cholesterol metabolism is far from complete, considerable advances have been made during the last decade, particularly by J.L. Goldstein and M.S. Brown, who were awarded the 1985 Nobel Prize for Medicine and Physiology. It is hoped that the following review of cholesterol metabolism might help to place the dietary cholesterol–blood cholesterol controversy in perspective.

The biosynthesis of cholesterol

Biosynthetic pathway

The biosynthetic pathway leading to the formation of cholesterol in animal tissues has been elucidated mainly by Bloch, Cornforth and Popjak and their respective colleagues (e.g. see Popjak, 1955; Cornforth, 1959; Bloch, 1965). The

27

administration of [1-^{14}C] or [2-^{14}C] acetate to rats and the subsequent isolation and systematic degradation of the liver cholesterol demonstrated that all of the carbon atoms of cholesterol were derived from acetate. Similar experiments showed that the carbon atoms of squalene, a minor component of rat liver lipids, were also derived from acetate. Robinson (1934) had already suggested that squalene could assume a folded structure from which cholesterol could be derived by cyclisation; this suggestion was verified by Langdon and Bloch (1953) who showed that [^{14}C]-squalene was utilised for the synthesis of cholesterol in the livers of rats and mice. It was also postulated that squalene originated biosynthetically from the condensation of six hypothetical 5-carbon isoprene units that in turn originated from the decarboxylation and dehydration of mevalonic acid, a 6-carbon compound known to be present in liver extracts. Experiments with ^{14}C-labelled substrates indeed confirmed the existence in rat liver of the overall reaction sequence, acetate → mevalonate → squalene → cholesterol. The details of this complex metabolic sequence have now been established and all the enzymes involved have been characterised. For convenience, this sequence may be divided into the four major stages presented in a much abbreviated form as follows:

1. *Conversion of acetate into mevalonate.* Three molecules of acetyl CoA condense to form 3-hydroxy, 3-methylglutaryl CoA which is then reduced to mevalonic acid.

2. *Conversion of mevalonic acid into 3-isopentenyl pyrophosphate.* Mevalonic acid is sequentially phosphorylated to form 5-phosphomevalonate and then 5-pyrophosphomevalonate which is decarboxylated to isopentenyl pyrophosphate. In the presence of isopentenyl pyrophosphate isomerase, isopentenyl pyrophosphate forms an equilibrium mixture with its isomer, 3,3-dimethylallyl pyrophosphate.

3. *Formation of squalene.* Isopentenyl pyrophosphate condenses with 3,3-dimethylallyl pyrophosphate to form geranyl pyrophosphate which in turn condenses with a second molecule of 3,3-dimethylallyl pyrophosphate to form farnesyl pyrophosphate. Two molecules of farnesyl pyrophosphate then condense to form squalene.

4. *Conversion of squalene into cholesterol.* A complicated series of reactions, including oxidative cyclisation, demethylation and double bond rearrangement result in the formation of cholesterol from squalene.

Site of cholesterol synthesis

Earlier investigations, which usually involved the measurement of the rate of incorporation of ^{14}C from [^{14}C] acetate into cholesterol by tissue slices *in vitro*, indicated that the liver contributed 80% or more of the total cholesterol synthesised in the body. This technique showed that in monkeys, for example, the liver and intestine accounted for 80% and 10% respectively of the total cholesterol synthesised in all tissues (Dietschy and Siperstein, 1967; Dietschy and Wilson,

1968). However, for the various reasons discussed by Dietschy and Spady (1984) this technique is now thought to exaggerate the hepatic contribution to total body cholesterol synthesis. More recently, rates of cholesterol synthesis have been measured by determining the incorporation of ^{3}H from [^{3}H]H$_2$O into cholesterol by various tissues *in vivo*. Using this more reliable procedure Spady and Dietschy (1983) have shown that in monkeys the liver and intestine contribute about 44% and 23% respectively of the total cholesterol synthesised in the whole body; thus, the contribution made by tissues other than the liver and intestine is considerable (i.e. about 33%) and is much greater than that revealed by earlier studies. The tissue distribution of synthetic activity in man is thought to be similar to that observed in monkeys.

At the subcellular level of distribution, the various enzymes that are involved in the synthesis of cholesterol from acetyl CoA are extramitochondrial, and many are associated with the microsomal fraction of low RNA content (Bucher and McGarrahan, 1956).

Regulation of cholesterol synthesis

The reduction of 3-hydroxy, 3-methylglutaryl CoA to mevalonic acid appears to be the rate limiting step in the synthesis of cholesterol in animal tissues (Ott and Lachance, 1981) and most factors that influence the rate of cholesterol synthesis do so either by increasing or by decreasing the activity of hydroxymethylglutaryl CoA reductase (HMG CoA-reductase). Thus, the activity of HMG CoA-reductase in many tissues changes in parallel with changes in the rate of incorporation of [^{14}C] acetate into cholesterol that occur under a wide variety of different physiological and nutritional conditions; under these conditions the rate of incorporation of [^{14}C] mevalonate into cholesterol is unaltered (Siperstein and Fagan, 1964, 1966).

Factors affecting the biosynthesis of cholesterol

Dietary cholesterol

The inclusion of cholesterol in the diet of man and many other mammalian species decreases the rate of cholesterol synthesis *de novo* in the liver (Gould, 1951; Siperstein, 1970). The effect of dietary cholesterol would seem to be a specific effect on sterol synthesis in that other synthetic processes in the liver (e.g. fatty acid and protein synthesis) are unaffected. Within 4–5 h of the administration of dietary cholesterol to rats, the rate of [^{14}C] acetate incorporation into cholesterol by the liver, and the activity of HMG CoA-reductase began to decrease, whilst the cholesterol content of the liver began to increase; the rate of [^{14}C] mevalonate incorporation into cholesterol remained unchanged (Shapiro and Rodwell, 1971). The initial effect of dietary cholesterol on hepatic cholesterol synthesis is thought to be due to inhibition of existing HMG CoA-reductase in the liver, but there is considerable evidence that subsequent effects of continued ingestion of cholesterol are due to the suppression of the synthesis of new enzyme (Higgins and Rudney, 1973; Edwards and Gould, 1974; Gould, 1977). There are indications from experiments with mouse hepatocytes *in vitro* that HMG CoA-reductase activity and the incorporation of [^{14}C] acetate into cholesterol are more strongly inhibited by certain analogues of cholesterol (e.g. 7-ketocholesterol, 7α-hydroxycholesterol, 7β-hydroxycholesterol and 25-hydroxycholesterol) than they are by cholesterol itself (Kandutsch and Chen, 1973, 1974; Kandutsch, Chen and Heiniger, 1978). However, there is as yet no proof that these analogues of cholesterol have any role in the physiological control of cholesterol synthesis *in vivo* (Bell, Sargeant and Watson, 1976).

The response to dietary cholesterol of small intestinal tissues is somewhat different from that of hepatic tissues, and there would appear to be species differences. Although the rate of cholesterol synthesis in the small intestinal tissue of the rat was not reduced significantly by supplementing the diet with 0.5% cholesterol, there was considerable stimulation of cholesterol synthesis in the cells of the small intestine when cholesterol absorption was inhibited by the administration of surfomer, a non-absorbable copolymer of α-olefin and maleic acid (Stange and Dietschy, 1983; Stange, Suckling and Dietschy, 1983). However as pointed out by Stange, Suckling and Dietschy (1983) the effect of dietary cholesterol on cholesterol synthesis in the tissues of the small intestine of the rat is complicated by the presence of three functionally different pools of cholesterol within the mucosal cells, and by the fact that cholesterol absorption occurs predominantly in the upper villus cells of the jejunum, whereas cholesterol synthesis occurs predominantly in the cells of the crypts and lower villi in the ileum. On the other hand, the inhibition by dietary cholesterol of cholesterol synthesis in intestinal tissues has been demonstrated in hamsters, guinea pigs, rabbits and dogs. For example, Anderson, Turley and Dietschy (1982) found that the supplementa-tion of the diet of rabbits with cholesterol decreased the rate of cholesterol synthesis throughout the whole length of the small intestine; the highest rate of cholesterol synthesis was observed in the region of the intestine proximal to the entry of the bile duct, i.e. an area not normally exposed to biliary cholesterol, and it was in this proximal section of the small intestine that the rate of cholesterol synthesis was most markedly depressed by dietary cholesterol. Using organ cultures of canine intestinal mucosa, Gebhard and Cooper (1978) showed that the addition of cholesterol to the medium resulted in significant suppressions of HMG CoA-reductase activity and rate of cholesterol synthesis; similar results were obtained with cultures of rabbit intestinal mucosa (Herold *et al.*, 1984).

Bile acids

Any procedure that interrupts the enterohepatic circulation of bile acids, e.g. the establishment of a bile fistula or the oral administration of cholestyramine, increases the rate of cholesterol synthesis in the liver and increases the activity of hepatic HMG CoA-reductase (Myant and Eder, 1961; Back, Hamprecht and Lynen, 1969). Supplementing the diet of rats with bile acids decreases the rate of cholesterol synthesis in the liver (Beher and Baker, 1959). The increased concentrations of bile acids in the liver do not inhibit the activity of existing HMG CoA-reductase, but suppress the synthesis of new enzyme (Barth and Hillmar, 1980). Although increased concentrations of bile acids in the hepatocyte may suppress the synthesis of HMG CoA-reductase directly, these are conditions under which the activity of cholesterol 7α-hydroxylase is known to be inhibited. Inhibition of the conversion of cholesterol to bile acids might be expected to increase the concentration of free cholesterol in the endoplasmic reticulum of the hepatocyte, and it is conceivable that this may be responsible for the suppression of HMG CoA-reductase synthesis that occurs when the concentrations of bile acids in the liver are increased (Myant and Mitropoulos, 1977). Experiments with rats, monkeys and man have shown that cholesterol synthesis in the small intestine is inhibited by bile acids. Thus, the rate of incorporation of [^{14}C] acetate into cholesterol by intestinal tissues of rats with bile fistulae is markedly greater than that in the intestinal tissues of control animals; intraduodenal infusions of bile acids into rats with bile fistulae reduces the rate of cholesterol synthesis in the intestine to that observed in control animals (Wilson, 1972). In their experiments with organ cultures of canine intestinal mucosa, Gebhard and Cooper (1978) found that, at equivalent concentrations in the medium, bile salts were more effective inhibitors of cholesterol synthesis than was cholesterol; moreover, the effects of cholesterol and bile acids on cholesterol synthesis were additive.

Hormones

The observed effects of various hormones on the rate of incorporation of [^{14}C] acetate into liver cholesterol are difficult to interpret since a number of these hormones e.g. glucagon, thyroxin, adrenalin and noradrenalin, increase the mobilisation of fatty acids from adipose tissues. This process increases the concentration of endogenous acetyl CoA in the liver which dilutes the exogenous [^{14}C] acetate used to measure the rate of cholesterol synthesis. Conversely, insulin inhibits the release of fatty acids from adipose tissues and would be expected to decrease the concentrations of endogenous acetyl CoA in the liver. Nevertheless, insulin, thyroxin, adrenalin and noradrenalin have been shown to stimulate the activity of HMG CoA-reductase, and by inference, the rate of cholesterol synthesis in the liver (Bortz, 1973; Rodwell, Nordstrom and Mitschelen, 1976). There is evidence that the effects of these hormones are mediated by the adenylcyclase system (Gibson and Ingebritsen, 1978).

Fasting

When food is withheld from rats for 5 h or so there is a pronounced decrease in the rate of synthesis of cholesterol from [^{14}C] acetate in the liver which coincides with a decrease in the activity of HMG CoA-reductase in the liver microsomes (Tomkins and Chaikoff, 1952; Bucher et al., 1959; Regen et al., 1966). Fasting has no effect on the incorporation of [^{14}C] mevalonate into liver cholesterol. It is possible that fasting suppresses the synthesis of HMG CoA-reductase, but there is also evidence that the livers of fasted rats contain a substance that inhibits existing HMG CoA-reductase (Migicovsky, 1955). The withholding of food from rats has little effect on the rate of synthesis of cholesterol from [^{14}C] acetate in the intestinal mucosa (Dietschy and Siperstein, 1967).

Dietary fat

The inclusion of fat, either saturated or unsaturated, in the diet of rats increases the rate of incorporation of [^{14}C] acetate into liver cholesterol (Linazasoro et al., 1958; Hill et al., 1960); this effect is associated with an increase in the activity of HMG CoA-reductase in the liver (Goldfarb and Pitot, 1972). Dietary fat also increases the rate of cholesterol synthesis in the small intestinal tissues of the rat (Stange, Suckling and Dietschy, 1983).

Intestinal absorption of cholesterol

Mechanism of absorption

Cholesterol in the diet of man is normally associated with other dietary lipids such as triglycerides and phospholipids. Only a relatively small proportion of dietary cholesterol is esterified (e.g. about 4% of the total cholesterol in egg yolk) and this esterified cholesterol must be hydrolysed before absorption can occur. Hydrolysis is catalysed in the lumen of the small intestine by pancreatic cholesteryl ester hydrolase. Exogenous free cholesterol of dietary origin mixes freely in the lumen of the small intestine with endogenous cholesterol of biliary origin. Biliary cholesterol is totally unesterified and the amount that is secreted into the small intestine of man varies between 750 and 1250 mg/d (Grundy and Metzger, 1972). In the small intestinal lumen free cholesterol is incorporated into mixed micelles containing phospholipids (mainly phosphatidyl choline but also some lysophosphatidyl choline), conjugated bile acids, 2-monoglycerides and fatty acids. Although conjugated bile acids and phospholipids enter the duodenal lumen via the bile, some phospholipid will be of dietary origin. A proportion of the phospholipids in the intestinal lumen is hydrolysed to lyso-compounds by pancreatic phospholipases A_1 and A_2. Hydrolysis of emulsified particles of dietary triglycerides by pancreatic lipase results in the formation of 2-monoglycerides and fatty acids. The incorporation of cholesterol into such micelles is a prerequisite step in the process of cholesterol absorption by the mucosal cells of the small intestine (Dietschy, 1978). The precise mechanism of cholesterol absorption is unknown, but it is conceivable that close association of the mixed micelle with the plasma membrane of the enterocyte promotes the transfer of cholesterol from the micelle into the lipid bilayer structure of the mucosal cell membrane and from there into the interior of the cell. The fatty acids, 2-monoglycerides and lysophospholipids in the micellar phase of the intestinal contents enter the mucosal cells by passive diffusion through the microvillus membrane. The absorption of cholesterol, 2-monoglycerides, fatty acids and lysophospholipids occurs mainly in the jejunum; there is little absorption of these lipid constituents after the digesta has reached the ileum.

Quantitative aspects

Much of the earlier work on quantitative aspects of cholesterol absorption in man suffered from inadequate methodology. However, the more recent application of combined sterol balance and isotopic tracer techniques (Quintao, Grundy and Ahrens, 1971a) has done much to dispel some of the uncertainty that had surrounded this aspect of cholesterol metabolism. In experiments with subjects maintained on liquid formula diets and given from 30 to 2936 mg/d of cholesterol dissolved in the oil phase of the diets, Quintao, Grundy and Ahrens (1971b) obtained a mean value of 38% for the efficiency of absorption; at the lower levels of intake, absorption efficiency increased to about 50% but decreased to about 25% at the higher levels of intake. In subjects consuming varying amounts of cholesterol as a natural component of their normal diets, Kudchodkar, Sodhi and Horlick (1973) found that between dietary intakes of 401 and 1214 mg/d the efficiency of cholesterol absorption remained unchanged at about 37%. Similar results have been reported by Connor and Lin (1974) and Whyte, Nestel and MacGregor (1977). Nevertheless, from the results reported from these and other studies it is clear that there is considerable variation between subjects in the efficiency with which cholesterol is absorbed. There are any number of factors that could account for this wide variation. For example, Mayer *et al.* (1985) have recently isolated from the small intestine a mucin that has a high binding affinity for cholesterol, and conclude that the mucin binding of cholesterol may represent a major diffusion limitation to cholesterol absorption; individual differences in the secretion of the mucin could well contribute to the variation in the efficiency of cholesterol absorption. There would also appear to be considerable variations between different populations in the efficiency of cholesterol absorption. For example, in an experiment with Tarahumara Indians of Mexico who habitually consume a low-cholesterol diet, McMurray *et al.* (1985) found that irrespective of dietary intake, the efficiency of cholesterol absorption remained low at 27%. There is evidence that endogenous (biliary) cholesterol is absorbed somewhat more efficiently than is exogenous cholesterol. This may be a reflection of the fact that dietary cholesterol must be transformed into a micellar state before absorption can occur whereas biliary cholesterol enters the intestinal lumen already in the form of a highly stable micellar solution. Even so, when the diet is completely free of cholesterol, only about 50% of the endogenous cholesterol entering the intestinal tract of man is reabsorbed (Quintao, Grundy and Ahrens, 1971b).

Factors affecting cholesterol absorption

Despite their structural similarity to cholesterol, plant sterols such as β-sitosterol are absorbed from the intestine only in trace amounts, and under certain conditions can markedly inhibit the absorption of cholesterol. According to Grundy and Mok (1976), the addition of 3 g/d of β-sitosterol to the diet of man resulted in a 50% reduction in the absorption of dietary cholesterol. The absorption of cholesterol can be effectively inhibited by very low doses of β-sitosterol administered in micellar solution directly into the duodenum (Grundy and Mok, 1977). Since it has been calculated that the diet of man contributes from 200 to 300 mg/d of plant sterols, it is conceivable that even as a normal course of events these phytosterols may play an important part in determining the efficiency of cholesterol absorption. The mechanisms whereby plant sterols inhibit cholesterol absorption have been discussed by Salen, Ahrens and Grundy (1970) and may involve the displacement of cholesterol from mixed micelles in the intestinal lumen, competition for uptake by the mucosal cell membrane and inhibition of cholesterol esterification within the mucosal cell.

In man and experimental animals the absorption of exogenous and endogenous cholesterol is increased by the addition of fat to the diet (Treadwell and Vahouny, 1968). This may be explained by the fact that the digestion of fat provides increased concentrations in the intestinal contents of those amphipathic molecules that promote the micellar solubilisation of cholesterol. In spite of claims to the contrary, there is no clear evidence that the degree of unsaturation of the dietary fat has any additional or unique effect on the absorption of exogenous or endogenous cholesterol. There is little, if any, firm evidence that the nature and amount of indigestible residues (i.e. fibre) in the diet have any direct influence on the intestinal absorption of cholesterol (Raymond *et al.*, 1977). It is also doubtful whether the intestinal absorption of cholesterol is influenced appreciably by gut microorganisms, for although these microorganisms can convert cholesterol into the non-absorbable coprostanol, this process is confined almost exclusively to the large intestine from which cholesterol is not absorbed.

Certain agents that reduce plasma cholesterol levels in man exert their effect, at least in part, by the direct inhibition of the intestinal absorption of cholesterol. Examples of such agents are neomycin (Sedaghat, Samuel and Crouse, 1975), sucrose polyester (Fallat, Glueck and Lutmer, 1976; Glueck, Mattson and Jandacek, 1979) and surfomer (Crouse, Grundy and Johnson, 1982). Although the administration of cholestyramine, which decreases the effective concentration of bile acids in the intestinal contents, might be expected to decrease the absorption of cholesterol indirectly, this effect is observed in some subjects but not in others (Miettinen, 1973).

Conversion of cholesterol into bile acids

Metabolic pathway and rate limiting step

The first proof that bile acids were derived metabolically from cholesterol was obtained by Bloch, Berg and Rittenberg (1943) who intravenously administered [^{3}H]-cholesterol to dogs and isolated [^{3}H]-cholic acid from the bile; the ^{3}H content of the isolated cholic acid indicated that cholesterol was the sole precursor of cholic acid. The biosynthesis of bile acids from cholesterol occurs only in the liver, and the metabolic pathway involved has now been fully elucidated from experiments in which isotopically labelled precursors were incubated with cell-free preparations obtained from the livers of experimental animals and man (Danielsson and Einarsson, 1969). The initial reaction is the conversion of cholesterol into 7α-hydroxycholesterol, a reaction catalysed by a microsomal 7α-hydroxylase. The 3β-hydroxyl group is then oxidised to a keto group by a microsomal Δ^5-3β-hydroxysteroid reductase, and under the influence of a microsomal Δ^5-3-ketosteroid isomerase, the Δ^5 double bond is isomerised to the Δ^4 position. The product of these two reactions (7α-hydroxycholest-4-en-3-one) may be hydroxylated in the 12α position by a microsomal 12α-hydroxylase to give 7α,12α-dihydroxycholest-4-en-3-one) which is then converted into 5β-cholestane-3α,7α,12α-triol by the sequential reactions catalysed by cytosolic Δ^4-3-ketosteroid-5β-reductase and 3α-hydroxysteroid ketoreductase. Alternatively these two enzymes may convert 7α-hydroxycholest-4-en-3-one into 5β-cholestane-3α,7α-diol. Modification of the steroid nucleus is followed by cleavage of the side chain which is initiated by hydroxylation at C_{26} to give the 3α,7α,12α,26-tetrol or the 3α,7α,26-triol. Oxidation at C_{26} leads to the formation of a carboxyl group which is esterified with CoA. Hydroxylation and oxidation at C_{24} is followed by thiolytic cleavage with CoA which results in the formation of propionyl-CoA and either cholyl-CoA or chenodeoxycholyl-CoA. The CoA esters of the two primary bile acids are then conjugated with either glycine or taurine to form glycocholic, taurocholic, glycochenodeoxycholic or taurochenodeoxycholic acids.

There is evidence that the rate limiting step in the synthesis of bile acids from cholesterol is the initial reaction catalysed by cholesterol 7α-hydroxylase. Physiological or experimentally induced changes in the rate of bile acid synthesis are invariably associated with corresponding changes in cholesterol 7α-hydroxylase activity, whereas there is no evidence of any such changes in the activities of the enzymes involved in the reaction sequence beyond 7α-hydroxycholesterol (Myant and Mitropoulos, 1977).

Enterohepatic circulation of bile acids

In man, the conjugated bile acids synthesised in and secreted by the liver enter the duodenal lumen via the common bile duct. Bile acids play an essential part in the digestion and absorption of cholesterol and other lipids in the proximal region of the small intestine and are subsequently reabsorbed, mainly by an active transport mechanism involving either conjugated or unconjugated acids, from the distal region of the ileum. The reabsorption of some unconjugated bile acids may also occur from the colon by a process that involves non-ionic diffusion. The reabsorbed bile acids are taken up into the portal blood system where they are transported as complexes with albumen. The bile acids in the portal blood are rapidly removed by the liver, and after appropriate modification, e.g. re-conjugation, are secreted into the bile and returned to the duodenal lumen. Under normal circumstances the enterohepatic circulation of bile acids is a highly efficient (95–98%) process in man and most experimental animals. For example, in man with a normal enterohepatic circulation 12–24 g/d of bile acids are secreted into the duodenal lumen, whereas the daily loss of bile acids by faecal excretion amounts to only 200–400 mg (Hofmann, 1977).

Probably by inhibiting the 7α-hydroxylation reaction, the bile acids taken up from the portal blood partially repress the hepatic synthesis of bile acids from cholesterol (Shefer et al., 1969). Thus, day to day changes in the size of the bile acid pool are small, with the amount of newly synthesised bile acids being equivalent to the amount lost by faecal excretion. However, if the enterohepatic circulation of bile acids is disrupted by decreasing the reabsorption from the distal ileum or colon, thereby decreasing the amount returning to the liver, cholesterol 7α-hydroxylase activity and thus the rate of bile acid synthesis are increased. This situation is most evident when bile acids are diverted through a bile fistula (Thompson and Vars, 1953), but is also observed when the reabsorption of bile acids is decreased by a number of factors that operate in the intestinal lumen.

The intestinal microflora is known to influence the enterohepatic circulation of bile acids (Fuller and Moore, 1971). The peptide bonds of the glycine- and taurine-conjugated cholic and chenodeoxycholic acids are hydrolysed by bacteria present in the lower ileum and large intestine. Intestinal bacteria may also modify the steroid nucleus, e.g. the 7α-hydroxyl groups may be removed from cholic and chenodeoxycholic acids resulting in the formation of deoxycholic and lithocholic acids, respectively. In addition, the 3α, 7α or 12α hydroxyl groups may be oxidised to the corresponding ketone groups. These and other bacterial transformations explain the fact that human faeces may contain as many as 20 different deconjugated bile acids. There is evidence that secondary bile acids (i.e. those resulting from bacterial transformation in the intestinal lumen) are not absorbed as readily as are the primary bile acids (i.e. cholic and chenodeoxycholic acids and their conjugates); this may be due, at least in part, to the fact that secondary bile acids are avidly adsorbed on to indigestible dietary residues. In germ-free animals, there is neither deconjugation nor modification of the steroid nucleus in the intestinal lumen (Linstedt and Norman, 1956; Gustafsson et al., 1957). Therefore the reabsorption of bile acids from the intestine and the inhibition of hepatic bile acid synthesis in germ-free animals is greater than in conventional control animals (Coates, Harrison and Moore, 1965); the rate of synthesis of cholic acid in conventional control animals is about twice that in germ-free animals (Kellog, 1971). Indigestible food constituents may also determine the extent to which primary bile acids are reabsorbed. Thus, the capacities of different types of dietary fibre to bind taurocholic acid *in vitro* correlate well with the abilities of these different fibrous materials to increase the faecal excretion of bile acids and to decrease plasma cholesterol levels when included in the diets of rats and rabbits (Moore, 1967; Kritchevsky, Tepper and Story, 1975). The oral administration of certain non-absorbable anion exchange resins, such as cholestyramine, causes the binding of bile acids in the intestinal lumen and a decrease in the extent of their reabsorption. This in turn results in an increase in the rate of synthesis of bile acids in the liver and also an increase in the rate of their excretion in the faeces.

Lipoproteins and the transport of cholesterol in the blood stream

In this section no attempt will be made to deal with all aspects of lipoprotein metabolism; more detailed accounts and full bibliographies are given in the many reviews that have been published on this subject, e.g. those by Brown and Goldstein (1983), Eisenberg (1976, 1984), Eisenberg and Levy (1975), Eisenberg *et al.* (1975), Goldstein and Brown (1977, 1984), Green and Glickman (1981), Hamilton (1978), Havel (1975, 1984), Mahley and Innerarity (1983), Mahley *et al.* (1984), Packard and Shepherd (1983) and Pittman and Steinberg (1984).

Synthesis of lipoproteins in the small intestine

Before utilisation for acylation reactions, the absorbed fatty acids must be converted to the CoA derivatives, the formation of which is catalysed by acyl CoA synthetase, an enzyme present in the microsomal fraction of the small intestinal mucosa. The synthesis of triglycerides in the enterocyte occurs mainly by the monoglyceride pathway but it can also occur by the α-glycerophosphate pathway. The synthesis of phospholipids in the mucosal cells occurs by the acylation of lysophospholipids absorbed from the intestinal lumen, but synthetic pathways involving choline phosphotransferase may also be utilised. The cells of the small intestine contain an enzyme, acyl CoA:cholesterol acyl transferase that catalyses the synthesis of cholesterol esters from absorbed or newly synthesised cholesterol and fatty acyl CoA derivatives. The lipid components (triglycerides, phospholipids, cholesterol and cholesterol esters) and a number of apoproteins synthesised in the enterocyte are there assembled into lipoprotein particles. The two main lipoproteins that are synthesised in the mammalian enterocyte are chylomicrons (density less than 0.93 g/ml, diameter 75–1000 nm) and very low density lipoproteins (VLDL, density 0.93–1.006 g/ml, diameter 25–75 nm). The approximate composition of chylomicrons is triglycerides, 84%; cholesteryl esters, 4%; cholesterol, 2%; phospholipids, 8%; protein 2%. The approximate composition of VLDL is triglycerides, 50%; cholesteryl ester, 16%; cholesterol, 6%; phospholipids, 18%; protein, 10%. In chylomicrons and VLDL the central core of the spherical particles contain virtually all of the constituent triglycerides and cholesteryl esters, about 30% of the free cholesterol but no phospholipid. The central core is surrounded by a surface film consisting of phospholipids, apoproteins and most of the free cholesterol which together form a monolayer with a constant thickness of about 2.2 nm. Since the thickness of the surface film remains constant, it is evident that there must be some variation in composition within the chylomicron and VLDL classes. Thus, as the diameter of the particle decreases, the proportions of the constituent apoproteins, phospholipids and free cholesterol increases, and the proportion of the triglycerides decreases. The demarcation between intestinal chylomicrons and VLDL particles is somewhat arbitrary and the composition of a small chylomicron is virtually the same as that of a large VLDL particle. The major apoproteins present in the surface film of intestinal chylomicrons and VLDL in man are apo-A (I, II and IV) and apo-B_{48}; these apoproteins are synthesised in the enterocyte.

Two factors appear to determine the proportion of chylomicrons and VLDL synthesised by intestinal cells. First, it is known that a large flux of triglycerides through the intestinal cells results in the formation of chylomicrons, whereas a small flux results in the formation of VLDL (Redgrave and Dunne, 1975). In man, lipid absorption is intermittent and relatively rapid during the period immediately after a meal. During this period, the rapid influx of large amounts of fatty acids and 2-monoglycerides into the enterocyte induces synthetic rates of core material (triglycerides) that are in excess of those of surface film components (phospholipids, cholesterol and apoproteins), which results in the assembly of the larger of the two classes of intestinal lipoproteins, i.e. chylomicrons. During starvation or between meals, lipid assimilation is relatively quiescent and is concerned only with the reabsorption and transport of endogenous lipids. Under these conditions, the synthesis of surface film components keeps pace with the synthesis of core material and this leads to the synthesis of the smaller intestinal lipoproteins, i.e. VLDL. Second, the type of fatty acid absorbed by the enterocyte exerts an influence on the type of lipoprotein particle synthesised. In experiments with rats, Ockner, Hughes and Isselbacher (1969) found that the absorption of saturated fatty acids resulted in the formation of VLDL whereas the absorption of equivalent amounts of unsaturated fatty acids resulted in the formation of chylomicrons.

Newly synthesised lipoprotein particles accumulate in the Golgi apparatus in the supranuclear region of the enterocyte. Migration of the Golgi vesicles to the basolateral region of the cell is followed by discharge of the lipoprotein particles into the intercellular space by reverse pinocytosis involving fusion of the Golgi membrane with the basolateral cell membrane. The intestinal lipoproteins then pass into the lacteals, and from there into the blood system via the intestinal and thoracic lymph ducts.

Synthesis of lipoproteins in the liver

The liver is the predominant source of plasma VLDL, although it has been estimated that the intestine may contribute up to 25% of the total plasma pool of VLDL. With the exception of certain of the apoproteins, the composition of hepatic VLDL is similar to that of intestinal VLDL. All of the lipid moieties of hepatic VLDL may be synthesised *de novo* in the liver cell. Fatty acids may be synthesised from glucose, but may be derived also from the unesterified fatty acids that circulate as a complex with albumen in the blood. Triglycerides are synthesised mainly by the α-glycerophosphate pathway, and phosphatidyl choline is synthesised by the choline phosphotransferase pathway. Cholesterol may be synthesised *de novo* and it is esterified by a hepatic acyl CoA:cholesterol acyl transferase. The major apoproteins present in the surface film of hepatic VLDL in man are apo-A (I, II and IV) and apo-B_{100}; in addition, hepatic VLDL contain apo-C (I, II and III), apo-E and apo-AIII which are all synthesised in the liver. Heimberg and

Wilcox (1972) and Wilcox, Dunn and Heimberg (1975) have reported that the VLDL secreted by rat livers after perfusion with unsaturated fatty acids consisted of larger particles containing higher proportions of triglycerides and smaller proportions of cholesterol and phospholipids than did VLDL secreted after perfusion with equivalent amounts of saturated fatty acids.

It appears that hepatic VLDL particles are manufactured in the endoplasmic reticulum and transported in Golgi vesicles to the sinusoidal surface before release into the circulation at the space of Diss. Plasma high density lipoproteins (HDL) originate mainly in the liver where they are synthesised as flat circular discs of 19 nm in diameter and 4.5 nm in thickness; these discs have a phospholipid-cholesterol bilayer structure with apo-A (I and IV), apo-C (I, II and III) and apo-E covering the hydrophobic edges. The composition of these HDL discs as formed in the liver is triglyceride, 1.4%; cholesterol esters, 4.3%; cholesterol, 16.0%; phospholipid, 39.9%; protein, 38.4%. These 'nascent' HDL discs are secreted by the liver into the blood stream together with the enzyme lecithin cholesterol acyl transferase (LCAT) in inactive form. The nascent HDL particles and LCAT immediately form a complex and the enzyme is activated specifically by apo-AI. LCAT catalyses the reaction

cholesterol + phosphatidyl choline →
                    cholesterol ester + lysophosphatidyl choline

Thus, molecules of cholesterol and phosphatidyl choline in the polar bilayer are utilised to synthesise non-polar core material, i.e. cholesterol esters, which accumulate in the hydrophobic region between the bilayer of the HDL disc. As the bilayer is gradually forced apart the particle becomes more spherical in shape and the apoproteins diffuse laterally to give a more even distribution throughout the polar surface film. The composition of plasma HDL (i.e. hepatic HDL after reaction with LCAT in the blood stream) is triglyceride, 1.2%; cholesterol ester, 23.6%; cholesterol, 5.1%; phospholipid, 25.9%; protein 44.3%.

Catabolism of lipoproteins and the removal of cholesterol from the blood stream

Low density lipoproteins

On entering the blood stream, the compositions of the surface films of the triglyceride-rich lipoproteins are modified by non-enzymic interactions with HDL. Apo-C (I, II, III) and apo-E are transferred from HDL to the surface films of chylomicrons and VLDL; at the same time, apo-A (I, II and IV), cholesterol and phospholipid are transferred from the surface films of chylomicrons and VLDL to HDL. This exchange process occurs to the extent that apo-C, apo-E and apo-B constitute the major apoproteins of serum chylomicrons and VLDL, which contrasts markedly with the apoprotein complement of 'nascent' chylomicrons and VLDL.

As chylomicrons and VLDL circulate in the blood supplying cardiac and skeletal muscle, adipose tissue, mammary tissue and other tissues, the constituent triglycerides are almost completely removed by the hydrolytic action of lipoprotein lipase, an enzyme located on the lumenal surface of the capillary endothelium permeating these tissues (e.g. Moore and Christie, 1981; Vernon, 1981). Lipoprotein lipase is activated by the apo-CII present in the surface film of the triglyceride-rich lipoproteins. The products of lipolysis (mainly fatty acids and 2-monoglycerides) are taken up by the various tissues for oxidation and the production of energy (muscle), and the synthesis of triglycerides for energy storage (adipose tissue) or secretion (mammary tissue). The hydrolytic action of lipoprotein lipase removes 80–90% of the triglycerides originally present in the chylomicrons and VLDL. This results in a considerable reduction in particle size, and an excess of cholesterol, phospholipids and apoproteins, since the thickness of the surface film remains constant. Excess cholesterol, phospholipid and apoproteins (mainly apo-C) are transferred to serum HDL_3, where LCAT transforms the additional surface film material (cholesterol and phospholipid) into core material (cholesteryl esters); HDL_3 is thereby converted into the larger HDL_2. It is important to stress that there is no loss of apo-B from the surface film and very little loss of cholesteryl esters from the apolar core of chylomicrons and VLDL undergoing lipolytic degradation; none of the cholesterol removed from the surface film is taken up by the various extrahepatic tissues. The degradation of triglyceride-rich lipoproteins by lipoprotein lipase ceases before the hydrolysis of the constituent triglycerides is complete. This is thought to be due to the fact that as the particles decrease in size, the apo-CII content decreases below levels that are sufficient to activate lipoprotein lipase. This first stage of the catabolism of chylomicrons and VLDL results in the formation of chylomicron remnants and intermediate density lipoproteins (IDL) which are similar in composition; the major apoproteins are apo-B and apo-E, and the apolar core contains about 65% triglyceride and 35% cholesteryl esters. Under normal circumstances, the transient appearance in the blood stream of chylomicron remnants and IDL in only very low concentrations is due to the rapidity with which they are further metabolised.

Although earlier studies indicated that the metabolism of intestinal and hepatic triglyceride-rich lipoproteins could both give rise to LDL, there is now evidence that in man and certain experimental animals such as the rabbit chylomicron remnants (containing apo-B_{48}) and IDL (containing apo-B_{100}) are metabolised by different pathways. Malloy et al. (1981) showed that a patient with normotriglyceridaemic abetalipoproteinaemia could synthesise chylomicrons (containing apo-B_{48}) but could not synthesise either VLDL or LDL. Moreover, it has been found that the LDL in normal human serum contains only apo-B_{100} and virtually no apo-B_{48} (Kane, Hardman and Paulus, 1980). This indicates that LDL cannot be derived from the catabolism of chylomicrons and intestinal VLDL which in man contain only apo-B_{48}. On the other hand, the results of trans-splanchnic arteriovenous difference studies in man (Turner et al., 1979) showed that IDL derived from hepatic VLDL (containing apo-B_{100}) were converted into LDL in the liver.

The rapid clearance of chylomicron remnants (and for that matter, IDL derived from intestinal VLDL) from the blood appears to involve the uptake of these particles totally by liver cells. There is evidence that apo-E is the component of the chylomicron remnant that is recognised and bound by a specific apo-E receptor on the plasma hepatic membrane. The particle is then 'internalised' by an endocytotic process and the components of the particle hydrolysed within the hepatocyte by lysosomal enzymes (e.g. acid lipase, monoglyceride lipase, phospholipases, proteolytic enzymes, cholesteryl ester hydrolase). It seems reasonable to suppose that apo-B_{48} also has some role in the recognition or binding of the chylomicron remnants to the apo-E receptor, but this role has yet to be defined. Alternatively, it could be argued that the apo-E receptor binds only those apo-E-containing lipoproteins that do not contain apo-B_{100}. Apo-C has been shown to inhibit the uptake of chylomicron remnants by the liver.

In man and rabbits, apo-B_{100} and apo-E are the predominant apoproteins of IDL derived from hepatic VLDL. Unlike the apo-B_{48}-containing chylomicron remnants which have only one metabolic fate, at least two mechanisms are available for the further metabolism of IDL containing apo-B_{100}. The first of these involves endocytotic uptake by, and catabolism within liver cells, and the second involves conversion into LDL. Experiments with Watanabe heritable hyperlipidaemic (WHHL) rabbits (Huettinger et al., 1984) have shown that the receptor responsible for the uptake by the liver of IDL containing apo-B_{100} is different from that responsible for the uptake of chylomicron remnants containing apo-B_{48}. The plasma hepatic membrane contains a second type of lipoprotein receptor (the apo-B,E or LDL receptor) and it is this receptor that mediates the uptake of IDL containing apo-B_{100}. However, as with chylomicron remnants, it would appear to be the apo-E of IDL that is recognised and bound by the apo-B,E receptor. The operation of this receptor will be discussed further in connection with the catabolism of LDL.

The apolar core of LDL contains about 93% cholesteryl esters and 7% triglycerides; apo-B_{100} is virtually the only apoprotein present in the surface film. In the conversion of IDL to LDL, the mean weight of the particles decreases from about 8.0 to 3.0 daltons $\times 10^{-6}$, a loss accounted for mainly by the removal of core triglycerides, but also surface film cholesterol, phospholipids and apo-E. There is no loss of apo-B_{100} from the surface film and very little loss of cholesteryl esters from the apolar core. The mechanism of this conversion is incompletely understood, but there is strong evidence that it involves the participation of hepatic endothelial lipase (HEL), an enzyme located on the surface of endothelial cells surrounding the liver sinusoids. Thus, when antiserum raised to purified HEL is injected into rats, the conversion of IDL into LDL is markedly inhibited (Grosser, Schrecker and Greten, 1981; Murase and Itakura, 1981). HEL hydrolyses phospholipids as well as triglycerides (Nikkila et al., 1984). It is conceivable that IDL is converted into LDL in the blood permeating the liver by a process analogous to that responsible for the conversion of VLDL into IDL in adipose tissue, for example. The IDL triglycerides may be hydrolysed by HEL located on the surface of the liver cells, and the products of hydrolysis taken up by the hepatocytes; redundant surface film material, i.e. phospholipid, cholesterol and apo-E, may then be transferred to HDL with the formation of HDL_1 (see later). However, since HEL can be detected in coated pits, coated vesicles and secondary lysosomes in liver endothelial cells, Kinnunen, Virtanen and Vainio (1983) have proposed that IDL binds to HEL and is internalised via coated pits and coated vesicles. Conversion into LDL occurs in secondary lysosomes which then open at the endothelial surface releasing LDL into the circulation.

In all mammalian species examined so far, it seems probable that a proportion of IDL is metabolised by each of the pathways outlined above, but the proportion varies between species. The conversion of IDL into LDL appears to be of minor importance in rats, guinea pigs and ruminant animals (Moore and Christie, 1984); this could be due to low HEL activity and/or high apo-B,E receptor activity in the liver of these species. In man, the pathway leading to LDL formation is of greater importance, but even so, there is considerable variation in the proportion of IDL metabolised by this pathway. According to Havel (1984), IDL produced from large

VLDL particles are more likely to be bound, internalised and catabolised in the liver cells, whereas IDL produced from small VLDL particles are more likely to be converted to LDL. The size of the VLDL particles is determined mainly by the relative rates of synthesis of core and surface film components. This difference in metabolic fate is likely to be due to the fact that IDL derived from large VLDL contains large amounts of apo-E per particle and this promotes rapid binding and endocytosis; whereas IDL derived from small VLDL contain smaller amounts of apo-E per particle and this presents a greater opportunity for conversion to LDL since binding to the apo-E receptor and endocytosis will occur less rapidly (Havel, 1984).

Investigations with a variety of experimental animals have shown that the liver removes about 60% of the LDL from the circulation each day. Other tissues that remove appreciable amounts of LDL from the blood are the adrenal gland, spleen and ovary (Brown and Goldstein, 1983; Pittman and Steinberg, 1984). The mechanism of the uptake of LDL from the blood was first elucidated with cultured mammalian fibroblasts and smooth muscle cells, and was shown to consist of an ordered sequence of events in which LDL is initially bound to a receptor on the cell surface, followed by endocytosis and degradation of the LDL particle by lysosomal enzymes (Goldstein and Brown, 1977). This process is known as the LDL pathway and has been shown to operate in most tissues of the body (Mahley and Innerarity, 1983). The human LDL receptor is a glycoprotein containing 839 amino acid residues which is synthesised in the rough endoplasmic reticulum and inserted at random in the plasma membrane. The LDL receptor then migrates laterally in the plane of the membrane until it encounters an indentation in the membrane coated on the cytoplasmic surface with a protein called clathrin; about 80% of the LDL receptors in the plasma membrane are concentrated in these 'coated pits' which cover only about 2% of the cell surface. Each LDL receptor is thought to possess two types of binding site; one is exposed on the external surface of the plasma membrane and is involved in binding lipoproteins, and the other is exposed on the cytoplasmic surface of the plasma membrane and binds to the clathrin coat, thereby fixing the position of the receptor in the coated pit. Earlier studies indicated that LDL were the only serum lipoproteins that would bind to this receptor, and it was assumed that the ligand for this binding was apo-B, virtually the only apoprotein present in LDL. However, it was subsequently discovered that the LDL receptor would also bind HDL_1 which also has an apolar core of cholesteryl esters and is about the same size as LDL. On the other hand, HDL_1 contains appreciable amounts of apo-E but no apo-B, whereas LDL contains appreciable amounts of apo-B but no apo-E. It is now known that the apo-B of LDL and the apo-E of HDL_1 bind to the same receptor site, and the LDL receptor is more recently referred to as the apo-B,E receptor. The mode of binding to the receptor is not the same for apo-B and apo-E, for there is evidence that each HDL_1 particle binds to four sites on each apo-B,E receptor, whereas each LDL particle binds to single sites on each apo-B,E receptor (Mahley and Innerarity, 1983). The fact that a lipoprotein particle contains apo-B and/or apo-E does not guarantee that it will bind to the apo-B,E receptor; binding efficiency may also depend on the lipid content or size of the particle. Normal VLDL containing apo-B and apo-E do not bind to the apo-B,E receptor, but can be induced to do so after the partial removal of core lipid by extraction with diethyl ether.

Binding of LDL to the apo-B,E receptor is followed by endocytosis and the formation of coated vesicles within the cell. These vesicles rapidly lose their clathrin coats and fuse together to form endosomes in which the LDL particles dissociate from the apo-B,E receptor. Most of the dissociated apo-B,E receptors return to the cell surface where they again assemble into coated pits. The endosomes fuse with primary lysosomes and the cholesteryl esters, phospholipids and apo-B contained in the LDL particles are hydrolysed by lysosomal cholesteryl ester hydrolase, phospholipase and proteolytic enzymes respectively. The free cholesterol so released may be utilised for expansion of the cell membrane, but when this requirement has been satisfied, the remaining cholesterol inhibits HMG CoA-reductase activity and this inhibits the endogenous synthesis of cholesterol within the cell. At the same time, acyl CoA:cholesterol acyl transferase is activated and cholesterol not required for the assembly of new cell membranes is re-esterified; when sufficient cholesterol has accumulated in the cell, the synthesis of the apo-B,E receptor, and the recycling of existing receptor between endosomes and the cell surface are both suppressed. This inhibits further uptake of LDL by the cell which is thereby protected against abnormal accumulation of cholesterol.

Under certain circumstances, the suppression of apo-B,E receptor activity can lead to the accumulation of high concentrations of LDL in the blood. This is most evident in patients with familial hypercholesterolaemia (FH), of which there are various types, but all are characterised by defective apo-B,E receptor activity. Depending on the type of FH, the absence of normal receptor activity has been shown to be due to a variety of metabolic errors such as a deficiency in receptor synthesis or in transport of receptor from the site of synthesis to the cell surface. In other types of FH, defective receptors are synthesised and transported to the plasma cell membrane; in one variant, the receptor binds normally with clathrin but is unable to bind with LDL, whereas in another variant, the receptor binds normally with LDL, but not with clathrin, so that the bound LDL particles cannot be internalised (Goldstein and Brown, 1984).

Quite apart from genetic abnormalities, the metabolic suppression or stimulation of apo-B,E receptor activity plays an important part in controlling LDL levels in the blood. This is well illustrated by the contrasting results obtained from experiments with rats and rabbits. When rabbits are given a diet supplemented with cholesterol, cholesterol accumulates in the liver and this suppresses hepatic HMG CoA-reductase activity and the synthesis of apo-B,E receptor in the liver cells. The uptakes of LDL (via apo-B) and IDL (via apo-E) are inhibited and as a result greater proportions of IDL are converted to LDL. Consequently, high concentrations of LDL accumulate in the blood (Kovanen et al., 1981). When rats are given a high cholesterol diet, cholesterol also accumulates in the liver and hepatic HMG CoA-reductase is inhibited, but apo-B,E receptor activity is not suppressed and LDL levels in the blood do not increase (Koelz et al., 1982). On the other hand, apo-B,E receptor activity in, and uptake of LDL by the liver can be stimulated by the administration of cholestyramine (Packard and Shepherd, 1983) which increases the conversion of cholesterol into bile acids and hence the demand for cholesterol by the liver. This effect is more pronounced if cholestyramine is administered together with compactin which inhibits HMG CoA-reductase and hence synthesis de novo of cholesterol in the liver (Kovanen et al., 1981). The administration of cholestyramine has been shown to decrease serum LDL levels in man and experimental animals (Levy and Langer, 1972; Kovanen et al., 1981; Packard and Shepherd, 1983).

By comparing the clearance rates of LDL in normal subjects with those in patients with FH and lacking apo-B,E receptor activity, Brown and Goldstein (1983) calculated that about 65% of the serum LDL in man is cleared by the receptor pathway; the remainder must be cleared by a mechanism that is independent of the LDL receptor. Chemical modification of the arginine and lysine residues of the apoprotein moieties of LDL and HDL_1 abolishes the binding of these lipoproteins to the apo-B,E receptor; comparison of the clearance rates of normal and chemically modified LDL has provided a technique for estimating the relative proportion of LDL catabolised by the receptor-dependent and the receptor-independent pathways. This technique has been used to demonstrate that 70% of LDL is cleared by the receptor-dependent pathway in rabbits, and about 50% in rats and monkeys (Mahley and Innerarity, 1983). The proportion of LDL taken up by the receptor-dependent and receptor-independent pathways also varies with tissues. For example, in experiments with hamsters Spady, Bilheimer and Dietschy (1983) found that more than 90% of the LDL taken up by the liver was by the receptor-dependent pathway, whereas the receptor independent-pathway accounted for 44% and 72% of the LDL taken up by the intestine and spleen. Little is known about the precise mechanism of LDL catabolism by the receptor-independent pathway.

High density lipoproteins

The time consuming elucidation of the metabolic pathways involving the low density group of lipoproteins was at least facilitated by techniques that utilised isotopic labelling of the constituent apo-B, an apoprotein known not to exchange between the various lipoprotein classes. The fact that both the lipid and apoprotein components of HDL exchange freely between the sub-groups within this class of lipoproteins and between HDL and the low density lipoproteins has hindered progress in the understanding of LDL catabolism. However, some progress has been made by the use of HDL in which the constituent apo-AI was labelled with [^{125}I] tyramine-cellobiose (Glass, Pittman and Steinberg, 1983) and the core cholesteryl esters with [^{3}H] cholesteryl ethers (Glass et al., 1983; Stein et al., 1983), the ether bond of which is not cleaved in animal tissues. In rats, the liver was found to be the major site of apo-AI and cholesteryl ester uptake from HDL, but the ovary and adrenal gland showed high levels of uptake when the results were expressed per gram of tissue. These experiments also showed that the uptake of cholesteryl esters from HDL by the liver, ovary and adrenal gland was disproportionately greater than the uptake of apo-AI. This finding was confirmed in studies with cultured rat adrenal cells and hepatocytes, and also with cultured human cells, and in which HDL containing only apo-AI and no apo-E was the only lipoprotein present in the culture medium (Pittman and Steinberg, 1984). Thus, the uptake of cholesteryl esters from HDL did not appear to involve internalisation of the whole HDL particle by the cells, which contrasts with the mechanism of uptake of LDL cholesteryl esters by various cell types.

   Glomset (1968) had proposed that cholesterol could be transferred from the membranes of cells in various tissues to the HDL (presumably HDL_3) that circulates in the interstitial fluid. The cholesterol so acquired by HDL could be esterified by LCAT, which is present in the interstitial fluid as well as in the blood plasma, and the resulting cholesteryl esters would be deposited in the apolar core of the HDL particles, i.e. HDL_3 would be transformed into HDL_2. Since HDL particles move freely between the interstitial fluid and blood plasma, this process seemed to provide a means whereby excess cholesterol in peripheral tissues could be transported to the liver and eliminated from the body.

More recently, Oram, Brinton and Bierman (1983) have obtained evidence of a specific receptor on the surface of cultured human fibroblasts that binds HDL without internalisation and degradation. If the fibroblasts are loaded with cholesterol by pre-incubation with LDL, the number of HDL binding sites is increased. The binding of HDL to these sites appears to be associated with the removal of cholesterol from the cells. Noting the apparent complementary nature of the findings of Glass et al. (1983), Oram et al. (1983) and Stein et al. (1983), Pittman and Steinberg (1984) proposed the following cyclic function of HDL in the transfer of cholesterol from peripheral tissues to the liver. Peripheral cells containing an excess of cholesterol bind HDL_3 via an apo-AI receptor; no internalisation of the HDL particle occurs, but binding is followed by the transfer of cholesterol from the cell to HDL. The additional cholesterol acquired by HDL is esterified by LCAT and forms part of the apolar core. The HDL_2 so formed is then transported via the interstitial fluid and blood to the liver where it is bound, possibly by an apo-AI receptor, but not internalised. Some of the core cholesteryl esters are taken up by the liver and the HDL particle now relieved of part of its cholesteryl ester load reverts to HDL_3 and is returned to the blood stream and interstitial fluid where it can participate again in the uptake of excess cholesterol from peripheral tissues.

When HDL contains sufficient apo-E, it can be catabolised by the pathway involving the apo-B,E receptor or the apo-E receptor (Mahley and Innerarity, 1983), but the concentration of apo-E in HDL varies considerably between species. Rat HDL contains appreciable amounts of apo-E and can thus be taken up and catabolised by the apo-B,E receptor (Drevon et al., 1981). In contrast, the concentration of apo-E in human HDL is normally insufficient to promote binding with the apo-B,E receptor. However, supplementation of the diet of man with cholesterol results in the appearance of an apo-E-rich HDL fraction, HDL_1, in the blood (Mahley, 1978, 1982) and HDL_1 can bind to the apo-B,E receptor or the apo-E receptor (see later).

Influence of dietary cholesterol on blood lipoproteins

The hypercholesterolaemia that can be induced by excessive dietary cholesterol is characterised by the appearance in the blood of β-VLDL, increased concentrations of IDL and LDL, decreased concentrations of HDL_2 and increased concentrations of HDL_1 (Mahley, 1978).

β-VLDL

β-VLDL are not normally detectable in the blood plasma of man and the commonly used experimental animals. This class of lipoprotein was first isolated from the plasma of patients with the genetic disease known as dysbetalipo-proteinaemia or type III hyperlipoproteinaemia. It was subsequently found that β-VLDL accumulates in the plasma of experimental animals given diets supplemented with cholesterol (Mahley, 1978, 1979; Mahley et al., 1980). There is evidence also for the presence of β-VLDL in the plasma of normal subjects given cholesterol-rich diets (Mistry et al., 1981; Nestel et al., 1982). In normal plasma VLDL, the diameters of the particles vary between 25 nm and 75 nm, and the apolar lipid core is composed of about 75% triglycerides and 25% cholesteryl esters; the predominant apoproteins are apo-B, apo-C and apo-E. The size of β-VLDL in the plasma of animals given cholesterol-rich diets is about the same as that of normal VLDL, but the apolar lipid core consists of about 15% triglyceride and 85% cholesteryl esters. In β-VLDL, apo-B and apo-E are the major apoproteins with apo-C present in much smaller concentrations than it is in normal VLDL (Mahley, 1978; Brown and Goldstein, 1983).

There is some uncertainty about the metabolic origin of β-VLDL. When Rhesus monkeys were given a diet containing 2% cholesterol, the β-VLDL that appeared in the plasma contained apo-B_{48}, but no apo-B_{100} and this led to the conclusion that β-VLDL originated from the cells of the intestinal mucosa (Lusk, Chung and Scanu, 1982). Lusk, Chung and Scanu (1982) point out that in man, Rhesus monkeys and rabbits given high-cholesterol diets, chylomicrons and intestinal VLDL obtained from thoracic lymph contain much higher proportions of cholesteryl esters than do the corresponding intestinal lipoproteins secreted under normal dietary conditions. When such VLDL enriched with cholesteryl esters enter the blood stream, there will be a rapid acquisition of apo-E from HDL and a concomitant transfer of apo-A to HDL, a process which could account for the formation of β-VLDL. In an analogous manner, cholesterol ester-rich chylomicrons could presumably give rise to β-VLDL after removal of most of the constituent triglycerides by the action of lipoprotein lipase. On the other hand, the work of Swift *et al.* (1982, 1984) indicates that in the hypercholesterolaemic rat, plasma β-VLDL can originate from hepatocytes as well as from enterocytes. The β-VLDL obtained from hypercholesterolaemic dogs was separated by Fainaru *et al.* (1982) into two fractions both containing predominantly apo-B and apo-E. However, fraction I contained both apo-B_{48} and apo-B_{100} and was thought to be derived from intestinal lipoproteins, whereas fraction II contained only apo-B_{100} and was probably of hepatic origin. Similarly the β-VLDL from patients with dysbetalipoproteinaemia was also found to be comprised of two fractions analogous to those found in hypercholesterolaemic dogs (Fainaru *et al.*, 1982).

Experiments in which [^{125}I] β-VLDL was injected into normal animals have shown that β-VLDL particles are rapidly removed from the blood circulation. This rapid removal is thought to involve binding to the apo-B,E receptor followed by endocytosis and catabolism, mainly in hepatocytes but also in extrahepatic cells (Brown and Goldstein, 1983). However, it is known that apo-B,E receptor activity is suppressed by cholesterol-rich diets and Kovanen *et al.* (1981) have shown that the addition of cholesterol to the diet of rabbits decreases the rate of uptake of β-VLDL by the liver *in vivo*. Thus the accumulation of β-VLDL in dietary-induced hypercholesterolaemia may be due to decreased rates of clearance as well as increased rates of synthesis.

There is another mechanism that may be partly responsible for the clearance of β-VLDL from the blood stream. Mouse peritoneal macrophages were found to possess binding sites that mediate the uptake and lysosomal catabolism of β-VLDL (Goldstein *et al.*, 1980). β-VLDL are the only class of naturally occurring lipoproteins (as distinct from chemically modified ones) that bind to macrophage receptors; macrophages obtained from other animals and from man have now been shown to exhibit β-VLDL receptor activity. The extent to which β-VLDL are cleared from the blood stream by the action of macrophage β-VLDL receptors is unknown. In experiments with dogs given cholesterol-rich diets, Mahley (1979) noted that when the plasma cholesterol level exceeded 750 mg/dl there was a simultaneous appearance of β-VLDL in the plasma and a marked deposition of cholesteryl esters in macrophages throughout the body. Based on this type of evidence, Brown and Goldstein (1983) conclude that the macrophage β-VLDL receptor probably functions as a reserve mechanism to clear β-VLDL from the blood when these lipoproteins cannot be removed, for whatever reason, by the apo-B,E receptors on hepatocytes and other cells. The cholesterol taken up by macrophages in this way may eventually be returned to the liver for excretion under more favourable conditions. In tissue culture, cholesterol-laden macrophages are known to secrete cholesterol and at the same time synthesise and secrete apo-E into the medium (Basu *et al.*, 1981, 1982). The secreted cholesterol and apo-E could be incorporated into HDL_1 which would provide a means of transporting cholesterol to the liver for uptake either via the apo-B,E or apo-E receptor mechanisms. The possible connection between cholesterol-laden macrophages and the foam cells of atherosclerotic plaques is discussed in detail by Brown and Goldstein (1983).

IDL and LDL

The increase in the concentrations of serum IDL and LDL that can be observed in man and some experimental animals when their diets are supplemented with cholesterol may be explained in terms of the repression of apo-B,E receptor activity. Mention has been made already of the work of Kovanen *et al.* (1981) and Koelz *et al.* (1982) who showed that cholesterol-rich diets increased the cholesterol content of the liver in both rabbits and rats, but that suppression of apo-B,E receptor activity occurred in rabbits but not in rats. This explains why the rat is particularly resistant to hypercholesterolaemia induced by dietary cholesterol, and why the addition of very small amounts of cholesterol to the diet of rabbits results in very large increases in serum cholesterol levels (Moore and Williams, 1964, 1966), characterised by large increases in the concentrations of IDL and LDL. Thus the plasma cholesterol level in rabbits on a control diet was 87 mg/dl, but this increased to 577 and 2105 mg/dl when the rabbits were given for one and six weeks respectively a diet containing 1% cholesterol. The corresponding values for plasma LDL concentrations were 38, 333 and 1165 mg/dl (Slater, Shepherd and Packard, 1982). After one and six weeks on the cholesterol-supplemented diet, apo-B,E receptor activity in the liver was suppressed to the extent of 83% and 88% respectively. There was no significant effect of dietary cholesterol on the receptor-independent uptake of LDL after one week, but after six weeks there was some repression of the receptor-independent pathway, but only in the liver and spleen.

   That high levels of dietary cholesterol can suppress apo-B,E receptor activity in man was shown by Applebaum-Bowden *et al.* (1984) in an experiment with six men and three women who were given diets contributing 137 mg/d or 1034 mg/d cholesterol; the additional cholesterol was derived from egg yolk. The supplementary cholesterol in the diet had no effect on the mean plasma cholesterol level, but it increased the mean concentration of plasma LDL and decreased the mean apo-B,E receptor activity determined in circulating mononuclear cells. Examination of the results from individuals revealed a striking linear correlation between the percentage increase in plasma LDL and the percentage suppression of apo-B,E receptor activity. For example, the additional dietary cholesterol given to one subject had very little effect on the plasma LDL level and only a 15% decrease in apo-B,E receptor activity, but in another subject it increased the plasma LDL level by 30% and decreased the apo-B,E receptor activity by almost 70%. Since LDL and IDL containing apo-B_{100} are catabolised via the same receptor (apo-B,E), suppression of the activity of this receptor may be expected to increase serum LDL levels for two reasons: first, receptor-mediated catabolism of IDL and LDL is decreased, and second, synthesis of LDL is increased as more IDL becomes available for conversion into LDL.

HDL_2 and HDL_1

The addition of cholesterol to the diets of various experimental animals brings about marked changes in the serum HDL fraction; the proportion of HDL_2 (diameter 8–11 nm) decreases and the proportion of the much larger HDL_1 (diameter 13–50 nm) increases (Mahley, 1978). HDL_1, sometimes referred to as HDL_C, normally constitutes only a very small proportion of mammalian serum HDL. Like HDL_2, HDL_1 contains apo-AI and no apo-B, but unlike HDL_2, HDL_1 contains apo-E. Continued administration of cholesterol-supplemented diets to animals causes an increase in size of the HDL_1 particles due to an increased accumulation of cholesteryl esters in the apolar core. The apo-E content of the particle also increases until it eventually becomes the predominant apoprotein present. According to Mahley (1978) HDL_1 is formed from HDL_2 which has acquired additional cholesterol and apo-E by transfer from other cholesterol-rich lipoproteins. Some of the additional cholesterol may also be acquired by transfer to HDL_2 in the interstitial fluid from tissue cells that contain an excess of cholesterol (Dory et al., 1983); LCAT catalyses the conversion of this additional cholesterol into core cholesteryl esters and HDL_2 is transformed into HDL_1 (Dory et al., 1985). The apo-E in HDL_1 may be derived by transfer from other lipoproteins in the blood, but there is also the possibility of a concomitant transfer of apo-E with cholesterol to HDL_2 in the interstitial fluid from tissue cells that are laden with cholesterol (Blue et al., 1983). Although it appeared originally that the liver was the predominant site of apo-E synthesis, Driscoll and Getz (1984) have demonstrated with rats and guinea pigs that apo-E is actively synthesised in most extrahepatic tissues, with the exception of the intestinal mucosa.

   Addition of cholesterol to the diet of man also results in the appearance of HDL_1 in the blood circulation. In an experiment reported by Mahley et al. (1978), the diet of five individuals was supplemented with cholesterol by gradually increasing the consumption of eggs up to 3/d during an 18 week period. At the beginning of the experiment, HDL_1 was barely detectable in plasma, but although the additional dietary cholesterol produced no significant change in the total plasma cholesterol concentration, it markedly increased the concentration of HDL_1 in the plasma.

   By virtue of the apo-E that it contains, HDL_1 can be taken up from the blood and catabolised in the liver by receptor-mediated processes that involve either the apo-E receptor or the apo-B,E receptor (Mahley and Innerarity, 1983). When blood and extrahepatic tissues contain excess cholesterol due to the absorption of large amounts of dietary cholesterol, it seems likely that HDL_1 becomes an important vehicle for the delivery of this excess cholesterol to the liver for excretion. Although the absorption of large amounts of dietary cholesterol leads to a decrease in apo-B,E receptor activity, the activity of the apo-E receptor is relatively unaffected (Mahley and Innerarity, 1983). Thus one of the two receptor-mediated pathways remains open for the disposal of HDL_1. The HDL_1 vehicle may also be important in the delivery of cholesterol to the liver for excretion in abetalipoproteinaemic patients who are unable to synthesise apo-B and, consequently, apo-B containing lipoproteins (Innerarity *et al.*, 1984).

Conclusions

Over the last 30 years or so there has been considerable controversy about the extent to which plasma cholesterol levels in man are influenced by dietary cholesterol. Since eggs constitute an important source of cholesterol (about 270 mg/egg) in the human diet, many investigators have concentrated on determining whether or not increased egg consumption results in a significant hypercholesterolaemic response. The results of many experiments (summarised by Glueck and Connor, 1978) with subjects in metabolic wards where nutrient intake can be standardised and measured with precision, showed that the consumption of one or two eggs/d resulted in an approximate 10% or 20% increase respectively in the concentration of cholesterol in the plasma. However, it must be emphasised that in all of these metabolic ward experiments the basal or control diets contained little or no cholesterol. It is perhaps more relevant to question whether plasma cholesterol levels are influenced by the addition of eggs to the normal mixed diets of adult man. Such diets contribute about 450 mg/d cholesterol. The answer to this question has been sought from experiments that have been conducted on an outpatient basis where it is inevitable that information on nutrient intake must lack precision. In most of these experiments no significant increases in plasma cholesterol levels resulted from the addition of one or two eggs/d to habitual mixed diets that already provided between 250 and 500 mg/d cholesterol (Kummerow *et al.*, 1977; Porter *et al.*, 1977; Bronsgeest-Schoute *et al.*, 1979; Flynn *et al.*, 1979; Buzzard *et al.*, 1982). In the few experiments in which a significant increase in plasma cholesterol was detected (Roberts, McMurray and Connor, 1981) the magnitude of this increase was small (i.e. less than 10%). Nevertheless, attention must be drawn to the results of at least two experiments (Applebaum-Bowden *et al.*, 1984; Sacks *et al.*, 1984) in which supplementary eggs in the diet did not significantly increase total plasma cholesterol levels but significantly increased plasma LDL cholesterol levels.

Translation of these findings, which are based on treatment means, into dietary advice that may be given to the general public is also complicated by the considerable variation that exists between individual subjects. For example, in the paper of Roberts, McMurray and Connor (1981), results are presented for eight normal healthy individuals whose customary diet was supplemented with a cholesterol-free egg substitute for four weeks, and then with eggs (supplying 500 mg/d cholesterol) for four weeks. In five of the subjects the plasma cholesterol level responded minimally or not at all (mean increase 4%), whereas in the other three subjects the plasma cholesterol level responded markedly (mean increase 22%). The wide variation that exists between individual subjects in their metabolic responses to increased intakes of dietary cholesterol has been recognised for some years. Thus, in individual subjects given a high-cholesterol diet, the efficiency of cholesterol absorption varied from 25% to 42%; the amount of cholesterol retained in the body tissues varied from 0 to 26% of that absorbed, and the amount of cholesterol re-excreted in the faeces varied from 31% to 68% of that absorbed (Quintao, Grundy and Ahrens, 1971b). In the same series of experiments, Quintao, Grundy and Ahrens (1971b) found that when a low-cholesterol diet was replaced by a high-cholesterol diet, the reduction in the rate of endogenous cholesterol synthesis in individual subjects varied from about 40 mg/d to about 750 mg/d, and that this variation was not related to variations in the efficiency of cholesterol absorption. This indicates that there must be large differences between individuals in the sensitivity of the feedback mechanism that controls the rate of endogenous cholesterol synthesis. More recently, the work of Applebaum-Bowden *et al.* (1984) has shown that when the natural diet of normal healthy individuals was supplemented with eggs (equivalent to about 900 mg/d cholesterol), suppression of apo-B,E receptor activity varied from 15% for one individual to 70% for another. When variations of this magnitude exist between apparently normal individuals in their metabolic responses to a challenge of dietary cholesterol, it is doubtful whether overall advice on cholesterol intake to large populations is possible or even desirable. Although it is clear that patients with FH and related errors of metabolism should be advised to reduce their intake of dietary cholesterol to the lowest possible levels, some have argued that this advice should be extended to the population as a whole. This is hardly justified since it would involve the elimination of some of the most nutritious components (e.g. eggs) from the human diet to accommodate the metabolic idiosyncrasies of what is probably a very small proportion of the total population. Quite apart from patients with FH in which there is a permanent deficiency of apo-B,E receptor activity, it now appears that there are in the population apparently healthy individuals who express normal apo-B,E receptor activity under conditions of moderate cholesterol intakes, but who respond to increased dietary cholesterol by severely suppressing apo-B,E receptor activity, which leads to significant increases in the levels of LDL cholesterol in the blood. Determination of plasma LDL cholesterol levels before and after a challenge of dietary cholesterol would identify those who should decrease their cholesterol intake.

References

ANDERSON, J.M., TURLEY, S.D. and DIETSCHY, J.M. (1982). Relative rates of sterol synthesis in the liver and various extrahepatic tissues of normal and cholesterol-fed rabbits. *Biochimica et Biophysica Acta*, **711**, 421–430

APPLEBAUM-BOWDEN, D., HAFFNER, S.M., HARTSOOK, E., LUK, K.H., ALBERS, J.J. and HAZZARD, W.R. (1984). Down-regulation of the low-density lipoprotein receptor by dietary cholesterol. *American Journal of Clinical Nutrition*, **39**, 360–367

BACK, P., HAMPRECHT, B and LYNEN, F. (1969). Regulation of cholesterol biosynthesis in rat liver: diurnal changes of activity and influence of bile acids. *Archives of Biochemistry and Biophysics*, **133**, 11–21

BARTH, C.A. and HILLMAR, I. (1980). Taurocholic acid inhibits the glucocorticoid-induced rise of 3-hydroxy-3-methylglutaryl-CoA reductase in primary cultures of hepatocytes. *European Journal of Biochemistry*, **110**, 237–240

BASU, S.K., BROWN, M.S., HO, Y.K., HAVEL, R.J. and GOLDSTEIN, J.L. (1981). Mouse macrophages synthesize and secrete a protein resembling apolipoprotein E. *Proceedings of the National Academy of Sciences of the USA*, **78**, 7545–7549

BASU, S.K., HO, Y.K., BROWN, M.S., BILHEIMER, D.W. and ANDERSON, R.S.W. (1982). Biochemical and genetic studies of the apoprotein E secreted by mouse macrophages and human monocytes. *Journal of Biological Chemistry*, **257**, 9788–9795

BEHER, W.T. and BAKER, G.D. (1959). Inhibition of cholesterol biosynthesis by cholic acid. *American Journal of Physiology*, **197**, 1339–1340

BELL, J.J., SARGEANT, T.E. and WATSON, J.A. (1976). Inhibition of 3-hydroxy-3-methylglutaryl coenzyme A reductase activity in hepatoma tissue culture cells by pure cholesterol and several cholesterol derivatives. *Journal of Biological Chemistry*, **251**, 1745–1758

BLOCH, K. (1965). The biological synthesis of cholesterol. *Science*, **150**, 19–28

BLOCH, K., BERG, B.N. and RITTENBERG, D. (1943). The biological conversion of cholesterol to cholic acid. *Journal of Biological Chemistry*, **149**, 511–517

BLUE, M.L., WILLIAMS, D.L., ZUCKER, S., KAHN, S.A. and BLUM, C.B. (1983). Apolipoprotein E synthesis in human kidney, adrenal gland and liver. *Proceedings of the National Academy of Sciences of the USA*, **80**, 283–287

BORTZ, W.M. (1973). On the control of cholesterol synthesis. *Metabolism*, **22**, 1507–1524

BRONSGEEST-SCHOUTE, D.C., HERMUS, R.J.J., DALLINGA-THIL, G.M. and HAUTVAST, J.G.A.J. (1979). Effect on serum cholesterol of removal of eggs from the diet of free-living habitually egg-eating people. *American Journal of Clinical Nutrition*, **32**, 2193–2197

BROWN, M.S. and GOLDSTEIN, J.L. (1983). Lipoprotein metabolism in the macrophage. *Annual Reviews of Biochemistry*, **52**, 223–261

BUCHER, N.L.R. and MCGARRAHAN, K. (1956). The biosynthesis of cholesterol from acetate-1-C^{14} by cellular fractions of rat liver. *Journal of Biological Chemistry*, **222**, 1–15

BUCHER, N.L.R., MCGARRAHAN, K., GOULD, E. and LOUD, A.V. (1959). Cholesterol biosynthesis in preparations of liver from normal, fasting, X-irradiated, cholesterol-fed, Triton, Δ^4-cholesten-3-one treated rats. *Journal of Biological Chemistry*, **234**, 262–267

BUZZARD, I.M., MCROBERTS, M.R., DRISCOLL, D.L. and BOWERING, J. (1982). Effect of dietary eggs and ascorbic acid on plasma lipid and lipoprotein cholesterol levels in healthy young men. *American Journal of Clinical Nutrition*, **36**, 94–105

COATES, M.E., HARRISON, G.F. and MOORE, J.H. (1965). Cholesterol metabolism in germ-free and conventional chicks. *Ernährungsforschung*, **10**, 251–256

CONNOR, W.E. and LIN, D.S. (1974). The intestinal adsorption of dietary cholesterol by hypercholesterolemic (type II) and normocholesterolemic humans. *Journal of Clinical Investigation*, **53**, 1062–1070

CORNFORTH, J.W. (1959). Biosynthesis of fatty acids and cholesterol considered as chemical processes. *Journal of Lipid Research*, **1**, 3–28

CROUSE, J.R., GRUNDY, S.M. and JOHNSON, J.H. (1982). Effects of AOMA on cholesterol metabolism in man. *Metabolism*, **31**, 733–739

DANIELSSON, H. and EINARSSON, K. (1969). Formation and metabolism of bile acids. In *The Biological Basis of Medicine, Volume 5*, (Bittar, E.E. and Bittar, N., eds), pp. 279–315. London, Academic Press

DIETSCHY, J.M. (1978). General principles governing movement of lipids across biological membranes. In *Disturbances in Lipid and Lipoprotein Metabolism*, (Dietschy, J.M., Gotto, A.M. and Ontko, J.A., eds), pp. 1–28. Bethesda, Maryland, American Physiological Society

DIETSCHY, J.M. and SIPERSTEIN, M.D. (1967). Effect of cholesterol feeding and fasting on sterol synthesis in seventeen tissues of the rat. *Journal of Lipid Research*, **8**, 97–104

DIETSCHY, J.M. and SPADY, D.K. (1984). Measurement of rates of cholesterol synthesis using tritiated water. *Journal of Lipid Research*, **25**, 1469–1476

DIETSCHY, J.M. and WILSON, J.D. (1968). Cholesterol synthesis in the squirrel monkey: relative rates of synthesis in various tissues and mechanisms of control. *Journal of Clinical Investigation*, **147**, 166–174

DORY, L., BOQUET, L.M., HAMILTON, R.L., SLOOP, C.H. and ROHEIM, P.S. (1985). Heterogeneity of dog interstitial fluid (peripheral lymph) high density lipoproteins: implications for a role in reverse cholesterol transport. *Journal of Lipid Research*, **26**, 519–527

DORY, L., SLOOP, C.H., BOQUET, L.M., HAMILTON, R.L. and ROHEIM, P.S. (1983). Lecithin:cholesterol acyltransferase-mediated modification of discoidal peripheral lymph high density lipoproteins: possible mechanism of formation of cholesterol-induced high density lipoproteins (HDL_C) in cholesterol-fed dogs. *Proceedings of the National Academy of Sciences of the USA*, **80**, 3489–3493

DREVON, C.A., ATTIE, A.D., PANGBURN, S.H. and STEINBERG, D. (1981). Metabolism of homologous and heterologous lipoproteins by cultured rat and human skin fibroblasts. *Journal of Lipid Research*, **22**, 37–46

DRISCOLL, D.M. and GETZ, G.S. (1984). Extrahepatic synthesis of apolipoprotein E. *Journal of Lipid Research*, **25**, 1368–1379

EDWARDS, P.A. and GOULD, R.G. (1974). Dependence of the circadian rhythm of hepatic β-hydroxy-β-methyl glutaryl coenzyme A on ribonucleic acid synthesis. A possible second site of inhibition by dietary cholesterol. *Journal of Biological Chemistry*, **249**, 2891–2896

EISENBERG, S. (1976). Mechanisms of formation of low density lipoproteins: metabolic pathways and their regulation. In *Low Density Lipoproteins*, (Day, C.E. and Levy, R.S. eds), pp. 73–92. New York, Plenum Press

EISENBERG, S. (1984). High density lipoprotein metabolism. *Journal of Lipid Research*, **25**, 1017–1058

EISENBERG, S. and LEVY, R.I. (1975). Lipoprotein metabolism. *Advances in Lipid Research*, **13**, 1–89

EISENBERG, S., RACHMILEWITZ, D., LEVY, R.I., BILHEIMER, D.W. and LINDGREN, F.T. (1975). Pathways of lipoprotein metabolism: integration of structure, function and metabolism. *Advances in Experimental Medicine and Biology*, **63**, 61–76

FAINARU, M., MAHLEY, R.W., HAMILTON, R.L. and INNERARITY, T.L. (1982). Structural and metabolic heterogeneity of β-VLDL from cholesterol-fed dogs and from humans with type III hyperlipo-proteinaemia. *Journal of Lipid Research*, **23**, 702–714

FALLAT, R.W., GLUECK, C.J. and LUTMER, R. (1976). Short term study of sucrose polyester a nonabsorbable fat-like material as a dietary agent for lowering plasma cholesterol. *American Journal of Clinical Nutrition*, **29**, 1204–1215

FLYNN, M.A., NOLPH, G.B., FLYNN, T.C., KAHRS, R. and KRAUSE, G. (1979). Effect of dietary egg on human serum cholesterol and triglyceride. *American Journal of Clinical Nutrition*, **32**, 1051–1057

FULLER, R. and MOORE, J.H. (1971). The effect on rabbit intestinal microflora of diets that influence serum cholesterol levels. *Laboratory Animals*, **5**, 25–30

GEBHARD, R.L. and COOPER, A.D. (1978). Regulation of cholesterol synthesis in cultured canine intestinal mucosa. *Journal of Biological Chemistry*, **253**, 2790–2796

GERTLER, M.M., GARN, S.M. and LERMAN, J. (1950). The interrelationships of serum cholesterol, cholesterol esters and phospholipids in health and in coronary artery disease. *Circulation*, **2**, 205–214

GIBSON, D.M. and INGEBRITSEN, T.S. (1978). Reversible modulation of liver hydroxymethyl-glutaryl CoA reductase. *Life Sciences*, **23**, 2649–2664

GLASS, C.K., PITTMAN, R.C. and STEINBERG, D. (1983). Tissue sites of apoprotein A-I in the rat. *Journal of Biological Chemistry*, **258**, 7161–7167

GLASS, C.K., PITTMAN, R.C., WEINSTEIN, D.B. and STEINBERG, D. (1983). Dissociation of tissue uptake of cholesteryl ester from that of Apo-AI in rat plasma high-density lipoprotein:selective delivery of cholesteryl ester to the liver, adrenal and gonads. *Proceedings of the National Academy of Sciences of the USA*, **80**, 5435–5439

GLOMSET, J.A. (1968). The plasma lecithin:cholesterol acyl-transferase reaction. *Journal of Lipid Research*, **9**, 155–167

GLUECK, C.J. and CONNOR, W.E. (1978). Diet–coronary heart disease relationships reconnoitered. *American Journal of Clinical Nutrition*, **31**, 727–737

GLUECK, C.J., MATTSON, F.H. and JANDACEK, R.J. (1979). The lowering of plasma cholesterol by sucrose polyester in subjects consuming diets with 800, 300 or less than 50 mg cholesterol per day. *American Journal of Clincal Nutrition*, **32**, 1636–1644

GOLDFARB, G. and PITOT, H.C. (1972). Stimulatory effect of dietary lipid and cholestyramine on hepatic HMG CoA reductase. *Journal of Lipid Research*, **13**, 797–801

GOLDSTEIN, J.L. and BROWN, M.S. (1977). The low density lipoprotein pathway and its relation to atherosclerosis. *Annual Reviews of Biochemistry*, **46**, 897–930

GOLDSTEIN, J.L. and BROWN, M.S. (1984). Progress in understanding the LDL receptor and HMG-CoA reductase, two membrane proteins that regulate the plasma cholesterol. *Journal of Lipid Research*, **25**, 1450–1461

GOLDSTEIN, J.L., HO, Y.K., BROWN, M.S., INNERARITY, T.L. and MAHLEY, R.W. (1980). Cholesteryl ester accumulation in macrophages resulting from receptor-mediated uptake and degradation of hypercholesterolemic canine β-VLDL. *Journal of Biological Chemistry*, **255**, 1839–1848

GOULD, R.G. (1951). Lipid metabolism and atherosclerosis. *American Journal of Medicine*, **11**, 209–227

GOULD, R.G. (1977). Some aspects of the control of hepatic cholesterol biosynthesis. In *Cholesterol Metabolism and Lipolytic Enzymes*, (Polonovsky, J., ed.), pp. 13–38. New York, Masson Publishing

GREEN, P.H.R. and GLICKMAN, R.M. (1981). Intestinal lipoprotein metabolism. *Journal of Lipid Research*, **22**, 1153–1173

GROSSER, J., SCHRECKER, O. and GRETEN, H. (1981). Function of hepatic triglyceride lipase in lipoprotein metabolism. *Journal of Lipid Research*, **22**, 437–486

GRUNDY, S.M. and METZGER, A.L.I. (1972). A physiological method for estimating hepatic secretion of biliary lipids in man. *Gastroenterology*, **62**, 1200–1217

GRUNDY, S.M. and MOK, H.Y.I. (1976). Effect of low dose phytosterols on cholesterol absorption in man. In *Lipoprotein Metabolism*, (Geten, H., ed.), pp. 112–118. Berlin, Springer-Verlag

GRUNDY, S.M. and MOK, H.Y.I. (1977). Determination of cholesterol absorption in man by intestinal perfusion. *Journal of Lipid Research*, **18**, 263–271

GUSTAFSSON, B.E., BERGSTROM, S., LINDSTEDT, S. and NORMAN, A. (1957). Turnover and nature of faecal bile acids in germ free and infected rats fed cholic acid-24-^{14}C. *Proceedings of the Society for Experimental Biology and Medicine*, **94**, 467–471

HAMILTON, R.L. (1978). Hepatic secretion and metabolism of high density lipoproteins. In *Disturbances in Lipid and Lipoprotein Metabolism*, (Dietschy, J.M., Gotto, A.M. and Ontko, J.A., eds), pp. 155–171. Bethesda, Maryland, American Physiological Society

HAVEL, R.J. (1975). Lipoproteins and lipid transport. *Advances in Experimental Medicine and Biology*, **63**, 37–59

HAVEL, R.J. (1984). The formation of LDL:mechanisms and regulation. *Journal of Lipid Research*, **25**, 1570–1575

HEIMBERG, M. and WILCOX, H.G. (1972). The effect of palmitic and oleic acids on the properties and composition of the very low density lipoproteins secreted by the liver. *Journal of Biological Chemistry*, **247**, 875–880

HEROLD, G., SCHNEIDER, A., DITSCHUNEIT, H. and STANGE, E.F. (1984). Cholesterol synthesis and esterification in cultured intestinal mucosa. *Biochimica et Biophysica Acta*, **796**, 27–33

HIGGINS, M. and RUDNEY, H. (1973). Regulation of rat liver β-hydroxy-β-methylglutaryl-CoA reductase activity by cholesterol. *Nature (New Biology)*, **246**, 60–61

HILL, R., WEBSTER, W.W., LINAZASORO, J.M. and CHAIKOFF, I.L. (1960). Time of occurrence of changes in the liver's capacity to utilize acetate for fatty acid and cholesterol synthesis after fat feeding. *Journal of Lipid Research*, **1**, 150–153

HOFMANN, A.F. (1977). The enterohepatic circulation of bile acids in man. *Clinics in Gastroenterology*, **6**, 3–24

HUETTINGER, M., SCHNEIDER, W.J., HO, Y.K., GOLDSTEIN, J.L. and BROWN, M.S. (1984). Use of monoclonal anti-receptor antibodies to probe the expression of the low density apoprotein receptor in tissues of normal and Watanabe heritable hyperlipidemic rabbits. *Journal of Clinical Investigation*, **74**, 1017–1026

INNERARITY, T.L., BERSOT, T.P., ARNOLD, K.S., WEISGRABER, K.H., DAVIS, P.A., FORTE, T.M. and MAHLEY, R.W. (1984). Receptor binding activity of high-density lipoproteins containing apoprotein E from abetalipoproteinemic and normal neonate plasma. *Metabolism*, **33**, 186–195

KANDUTSCH, A.A. and CHEN, H.W. (1973). Inhibition of sterol synthesis in cultured mouse cells by 7α-hydroxycholesterol, 7β-hydroxycholesterol, and 7-ketocholesterol. *Journal of Biological Chemistry*, **248**, 8408–8417

KANDUTSCH, A.A. and CHEN, H.W. (1974). Inhibition of sterol synthesis in cultured mouse cells by cholesterol derivatives oxygenated in the side chain. *Journal of Biological Chemistry*, **249**, 6057–6061

KANDUTSCH, A.A., CHEN, H.W. and HEINIGER, H.J. (1978). Biological activity of some oxygenated sterols. *Science*, **201**, 498–501

KANE, J.P., HARDMAN, D.A. and PAULUS, H.E. (1980). Heterogeneity of apoliprotein B: isolation of a new species from human chylomicrons. *Proceedings of the National Academy of Sciences of the USA*, **77**, 2465–2469

KELLOG, T.F. (1971). Microbiological aspects of enterohepatic neutral sterol and bile acid metabolism. *Federation Proceedings*, **30**, 1808–1814

KINNUNEN, P.K.J., VIRTANEN, J.A. and VAINIO, P. (1983). Lipoprotein lipase and hepatic endothelial lipase: their roles in plasma lipoprotein metabolism. *Atherosclerosis Reviews*, **11**, 64–85

KOELZ, H.R., SHERRILL, B.C., TURLEY, S.D. and DIETSCHY, J.M. (1982). Correlation of low and high density lipoprotein binding *in vivo* with rates of lipoprotein degradation in the rat. *Journal of Biological Chemistry*, **257**, 8061–8072

KOVANEN, P.T., BROWN, M.S., BASU, S., BILHEIMER, D.W. and GOLDSTEIN, J.L. (1981). Saturation and suppression of hepatic lipoprotein receptors: a mechanism for the hypercholesterolemia of cholesterol-fed rabbits. *Proceedings of the National Academy of Sciences of the USA*, **78**, 1396–1400

KRITCHEVSKY, D., TEPPER, S.A. and STORY, J.A. (1975). Non-nutritive fibre and lipid metabolism. *Journal of Food Science*, **40**, 8–11

KUDCHODKAR, B.J., SODHI, H.S. and HORLICK, L. (1973). Absorption of dietary cholesterol in man. *Metabolism*, **22**, 155–163

KUMMEROW, F.A., KIM, Y., HULL, H.H., POLLARD, J., ILINOV, P., DOROSSIEV, D.L. and VALEK, J. (1977). The influence of egg consumption on the serum cholesterol level in human subjects. *American Journal of Clinical Nutrition*, **30**, 664–673

LANGDON, R.G. and BLOCH, K. (1953). The utilization of squalene in the biosynthesis of cholesterol. *Journal of Biological Chemistry*, **200**, 135–144

LEVY, R.I. and LANGER, T. (1972). Hyperlipidemic drugs and lipoprotein metabolism. *Advances in Experimental Medicine and Biology*, **26**, 155–163

LINAZASORO, J.M., HILL, R., CHEVALLIER, F. and CHAIKOFF, I.L. (1958). Regulation of cholesterol synthesis in the liver: the influence of dietary fat. *Journal of Experimental Medicine*, **107**, 813–820

LINDSTEDT, S. and NORMAN, A. (1956). The excretion of bile acids in rats treated with chemotherapeutics. *Acta Physiologica Scandinavica*, **38**, 129–134

LUSK, L., CHUNG, J. and SCANU, A.M. (1982). Properties and metabolic fate of two very low density lipoprotein subfractions from rhesus monkey serum. *Biochimica et Biophysica Acta*, **710**, 134–142

MAHLEY, R.W. (1978) Alterations in plasma lipoproteins induced by cholesterol feeding in animals including man. In *Disturbances in Lipid and Lipoprotein Metabolism*, (Dietschy, J.M., Gotto, A.M. and Ontko, J.A., eds) pp. 181–197. Bethesda, Maryland, American Physiological Society

MAHLEY, R.W. (1979). Dietary fat, cholesterol and accelerated atherosclerosis. *Atherosclerosis Reviews*, **5**, 1–34

MAHLEY, R.W. (1982). Atherogenic hyperlipoproteinemia: the cellular and molecular biology of plasma lipoproteins altered by fat and cholesterol. *Medical Clinics of North America*, **66**, 375–402

MAHLEY, R.W. and INNERARITY, T.L. (1983). Lipoprotein receptors and cholesterol homeostasis. *Biochimica et Biophysica Acta*, **737**, 197–222

MAHLEY, R.W., INNERARITY, T.L., BERSOTT, T.P., LIPSOM, A. and MARGOLIS, S. (1978). Alterations in human high density lipoproteins with or without increased plasma cholesterol induced by diets high in cholesterol. *Lancet*, **ii**, 807–809

MAHLEY, R.W., INNERARITY, T.L., BROWN, M.S., HO, Y.K. and GOLDSTEIN, J.L. (1980). Cholesterol ester synthesis in macrophages: stimulation by β-very low density lipoproteins from cholesterol-fed animals of several species. *Journal of Lipid Research*, **21**, 970–980

MAHLEY, R.W., INNERARITY, T.L., RALL, S.C. and WEISGRABER, K.H. (1984). Plasma lipoproteins; apolipoprotein structure and function. *Journal of Lipid Research*, **25**, 1277–1294

MALLOY, M.J., KANE, J.P., HARDMAN, D.A., HAMILTON, R.L. and DALAL, K.B. (1981). Normotriglyceridemic abetalipoproteinemia. Absence of the B_{100} apolipoprotein. *Journal of Clinical Investigation*, **67**, 1441–1450

MAYER, R.M., TREADWELL, C.R., GALLO, L.L. and VAHOUNY, G.V. (1985). Intestinal mucins and cholesterol uptake *in vitro*. *Biochimica et Biophysica Acta*, **833**, 34–43

MCMURRAY, M.P., CONNOR, W.E., LIN, D.S., CERQUEIRA, M.T. and CONNOR, S.J. (1985). The absorption of cholesterol and the sterol balance in the Tarahumara Indians of Mexico fed cholesterol-free and high cholesterol diets. *American Journal of Clinical Nutrition*, **41**, 1289–1298

MIETTINEN, T.A. (1973). Clinical implications of bile acid metabolism in man. In *The Bile Acids, Chemistry, Physiology and Metabolism, Volume 2, Physiology and Metabolism*, (Nair, P.P. and Kritchevsky, D., eds), pp. 191–247. New York, Plenum Press

MIGICOVSKY, B.B. (1955). Inhibition of cholesterol formation by rat liver homogenates. *Canadian Journal of Biochemistry and Physiology*, **33**, 135–138

MISTRY, P., MILLER, N.E., LAKER, M., HAZZARD, W.R. and LEWIS, B. (1981). Individual variation in the effects of dietary cholesterol on plasma lipoproteins and cellular cholesterol homeostasis in man. *Journal of Clinical Investigation*, **67**, 493–502

MOORE, J.H. (1967). The effect of the type of roughage in the diet on plasma cholesterol levels and aortic atherosis in rabbits. *British Journal of Nutrition*, **21**, 207–215

MOORE, J.H. and CHRISTIE, W.W. (1981). Lipid metabolism in the mammary gland of ruminant animals. In

Lipid Metabolism in Ruminant Animals, (Christie, W.W., ed.), pp. 227–277. Oxford, Pergamon Press

MOORE, J.H. and CHRISTIE, W.W. (1984). Digestion, absorption and transport of fats in ruminant animals. In *Fats in Animal Nutrition*, (Wiseman, J., ed.), pp. 123–149. London, Butterworths

MOORE, J.H. and WILLIAMS, D.L. (1964). The relationship between diet, plasma lipid composition and aortic atherosis in rabbits. *British Journal of Nutrition*, **18**, 431–448

MOORE, J.H. and WILLIAMS, D.L. (1966). The effect of an atherogenic diet on plasma lipid composition and aortic atherosis in two strains of New Zealand White rabbit. *British Journal of Nutrition*, **20**, 571–580

MURASE, G. and ITAKURA, H. (1981). Accumulation of an intermediate density lipoprotein in plasma after administration of hepatic triglyceride lipase antibody into rats. *Atherosclerosis*, **39**, 293–300

MYANT, N.B. and EDER, H.A. (1961). The effect of biliary drainage upon the synthesis of cholesterol in the liver. *Journal of Lipid Research*, **2**, 363–368

MYANT, N.B. and MITROPOULOS, K.A. (1977). Cholesterol 7α-hydroxylase. *Journal of Lipid Research*, **18**, 135–153

NESTEL, P., TADA, N., BILLINGTON, T., HUFF, M. and FIDGE, N. (1982). Changes in very low density lipoproteins with cholesterol loading in man. *Metabolism*, **31**, 398–405

NIKKILA, E.A., KUUSI, T., TASKINEN, M.J. and TIKKANEN, M.J. (1984). Regulation of lipoprotein metabolism by endothelial lipolytic enzymes. In *Treatment of Hyperlipoproteinemia* (Carlson, L.A. and Olsson, A.G., eds), pp. 77–83. New York, Raven Press

OCKNER, R.K., HUGHES, F.B. and ISSELBACHER, K.J. (1969). Very low density lipoproteins in intestinal lymph: role in triglyceride and cholesterol transport during fat absorption. *Journal of Clinical Investigation*, **48**, 2367–2373

ORAM, J.F., BRINTON, E.A. and BIERMAN, E.L. (1983). Regulation of high density lipoprotein receptor activity in cultured human skin fibroblasts and human anterial smooth muscle cells. *Journal of Clinical Investigation*, **72**, 1611–1621

OTT, D.B. and LACHANCE, P.A. (1981). Biochemical controls of liver cholesterol biosynthesis. *American Journal of Clinical Nutrition*, **34**, 2295–2306

PACKARD, C.J. and SHEPHERD, J. (1983). Low-density lipoprotein receptor pathway in man: its role in regulating plasma low-density lipoprotein levels. *Atherosclerosis Reviews*, **11**, 29–63

PITTMAN, R.C. and STEINBERG, D. (1984). Sites and mechanisms of uptake and degradation of high density and low density lipoproteins. *Journal of Lipid Research*, **25**, 1577–1585

POPJAK, G. (1955). Chemistry, biochemistry and isotopic tracer techniques. *Royal Institute of Chemistry Lecturers, Monographs and Reports, No. 2*, 59–78

PORTER, M.W., YAMANAKA, W., CARLSON, S.D. and FLYNN, M.A. (1977). Effect of dietary egg on serum cholesterol and triglyceride in human males. *American Journal of Clinical Nutrition*, **30**, 490–495

QUINTAO, E., GRUNDY, S.M. and AHRENS, E.H. (1971a). An evaluation of four methods of measuring cholesterol absorption by the intestine of man. *Journal of Lipid Research*, **12**, 221–232

QUINTAO, E., GRUNDY, S.M. and AHRENS, E.H. (1971b). Effects of dietary cholesterol on the regulation of total body cholesterol in man. *Journal of Lipid Research*, **12**, 233–247

RAYMOND, T.L., CONNOR, W.E., LIN, D.S., WARNER, S., FRY, M.M. and CONNOR, S.L. (1977). The interaction of dietary fibres and cholesterol upon the plasma lipids and lipoproteins, sterol balance and bowel functions in human subjects. *Journal of Clinical Investigation*, **60**, 1429–1437

REDGRAVE, T.G. and DUNNE, K.B. (1975). Chylomicron formation and composition in unanesthetized rabbits. *Atherosclerosis*, **22**, 389–400

REGEN, D., RIEPERTINGER, C., HAMPRECHT, B. and LYNEN, F. (1966). The measurement of β-hydroxy-β-methylglutaryl CoA reductase in rat liver; effects of fasting and refeeding. *Biochemische Zeitschrift*, **346**, 78–84

ROBERTS, S.L., MCMURRAY, M.P. and CONNOR, W.E. (1981). Does egg feeding (i.e. dietary cholesterol) affect plasma cholesterol levels in humans? The results of a double-blind study. *American Journal of Clinical Nutrition*, **34**, 2092–2099

ROBINSON, R. (1934). Structure of cholesterol. *Chemistry and Industry*, **53**, 1062–1063

RODWELL, V.W., NORDSTROM, J.L. and MITSCHELEN, J.J. (1976). Regulation of HMG-CoA reductase. *Advances in Lipid Research*, **14**, 1–74

SACKS, F.M., SALAZAR, J., MILLER, L., FOSTER, J.M., SUTHERLAND, M., SAMONDS, K.W., ALBERS, J.J. and

KASS, E.H. (1984). Ingestion of egg raises plasma low density lipoproteins in free-living subjects. *Lancet*, **i**, 647–649

SALEN, G., AHRENS, E.H. and GRUNDY, S.M. (1970). Metabolism of β-sitosterol in man. *Journal of Clinical Investigation*, **49**, 952–967

SEDAGHAT, A., SAMUEL, P. and CROUSE, J.R. (1975). Effects of neomycin on absorption, synthesis and/or flux of cholesterol in man. *Journal of Clinical Investigation*, **55**, 12–21

SHAPIRO, D.J. and RODWELL, V.W. (1971). Regulation of hepatic 3-hydroxy-3-methylglutaryl coenzyme A reductase and cholesterol synthesis. *Journal of Biological Chemistry*, **246**, 3210–3216

SHEFER, S., HAUSER, S., BEKERSKY, I. and MOSBACH, E.H. (1969). Feedback regulation of bile acid biosynthesis in the rat. *Journal of Lipid Research*, **10**, 646–655

SIPERSTEIN, M.D. (1970). Regulation of cholesterol biosynthesis in normal and malignant tissues. In *Current Topics in Cellular Regulation, Volume 2*, (Horecker, B.L. and Stadtman, E.R., eds), pp. 65–100. New York, Academic Press

SIPERSTEIN, M.D. and FAGAN, V.M. (1964). Studies on the feedback regulation of cholesterol synthesis. *Advances in Enzyme Regulation*, **2**, 249–264

SIPERSTEIN, M.D. and FAGAN, V.M. (1966). Feedback control of mevalonate synthesis by dietary cholesterol. *Journal of Biological Chemistry*, **241**, 602–609

SLATER, H.R., SHEPHERD, J. and PACKARD, C.J. (1982). Receptor-mediated catabolism and tissue uptake of human low density lipoprotein in the cholesterol-fed, atherosclerotic rabbit. *Biochimica et Biophysica Acta*, **713**, 435–445

SPADY, D.K. and DIETSCHY, J.M. (1983). Sterol synthesis *in vivo* in 18 tissues of the squirrel monkey, guinea pig, rabbit, hamster and rat. *Journal of Lipid Research*, **24**, 303–315

SPADY, D.K., BILHEIMER, D.W. and DIETSCHY, J.M. (1983). Rates of receptor-dependent and independent low density lipoprotein uptake in the hamster. *Proceedings of the National Academy of Sciences of the USA*, **80**, 3499–3503

STANGE, E.F. and DIETSCHY, J.M. (1983). Cholesterol synthesis and low density lipoprotein uptake are regulated independently in rat small intestinal epithelium. *Proceedings of the National Academy of Sciences of the USA*, **80**, 5739–5743

STANGE, E.F., SUCKLING, K.E. and DIETSCHY, J.M. (1983). Synthesis and coenzyme A-dependent esterification of cholesterol in rat intestinal epithelium. *Journal of Biological Chemistry*, **258**, 12868–12875

STEIN, Y., DABACH, Y., HOLLANDER, G., HALPERIN, G. and STEIN, O. (1983). Metabolism of HDL cholesteryl ester in the rat, studied with a non-hydrolyzable analog, cholesteryl linoleyl ether. *Biochimica et Biophysica Acta*, **752**, 98–105

SWIFT, L.L., MANOWITZ, N.R., DUNN, G.D. and LE QUIRE, V.S. (1982). Isolation and characterization of hepatic Golgi lipoproteins from hypercholesterolemic rats. *Journal of Lipid Research*, **23**, 962–971

SWIFT, L.L., SOULE, P.D., GRAY, M.E. and LE QUIRE, V.S. (1984). Intestinal lipoprotein synthesis. Comparison of nascent Golgi lipoproteins from chow-fed and hypercholesterolemic rats. *Journal of Lipid Research*, **25**, 1–13

THOMPSON, J.C. and VARS, H.M. (1953). Biliary excretion of cholic acid and cholesterol in hyper-, hypo- and euthyroid rats. *Proceedings of the Society for Experimental Biology and Medicine*, **83**, 246–248

TOMKINS, G.M. and CHAIKOFF, I.L. (1952). Cholesterol synthesis by liver. Influence of fasting and of diet. *Journal of Biological Chemistry*, **196**, 569–573

TREADWELL, C.R. and VAHOUNY, G.V. (1968). Cholesterol absorption. In *Handbook of Physiology, Section 6, Volume 3*, (Code, C.F., ed.), pp. 1407–1438. Washington, American Physiology Society

TURNER, P.R., COLTART, J., HAZZARD, W.R., BACCHUS, R., NICOLL, A., MILLER, N.E. and LEWIS, B. (1979). Production and conversion of lipoproteins: trans-splanchnic arteriovenous difference studies in man. *European Journal of Clinical Investigation*, **9**, 36

VERNON, R.G. (1981). Lipid metabolism in the adipose tissue of ruminant animals. In *Lipid Metabolism in Ruminant Animals*, (Christie, W.W., ed.), pp. 279–362. Oxford, Pergamon Press

WHYTE, M., NESTEL, P. and MACGREGOR, A. (1977). Cholesterol metabolism in Papua New Guineans. *European Journal of Clinical Investigation*, **7**, 53–60

WILCOX, H.S., DUNN, G.D. and HEIMBERG, M. (1975). Effects of several common long chain fatty acids on the properties and lipid composition of the very low density lipoproteins secreted by the liver. *Biochimica et Biophysica Acta*, **398**, 39–54

WILSON, J.D. (1972). The role of bile acids in the overall regulation of steroid metabolism. *Archives of Internal Medicine*, **130**, 493–505

Chapter 4

Cholesterol in the human diet: a medical viewpoint

H. Tunstall-Pedoe

Introduction—the importance of coronary heart disease

Unlike cigarette smoking which relates to a number of different diseases, and blood pressure which is also a risk factor for several diseases apart from coronary heart disease, cholesterol's role as a risk factor relates almost exclusively to the arterial disease that causes coronary heart disease so that the first question that might be asked about it is 'Why bother?'.

Diseases of the heart and blood vessels account for about half of all deaths in most industrialised countries and coronary heart disease accounts for a half of this total. More important than the proportion at all ages, as everybody has to die eventually of something, is the impact of coronary heart disease in causing premature death and disability. In men the effect is greater than that from cancer, and in women it is about the same as that from breast cancer (Tunstall-Pedoe, 1983). In Scotland, at current rates about one man in ten will die from coronary heart disease before the age of 65 and an equivalent proportion will have non-fatal heart attacks. The impact on women is about a third as much but becomes more equal at older ages. This makes coronary heart disease the dominant cause of death and disability before old age and the most likely cause of a man being struck down in his prime. Rates in England and Wales are slightly lower, but those in the United Kingdom are among the highest in the world for both men and women (Pisa and Uemura, 1982; Tunstall-Pedoe, 1982; Smith and Tunstall-Pedoe, 1984; Uemura and Pisa, 1985).

Treatment of coronary heart disease has improved considerably over the years but there is no cure and some of the more successful techniques such as coronary artery surgery and angioplasty are, and will continue to be, a heavy burden on the health service. Most coronary deaths occur suddenly and out of reach of medical or resuscitation services. There is therefore an overwhelming case for complementing expensive and often unsuccessful treatments with strategies for preventing the onset and progression of the disease, provided that these can be shown to be sensible, acceptable and safe and with a reasonable prospect of success (Tunstall-Pedoe, 1982, 1983).

Serum cholesterol as a risk factor for coronary heart disease

As was discussed in Chapter 3, cholesterol is an essential component of the animal cell membrane and also a precursor substance for the synthesis of various hormones so that it has an essential role in cellular metabolism (Grundy, 1979; Myant, 1981; Gallo, 1983). However, in a number of human disease processes it accumulates in different parts of the body. In coronary heart disease (and in one of the major varieties of stroke, and of diseases of the arteries of the legs leading to amputation), cholesterol becomes deposited in complicated thickenings called atheromatous plaques in the walls of certain arteries, causing narrowing, obliteration or thrombosis. It has been shown that the cholesterol in these plaques comes from the cholesterol circulating in the blood. It is the plaques, called atheroma, that lead to the coronary heart disease manifestations of angina pectoris, cardiac or myocardial infarction and sudden death, known also as heart attacks (Tunstall-Pedoe, 1983).

Since the early 1950s numerous epidemiological studies have been mounted to investigate the relationship between blood levels of cholesterol, usually measured as serum but sometimes as plasma, and risk of coronary heart disease. These studies, of which the Framingham study is the best known (Dawber, 1980), have consistently and virtually unanimously implicated serum cholesterol with cigarette smoking and blood pressure as the three dominant factors that can be measured in individuals and powerfully predict future risk of developing cardiac infarction or sudden death (Pooling Project Research Group, 1978). Debates of 20 or 30 years ago as to whether serum cholesterol predicted risk at all now seem to have been replaced by arguments as to whether the bottom end of the curve is flat, rising or falling, that is whether there is a threshold effect or not. (A recent set of results from a very large study suggests there is not.) While this is of considerable theoretical importance it does mean that hardly anyone is now arguing as to whether serum cholesterol is a risk factor over most of its range; the evidence is generally accepted.

Less common and more expensive have been comparisons of different populations in different countries. The largest and best known of these has been the Seven Countries Study initiated by Keys (1980). The importance of this study has been in showing that there are populations in certain countries in which levels of blood pressure and cigarette smoking are as high as those in Western industrialised countries, but in which coronary heart disease is rare. According to his results, which have been criticised but never supplanted by better evidence or an alternative explanation, the underlying determinant of whether a population experiences coronary heart disease as a major cause of death is the level in that population of the serum cholesterol. As will be discussed later, the major environmental determinant of that is the local diet.

It is not possible to review the whole of cardiovascular epidemiology in this preamble to discussion of dietary cholesterol but studies of migrants in different countries suggest that environmental factors, including diet, are more important that genetic factors in determining the susceptibility of a population group to coronary heart disease (Anon, 1976). Major changes of disease rates occurring within one generation also suggest that coronary heart disease is not inevitable and predetermined but must be powerfully affected by changes of environment and life style within one country (Uemura and Pisa, 1985).

Measurement of diet of individuals and populations and its relationship to serum cholesterol and coronary heart disease

Serum cholesterol is a major individual determinant of coronary risk but although, as will be shown, serum cholesterol relates to diet, epidemiologists have been far less successful in demonstrating that individual differences in diet relate to coronary risk or indeed to serum cholesterol. Measurement of the average diet of populations is difficult (Bingham, 1983; Medical Research Council Environmental Epidemiology Unit, 1983), the characterisation of individual diet is very much more so (Marr, 1981; Todd, Hudes and Calloway, 1983; Yarnell et al., 1983; Gordon, Fisher and Rifkind, 1984) and creates particular problems for the statistician (Liu et al., 1978; Jacobs, Anderson and Blackburn, 1979; Lozy, 1983). The reason for this lies in the day to day variation in what is eaten and the long periods of time that the diet needs to be studied in order to distinguish one person from another.

Crude comparisons of commodity consumption in different countries can come up with a lot of different correlations. If people eat more of one thing they eat less of another (Armstrong et al., 1975; Knox, 1977). The same problem also arises when time trends of eating habits are examined within one country (Harper, 1983). There are problems with relating food 'disappearance' to what people actually eat.

Full dietary surveys on large population groups are comparatively rare. Some studies have had difficulty in demonstrating a relationship between individual dietary data and serum cholesterol on the one hand or between that and subsequent risk of coronary disease (Nichols et al., 1976; Dawber et al., 1982). Others have found a role for fats perhaps but not dietary cholesterol (Morris, Marr and Clayton, 1977). However, a considerable number of studies are now reporting correlations between dietary measurements thought to relate to serum cholesterol and subsequent coronary heart disease mortality or incidence, although other factors such as calorie intake, alcohol and fish are sometimes coming out more strongly than the factors which dietary experiments (see below) relate to serum cholesterol (Gordon et al., 1981; Shekelle et al., 1981; Kromhout, 1983; McGee et al., 1984; Kromhout, Bosschieter and Coulander, 1985; Kushi et al., 1985). When some studies show correlations and others do not it is possible for the partisan interpreter to take sides, either claiming that those done properly were positive (a potentially circular argument) or that results are inconsistent and correlations are weak, although the latter is predictable given the problems of measurement.

Measurement of differences between individuals is difficult because within one culture diet tends to be fairly homogeneous. Differences between heterogeneous subcultures show up fairly well in that vegans and vegetarians and omnivores show the lipid differences that would be predicted from their diets. In the Seven Countries Study (Keys, 1980) the differences in serum cholesterol levels between national population groups could be correlated fairly closely with their measured dietary patterns (which also included some laboratory analyses of replicate diets). While individual differences in serum cholesterol within populations may be small or insignificant compared with what is predicted from dietary measurements, those between populations in this study were rather greater than theory would have predicted from the dietary measurements.

Diet and serum cholesterol—results of experiments

Not only do natural diets vary considerably from day to day, but so do the serum cholesterol measurements in individuals so that it needs a series of measurements to get a good estimate of what one person's average level truly is. Different individuals will stabilise at different levels of serum cholesterol when they are fed an identical diet and different individuals will also vary in their serum cholesterol response to change in the diet (Mistry *et al.*, 1981; Jacobs *et al.*, 1983; Turner *et al.*, 1984). With all these potential sources of variation it is not surprising that the most definitive information on the relationship between diet and serum cholesterol has come from dietary experiments in metabolic wards, done under carefully controlled conditions using crossover and latin square designs, and frequently, liquid formula diets.

Originally total fat intake was thought to determine serum cholesterol. Later came the realisation that some animal and vegetable fats behaved differently; then that the source of the fat was less important than its nature in that saturated fats tended to raise serum cholesterol levels and polyunsaturated fats to lower them. Now different fatty acids of different chain length are considered to have different effects within the saturated or polyunsaturated series. Cholesterol itself, found only in animal products, and usually associated with other fats, was thought by some observers, paradoxically, to have no effect in itself. This was despite the fact that in many animal feeding experiments it is difficult to raise serum cholesterol without feeding cholesterol with the other fats, and it was disputed (Wells and Bronte Stewart, 1963). However, large numbers of experiments were summarised in the 1960s using predictive formulae. One developed by Keys and coworkers (Keys, Anderson and Grande, 1965) suggested that, quite independently of the large effects of saturated fat in raising serum cholesterol and the lesser effect of polyunsaturated fats in lowering it, dietary intake of cholesterol had an effect that was related to the square root of the amount consumed. In other words, the effect was not proportional; beyond a certain point additional amounts had decreasing effects. A second group (Hegsted *et al.*, 1965) derived a rather similar formula, again suggesting that the cholesterol effect was independent but that it was linear; double the increase and the serum cholesterol increase is doubled. Despite these differences, in terms of usual dietary manipulations the two formulae often come up with very similar answers and 20 years later both formulae are still being used.

When the effects of adding or subtracting the cholesterol were tried in free-living subjects in the general population (able to compensate or cheat), a number of negative trials were reported. The subject has recently received a considerable amount of attention not just to know whether dietary cholesterol changes serum cholesterol but also to understand what the metabolic effects on the patient are other than in the blood.

Recent reports and reviews of this subject can be taken alphabetically.

Applebaum-Bowden *et al.* (1984) fed nine adults in a crossover trial on a diet with 40% calories from fat and either 137 or 1034 mg cholesterol daily. There was an 11% change in the serum cholesterol component thought to promote arterial disease (low density lipoprotein cholesterol). The increase in total cholesterol was not significant (11 mg/100 ml) but there were major changes in the cellular uptake of cholesterol measured as receptor activity in mononuclear cells.

Beynen and Katan (1985) fed six subjects a normal diet with no eggs and then tried the effect of six eggs daily. Serum cholesterol rose 13%. There was considerable variation in response both within and between individuals so that it was not possible to categorise them with certainty as either hyper- or hypo-responders.

Cole *et al.* (1983) claim that the effects of adding to dietary cholesterol vary with the fats that are being eaten at the time. In other words there is an interaction not alluded to in the Keys or the Hegsted equations. Cole *et al.* (1985) tried the effect of a high cholesterol and high fat diet on patients with a genetically impaired ability to handle cholesterol. Diet-induced change was resisted metabolically to some extent and the mechanism is not known. Connor and Connor (1983) review the literature on experiments involving dietary cholesterol up to 1983.

Flynn *et al.* (1984) tried the effect of eggs in the diet and examination stress on the serum cholesterol levels of students. Eggs had more effect. Katan and Beynen (1983, 1984) investigated the effects of dietary cholesterol on different lipids in the blood. They also were unable to do an egg tolerance test to distinguish those subjects who responded a lot from those who did not as they found that responses were not consistent on different occasions.

Keys (1984) reviews much experimental data accumulated since his group published its 1965 predictive formula and again states that there is a square root relationship between the amount of cholesterol consumed and the serum cholesterol response. He was challenged by McNamara (1985) on the grounds of individual variability and Keys (1985) responded. McGill (1979) published a major review of the subject of dietary cholesterol at that time.

Mistry *et al.* (1981) sought to explain individual differences in the response to dietary cholesterol in terms of down-regulation of the cellular receptors that bind low density lipoprotein.

Packard *et al.* (1983) fed six eggs a day to investigate what happened to metabolic processes and receptor activity. They showed an increase in low density lipoprotein synthesis and that non-receptor mediated pathways were involved in its degradation.

Quig *et al.* (1983) fed four additional eggs a day to each of 23 subjects and showed that total cholesterol rose by 32 mg/100 ml.

Rhomberg and Braunsteiner (1976) in an older case report tell of a patient who was on a slimming diet involving 8–12 eggs daily whose cholesterol level was 24.4 mmol (949 mg/100 ml). There was a dramatic decline on stopping the eggs.

Sacks *et al.* (1984) in contrast to all the multiple egg experiments tried the effect of adding a single egg/d to the diet of 17 lactovegetarian students. Mean cholesterol rose 17 mg/100 ml but this was not statistically significant, although there were significant changes in other lipid components of the blood. This report was followed by some fierce letters in the correspondence columns, which were answered.

Evidence of reversibility of coronary risk through control of serum cholesterol

Dietary experiments to control serum cholesterol and therefore coronary heart disease have not produced conclusive answers. Dietary change is difficult to initiate and sustain outside institutions (Reeves *et al.*, 1983) and in some intervention studies serum cholesterol change has been very disappointing (World Health Organisation European Collaborative Group, 1983). However, in the short term it has been shown that the diets and the serum cholesterol levels of different populations are interchangeable, as evidenced by the crossover of Finnish and Italian diets (Ehnholm *et al.*, 1982; Puska *et al.*, 1983) and where diets are sustained the effect on serum cholesterol is also sustained (Grande, 1975). There has been no large scale test of the dietary theory but a number of near misses. In the Oslo study

(Hjermann *et al.*, 1981) intervention was on high serum cholesterol and on smoking with an apparent halving of coronary events in a rather small study. In the Leiden trial (Arntzenius *et al.*, 1985) a vegetarian diet seemed to be associated with lack of progression of coronary artery disease. A trial of serum cholesterol lowering using a drug that is not absorbed produced evidence of benefit (Lipid Research Clinics Progam, 1984). A population intervention programme using diet as well as anti-smoking propaganda and blood pressure control was associated with a significant fall in disease incidence (Puska *et al.*, 1981). However, there has been no pure test of dietary intervention alone and to set against the above apparent successes are the results of the Multiple Risk Factor Intervention Trial Research Group (1982) in which apparently adequate reductions in risk factor levels in high risk men, including dietary control of serum cholesterol, produced no significant overall benefit although there was some in some sub-groups.

Conclusion

Dietary intervention has not been proved to control coronary heart disease but there is a lot of circumstantial evidence and there are scientific grounds for considering that the definitive experiments would be almost impossible to carry out. The dietary theory of coronary disease causation (reviewed or stated by Malmros, 1969; Tunstall-Pedoe and Rose, 1979; Stamler, 1979, 1980, 1982; Grundy *et al.*, 1982; Kritchevsky, 1983) has its hostile critics (Reiser, 1973, 1984; Brisson, 1981), purists who are awaiting complete proof (Mitchell, 1984), those who accept it in part or for certain people only (Oliver, 1976, 1978, 1981, 1983; Samuel, McNamara and Shapiro, 1983) and its enthusiastic supporters (Blackburn, 1979; Stamler, 1983a, 1983b). It now forms the basis of large numbers of official reports and recommendations for the control of coronary heart disease, some of which recommend intervention on dietary fats and cholesterol (WHO, 1982; Nutrition Committee and Council on Arteriosclerosis of the American Heart Association, 1984; WHO Regional Office for Europe, 1985), and some of which make no specific recommendation on cholesterol in the diet (Shaper and Marr, 1977; Committee on Medical Aspects of Food Policy—COMA, 1984).

While all the reports are unanimous in recommending a reduction in the quantity of saturated fats consumed, they are less so in terms of dietary cholesterol, and also of increasing polyunsaturated fats (Sinclair, 1980; Renaud *et al.*, 1981; Woodcock *et al.*, 1984).

In fact, it would be very difficult to eat less saturated fat, which is largely of animal origin, without a substantial reduction in cholesterol intake. Most dietary cholesterol is associated with saturated fat. (Similarly a reduction of saturated fat leads to a relative increase in the polyunsaturated to saturated fat ratio.) There are, however, some foodstuffs in which cholesterol is less associated with saturated fat so what the dietary guidelines say or do not say becomes important. These are shellfish, offal such as liver, and eggs. In terms of intake of cholesterol, eggs are by far the most important, as they account for about 40% of the average person's intake.

From the published data it would appear that reducing the average British person's egg consumption from three to four a week to a lower average is unlikely to make a major change in population serum cholesterol levels, which are too high and should be lowered primarily by a reduction in saturated fat consumption. On the other hand, it cannot be claimed that the cholesterol in eggs is either necessary or healthy. At present egg consumption in the UK is fairly modest and the egg industry is not a prime target for coronary prevention campaigns. However, this situation could change if the egg industry adopted too high a profile in recommending a major increase in consumption or in stating that eggs were good for, or essential for, health. It should also be remembered that there are those whose blood cholesterol levels are much too high, who may be eating more eggs than they can cope with, and who may have to be told to cut their consumption drastically. The relative importance of eggs as a contributor to British cholesterol levels could change with other changes in the diet.

As someone who enjoys an occasional egg boiled or fried, or an omelette, but not frequently, I suggest that the industry accepts that the cholesterol content of eggs has to be accepted as a potential disadvantage, but that there are any number of foodstuffs which contain components which may be harmful to some people or in excess. Eggs contain excellent proteins and have great culinary advantages. Perhaps thought should be given to taking a tip from the dairy farmers who are selling milk with reduced fat content. Perhaps eggs should be marketed with reduced yolk content or ready separated.

Finally, coronary prevention campaigns are not all bad news for the poultry farmer as a major recommendation of most of them is to substitute chicken or turkey (or fish) for red meat.

References

ANON (1976). Migrants and cardiovascular disease. *British Medical Journal*, **2**, 1423–1424

APPLEBAUM-BOWDEN, D., HAFFNER, S.M., HARTSOOK, E., LUK, K.H., ALBERS, J.J. and HAZZARD, W.R. (1984). Down-regulation of the low-density lipoprotein receptor by dietary cholesterol. *American Journal of Clinical Nutrition*, **39**, 360–367

ARMSTRONG, B.K., MANN, J.I., ADELSTEIN, A.M. and ESKIN, F. (1975). Commodity consumption and ischaemic heart disease with special reference to dietary practices. *Journal of Chronic Diseases*, **28**, 455–469

ARNTZENIUS, A.C., KROMHOUT, D., BARTH, J.D., REIBER, J.H.C., BRUSCHKE, A.V.G., BUIS, B., van GENT, C.M., KEMPEN-VOOGD, N., STRIKWERDA, S. and van der VELDE, E.A. (1985). Diet, lipoproteins and the progression of coronary atherosclerosis. The Leiden Intervention Trial. *New England Journal of Medicine*, **312**, 805–811

BEYNEN, A.C. and KATAN, M.B. (1985). Effect of egg yolk feeding on the concentration and composition of serum lipoproteins in man. *Atherosclerosis*, **54**, 157–166

BINGHAM, S. (1983) Premise and methods. In *Surveillance of Dietary Habits of the Population with Regard to Cardiovascular Diseases*, (de Backer, G.G., Tunstall-Pedoe, H. and Ducimetiere, P., eds), pp. 21–42. Report of an EEC Workshop, Ghent, Belgium. Wageningen, EURONUT

BLACKBURN, H. (1979). Diet and mass hyperlipidaemia: public health considerations—a point of view. In *Nutrition, Lipids and Coronary Heart Disease,* (Levy, R.I., Rifkind, B.M., Dennis, B. and Ernst, N.D., eds), pp. 309–347. New York, Raven Press

BRISSON, G.J.S. (1981). *Lipids in Human Nutrition. An Appraisal of some Dietary Concepts.* Lancaster, MTP Press

COLE, T.G., PATSCH, W., KUISK, I., GONEN, B. and SCHONFELD, G. (1983). Increases in dietary cholesterol and fat raise levels of apoprotein E-containing lipoproteins in the plasma of man. *Journal of Clinical Endocrinology and Metabolism*, **56**, 1108–1115

COLE, T.G., PFLEGER, B., HITCHINS, O. and SCHONFELD, G. (1985). Effects of high cholesterol high fat diet on plasma lipoproteins in familial hypercholesterolemia. *Metabolism*, **34**, 486–493

COMMITTEE ON MEDICAL ASPECTS OF FOOD POLICY—COMA (1984). *Diet and Cardiovascular Disease.* Department of Health and Social Security. London, HMSO

CONNOR, S.L. and CONNOR, W.E. (1983). The importance of dietary cholesterol in coronary heart disease. *Preventive Medicine*, **12**, 115–123

DAWBER, T.R. (1980). *The Framingham Study. The Epidemiology of Atherosclerotic Disease*. Cambridge, Mass., Harvard University Press

DAWBER, T.R., NICKERSON, R.J., BRAND, F.N. and POOL, J. (1982). Eggs, serum cholesterol and coronary heart disease. *American Journal of Clinical Nutrition*, **36**, 617–625

EHNHOLM, C., HUTTUNEN, J.K., PIETINEN, P., LEINO, U., MUTANEN, M., KOSTIAINEN, E., PIKKARAINEN, J., DOUGHERTY, R., IACANO, J. and PUSKA, P. (1982). Effect of diet on serum lipoproteins in a population with a high risk of coronary heart disease. *New England Journal of Medicine*, **307**, 850–855

FLYNN, M.A., ANDERSON, A., RUTLEDGE, M., NOLPH, G.B., KRAUSE, G. and ELLERSIECK, M.R. (1984). Eggs, serum lipids, emotional stress, and blood pressure in medical students. *Archives of Environmental Health*, **39**, 90–95

GALLO, L.L. (1983). Cholesterol and other sterols: absorption, metabolism, roles in atherogenesis. In *Nutrition and Heart Disease*, (Feldman, E.B., ed.), pp. 83–109. New York, Churchill Livingstone

GORDON, T., FISHER, M. and RIFKIND, B.M. (1984). Some difficulties inherent in the interpretation of dietary data from free-living populations. *American Journal of Clinical Nutrition*, **39**, 152–156

GORDON, T., KAGAN, A., GARCIA-PALMIERI, M., KANNEL, W.B., ZUKEL, W.J., TILLOTSON, J. *et al.* (1981). Diet and its relation to coronary heart disease and death in three populations. *Circulation*, **63**, 500–514

GRANDE, F. (1975). Prolonged dietary experiments in man. In *Proceedings of the 9th International Congress of Nutrition, Mexico 1972*, (Chavas, A., Bourges, H. and Baston, S., eds). Basel, Karger

GRUNDY, S.M. (1979). Dietary fats and sterols. In *Nutrition, Lipids and Coronary Heart Disease*, (Levy, R.I., Rifkind, B.M., Dennis, B.H., Ernst, N.D. eds), pp. 89–118. New York, Raven Press

GRUNDY, S.M., BILHEIMER, D., BLACKBURN, H., BROWN, W.V., KWITEROVICH, P.O., MATTSON, F. *et al.* (1982). Rationale of the Diet-Heart Statement of the American Heart Association. Report of the Nutrition Committee. *Circulation*, **65**, 839A–854A

HARPER, A.E. (1983). Coronary heart disease—an epidemic related to diet? *American Journal of Clinical Nutrition*, **37**, 669–681

HEGSTED, D.M., MCGANDY, R.B., MYERS, M.L. and STARE, F.J. (1965). Quantitative effects of dietary fat on serum cholesterol in man. *American Journal of Clinical Nutrition*, **17**, 281–295

HJERMANN, I., VELVE BYRE, K., HOLME, I. and LEREN, P. (1981). Effect of diet and smoking intervention on the incidence of coronary heart disease. Report from the Oslo Study Group of a randomised trial in healthy men. *Lancet*, **ii**, 1303–1310

JACOBS, D.R. JR., ANDERSON, J.T. and BLACKBURN, H. (1979). Diet and serum cholesterol, do zero correlations negate the relationship? *American Journal of Epidemiology*, **110**, 77–87

JACOBS, D.R. JR., ANDERSON, J.T., HANNAN, P., KEYS, A. and BLACKBURN, H. (1983). Variability in individual serum cholesterol response to change in diet. *Arteriosclerosis*, **3**, 349–356

KATAN, M.B. and BEYNEN, A.C. (1983). Hyper-response to dietary cholesterol in man. *Lancet*, **i**, 1213

KATAN, M.B. and BEYNEN, A.C. (1984). HDL cholesterol, LDL receptor activity and response to dietary cholesterol. *Atherosclerosis*, **52**, 357–358

KEYS, A. (1980). *A Multivariate Analysis of Death and Coronary Heart Disease*. Cambridge, Harvard University Press

KEYS, A. (1984). Serum cholesterol response to dietary cholesterol. *American Journal of Clinical Nutrition*, **40**, 351–359

KEYS, A. (1985). Serum cholesterol response to dietary cholesterol. *American Journal of Clinical Nutrition*, **41**, 658–659

KEYS, A., ANDERSON, J.T. and GRANDE, F. (1965). Serum cholesterol response to changes in the diet. *Metabolism*, **14**, 748–758, 759–765, 766–775, 776–787

KNOX, E.G. (1977). Foods and diseases. *British Journal of Preventive and Social Medicine*, **31**, 71–80

KRITCHEVSKY, D. (1983). Nutritional theories of atherogenesis. In *Nutrition and Heart Disease*, (Feldman, E.B., ed.), pp. 29–44. New York, Churchill Livingstone

KROMHOUT, D. (1983). Body weight, diet, and serum cholesterol in 871 middle-aged men during 10 years of follow-up (the Zutphen Study). *American Journal of Clinical Nutrition*, **38**, 591–598

KROMHOUT, D., BOSSCHIETER, E.B. and COULANDER, C. de L. (1985). The inverse relationship between fish consumption and 20-year mortality from coronary heart disease. *New England Journal of Medicine*, **312**, 1205–1209

KUSHI, L.H., LEW, R.A., STARE, F.J., ELLISON, C.R., LOZY, M.EL., BOURKE, G., DALY, L., GRAHAM, I., HICKEY, N., MULCAHY, R. and KEVANEY, J. (1985). Diet and 20 year mortality from coronary heart disease. The Ireland-Boston Diet-Heart Study. *New England Journal of Medicine*, **312**, 811–818, 851–853

LIPID RESEARCH CLINICS PROGRAM (1984). The Lipid Research Clinics coronary primary prevention trial results. I. Reduction in incidence of coronary heart disease. *Journal of the American Medical Association*, **251**, 351–364

LIU, K., STAMLER, J., DYER, A., MCKEEVER, J. and MCKEEVER, P. (1978). Statistical methods to assess and minimize the role of intra-individual variability in obscuring the relationship between dietary lipids and serum cholesterol. *Journal of Chronic Diseases*, **31**, 399–418

LOZY, M.EL (1983). Dietary variability and its impact on nutritional epidemiology. *Journal of Chronic Diseases*, **36**, 237–249

MALMROS, H. (1969). Dietary prevention of atherosclerosis. *Lancet*, **ii**, 479–484

MARR, J.W. (1981). Individual variation in dietary intake. In *Preventive Nutrition and Society*, (Turner, M.R., ed.), pp. 77–83. London, Academic Press

MCGEE, D.L., REED, D.M., YANO, K., KAGAN, A. and TILLOTSON, J. (1984). Ten-year incidence of coronary heart disease in the Honolulu Heart Program. Relationship to nutrient intake. *American Journal of Epidemiology*, **119**, 667–676

MCGILL, H.C., JR. (1979). The relationship of dietary cholesterol to serum cholesterol concentration and to atherosclerosis in man. *American Journal of Clinical Nutrition*, **32**, 2664–2702

MCNAMARA, D.J. (1985). Prediction of plasma cholesterol response to dietary cholesterol. *American Journal of Clinical Nutrition*, **40**, 351–359

MEDICAL RESEARCH COUNCIL ENVIRONMENTAL EPIDEMIOLOGY UNIT (1983). *The Dietary Assessment of Populations*. Conference Report, Southampton

MISTRY, P., MILLER, N.E., LAKER, M., HAZZARD, W.R. and LEWIS, B. (1981). Individual variation in the effects of dietary cholesterol on plasma lipoproteins and cellular cholesterol homeostasis in man. Studies of low density lipoprotein receptor activity and 3-hydroxy-methylglutaryl coenzyme A reductase activity in blood mononuclear cells. *Journal of Clinical Investigation*, **67**, 493–502

MITCHELL, J.R.A. (1984). What constitutes evidence on the dietary prevention of coronary heart disease? Cosy beliefs or harsh facts? *International Journal of Cardiology*, **5**, 287–298

MORRIS, J.N., MARR, J.W. and CLAYTON, D.G. (1977). Diet and heart: a postscript. *British Medical Journal*, **2**, 1307–1314

MULTIPLE RISK FACTOR INTERVENTION TRIAL RESEARCH GROUP (1982). Multiple Risk Factor Intervention Trial: risk factor changes and mortality results. *Journal of the American Medical Association*, **248**, 1465–1477

MYANT, N.B. (1981). *The Biology of Cholesterol and Related Sterols*. London, Heinemann

NICHOLS, A.B., RAVENSCROFT, C., LAMPHIEAR, D.E. and OSTRANDER, L.D. (1976). Independence of serum lipid levels and dietary habits. The Tecumseh Study. *Journal of the American Medical Association*, **236**, 1948–1953

NUTRITION COMMITTEE AND COUNCIL ON ARTERIOSCLEROSIS OF THE AMERICAN HEART ASSOCIATION (1984). Recommendations for the treatment of hyperlipidaemia in adults. *Circulation*, **69**, 444A–468A

OLIVER, M.F. (1976). Dietary cholesterol, plasma cholesterol and coronary heart disease. *British Heart Journal*, **38**, 214–218

OLIVER, M.F. (1978). Diet and coronary heart disease. In *Diet of Man: Needs and Wants*, (Yudkin, J., ed.), pp. 69–88. London, Applied Science

OLIVER, M.F. (1981). Diet and coronary heart disease. *British Medical Bulletin*, **37**, 49–58

OLIVER, M.F. (1983). The cholesterol–coronary question: why not a policy of selective intervention? *International Journal of Cardiology*, **4**, 201–206

PACKARD, C.J., MCKINNEY, L., CARR, K. and SHEPHERD, J. (1983). Cholesterol feeding increases low density lipoprotein synthesis. *Journal of Clinical Investigation*, **72**, 45–51

PISA, Z. and UEMURA, K. (1982). Trends of mortality from ischaemic heart disease and other cardiovascular diseases in 27 countries 1968–77. *World Health Statistics Quarterly*, **35**, 11–47

POOLING PROJECT RESEARCH GROUP (1978). Relationship of blood pressure, serum cholesterol, smoking habits, relative weight and ECG abnormalities to incidence of major coronary events: final report of the Pooling Project. *Journal of Chronic Diseases*, **31**, 201–306

PUSKA, P., IACONO, J.M., NISSINEN, A., KORHONEN, H.J., VARTIAINEN, E., PIETINEN, P., DOUGHERTY, R., LEINO, U., MUTANEN, M., MOISIO, S. and HUTTUNEN, J. (1983). Controlled, randomised trial of the effect of dietary fat on blood pressure. *Lancet*, **i**: 1–5

PUSKA, P., TUOMILEHTO, J., SALONEN, J., NISSINEN, A., VIRTAMO, T., BJÖRKQVIST, S. *et al.* (1981). Community control of cardiovascular diseases. The North Karelia Project. Copenhagen, WHO Regional Office for Europe

QUIG, D.W., THYE, F.W., RITCHEY, S.J., HERBERT, W.G., CLEVIDENCE, B.A., REYNOLDS, L.K. and SMITH, M.C. (1983). Effects of short-term aerobic conditioning and high cholesterol feeding on plasma total and lipoprotein cholesterol levels in sedentary young men. *American Journal of Clinical Nutrition*, **38**, 825–834

REEVES, R.S., FOREYT, J.P., SCOTT, L.W., MITCHELL, R.E., WOHLLEBB, J. and GOTTO, A.M. JR. (1983). Effects of a low cholesterol eating plan on plasma lipids: results of a three year community study. *American Journal of Public Health*, **73**, 873–877

REISER, R. (1973). Saturated fat in the diet and serum cholesterol concentration: a critical examination of the literature. *American Journal of Clinical Nutrition*, **26**, 524–555

REISER, R. (1984). A commentary on the Rationale of the Diet–Heart Statement of the American Heart Association. *American Journal of Clinical Nutrition*, **40**, 654–658

RENAUD, S., MORAZAIN, R., GODSEY, F., DUMONT, E., SYMINGTON, I.S., GILLANDERS, E.M. and O'BRIEN, J.R. (1981). Platelet function in relation to diet and serum lipids in British farmers. *British Heart Journal*, **46**, 562–570

RHOMBERG, H.P. and BRAUNSTEINER, H. (1976). Excessive egg consumption, xanthomatosis and hypercholesterolaemia. *British Medical Journal*, **1**, 1188–1189

SACKS, F.M., SALAZAR, J., MILLER, L., FOSTER, J.M., SUTHERLAND, M., SAMONDS, K.W., ALBERS, J.J. and KASS, E.H. (1984). Ingestion of egg raises plasma low density lipoproteins in free-living subjects. *Lancet*, **i**, 647–649, 1127–1128, 1191

SAMUEL, P., MCNAMARA, D.J. and SHAPIRO, J. (1983). The role of diet in the etiology and treatment of atherosclerosis. *Annual Reviews of Medicine*, **34**, 179–194

SHAPER, A.G. and MARR, J.W. (1977). Dietary recommendations for the community towards the postponement of coronary heart disease. *British Medical Journal*, **1**, 867–871

SHEKELLE, R.B., SHRYOCK, A.M., PAUL, O., LEPPER, M., STAMLER, J., LIU, S. and RAYNOR, W.J., JR. (1981). Diet, serum cholesterol, and death from coronary heart disease. The Western Electric Study. *New England Journal of Medicine*, **304**, 65–70

SINCLAIR, H.M. (1980). Prevention of coronary heart disease: the role of essential fatty acids. *Postgraduate Medical Journal*, **56**, 579–584

SMITH, W.C. and TUNSTALL-PEDOE, H. (1984). European regional variation in cardiovascular mortality. *British Medical Bulletin*, **40**, 374–379

STAMLER, J. (1979). Population studies. In *Nutrition, Lipids and Coronary Heart Disease*, (Levy, R.I., Rifkind, B.M., Dennis, B.H. and Ernst, N.D., eds), pp. 25–88. New York, Raven Press

STAMLER, J. (1980). The established relationship among diet, serum cholesterol and coronary heart disease. *Acta Medica Scandinavica*, **207**, 433–446

STAMLER, J. (1982). Diet and coronary heart disease. *Biometrics* (Supplement: Current topics in biostatistics and epidemiology), **38**, 95–114

STAMLER, J. (1983a). Does cholesterol change alter coronary artery disease risk? Epidemiological evidence. In *The Decline in Coronary Heart Disease Mortality—the Role of Cholesterol Change*, pp. 27–45. Columbia University College of Physicians and Surgeons. Mead Johnson

STAMLER, J. (1983b). The prevention and control of epidemic coronary heart disease: scientific foundations and strategic approaches. *International Journal of Cardiology*, **4**, 207–215

TODD, K.S., HUDES, M. and CALLOWAY, D.H. (1983). Food intake measurement: problems and approaches. *American Journal of Clinical Nutrition*, **37**, 139–146

TUNSTALL-PEDOE, H. (1982). Coronary heart disease prevention. In *Recent Advances in Community Medicine*, (Smith, A., ed.), pp. 95–110. Edinburgh, Churchill Livingstone

TUNSTALL-PEDOE, H. (1983). Coronary heart disease. In *Epidemiology of Diseases*, (Miller, D.L. and Farmer, R.D.T., eds), pp. 136–145. Oxford, Blackwell Scientific

TUNSTALL-PEDOE, H.D. and ROSE, G. (1979). Atherosclerosis as related to diet. In *International Review of Biochemistry: Biochemistry of Nutrition. I.*, (Neuberger, A. and Jukes, T.H., eds), pp. 245–279. Baltimore, University Park Press

TURNER, P.R., KONARSKA, R., REVILL, J., MASANA, L.I., LA VILLEA, A., JACKSON, P., *et al.* (1984). Metabolic study of variation in plasma cholesterol in normal man. *Lancet*, **ii**, 663–665

UEMURA, K. and PISA, Z. (1985). Recent trends in cardiovascular disease mortality in 27 industrialized countries. *World Health Statistics Quarterly*, **38**, 142–162

WELLS, V.M. and BRONTE-STEWART, B. (1963). Egg yolk and serum-cholesterol levels: importance of dietary cholesterol intake. *British Medical Journal*, **1**, 577–580

WOODCOCK, B.E., SMITH, E., LAMBERT, W.H., JONES, W.M., GALLOWAY, J.H., GREAVES, M. and PRESTON, F.E. (1984). Beneficial effect of fish oil on blood viscosity in peripheral vascular disease. *British Medical Journal*, **288**, 592–594

WORLD HEALTH ORGANISATION (1982). *Prevention of Coronary Heart Disease.* Report of a WHO Expert Committee. Technical Report Series 678. Geneva, WHO

WORLD HEALTH ORGANISATION EUROPEAN COLLABORATIVE GROUP (1983). Multifactorial trial in the prevention of coronary heart disease. 3. Incidence and mortality results. *European Heart Journal*, **4**, 141–147

WORLD HEALTH ORGANISATION REGIONAL OFFICE FOR EUROPE (1985). Primary prevention of coronary heart disease. Anacapri 15–19 October 1984. EURO reports and studies 98. Copenhagen, WHO

YARNELL, J.W.G., FEHILY, A.M., MILBANK, J.E., SWEETNAM, P.M. and WALKER, C.L. (1983). A short dietary questionnaire for use in an epidemiological survey: comparison with weighed dietary records. *Human Nutrition: Applied Nutrition*, **37A**, 103–112

Part II

Methods of egg quality assessment

Chapter 5

Evaluation of egg quality in commercial practice

N.D. Overfield

Introduction

Eggs are food. In 1984 expenditure on eggs by UK consumers is estimated at £1000m (Annual Review of Agriculture, 1985). Eggs have to compete successfully with other foods if the egg industry is to remain viable. National figures indicate that egg consumption per person has fallen substantially during the last 15 years (National Food Survey, 1984). One of the reasons offered for the decline in egg consumption is that average quality has not been maintained at a level sufficient to satisfy modern consumers. Many competitive foods are manufactured under carefully controlled conditions tailored to a programme based on consumer requirements and production efficiencies. These programmes are normally monitored by comprehensive quality control techniques. As an agricultural product the egg is produced efficiently and in many ways the egg industry has been the technological leader in animal production methods. As with most other agricultural products the fragmented nature of the egg industry and the natural variability of its product create difficulties when production technology has to be modified to meet consumer needs. Fundamental to the successful change of emphasis is the ability to monitor progress with techniques capable of assessing egg quality. The object of this chapter is to review the success of the industry in evaluating egg quality in commercial practice.

Principles of quality grading

Quality control is an essential part of the marketing process for any product. It can be defined as the maintenance of the characteristics of a product at levels and tolerances acceptable to the end user. For most products a specification is determined prior to manufacture based on the established requirements and production efficiencies. The quality constraints are clearly determined and the tolerances are within narrow limits. For other products this approach is impractical or impossible. Most agricultural products with their inherent variation fall into this category. In these circumstances a system of grading is often adopted. Grading is a form of quality control used to divide a variable commodity or product into a number of classes. It is a process of identification, classification and separation. The advantages of grading can be listed as follows.

(1) Grading allows the consumer to exercise a preference in relation to quality which in turn may stimulate increased prices and sales.
(2) The grade price differentials that develop provide an incentive to the producer to adjust his production methods.
(3) Setting and maintaining a reliable standard gives confidence in the product and a favourable reputation is established safeguarding the market.
(4) Grading facilitates the mechanical processes of packaging and distribution and often enhances the appearance of the product.
(5) Grading systems can be used to establish minimum characteristics for the protection of the end user.

Grading systems can have certain disadvantages.

(1) Grading almost by definition is wasteful. It has no immediate influence on the nature of the heterogenous population on which it must select. Consequently, matching supply to demand is difficult and in the short term impossible.
(2) A grading system tends to be rigid and slow to react to market changes.
(3) A compulsory national grading system designed for consumer protection and for the standardisation of commercial practices may inhibit attempts to stimulate and develop demand.

Egg quality grading systems

The importance of grading in egg marketing was reviewed by Low (1970).

Following a review of the state of the post First World War egg industry a report by the Marketing Division of the Ministry of Agriculture in 1926 concluded that the most promising prospect for improving the profitability of egg production was in raising the reputation of UK eggs through a voluntary system of grading with the objective of attracting higher prices for quality produce (Ministry of Agriculture and Fisheries, 1926). Their recommendations were put into effect for England and Wales in the National Mark Egg Scheme in 1929. The quality grading scheme at present operated in the UK and throughout the European Economic Community (EEC) is remarkably similar to that introduced in 1929. The principle stages in the development of the official definition of first quality eggs can be summarised as follows.

Official definition of first quality eggs

1. National Mark Approved Scheme 1929

The egg must not have been preserved by any process; the shell must be clean and sound, yolk translucent or faintly but not clearly visible on candling, the white translucent and firm and the air space must not exceed a depth of 0.25 in (6.35 mm).

2. The Agricultural Produce (Grading and Marking) (Eggs) Regulations 1936

The egg must not have been preserved by any process and must be free from taint; the shell must be clean, sound, of good texture and shape. The contents must be free from blemish, the yolk central and translucent or faintly but not clearly outlined by the candling light, the white must be translucent and the air space must not exceed a depth of 0.25 in (6.35 mm).

3. The Eggs (Amendment 4) Order 1953

Fresh eggs free from tainting. Shell clean and unstained, sound and of good texture and shape. Contents free from visible blemish and discoloration. Yolk central, translucent, faintly but not clearly defined on candling. White translucent. Air space not exceeding a depth of 0.25 in (6.35 mm).

4. Regulation (EEC) No 2772/75 on marketing standards for eggs Article 7

Fresh eggs free from extraneous odour. Shell and cuticle normal, clean and undamaged. Albumen clear, limpid, of gelatinous consistency, free of extraneous matters of any kind. Yolk visible on candling as a shadow only, without clearly discernible outline not moving appreciably away from the centre of the egg on rotation, free from extraneous matters of any kind. Germ cell, imperceptible development. Air space stationary not exceeding a height of 6 mm.

The present quality regulations concerning first quality (Grade A) eggs prohibit cleaning, preservation or refrigerated cooling to temperatures maintained at less than 8 °C. However, there is the proviso in Article 19 of the same regulation to permit a special higher quality egg to be marketed as 'extra' fresh provided the height of the air space of these eggs is less than 4 mm at the time of packing, and certain other requirements are fulfilled concerning registration, collection, packaging and inspection tolerances.

Prior to the introduction of the EEC Regulations any producer wishing to sell directly to the retailer or to the consumer was free to grade or not to grade. Since 1 February 1973 all eggs marketed in the UK (other than those sold direct to the consumer, on the producers' premises or on a market stall) must be graded to EEC standards, on approved premises by registered packers. The premises, eggs and packaging are regularly inspected by statute at packing station and wholesale level.

Assessing the success of egg quality grading

Although present egg quality grading is adequately controlled and monitored surprisingly little effort has been made by the egg industry to assess its value in the wider context of egg marketing.

Incidence of downgrading

In relation to egg quality grading the proportion of eggs downgraded as ineligible for first quality should serve as a useful indication of trends in commercial practice. In the UK these figures are obtained by compiling the returns made by a representative sample of registered egg packing stations to the Eggs Authority or its predecessor the British Egg Marketing Board (BEMB). The trend in downgrading during the last 27 years is shown in Table 5.1.

Very few observations on the trend of downgrading have been published. After reviewing the factors influencing downgrading prior to 1970 it was tentatively concluded that the steady rise was due to the practice of increasing the flock laying life and the widespread introduction of the battery cage system during the 1960s

Table 5.1 The annual pattern of downgrading of eggs in the UK

Year	Percentage downgraded	Year	Percentage downgraded
1958	4.1	1972	7.3
1959	4.4	1973	7.3
1960	4.7	1974	7.0
1961	4.9	1975	7.1
1962	5.2	1976	7.1
1963	5.1	1977	7.3
1964	6.4	1978	7.4
1965	6.6	1979	7.8
1966	6.5	1980	7.2
1967	6.9	1981	7.0
1968	6.9	1982	6.7
1969	7.0	1983	6.5
1970	—	1984	6.5
1971	7.0		

(Overfield, 1970). Field studies in the USA yielded similar conclusions (Bezpa, 1974). The decline in the incidence of downgrading since 1979 may be associated with the nationwide adoption of brown eggs.

Estimates of the incidence of downgrading made in Europe (Folkerts, 1976) and the USA (Roland, 1977) are similar to those experienced in the UK. National estimates almost certainly underestimate the true level. Results from surveys of individual farms (Maddison, 1970) and laying trials (Overfield, 1970) suggest the total figure is higher because the national estimates do not include damaged and soiled eggs which many producers frequently remove prior to forwarding the batch for grading. Well planned field surveys of downgrading are few, consequently little published information is available on the breakdown of downgraded eggs into various categories of quality. A UK survey involving 685 production units revealed that among eggs downgraded by packing stations shell faults accounted for 87.37% (Maddison, 1970). A further 10.01% were downgraded because of the presence of blood and meat spots in the eggs. When the eggs downgraded on the farms were added to those downgraded at the packing stations the proportion of eggs with shell faults was 90.54%.

The majority of eggs which will be ultimately downgraded are cracked before they are collected from the battery cage (Bowman and Challender, 1963; Shrimpton and Hann, 1967; Leech and Knowles, 1969). More recent results from the USA indicate mechanical egg collection and egg washing can have a marked influence on the incidence of cracked eggs (Eggleton and Ross, 1971; Berry, 1976; Thompson, Hamilton and Grunder, 1985).

Grading standards achieved in relation to standards set

When the National Mark Scheme was introduced in 1929 the home produced egg had a relatively poor image in towns as compared with the imported egg. This situation improved substantially prior to the Second World War and the Scheme undoubtedly made a major contribution. In 1929 National Mark Standard eggs commanded a price higher than their Danish equivalents, which were considered the best imported eggs. By the mid 1930s the margin had widened further and the trend continued.

By 1937 the National Mark egg had captured 15% of the home market involving 168 packing stations. Some thought this was disappointing (Ministry of Agriculture and Fisheries, 1947). However, the achievement of the Scheme in establishing a network of packing stations equipped to grade and test eggs can now be seen to have been of particular significance in the development of the egg industry.

Although the minimum standard achieved ensured that only wholesome eggs were passed on to the consumer, problems in relation to the standard set did occur and many have persisted to this day. It is relatively easy to separate damaged, dirty and rotten eggs but much more difficult to grade batches of eggs of marginal quality differences. Almquist (1933) critically examined the relationship between the standards set for classifying eggs of intermediate quality and the ability to grade to those standards. Many other workers have published evidence highlighting the difficulties of assessing individual components of quality as defined in the standards (Coles, 1940; Romanoff and Romanoff, 1949; Jensen, Sauter and Stadelman, 1952; Sauter, Stadelman and Carver, 1952; Baker and Vadehra, 1972; Moats, 1982).

Field experience has demonstrated that outbreaks of so-called 'watery-whites' in fresh eggs are either inadvertently overlooked or exaggerated by many packing stations (Anderson, 1936; Overfield, 1976). Since 1936 the UK standards require that an egg should not be tainted, yet no method of identifying taints has been devised other than breaking out the egg. In 1971 in the United Kingdom there were numerous complaints of tainted eggs from producers who sold their eggs direct to consumers. Large packing stations did not report a problem.

Low (1970) explored the apparent dilemma of reconciling relatively stable downgrading figures with a frequently expressed view at that time that egg quality in general was in decline and in particular those marketed through the BEMB. Among several factors considered was the possibility that relatively more eggs with marginal quality close to the minimum standard and least easily detected by grading were passing through as first quality. Producer/retailers were by-passing the BEMB's packing stations. The report of the Reorganisation Commission for Eggs (1968) suggested that though they may be judged irrational many people considered the Lion egg (i.e. one that carried the BEMB 'Little Lion' symbol of quality) stale and produced in an egg factory. The BEMB itself was aware that quality aspects were not entirely satisfactory and had considered amending the grading system. During the 1960s the BEMB had seriously considered introducing sample break-out tests. In 1985 a testing system supplementary to egg candling has still not been introduced at national level although many packing stations voluntarily break out samples of eggs to assist in quality control.

Quality grading and laboratory tests

Many research workers justify shell orientated research on the basis of the financial loss to the egg industry due to downgrading. As the vast majority of eggs are downgraded because of shell faults initial strength of the shell is of fundamental importance. Attempts to relate various measures of shell strength to the incidence of cracked or downgraded eggs have not always been successful.

A variety of methods have been used in the laboratory to measure various egg shell characteristics associated with resistance to breakage and these have been regularly reviewed (Tyler, 1961; Wells, 1968; Hamilton, 1982).

Bowman and Challender (1963) emphasised the limited value of laboratory tests on shells unless they relate fairly closely to the proportion of cracks in eggs under commercial conditions. Information concerning this relationship is inadequate.

McNally (1965) demonstrated a logarithmic increase in cracking with a decrease in shell weight over a wide range. Tyler and Geake (1960) found a similar increase with thinner shells measured as shell weight/unit area. Wells (1967a) found there was a nearly perfect curvilinear relationship between percentage cracks and shell thickness measured as egg specific gravity. When eggs were subjected to tests that simulated the treatment they would have received if laid in battery cages or roughly handled in transit, the shell strength of cracked eggs was significantly less ($P<0.01$) than sound eggs (Wells, 1967b). Wells (1967a) used four techniques to measure shell strength of eggs produced during a 24-week period by 25 individually caged birds. The total percentage of cracks was 11.72 and the correlations between the percentage of cracked eggs and each of the four measurements ranged from -0.678 to -0.769. Similar correlations were obtained based on shell thickness measured directly and indirectly and the number of cracked eggs produced on the farm and in transit to the packing station (Bowman and Challender, 1963). Holder and Bradford (1979) measured the specific gravity of eggs before passing them through a grading machine. There was a significant decrease in the number of cracked eggs as specific gravity increased.

Other workers have demonstrated a less clear-cut relationship between shell strength as measured and the incidence of cracks. Shrimpton and Hann (1967) found shell strength assessed by deformation was of limited value in predicting subsequent breakage during transit. When eggs were repeatedly passed through egg washing equipment shell strength measured by several methods was found to be significantly higher ($P<0.05$) for the intact eggs than for the cracked eggs, but the range in values almost completely overlapped (Thompson, Hamilton and Grunder, 1985).

Measurements of shell strength as a means of predicting shell breakage are only likely to be of value if the eggs under test spread over a wide range of shell strength, or under controlled conditions when factors likely to influence breakage are constant. Under commercial conditions the relationship between shell strength and downgrading is not close because frequently the challenge or environmental insult is in excess of the variation in shell strength (Carter, 1970).

Overfield (1976) reported unpublished field work which demonstrated that shell thickness, albumen quality and yolk colour scores for batches of eggs passing through a packing station showed little or no relationship with downgrading. Only a limited number of workers have attempted to review factors affecting shell damage under commercial conditions (Overfield, 1970; Hamilton et al., 1979; Washburn, 1982).

Quality grading in relation to the consumer

One of the fundamental objectives of egg grading is to meet the requirements of the consumer. As the quality grading system at present applied to eggs is not markedly different to that introduced with the National Mark Scheme in 1929, it is difficult to conclude other than that the existing system is not ideal.

Certainly, the original grading system increased demand for home produced eggs and now very few bad quality eggs reach the consumer. However, by the late 1960s the BEMB was aware that there was an increasing insistence on a choice and the development of a preference for higher quality eggs. These preferences undoubtedly encouraged an increase in the trade of non-BEMB eggs (Low, 1970). Evidence obtained at that time from consumer organisations indicated that UK housewives prefer an egg which first and foremost is fresh, but also has a strong shell and a firm albumen. They also prefer brown shells and dark coloured yolks (Reorganisation Commission for Eggs, 1968). The BEMB considered carefully the possibility and advisability of amending the quality grading system. The reasons given for not implementing changes in part reflect the inflexibility of a national system but also the BEMB's belief that the function of specialised grading was outside its control, and the responsibility of the market.

In exploring the future Low (1970) anticipated that the emphasis on quality criteria would continue and anticipated that attempts to establish markets for brown, under 48 h old, and free range eggs could increase as suppliers developed their own markets and brands, and retailers tried to increase their sales by establishing a reputation for quality. Since the demise of the BEMB many changes have occurred. Almost all eggs produced in the UK are brown and EEC Marketing Regulations permit the sale of eggs as extra fresh or free range. However, egg consumption per person has fallen and many believe that inadequate quality is partly responsible.

Consumer requirements change and only comprehensive consumer surveys will reveal the demands and preferences of the public. It is difficult to establish suitable techniques for assessing preferences but it is fundamental to marketing that the industry produces what is wanted. Published results of consumer surveys are scant and are limited in content (Overfield, 1976). Most survey organisers probably correctly assumed that consumers would expect eggs they purchased to be clean, intact, edible and free from taint and unsightly inclusions. Preferences which repeatedly ranked high were: freshness, dark yolk colour, firmness of albumen. Surveys on individual components have indicated fairly precise preferences for shell colour, yolk colour and albumen quality. However, factors other than the physical attributes of the egg are important in influencing consumers and systems of production are an important consideration. It must be emphasised that preferences not only vary in different countries and regions but within an individual survey. Specific requirements by minorities and extremes often provide a lucrative market. Alternatively, some may believe that certain apparent illogical preferences may be overcome by a programme of consumer education (Hughes, 1982).

Quality grading and egg candling

The success of a quality control system depends not only upon the standards set but the ability to identify and measure each component monitored within the parameters originally established. The focal point of egg quality grading is the practice known as egg candling. Since the introduction of the National Mark Scheme in 1929 egg candling has played a fundamental role in the marketing of eating eggs.

A brief history of egg candling highlights how the basic principle of shining a light through an egg in order to assess the condition of the shell and contents has not changed since ancient times (Overfield, 1974).

Originally, eggs were candled individually and the technique is still invaluable to advisers, inspectors, managers and trainees. It is a condition of the EEC Egg Marketing Regulations that grading equipment should include an independent candling lamp. In the hands of an experienced operator individual egg candling can achieve remarkable accuracy for several components of quality. On a commercial scale eggs pass in front of the candler in up to 12 parallel rows. As many as 150 eggs can be illuminated at any one time. Up to 25 000 eggs/h can pass before the eyes of an individual candler. Modern engineering principles and more sophisticated lighting techniques have been used to assist the candler but at best the assessment of egg quality by mass candling is extremely subjective and for certain aspects of quality impossible.

As the speeds of egg candling have increased the nature of complaints concerning the associated difficulties have changed. Earlier problems were associated with the differentiation of individual components of, in particular, internal quality and the correlation between observations made and the component being assessed. Recent problems involve the difficulty of recognising some of the previously more obvious faults which in part is due to high machine speeds and brown shells.

Almquist (1933) highlighted the complex relationship of the candling appearance of eggs to their real quality. The assumption that the yolk shadow was a major indication of the liquefaction of the albumen was explored and the results cast considerable doubt on the value of the yolk shadow. Size and defects of the air space were also examined critically. He concluded that candling may be successful with eggs of extreme quality but it was not reliable in making fine distinctions in quality that are supposed to be discernible in intermediate egg grades. Similar conclusions on yolk quality and egg candling were reached by Coles (1940). The relationship between candling and various assessments of albumen quality is not well correlated (Baker and Vadehra, 1972). Other workers have highlighted problems in identifying blood and meat spots (Jenson, Sauter and Stadelman, 1952; Sauter, Stadelman and Carver, 1952). The difficulty of identifying hair cracks in shells has been noted (Moats, 1982). Brant and Norris (1954) concluded that candling accuracy in the USA had not improved since given formal recognition in 1923, and that the discrimination standards required of candling exceed its known limitations.

The dilemma facing modern candlers was underlined by Anderson, Carter and Morley Jones (1969) when an experiment planned to demonstrate factors affecting downgrading in transit included four experienced candlers. The most striking difference revealed was that between candlers. Highly significant differences were detected among three experienced candlers determining internal egg quality by Baker and Vadehra (1972). In a brave attempt to identify factors influencing mass candling performance the effects of five variables were assessed with 12 professional candlers (Oosterwoud, Frijters and Davids, 1976). The results were inconclusive and served to emphasise the complexity of the problem.

The author recently invited observations from egg candlers and their supervisors on the difficulties they experience when mass candling. The following list is compiled from their comments.

(1) Brown eggs are extremely difficult to penetrate with light if glare around the egg is to be avoided.
(2) Fine cracks in fresh eggs are not visible until moisture from the egg moves into the crack which is a frustrating problem for integrated production and packing units.
(3) Scratch marks and weaknesses in the shell are confused with hair cracks.
(4) Speckled brown shells are frequently identified as dirty eggs.

(5) Only extremes in air space can be identified.
(6) Many blood spots are recognised but small blood and meat spots, particularly those associated with the yolk and chalazae, escape detection.
(7) The condition of the albumen is particularly difficult to ascertain.
(8) As the percentage of faults in a batch increases there is a tendency for the candler to subconsciously concentrate on a particular type of fault.
(9) As faults approach 10% the task of physically removing the downgraded eggs becomes increasingly difficult in the time available.
(10) Finally, there is the problem of candlers removing eggs with no faults, due to false identification. Eggs removed as 'phantom' faults can approach 2–3%.

There are close parallels with grading fruit. The grading efficiency falls almost linearly with each additional fault being sought. If objects are being examined for two faults instead of one the efficiency drops by 3% in citrus fruit grading (Malcolm and De Garmo, 1953).

Despite the difficulties associated with egg candling packers achieve on most occasions the necessary official minimum standards. It is when the packer wishes to adopt a more positive attitude to quality control, or is even obliged to meet more stringent requirements for the perceptive buyer, that the inadequacy of the candling system is exposed.

To assist mass candlers the feasibility of staining eggs to make cracks more visible has been tested (Moats, 1982). Equipment for electronically labelling defective eggs which can be removed automatically after grading also assists the candler (Carlow, 1983). In the short term improvements to candling will continue but it will remain the fundamental weakness of the existing quality grading system.

Long term a more radical approach involving alternatives to egg candling seems inevitable (Brant and Norris, 1954; Overfield, 1976; Hughes, 1982; N.D. Overfield, 1981, 1984, unpublished data).

Break-out tests to supplement egg candling

When the BEMB considered break-out tests they envisaged them being used after candling had disclosed a high proportion of faulty or marginal quality eggs. The BEMB anticipated that the tests would provide information on the colour, position and acceptability of the yolk, the presence of thick white, the presence of blood and meat spots and the thickness of the shell. Many packers now voluntarily break out samples of eggs but contrary to the BEMB plans the sample is taken and tested prior to candling. The object is to identify poor quality batches so that machine speeds and numbers of candlers can be adjusted. Generally, the conclusion has been that the extra effort and cost was offset by the ability to more readily recognise sub-standard batches and make recommendations to the producers concerned. A second more positive reason for break-out tests is to supplement the information provided by candling which alone is inadequate. Additional information is considered vital by some quality conscious retailers and supplementary grading is used to achieve the standards required by the contract. Improved quality control allows the packer to meet market requirements with more confidence. Ultimately, it allows the packer to devise quality bonus schemes to reward the successful producer.

In the USA quality grading system a superior AA grade (known as 'fresh fancy') was introduced in 1959. In addition to fulfilling certain husbandry and packaging requirements a sample break-out test is carried out on all Grade AA batches prior to normal candling (Gulich and Fitzgerald, 1969). A flock may be eligible for the grade when a random sample of 25 eggs averages 76 Haugh units (a measurement of albumen quality) and may remain in the grade so long as a moving average of at least 74 Haugh units is maintained. Flocks failing to maintain this average are excluded from the grade but may be reinstated if the original sampling conditions are met.

It should be emphasised that break-out tests can only supplement egg candling; they are not a substitute. Sample tests give an indication of the average quality for each component tested. Although the average may meet the required standard, almost certainly some individual eggs in the batch will not meet the official minimum requirements.

Because eggs are so variable sampling is a problem. It must be on a flock basis. Fortunately, modern production methods result in a relatively consistent quality for a given flock at a given age. Consequently, a fairly small sample of eggs can provide a meaningful indication of the average quality of the component under consideration. The degree of accuracy required depends on the objective of the measurement. A grossly inferior batch of eggs can be identified by examining very few eggs. If in doubt the packer will take a further larger sample. On this basis alone a whole batch may be downgraded. More precise information and an estimate of the range of quality requires more careful sampling. Overfield (1981) presented typical figures for the means and ranges of each of several quality components of fresh eggs from birds 30 weeks of age. The degree of accuracy required and the inherent variation of the individual component under consideration will influence the size of the sample that must be taken. Sampling is further complicated by the age of the flock producing the eggs. Many important egg quality components deteriorate and become more variable with age of bird. Additionally, the average quality of albumen falls and the variation increases with age of egg (Hill and Hall, 1980). Superimpose the effects of disease, nutrition and other environmental factors and it soon becomes apparent that sample break-out tests are fraught with variables. Supplementary tests must be assessed within the overall context of monitoring egg quality. With experience an egg packer can make important commercial decisions based on the information obtained.

A further problem associated with break-out tests is the lack of suitable measuring equipment. Conventional laboratory equipment used by the researcher is rarely suitable for quality control in a commercial operation. Relatively simple, robust, electronic equipment linked to a desk computer is essential to overcome the laborious nature of break-out tests. Hughes (1982) gave examples of equipment which may be suitably adapted.

Alternatives to egg candling

The inadequacies of egg candling frustrated the USA egg industry to such an extent that in 1949 a research programme was inaugurated to direct effort towards developing mechanical and automatic methods of detecting egg quality in intact eggs (Brant and Norris, 1954). A review of the techniques available at that time and promising developments in the fields of sonics, ultrasonics and microwaves prompted the researchers to conclude that suitable detection devices were feasible.

Table 5.2 List of references to work on mechanical and automatic methods of detecting egg quality

Testing technique	Quality component	Researchers
1. Ultrasonics	Shell thickness	Gould (1972)
		Voisey and Hamilton (1976)
	Albumen	Mayer and Heidemann (1958)
		Wilkinson (1978)
		Povey and Wilkinson (1980)
2. Microwave	Albumen	Yen Fu Bow (1958)
3. Spectrophotometry	Shell colour	Brant (1953)
	Yolk colour	Philip, Webber and Berry (1976)
	Blood and meat spots	Brant, Norris and Chin (1953)
		Hamann (1957)
		Norris and Rowan (1962)
		Jong (1981)
		Sherman (1981)
	Shell cracks	Sherman (1981)
4. Radiofrequency	Albumen	Norris and Brant (1952)
5. Radiation	Shell strength	James and Pressly (1979)
6. Viscometry	Albumen	Tung, Watson and Richards (1971)
7. Ultraviolet	Rots	Norris, Brant and Chin (1953)
8. Laser scanning	Shell cracks	Bol (1981)

Progress has been extremely slow. No device has been permanently adopted and candling as a means of egg quality control is still universal. A recent review of the literature highlights the lack of research emphasis in this field. The diversity of the techniques listed in *Table 5.2* and the wide and irregular time scale make it apparent that following the 1949 initiative there has been no concerted effort and the limited progress achieved relied on the enthusiasm of the individual researcher.

Although certain of the earlier techniques may be adapted for investigating specific problems, it is unlikely that any but the most recent have the potential for comprehensively assessing egg quality under commercial conditions.

In 1982 a collaborative group representing Ministry of Agriculture, Fisheries and Food researchers and advisers recommended that the various aspects of the subject of alternatives to egg candling should be reviewed including the feasibility of applying modern analytical techniques to egg quality grading. A discussion document based on the investigation was subsequently distributed to interested parties (Overfield, 1984). The conclusion was tentatively reached that the unique nature of the egg and the interrelationship of numerous quality factors would require, for the foreseeable future, 'visual' inspection of the egg. However, the human eye would be replaced by electronic viewers allowing the egg to be subjected to extremes of intense light modified to emphasise essential aspects of the egg. Already a prototype system was being tested in a United Kngdom packing station. High resolution cameras resistant to blooming (glare) and with the optimum spectrum for viewing eggs were each capable of inspecting six rows of eight eggs to give a matrix of 48 eggs passing along conventional conveyors at normal speeds. The picture is projected on a television screen in another room. An electronic model for each matrix allows the operators to touch the problem egg on the screen with a light pen resulting in the egg on the screen being electronically labelled. The egg is automatically discharged from the conveyor at a later stage. The potential advantages are that the operator is in comfortable surroundings, the view of the egg is enhanced by the camera, and the eggs are automatically discharged later. A similar principle of labelling and automatically discharging faulty products including eggs has been developed (Carlow, 1983). The system was included as an option in commercial grading in 1983. The candling booth is conventional, with an eight channel egg conveyor passing through it. Lights below the conveyor pass through an almost transparent matrix of thin coils. The candler is provided with a hand held 'wand' with which to touch defective eggs. The wand emits a signal which is picked up in the matrix and stepped with the movement of the conveyor until the segregating equipment rejects all eggs which have been touched. Advantages include the reduction of glare because defective eggs remain on the conveyor. The wand is smaller than the hand and consequently obscures less of the field of vision. Eggs do not have to be physically removed allowing more time for inspection.

In the short term, it appears that suitable labelling and sorting systems are available and in service. If the use of specialised cameras successfully enhances the view of the egg and consequently improves the standard of quality grading, a major first step will have been taken.

In the long term, it seems inevitable that the human eye will be replaced if the accuracy and speeds of inspection are to be improved. Other produce, including food, is being inspected by image analysis systems. These include scanning systems which are particularly suitable for assessing size and shape of objects. The information is translated by a microprocessor and the appropriate instruction is passed to the sorting mechanism (Chuma, Kawano and Sein, 1976; Danno, Miyazato and Ishiguro, 1978; Ikeda, Yamashita and Matsua, 1981). Image analysis is already used to explore the proportions of fat and lean on the surface of meat. Image analysis systems are available at relatively low cost and the speed of processing complex images is high enough for them to be considered as part of an automatic vision inspection system for eggs. An enormous advantage over human visual inspection is the ability to use more intense light sources. Bol (1981) has developed a laser scanning system as a means of detecting hair cracks in eggs.

At the present time image analysis appears to offer most hope as a possible alternative to egg candling but it would be premature to neglect other sensor systems which are available for adaptation to agriculture (ARC Working Party, 1982). Infrared transmission spectroscopy has been used for compositional analysis of liquid egg products (Osborne and Barrett, 1984) and ultrasonics are being used to assess albumen quality (Povey and Wilkinson, 1980). Nuclear magnetic resonance has been successfully employed to study embryo development in eggs (Belton et al., 1983) and in pilot studies to assess albumen quality in intact eggs.

Discussion and conclusions

Grading products as a method of quality control is a wasteful process but with agricultural products including eggs there is little alternative because of the variable nature of the products. With eggs there is ample scope for more precise production methods carefully programmed to meet specific demands but inevitably it will be necessary to grade.

The history of egg quality grading highlights its weakness from the outset when the standards set could not be achieved. However, the initial range in quality was so great that success was obtained in uplifting the overall quality of eggs available to the consumer with consequent uplift in sales and prices. Although the standard definition of first quality has been expanded in detail, the basic principles are essentially the same after 55 years. The predominance of shell faults almost to the exclusion of other faults does not necessarily mean that yolk and albumen faults do not exist in eggs from modern poultry flocks. More likely, it reflects the weakness of candling in assessing internal faults. Egg quality research has persisted in pursuing the science of the egg, and in particular the shell, almost in isolation to the problems of quality experienced by the industry in practice. The relationship between shell faults and shell strength is rarely close and the influence of other quality components on downgrading is minimal. The dilemma is the weakness of the grading system which successfully segregates most damaged, dirty and severely deteriorated eggs but cannot categorise those quality components which can be measured in the laboratory, and frequently form the basis of consumer preferences. At best the grading system achieves the official minimum standards but is incapable of meeting higher standards demanded by the more discerning buyers. As a food competing for sales the egg is placed at a serious disadvantage due to inadequate quality control.

Egg candling is the stumbling block. It was never a precise tool, relying on interpretation of imprecise observations. The development of modern machinery with electronic egg weight grading has emphasised the fundamental weakness of egg candling as a quality control technique. Sample break-out tests are essential to supplement egg candling information but they should be seen as an interim tool used until alternative methods of quality grading became available. There is a resurgence of interest in alternatives to egg candling. The development of an assortment of sensor systems and computer technology already employed in industry, including quality control in some food manufacturing, should serve to stimulate research and development. Success would be a major step in safeguarding the future of the egg industry. It will require the full commitment of the industry and its resources.

What are the implications of a radical improvement in egg quality grading? It will fulfil a basic requirement of grading in allowing the consumer to exercise a preference. Production efficiencies will have to accommodate quality objectives. Production methods will be manipulated to meet a more precise demand. Identification of quality will lead to higher rewards for the successful producers. These are the first steps in reorientating a production conscious industry towards the consumer.

References

ALMQUIST, H.J. (1933). Relation of the candling appearance of eggs to their quality. *California Agricultural Experimental Station Bulletin*, **561**, 3–31

ANDERSON, C.F. (1936). Investigations into the condition known as 'watery-white' in eggs. Bulletin No. 308. Department of Agriculture, Adelaide, South Australia

ANDERSON, G.B., CARTER, T.C. and MORLEY JONES, T. (1969). Some factors affecting downgrading in eggs, especially damage in transit. *British Poultry Science*, **10**, 45–52

ANNUAL REVIEW OF AGRICULTURE (1985). Ministry of Agriculture, Fisheries and Food, Cmmd. 9423. London, HMSO

ARC WORKING PARTY (1982). *Sensors in Agriculture*. National Institute of Agricultural Engineering, Wrest Park, Silsoe, Bedford

BAKER, R.C. and VADEHRA, D.V. (1972). A comparison of candling eggs with other methods of determining internal egg quality. *Poultry Science*, **51**, 991–994

BELTON, P.S., GORDON, R.E., JONES, J.N. and SHAW, D. (1983). A ^{31}P topical magnetic resonance study of embryonic development in hens' eggs. *British Poultry Science*, **24**, 429–433

BERRY, J.G. (1976). Extending egg shell damage survey results into the field. *Poultry Science*, **55**, 758–761

BEZPA, J. (1974). Field studies on eggshell damage and bloodspot detection. *Extension Bulletin. Co-operative Extension Service, Cook College, Rutgers University, New Brunswick, New Jersey*, **403**, 3–24

BOL, J. (1981). Laser scanning system for the automated inspection of eggs for haircracks. In *Quality of Eggs*, Proceedings of 1st European Egg Quality Symposium (Group 4), (Beuving, G.M., Scheele, C.W. and Simons, P.C.M., eds), pp. 84–93. Beekbergen, Spelderholt Institute of Poultry Research

BOWMAN, J.C. and CHALLENDER, N.I. (1963). Egg shell strength. A comparison of two laboratory tests and field results. *British Poultry Science*, **4**, 103–116

BRANT, A.W. (1953). Machine sorts eggs for shell colour. USDA. *Poultry Processing and Marketing*, **59**, 12–13

BRANT, A.W. and NORRIS, K.H. (1954). Mechanising the determination of quality in shell eggs. In *Proceedings of 10th World Poultry Congress, Edinburgh*, (Wilson, J.E., ed.), pp.335–338. Edinburgh, Department of Agriculture for Scotland

BRANT, A.W., NORRIS, K.H. and CHIN, G. (1953). A spectrophotometric method for detecting blood in white-shelled eggs. *Poultry Science*, **32**, 357–363

CARLOW, C.A. (1983). An instructible rejection system for quality grading of potatoes and other produce. *Journal of Agricultural Engineering Research*, **28**, 373–383

CARTER, T.C. (1970). Why do egg shells crack? *World's Poultry Science Journal*, **26**, 549–561

CHUMA, Y., KAWANO, S. and SEIN, K. (1976). Optical properties of fruits to serve the automatic selection in the packing house line (2)—Light reflectance of satsuma orange. *Journal of the Society of Agricultural Machinery, Japan*, **37**, 587–592

COLES, R. (1940). Egg candling and yolk quality. *USA Egg and Poultry Magazine*, **46**, 92–95

DANNO, A., MIYAZATO, M. and ISHIGURO, E. (1978). Quality evaluation of agricultural products by infrared imaging method. 1. Grading of fruits for bruise and other surface defects. *Memoirs of the Faculty of Agriculture, Kayoshima University*, **14**, 123–138

EGGLETON, L.Z. and ROSS, W.J. (1971). Observed shell damage in a mechanical gathering system. *Poultry Science*, **50**, 1008–1013

FOLKERTS, J. (1976). Influence of feeding and husbandry on egg shell quality. In *Proceedings of 5th European Poultry Conference, Malta*, pp. 580–593.

GOULD, R.W. (1972). Non-destructive egg shell thickness measurement using ultrasonic energy. *Poultry Science*, **51**, 1460–1461

GULICH, A.R. and FITZGERALD, J.C. (1969). *Egg Grading Handbook*. USDA Consumer Market Service, Agriculture Handbook 75

HAMANN, J.H. (1957). *Electronic Detection of Blood Spots in Eggs*. Agricultural Marketing, USDA Agriculture Marketing Service

HAMILTON, R.M.G. (1982). Methods and factors that affect the measurement of egg shell quality. *Poultry Science*, **61**, 2022–2039

HAMILTON, R.M.G., HOLLANDS, K.G., VOISEY, P.W. and GRUNDER, A.A. (1979). Relationship between egg shell quality and shell breakage and factors that affect shell breakage in the field. A review. *World's Poultry Science Journal*, **35**, 177–190

HILL, A.T. and HALL, J.W. (1980). Effects of various combinations of oil spraying, washing, sanitising, storage time, strain, and age of layer upon albumen quality changes in storage and minimum sample sizes required for their measurement. *Poultry Science*, **59**, 2237–2242

HOLDER, D.P. and BRADFORD, M.V. (1979). Relationship of specific gravity of chicken eggs to number of cracked eggs and per cent shell. *Poultry Science*, **58**, 250–251

HUGHES, R.J. (1982). Egg quality control in Australia. *World's Poultry Science Journal*, **38**, 186–193

IKEDA, Y., YAMASHITA, R. and MATSUA, Y. (1981). On the system evaluating the shape of products via image processing techniques (Part 2). *Research Report on Agricultural Machinery, Japan*, **11**, 83–93

JAMES, P.E. and PRESSLY, R.S. (1979). A comparison of beta back-scatter gauges for measuring egg shells. *Poultry Science*, **58**, 361–364

JENSEN, L.S., SAUTER, E.A. and STADELMAN, W.J. (1952). The detection and disintegration of blood spots as related to age of eggs. *Poultry Science,* **31**, 381–387

JONG, DE L.P. (1981). Electro-optical blood-spot detection in intact eggs. In *Quality of Eggs,* Proceedings of 1st European Egg Quality Symposium (Group 4), (Beuving, G., Scheele, C.W. and Simons, P.C.M., eds), pp. 94–102. Beekbergen, Spelderholt Institute of Poultry Research

LEECH, E.M. and KNOWLES, N.R. (1969). An investigation on commercial farms on factors thought to contribute to egg cracking. *British Poultry Science,* **10**, 139–147

LOW, E.M. (1970). The importance of grading in egg marketing. In *Factors Affecting Egg Grading,* (Freeman, B.M. and Gordon, R.F., eds), pp. 3–16. Edinburgh, British Poultry Science

MADDISON, A.E. (1970). The incidence of downgrading at the present time. In *Factors Affecting Egg Grading,* (Freeman, B.M. and Gordon, R.F., eds), pp. 17–26. Edinburgh, British Poultry Science

MALCOLM, D.G. and DE GARMO, E.P. (1953). *Visual Inspection of Products for Surface Characteristics in Grading Operations.* USDA Marketing Research Report No. 45, Washington DC

MAYER, W.G. and HEIDEMANN, E.A. (1958). On the feasibility of ultrasonic grading of shell eggs. *Food Research,* **24**, 97–103

MCNALLY, E.H. (1965). The relationship of egg shell weight to cracked eggs. *Poultry Science,* **44**, 1513–1518

MINISTRY OF AGRICULTURE AND FISHERIES (1926). *Report on Egg Marketing in England and Wales.* Economic Series, No. 10

MINISTRY OF AGRICULTURE AND FISHERIES (1947). *The Report of the Committee Appointed to Review the Working of the Agricultural Marketing Acts.* Economic Series, No. 48

MOATS, W.A. (1982). A staining procedure for detecting cracked eggs. *Poultry Science,* **61**, 1007–1008

NATIONAL FOOD SURVEY (1984). *Household Food Consumption and Expenditure.* Annual Report of the National Food Survey Committee. Ministry of Agriculture, Fisheries and Food. London, HMSO

NORRIS, K.H. and BRANT, A.W. (1952). Radio frequency as a means of grading eggs. *Food Technology,* **6**, 204–208

NORRIS, K.H. and ROWAN, J.D. (1962). Automatic detection of blood in eggs. *Agricultural Engineering,* **43**, 154–159

NORRIS, K.H., BRANT, A.W. and CHIN, G. (1953). Principles for automatic detection of *Pseudomonas* fluorescence (green rot) in shell eggs. *Poultry Science,* **32**, 918–919

OOSTERWOUD, A., FRIJTERS, J.E.R. and DAVIDS, C. (1976). Some factors affecting mass candling performance of eggs. *British Poultry Science,* **17**, 249–260

OSBORNE, B.G. and BARRETT, G.M. (1984). Compositional analysis of liquid egg products using infrared transmission spectroscopy. *Journal of Food Technology,* **19**, 349–353

OVERFIELD, N.D. (1970). Factors affecting egg quality—field observations. In *Factors Affecting Egg Grading,* (Freeman, B.M. and Gordon, R.F., eds), pp. 29–52. Edinburgh, British Poultry Science

OVERFIELD, N.D. (1974). *Quality Testing of Eggs.* Ministry of Agriculture, Fisheries and Food, Reference Book 428. London, HMSO

OVERFIELD, N.D. (1976). General aspects of egg quality. In *Proceedings of 5th European Poultry Conference, Malta,* pp.569–579

PHILIP, T., WEBER, C.W. and BERRY, J.W. (1976). Rapid measurement of egg yolk colour. *Food Technology,* **33**, 58–59

POVEY, M.J.W. and WILKINSON, J.M. (1980). Application of ultrasonic pulse-echo techniques to egg albumen quality testing: a preliminary report. *British Poultry Science,* **21**, 489–495

REORGANISATION COMMISSION FOR EGGS (1968). Report. Ministry of Agriculture, Fisheries and Food. London, HMSO

ROLAND, D.A. (1977). The extent of uncollected eggs due to inadequate shell. *Poultry Science,* **56**, 1517–1521

ROMANOFF, A.L. and ROMANOFF, A.J. (1949). *The Avian Egg.* New York, Wiley

SAUTER, E.A., STADELMAN, W.J. and CARVER, J.S. (1952). Factors affecting the incidence of blood spots and their detection in hen's eggs. *Poultry Science,* **31**, 1042–1049

SHERMAN, R.C. (1981). An automatic egg candler. In *Quality of Eggs,* Proceedings of 1st European Egg Quality Symposium (Group 4), (Beuving, G., Scheele, C.W. and Simons, P.C.M., eds), pp. 77–83. Beekbergen, Spelderholt Institute of Poultry Research

SHRIMPTON, D.H. and HANN, C.M. (1967). Shell deformation in predicting breakage due to transport and handling. *British Poultry Science,* **8**, 317–320

THOMPSON, B.K., HAMILTON, R.M.G. and GRUNDER, A.A. (1985). The relationship between laboratory measures of egg shell quality and breakage in commercial egg washing and candling equipment. *Poultry Science,* **64**, 901–909

TUNG, M.A., WATSON, E.L. and RICHARDS, J.F. (1971). Rheology of egg albumen. *Transactions of the American Society of Agricultural Engineers,* No. 69.874

TYLER, C. (1961). Shell strength: its measurement and its relationship to other factors. *British Poultry Science,* **2**, 3–18

TYLER, C. and GEAKE, F.H. (1960). Studies on egg shells. XIII—Influence of individuality, breed, season and age on certain characteristics of egg shells. *Journal of the Science of Food and Agriculture,* **11**, 535–547

VOISEY, P.W. and HAMILTON, R.M.G. (1976). Ultrasonic measurement of egg shell thickness. *Poultry Science,* **55**, 1319–1324

WASHBURN, K.W. (1982). Incidence, cause and prevention of egg shell breakage in commercial production. *Poultry Science,* **61**, 2005–2012

WELLS, R.G. (1967a). Egg shell strength. 1. The relationship between egg breakage in the field and certain laboratory assessments of shell strength. *British Poultry Science,* **8**, 131–139

WELLS, R.G. (1967b). Egg shell strength. 2. The relationship between egg specific gravity and egg shell deformation and their reliability as indicators of shell strength. *British Poultry Science,* **8**, 193–199

WELLS, R.G. (1968). The measurement of certain egg quality characteristics: a review. In *Egg Quality. A Study of the Hen's Egg,* (Carter, T.C., ed.), pp. 207–250. Edinburgh, Oliver and Boyd

WILKINSON, J.M. (1978). Application of ultrasonic pulse echo techniques to albumen quality testing of the hen's egg. MSc Thesis. University of Leeds, England

YEN FU BOW (1958). Microwaves as a means of grading eggs. *Food Research,* **24**, 104–111

Chapter 6

Laboratory evaluations of egg quality

Peter Hunton

Introduction

Laboratories of many kinds concern themselves with measurements of egg quality. While they do this for a variety of reasons, it is important to remember that a common factor in all evaluations is a relationship to some aspect of consumer satisfaction. This may be as simple as evaluating shell or yolk colour because consumers are known to have preferences. Conversely, it may relate to drug residues, complex changes resulting from the nutrition of the hen or a combination of these and other factors. In view of this, it is therefore vital that an understanding exists of the correlation, or the cause and effect relationship, between what is measured in the laboratory and what consumers perceive as desirable quality attributes. It is also important to realise that in many cases there will be a two stage process relating laboratory measurements to consumer perception, since the actual evaluation of market eggs is mediated through a field grading procedure, which is dealt with in a separate chapter. The existence of a feedback mechanism, whereby consumer requirements may be translated into laboratory measurements, is important in any discussion of existing or new methods for evaluating egg quality.

It is worthwhile considering a few of the major contributors to laboratory egg quality evaluation. Breeding companies are vitally concerned with measuring egg quality in nucleus or pedigreed populations. This is because, in most cases, commercial chickens in the field can produce eggs of a quality only equal to that recorded in their pedigree ancestors. Most of the traits which consumers believe to be important have been studied by geneticists and many have been found to have moderate to intermediate heritabilities. While in many instances breeders have been content to preserve the existing level of quality for various traits, considerable progress has been necessary, and in many cases has been achieved, in the area of egg shell quality. The methods used will be discussed later. Breeders are, however, faced with the limitation that egg quality evaluation among nucleus stocks can usually be made only at a few locations, while commercial expression of egg quality will be on a worldwide basis. Nutrition, environment and disease will influence field results. Nevertheless, recording acceptable standards among the nucleus flocks will give a breeder confidence in placing birds in the field to meet those challenges. Besides shell quality, breeders have been concerned with albumen quality, yolk quality and the absence of inclusions, among other traits.

Both commercial and institutional laboratories concerned with evaluation of feedingstuffs will have an interest in egg quality. Measurement of egg shell quality, yolk and albumen quality and composition are almost standard procedures where new ingredients or new feeding programmes are under investigation. In the special area of yolk pigmentation, natural feed ingredients and additives must be evaluated before they can be used commercially. There is also the risk that novel feed ingredients may precipitate off-flavours, such as occurred with the use of rapeseed meal.

The production and marketing of drugs, feed additives, and biological products can take place only after rigorous testing in the potential subject species; in the case of laying hens, this would include evaluations of egg quality. Emphasis would be placed on special attributes such as the presence of residues, a possibility of unusual effects such as yolk mottling, and other more subtle changes which might result from the treatment of hens with these new products.

Finally, and of great importance to us all, is the fact that consumers are quite entitled to make laboratory evaluations of the final product of our industry. To my personal knowledge, very little work has been done at the consumer level to evaluate the quality of eggs at the retail stage or beyond. Nevertheless, it is important that methods for measuring egg quality at this level should be available, and that they should be in harmony with those used in other areas of the industry.

The yolk

Yolk colour

The yolk accounts for slightly over 30% of the total weight of the egg, yet comparatively few of its features are the subject of routine qualitative analysis. The most important of these traits is the colour of the egg yolk. The physical shape of the yolk is also important, but Wells (1968) concluded from his review of the literature that yolk shape or yolk index was mainly a function of albumen quality, and therefore measuring it as an independent trait was of limited value.

The measurement of yolk colour, however, is of considerable importance. Consumers have strong preferences for specific yolk colours, and these vary in different parts of the world. Yolk colour is extremely sensitive to the presence of carotenoids or their precursors in the diet, and must therefore be critically examined by those involved in the development of feeding programmes.

Most assessments of egg yolk colour have been made by means of visual comparisons with prepared standards. Optical evaluation of extracted pigment and light reflectance have also been used. For many years, the Heiman–Carver Colour Rotor (Heiman and Carver, 1935) was used as an industry standard. This consisted of 24 painted watch glasses ranging in colour from light creamy white through yellow and orange to orange-red. Although various other groups developed colour standards, the Heiman–Carver system was given official sanction in the USA. In 1956, F. Hoffmann-LaRoche Company Limited produced the first of their colour fans. This consisted of a series of 12 coloured sheets, 3 cm × 16 cm with a triangular notch at one end. This was replaced approximately 10 years later by the Roche Yolk Colour Fan edition 1965, described by Vuilleumier (1969). This has largely replaced all the earlier colour standards for comparative evaluations of yolk colour. It consists of 15 colour standards corresponding to the range normally found in egg yolks. Although technically superior to the earlier versions, the current Roche scale suffers the same disadvantages. These include failure to reproduce exactly the actual colour (wavelength) of the egg yolks to be compared, and the element of subjectivity involved in making comparisons of sample material with a prepared standard. Nevertheless, the Roche Fan is widely used and for most purposes, in competent and experienced hands, can provide useful results. (Since the manuscript for this review was prepared, the Roche company has released a further improved version of their fan.)

The standard colorimetric method (AOAC, 1980) involves extracting the pigments from the yolk material with acetone, measuring light absorbance, and comparing with a standard curve to determine beta-carotene equivalents. While this clearly eliminates the subjective element of the visual comparison, it is also open to the objection that it may not be sensitive to all of the pigments which make up yolk colour. Indeed, Fletcher (1980) in a major review of the AOAC method, produced yolk samples giving beta-carotene equivalent values of 14.3 and 14.2 μg/g, while the same samples visually scored using the Roche Colour Fan gave values of 7 and 15 respectively.

The measurement of light reflected from egg yolk surfaces represents an alternative to both visual scoring and pigment extraction. Several methods have been described in the literature, and were reviewed by Wells (1968) but since then a new method has been reported by Hinton et al. (1970) and McReady et al. (1973). This method uses the IDL Color-Eye® to measure reflectance. It provides estimates of dominant wavelength and excitation purity values, parameters which, together, seem to define egg yolk pigmentation quite precisely. These parameters were also quoted by earlier workers (Hartfiel and Schmitten, 1965) as essential. Hinton, Fry and Harms (1973) used the IDL Color-Eye® to classify for yolk colour, eggs which had previously been candled and graded on the basis of yolk shadow. Wide variation in pigmentation had been achieved by supplementing the hens' diets with two different xanthophyll pigments. The colour and intensity variations were clearly reflected in candling grade. As the colour changed from yellow to reddish orange, so the intensity of yolk shadow increased. This would have increased downgrading in markets where deeply pigmented yolks were not required.

Fletcher (1980) used different equipment, but measured the same parameters in a comparison of the AOAC procedure, visual comparisons and colorimetry. In addition to dominant wavelength and excitation purity, Fletcher measured luminosity and the 1976 CIE values of L^* (lightness), a^* (+ = redness) and b^* (+ = yellowness). In this experiment, xanthophyll-free yolks and pigmented yolks from hens fed yellow corn were blended with Canthaxanthin to give varying intensities of yellow, red and orange pigmentation. Both the Roche Colour Fan and the colour reflectance techniques were able to identify differences in redness and yellowness, while the AOAC method, as noted above, did not. In a second part of the experiment, 32 diets with different xanthophyll contents and sources were used to produce different coloured yolks. Results from these essentially repeated those from the artificially created yolk mixtures in the first part of the study. It was concluded that the AOAC procedure of beta-carotene equivalents was inadequate in describing yolk colours produced from different xanthophyll sources. The reflectance colorimetry and Roche Colour Fan evaluations were in close agreement, and gave results which could be applied over a wide range of pigment sources.

Although considerable progress has been made in evaluating egg yolk pigmentation, as late as 1984 Karunajeewa et al. stated: 'There is clearly a need for the development of more precise and rapid methods for the objective measurement of yolk colour.'

As others have pointed out, the evaluation of egg yolk colour by consumers is itself subjective, and we may therefore apply subjective evaluations in the laboratory with a little more confidence.

Yolk mottling

Mottling of egg yolks has been identified as a problem for many years. A review of factors influencing egg yolk mottling by Cunningham and Sanford (1974) identified both chemical and physical factors which would influence the extent of mottling. However, neither in their paper nor in any other which has reached the author's attention has there been any method for describing the severity of mottling except by counting eggs or by scoring individual eggs. The study by Cunningham (1976) of composition and functional properties of mottled egg yolks showed that the difference is much deeper than merely visual. Significant differences between control and mottled yolks were observed in moisture, fat, protein, ash, calcium, phosphorus and iron content as well as colour evaluated by the pigment extraction method (AOAC, 1980). Similar differences were noted in functional properties such as emulsifying capacity, viscosity and foaming. It would thus appear that several marker characteristics may exist which might be used to obtain numerical definitions of mottling, if this were needed. Clearly, where eggs are being used for industrial purposes, such qualitative distinctions may have to be made.

Egg taints

Although the presence of fishy taints or off-flavour in eggs was reported many years ago (Vondell, 1932; Hutt, 1949), during the past decade this phenomenon has achieved added commercial significance. This was associated with the increased use of rapeseed meal as a component of layer diets. While rapeseed meal has been the prime ingredient involved, the problem is not restricted to it. Fish meals have also been implicated (Pearson *et al.*, 1983). From a practical point of view, the determination of taint in eggs becomes an all-or-none characteristic; the egg is either tainted or it is not. This distinction is usually made by trained laboratory technicians. Some workers (e.g. Bolton, Carter and Morley Jones, 1976) have assigned scores to the degree of tainting. In biochemical studies, the concentration of trimethylamine in the egg yolk may be determined. While a full discussion of the problem of fishy taint in eggs lies outside the scope of this chapter, an excellent review by Butler and Fenwick (1984) is available.

Miscellaneous yolk characteristics

As technology becomes more sophisticated, more and more characteristics of the egg yolk become of interest. As concern increases over cholesterol, so determinations of the cholesterol content of egg yolks becomes commonplace.

The use of polyacrylamide gel electrophoresis has permitted the identification of many proteins unique to the egg yolk. Several of these have been identified as genetic polymorphisms but the exact significance of these is not yet clear (e.g. Tanabe and Ogawa, 1982).

The albumen

Although the albumen or white represents the largest proportion (approximately 58.5%) of the whole egg, it also includes the highest proportion (approximately

88.5%) of water. While much attention has been paid in the egg yolk to its chemical composition, the most important characteristics of the albumen are largely physical. This is because the physical form of the albumen largely determines that of the entire egg, once it has been removed from the egg shell. Since 1937, when its inventor, Haugh, first described it, the Haugh unit has become the almost universal method of evaluating albumen quality. This has occurred in spite of the fact, noted by Wells (1968), that it bears little relation to any known standard established by consumers. The Haugh unit relates well to pictorial standards sometimes used to identify quality characteristics. However, even if the precautions reviewed by Wells (1968) are carefully observed, there may still be observer effects in the evaluation of albumen by Haugh units, and it is therefore important for measurements in a series within which comparisons are to be made, to be taken by the same operator. One important improvement in technique resulted from the invention by Buckley and Reid (1971) of a new apparatus to measure albumen height. Previous methods, using a standard tripod micrometer, were subject to error in determining the exact point when the measuring rod touched the albumen. This also made the measurement extremely time consuming. The method of Buckley and Reid (1971) avoids this problem by using electronic circuitry. The circuit is completed when the measuring rod touches the albumen, and the digital readout 'freezes' at exactly this point. A later model claiming improved long term reliability was described by Buckley, St. Amour and Fairfull (1981). Both these gauges have the advantage that the digital readout may be automatically entered on an external data recording device. Thus, if the weight of the egg were also to be read by an external device, the Haugh unit calculation could be computed automatically.

The manufacturers of the original tripod micrometer, B.C. Ames Company, Waltham, Massachusetts, have modified their albumen height gauge so that if it is preset to the weight of the egg, Haugh units are read directly on the dial scale.

As an aid to Haugh unit calculation, where egg weight and albumen height are measured independently, Roush (1981) published the program coding for the TI-59 Programmable Calculator, allowing automatic computation of the Haugh unit values.

A factor frequently ignored in studies which have used the Haugh unit as a method of evaluating albumen quality is that, as the Haugh unit level deteriorates, variation in the Haugh unit value of individual eggs tends to increase. Thus, the sample size required to obtain results of a given precision will vary. Hill and Hall (1980) and Hill et al. (1980) studied this at length. Eggs were sampled from two genotypes of layers varying in age from 30 to 78 weeks. Haugh units were measured on oiled and unoiled eggs, 1, 7 or 14 d after lay. The criteria they set were to measure Haugh units ±2.5 with a probability of 0.90. To meet these criteria with fresh (1 d old) eggs required sample sizes varying from 18 for young pullets to 28 for old hens. When measured at 7 and 14 d, sample sizes required were slightly larger, varying from 20 to 30. To predict the Haugh unit after 7 or 14 d, samples of approximately 50 eggs should be measured at 1 d.

While Haugh units remain the standard evaluation for albumen quality, the underlying biochemical changes have received some study, although these have not so far yielded any objective measurement which might replace the Haugh unit. The changes which occur in albumen quality are accompanied by major changes in the pH of the albumen. The pH of the albumen in a normal freshly laid egg is approximately 7.8. This rises over time to a maximum of 9.7, and has been described (Sharp and Powell, 1931) as the most alkaline biological product in nature. The rise in pH leads to deterioration of the physical characteristics of both the yolk and the albumen (Fromm and Gammon, 1968) and is caused primarily by the loss of CO_2 through the outer membranes and the egg shell. Thus a measurement of albumen pH would also represent an important quality indicator.

The development of alternative physical measures of albumen quality has proved a daunting task. Two attempts have been made to study physical properties of egg albumen, but neither has resulted in any sustained progress. Misra *et al.* (1980) used pulse nuclear magnetic resonance techniques to study differences in the properties of albumen water between thick and thin albumen. Significant differences in nuclear magnetic resonance relaxations were observed between thick and thin albumen. These authors also detected differences in nuclear magnetic resonance responses of thick albumen during the thinning process. While this work served to confirm the already observed differences, no further developments using the technique have been reported.

Povey and Wilkinson (1980) used ultrasonic pulse echo techniques to study thick and thin albumen. They showed that the acoustic properties of thick and thin albumen differed, were distinguishable and measurable. However, this work was only conducted on broken out, separated albumen material. The authors concluded that intact eggs could be measured using the same techniques, provided that many uncontrolled factors, e.g. yolk characteristics, remained constant. Recently Povey (1985, personal communication) has indicated that the technique can select high quality eggs, i.e. those with a high proportion of thick albumen, but that its use in grading lower quality eggs is problematic. It was pointed out that the same technique, if used on intact eggs, could also provide estimates of egg shell thickness as described by Gould (1972). However, no further work on this technique has been reported to date.

We must therefore, arrive at the conclusion, as Wells did in 1968, that no clear challenger to the Haugh unit has so far emerged. Perhaps the unique characteristics of egg albumen, with its subdivision into various components whose proportions change over time, have discouraged attempts at physical or other definitions. Whatever the reason, it appears to this author that the Haugh unit continues to be the preferred measurement, with all its limitations.

Using methods similar to those used in the study of yolk proteins, many genetic polymorphisms have been discovered amongst egg albumen proteins. Various authors have attempted to identify associations between these and other characteristics, without consistent success (Ermenkova, 1978, 1979).

An interesting development in the utilization of eggs in recent years is the extraction of lysozyme for pharmaceutical purposes. While the amount of lysozyme does not appear to affect the physical quality of the egg, it has been shown (Melek, 1977) to vary between breeds, and between individuals having different albumen protein polymorphisms.

The shell

Structure

By its nature, the shell is the most visible and vulnerable component of the egg. Cracked and broken shells, whether caused by quality variation or other factors, lead to a great reduction in the value of the egg if it is salvaged, or total loss in the case where the egg fails to be collected. Various estimates of the financial loss caused by shell breakage have been made. Carter (1971) estimated a loss of £5 million for the UK; Hamilton (1982) estimated a loss of $110 million for the US and Canada. Using the latter figure, and estimates of egg production in the major producing countries reporting to the International Egg Commission, it is estimated that worldwide losses from egg shell breakage alone probably exceed $600 million. This estimate does not include the USSR, South America and Asia (except Japan).

The shell comprises between 8 and 9% of the weight of the fresh egg. This parameter is sometimes used as an indicator of shell quality. It is criticised on the grounds that percentage shell may be related to egg weight; larger eggs frequently have proportionately less shell.

In his 1968 publication, Wells reviewed many methods for estimating egg shell quality. These included falling steel balls, crushing and puncturing, hydraulic pressure, non-destructive deformation, shell thickness, percentage shell, specific gravity, and lastly, backscatter of beta particles. He also reviewed studies which attempted to relate these measurements to breakage in the laboratory and in the field. An important conclusion reached here was that the correlation between shell thickness and breakage was usually greater than the correlation between other estimates of strength and shell damage.

The egg shell has been intensively studied over the past two decades. The design and structure of the different parts of the egg shell are now understood more clearly. The relationship of structure to function and to quality, while still not completely understood, has been the subject of much research. A wide variety of methods for measuring different properties of egg shells is now available.

While the study of the structure of the egg shell began more than a century ago, the advent of electron microscopes has enabled us to develop a much more accurate and realistic description of the different parts of the shell. While various other laboratories preceded it, the work of Fujii and Tamura (1969), Simons and Wiertz (1970) and Simons (1971) provide a detailed description of the ultrastructure of the hen's egg shell. Fujii and Tamura (1970) and Fujii, Tamura and Okamoto (1970) used similar techniques to study shell and membrane formation in eggs removed from various locations in the oviduct. Simons (1971) used both transmission and scanning electron microscopes to produce electron micrographs of all components of the egg shell. These were discussed in detail, and interpreted in terms of the physiology of shell formation. The data were also interpreted in terms of the relationship between structure and strength, and the changes which occur during incubation. These publications have formed the basis for considerable subsequent work on various aspects of shell structure and strength. Although time and space do not permit a detailed review of this work here, a description of the shell structure may help in understanding the discussion of quality evaluation which will follow.

Starting from the interior of the egg shell, the two membranes form the foundation for its structure. The inner membrane is thinner and denser than the outer one. Simons (1971) found the inner membrane to have a thickness of 22 µm and the outer one 48 µm. The outer membrane is much more irregular because it contains the bases of the mammillary layer, and some of its fibres actually enter the calcified part of the shell. The anchorage of the shell in this outer membrane is further strengthened by the penetration of calcium deposits into the meshes of the fibre network. The membrane fibres do not extend far into the crystalline part of the egg shell, but an organic matrix exists through the calcified layers of the shell.

The mammillary layer consists of basal caps, occupying 20 µm, and the cone-shaped crystals, 90 µm of the total shell thickness. The thickest portion, the palisade or spongy layer, consists of crystal columns perpendicular to the shell surface. It is approximately 200 μm in thickness.

In the calcified layers Simons found differences in the direction of fractures which must be relevant to shell strength and breakage studies to be dealt with later. In the mammillary layer almost all fractures appear to be radial, that is at right angles to the shell surface. In the palisade some transverse breaks occur which are parallel to the shell surface. These fractures are thought to reflect the different crystalline structure of these two layers.

The thin surface crystal layer is of different crystalline structure from the palisade layer, and according to Simons varies from 3–8 μm in thickness. This layer is comparatively rich in organic matter and on its outer surface possesses a thin, irregular membrane which makes contact with the cuticle.

The cuticle is an organic layer of irregular thickness covering the entire shell surface. It extends over the pores and in fact plugs their openings with organic material.

While later studies may call into question some of the structural details described by Simons, they do, in general, form a good foundation for an understanding of egg shell structure and quality evaluation.

Numerous new laboratory techniques for measuring egg shell quality have been reported since 1967. Until that time most evaluations were based on shell thickness (or specific gravity, an accurate predictor of thickness), or egg shell deformation by the method of Schoorl and Boersma (1962). A method for estimating shell strength had also been reported by Brooks and Hale (1955) but was not widely used. Since then, methods of puncturing and fracturing the egg shell, other strength testing procedures with and without breakage, and bombardment of the egg with ultrasound or beta particles have all been used to estimate the strength or thickness of the shell.

A major centre for the study of the mechanical properties of egg shells has been the Engineering and Statistical Research Service, and the Animal Research Centre of Agriculture Canada in Ottawa. Beginning in 1964, Voisey, Hamilton and their associates published a variety of papers dealing with the mechanical and engineering aspects of egg shell strength testing and also the mechanical properties of the egg itself. They developed their own testing apparatus and compared it with other methods being reported in the literature during this period (Voisey and Hunt, 1964, 1967, 1973, 1974; Voisey, Hunt and James, 1969; Voisey and Robertson, 1969; Voisey, 1975a, 1975b; Voisey and Hamilton, 1975, 1976a, 1976b, 1977a, 1977b, 1977c; Hamilton et al., 1979; Voisey, Hamilton and Thompson, 1979; Hamilton, 1982). Simultaneously with the work in Ottawa, Carter at the Poultry Research Centre, Edinburgh, was also involved in developing techniques to describe the hen's egg shell and for evaluating quality.

Both free falling objects and quasi-static compression tests have been used to measure egg shell strength in terms of the mechanical force required to fracture the shell. As might be expected, these two methods measure quite different properties of the egg shell, and this can be determined by studying the type of fracture which they cause in the shell.

The simplest and traditional method of evaluating egg shells is to measure their thickness, either directly, or indirectly by means of specific gravity. Direct measurements require that the shell be broken and are subject to error because of variations in thickness at different points on the egg shell. Nevertheless, the use of a micrometer or dial gauge comparator offers a rapid method of egg shell evaluation.

The measurement of specific gravity avoids breaking the egg and has been used by many researchers, particularly those investigating treatments likely to affect the thickness of the egg shell. Even specific gravity, however, is subject to errors in measurement, as described by Voisey and Hamilton (1976a, 1977a). They identified the sources of error as: the effect of temperature on the specific gravity of the test solutions; errors in calibration and reading hydrometers; hair-line cracks in the egg shell; cooling of the solutions by stored eggs; calibration of hydrometers at a standard temperature of 15.6 °C and use at another temperature. These authors concluded that errors up to 0.006 in the specific gravity of individual eggs could occur as a result of these factors.

Many of the methods used to evaluate shell strength test the eggs under quasi-static compression. In this procedure the egg is compressed between flat parallel surfaces. One of these is moved slowly toward the other at a fixed rate. An electronic force transducer is normally used to measure the force required to fracture the egg shell. The same equipment may also be used to measure egg shell deformation prior to fracture.

Many factors influence the behaviour of the egg shells and results obtained from quasi-static compression tests. These were reviewed by Voisey and Hunt (1974). One of the most important factors is the rate of compression, and because this has not been standardised, results obtained by different laboratories may not be strictly comparable. Voisey and Hunt state that the optimum compression speed is in the order of 20 cm/min but point out that this speed requires high frequency response recording apparatus, which may create economic problems because of cost and the use of large quantities of recording chart paper. Using a microcomputer instead of strip chart recording overcomes this problem.

Because quasi-static compression may bear little relation to the type of stress likely to be encountered in the field, other mechanical methods have also been developed to measure shell strength. Impact tests, in which heavy objects are dropped upon the egg, have also been widely studied. A variety of different techniques, each with its own shortcomings, has been developed and these were reviewed by Voisey and Hunt (1974). Their own system involved dropping a force or acceleration transducer onto the shell, mounted at the end of a rod, from a constant height. The force required to fracture the egg shell was measured. Although quasi-static compression and puncture strength are thought to measure tensile stress and shear strength forces respectively, the correlation between these values is quite high ($r = +0.7$; Voisey, Hamilton and Thompson, 1979). Indeed, it is a feature of the reported data that all of the different measures of shell strength seem to be correlated with each other, although not always at such high levels. Since each accident which leads to shell fracture in the field is unique to that particular occasion, the view has been taken that experimental convenience can play a part in deciding which of the many measures of shell strength to use in any particular circumstance. Thus, those methods which are relatively inexpensive and rapid have tended to be given priority.

The egg shell deformation apparatus of Schoorl and Boersma (1962) has been widely used in the field. However, Voisey and Foster (1970) identified some measurement errors associated with this apparatus and designed their own modification. Instead of using a mechanical dial gauge to indicate deformation, electronic circuitry is used to provide a readout using a digital voltmeter.

In addition to modifying the Instron testing machine (Voisey and Hamilton, 1976b), the Ottawa group developed a new egg shell tester (Voisey and

MacDonald, 1978) which can be used to measure both non-destructive deformation and force at fracture. Together, these can be used to estimate the stiffness of the egg shell.

Carter approached the description of the egg as a biologist rather than as an engineer. These studies provide a major contribution to the understanding of the egg shell, and inspired many others to include his considerations in their own work. Beginning in 1968, Carter has provided us with precise definitions of egg shape and curvature, methods of estimating mean shell thickness for both flocks and individuals, and considerable insight into the nature and causes of egg shell damage (Carter, 1968, 1969, 1971, 1975a, 1975b; Carter and Morley Jones, 1970; Anderson, Carter and Morley Jones, 1970a, 1970b). Much of this work was concerned with shell thickness; this characteristic has been avoided by many researchers because in order to make a measurement the egg must be broken. Many of the alternatives have been developed to estimate shell thickness without breaking the egg. If, however, the egg is to be broken for other purposes, for example the evaluation of its contents, then the measurement of shell thickness may still be the one of choice. Carter (1975a) reinforced this view. In a study of data from random sample tests, including a large range of varieties, it was concluded that egg shell colour (in brown eggs only) and shell thickness were the traits mainly responsible for variations in egg shell breakage.

Carter (1968) compared a variety of direct and indirect measurements used to estimate mean thickness of an individual egg. Among these was egg shell deformation using the method of Schoorl and Boersma (1962) described elsewhere in this paper. Carter found systematic errors in the Marius machine as did Voisey (see above) but considered it useful particularly if multiple measures, at the pole and the equator, were used. The estimate of shell thickness by this method could be improved by the inclusion of shell curvature. Estimation of shell curvature was described by Carter (1968) and Carter and Morley Jones (1970).

The 1970 paper also provides a method for obtaining a complete definition of shell shape. While the measurements and computations involved in this are highly complex, Carter emphasised that the former could be automated and the latter computerised, to provide acceptable speed and precision for many applications.

Another aspect of egg shell thickness which may influence strength and shell breakage is the organic content of the shell material. Various earlier workers had associated organic content with shell strength. Carter (1969) showed that once membranes were removed, the organic content of incremental shell material seemed to be constant at 0.68% by weight. However, variation in the overall organic content of the egg shell was due to variation in the thickness of the cuticle and it was felt that this might be responsible for variation in shell strength. This was also noted by Simons (1971) and further studied by Belyavin and Boorman (1980), who concluded that while the cuticle made a significant contribution to shell thickness, its influence on shell strength *per se* may be unimportant.

While this chapter deals with shell quality, it should not be assumed that this is the only factor involved in egg breakage. This was emphasised by Carter (1971) who showed that in fact the characteristics of the insult (a term which he coined) to the shell had far more influence on the incidence of breakage than the shell's own properties. This study showed that while the incidence of cracks was slightly influenced by mean shell thickness and curvature, the most important determinants were mean drop height during oviposition and effective cage floor mass.

As an alternative to the use of shell thickness, several laboratories have used shell weight/unit surface area as an index of egg shell quality (e.g. Garlich *et al.*, 1984). This necessitates drying and weighing the individual egg shells and estimating surface area. The former procedure is time consuming but may be practicable in some circumstances. Estimation of surface area can be accomplished by means of algorithms using the weight and/or length and/or breadth of the fresh egg. Five such algorithms were compared by Hughes (1984) who concluded from his data that the extra effort needed to measure length and breadth was not justified, and that surface area was accurately estimated from egg weight alone.

Most of the methods available to measure shell characteristics in the laboratory have been included in the above review. However, a few others have been used occasionally and should not be ignored. For instance, Wells (1968) referred to the use of the beta-backscatter technique (James and Retzer, 1967). While this method has been shown to provide acceptable predictions of egg shell thickness, it has not been widely used. Part of the reason for this is that the measurement tends to be somewhat time consuming, and the equipment more expensive than for some other methods. Further, Voisey and James (1970) concluded that additional research was required to determine the optimum radioactive source and the errors inherent in the measurement. In a comparison of beta-backscatter with non-destructive deformation, shell thickness, and quasi-static compression, Hunton (1969) found that backscatter count yielded low coefficients of variation and did not detect differences between inbred lines which could be demonstrated by the other methods. A similar experience with the beta-backscatter technique was reported by Garwood, Lowe and Haugh (1979), who reported another method for assessing shell strength. This was referred to as 'random impact loading' and consisted of placing 25 eggs in a 305 mm × 305 mm × 50 mm deep, smooth floored wooden box, which was then 'shaken' through a 75 mm distance for 2 min at 60 cycles/min. This procedure broke approximately one-third of the eggs and this proportion was used to describe each 25 egg sample. Using this technique to evaluate eggs representing sire families, the authors showed that bi-directional selection for a single generation was effective in changing shell strength. A correlated response in shell thickness was noted, and heritability of the measurement estimated as 0.48 ± 0.05. Buss (1985, personal communication) has used similar equipment in his laboratory with essentially the same results.

Van Toledo, Parsons and Combs (1980, 1982) demonstrated a relationship between ultrastructure of the egg shell and its breaking strength. Using genetic lines differentiated for shell strength by direct selection, they examined the size and density of the mammillary knobs. This was accomplished by examining epoxy resin casts made from the egg shell mammillary layer, using a scanning electron microscope. While costly and time consuming, these observations have the advantage that they do not involve mechanical measurements, which may be influenced by a combination of many variables. They concluded (Van Toledo, Parsons and Combs, 1980) that variation in mammillary knob density might account for 20% of the variation in shell strength, compared with 60% for shell thickness.

Vikram, Vedam and Buss (1980) described a method of determining egg shell strength using holographic interferometry. This method employs a laser beam to illuminate the egg and produce a 'hologram'. The procedure may then be repeated with the egg under mechanical load or deformation, and a second exposure superimposed on the first. Easily visible differences were observed between eggs known to have different shell strengths, although quantification of such variation might prove difficult.

Gould (1972) used ultrasonic energy to estimate egg shell thickness without breaking the eggs. A beam of ultrasonic energy is directed into the egg and reflected from the shell/liquid interface. When compared with thickness measurements made using a standard dial gauge micrometer, the ultrasonic method predicted thickness within 0.01 mm, an acceptable precision. One of the factors which may have discouraged its widespread acceptance is that of cost; Gould (1972) quotes approximately $2500 for the ultrasonic instrument. Voisey and Hamilton (1976b) also used an ultrasonic technique to estimate shell thickness but concluded that, while the method had potential, others gave equal or greater precision at lower cost.

An important consideration when comparing methods of shell quality assessment is how they relate to shell performance in the field. This was reviewed by Hamilton *et al.* (1979) and was also the subject of a critical experiment (Thompson, Hamilton and Grunder, 1985). In the latter study, individual hens were assessed for shell strength using quasi-static fracture force, deformation, shell weight and thickness. Subsequent eggs from the same hens were then examined for breakage in commercial washing and candling equipment. In all cases, breakage was higher in eggs from hens judged to produce eggs of lower shell strength and quality. However, the range of values for quality among hens laying intact and broken eggs completely overlapped, confirming Carter's (1971) contention that variation in the insults is more important than variation in the shells, in determining whether eggs fail during handling.

The cost of equipment needed to measure shell quality may influence the choice of method. Current approximate prices for some of the equipment reviewed here are given in *Table 6.1*.

Table 6.1 Egg shell quality—equipment price comparisons[a]

	$
Ottawa egg shell tester	8500
Dial gauge comparator	450–1000
Pocket shell thickness gauge	55
Specific gravity	250
Beta-backscatter	1200
Marius—deformation	2000
Instron—breaking strength	11700
Ultrasound	4000

[a]Prices are approximate, expressed in US dollars, Spring 1985.

The method chosen to measure shell quality will depend on many factors. Of 120 studies revealed in a literature search, undertaken for this chapter, 95 used shell thickness to illustrate variation in egg shell quality, 47 used specific gravity, and a similar number estimated breaking strength or fracture force with a variety of instruments. Next in popularity was shell weight or shell weight/unit of surface area, followed by non-destructive deformation and percentage shell. Many studies reported two or three different parameters.

In feeding or nutrition studies, where variation in the absolute quantity of shell material deposited may be important, shell thickness and/or shell weight are probably essential measurements. These require that the egg be broken.

In genetic or breeding experiments, the use of non-destructive deformation or specific gravity may be appropriate, particularly in the case of pedigree eggs required for incubation. These measurements also have the advantage that they can be made relatively quickly, allowing large numbers of eggs to be evaluated.

Egg shell colour

Consumer preferences for different coloured egg shells continue to polarise. The laboratory assessment of shell colour continues to be by the reflectance method described by Hunton (1962) with modifications reported by Gowe, Budde and McGann (1965). Recent versions of this equipment have replaced the moving coil galvanometer with a digital readout.

Acknowledgements

I would like to acknowledge the following who helped in the preparation of this chapter by providing facilities and/or photographs illustrating various aspects of egg quality measurement: Dr R.M.G. Hamilton, Agriculture Canada, Ottawa; Dr E.G. Buss, Penn. State University; Dr Alan Emsley, I.S.A. Babcock, Ithaca, NY; Dr Howard French, Shaver Poultry Breeding Farms Ltd, Cambridge, Ontario; Dr Al Kulenkamp, Shaver Poultry Breeding Farms Ltd, Cambridge, Ontario; Instron Canada Ltd, Oakville, Ontario.

I am also extremely grateful to the Ontario Egg Producers' Marketing Board for allowing me the time, and providing clerical services, to prepare this chapter.

References

ANDERSON, G.B., CARTER, T.C. and MORLEY JONES, R. (1970a). Some factors affecting the incidence of cracks in hens' egg shells. *British Poultry Science*, **11**, 103–116

ANDERSON, G.B., CARTER, T.C. and MORLEY JONES, R. (1970b). Some factors affecting dynamic fracture of egg shells in battery cages. In *Factors Affecting Egg Grading*, (Freeman, B.M. and Gordon, R.F., eds), pp. 53–69. Edinburgh, British Poultry Science

AOAC (1980). *Official Methods of Analysis, 13th Edition*. Washington, DC, Association of Official Analytical Chemists

BELYAVIN, C.G. and BOORMAN, K.N. (1980). The influence of the cuticle on egg-shell strength. *British Poultry Science*, **21**, 295–298

BOLTON, W., CARTER, T.C. and MORLEY JONES, R. (1976). The hen's egg: Genetics of taints in eggs from hens fed on rapeseed meal. *British Poultry Science*, **17**, 313–320

BROOKS, J. and HALE, H.P. (1955). Strength of the shell of the hen's egg. *Nature (London)*, **175**, 848–849

BUCKLEY, D.J. and REID, W.S. (1971). A digital egg albumen height measurement gauge. *Poultry Science*, **50**, 1326–1330

BUCKLEY, D.J., ST. AMOUR, G. and FAIRFULL, R.W. (1981). An improved electronic gauge for measuring egg albumen height. *Poultry Science*, **60**, 777–780

BUTLER, E.J. and FENWICK, G.R. (1984). Trimethylamine and fishy taint in eggs. *World's Poultry Science Journal*, **40**, 38–51

CARTER, T.C. (1968). The hen's egg: Estimation of egg mean and flock mean shell thickness. *British Poultry Science*, **9**, 343–357

CARTER, T.C. (1969). The hen's egg: Relationship between thickness and the amount of organic matter in the shell. *British Poultry Science*, **10**, 165–174

CARTER, T.C. (1971). The hen's egg: Shell cracking at oviposition in battery cages and its inheritance. *British Poultry Science*, **12**, 259–278

CARTER, T.C. (1975a). The hen's egg: A rapid method for routine estimation of flock mean shell thickness. *British Poultry Science*, **16**, 131–143

CARTER, T.C. (1975b). The hen's egg: Relationship of seven characteristics of the strain of hen to the incidence of cracks and other shell defects. *British Poultry Science*, **16**, 289–296

CARTER, T.C. and MORLEY JONES, R. (1970). The hen's egg: Shell shape and size parameters and their interrelations. *British Poultry Science*, **11**, 179–188

CUNNINGHAM, F.E. (1976). Composition and functional properties of mottled yolks. *Poultry Science*, **55**, 994–998

CUNNINGHAM, F.E. and SANFORD, P.E. (1974). A review of factors influencing egg yolk mottling. *World's Poultry Science Journal*, **30**, 103–114

ERMENKOVA, L. (1978). Sexual maturity of pullets with different blood-group B phenotypes and ovoglobulin genotypes. *Zhivotnov "dni Nauki*, **15**, 79–84

ERMENKOVA, L. (1979). Genetic polymorphisms of egg albumen in two lines of White Plymouth Rock Hens, and the relationship with some morphological characters of eggs. *Zhivotnov "dni Nauki*, **16**, 73–79

FLETCHER, D.L. (1980). An evaluation of the A.O.A.C. method of yolk colour analysis. *Poultry Science*, **59**, 1059–1066

FROMM, D. and GAMMON, S.U. (1968). Specific gravity and volume of the hen's egg yolk as influenced by albumen pH and storage age of the egg. *Poultry Science*, **47**, 1191–1196

FUJII, S. and TAMURA, T. (1969). Scanning electron microscopy of the hen's egg shell. *Journal of the Faculty of Fisheries and Animal Husbandry, Hiroshima University*, **8**, 85–98

FUJII, S. and TAMURA, T. (1970). Scanning electron microscopy of shell formation in hen's eggs. *Journal of the Faculty of Fisheries and Animal Husbandry, Hiroshima University*, **9**, 65–81

FUJII, S., TAMURA, T. and OKAMOTO, T. (1970). Scanning electron microscopy of shell membrane formation in hen's eggs. *Journal of the Faculty of Fisheries and Animal Husbandry, Hiroshima University*, **9**, 139–150

GARLICH, J., BRAKE, J., PARKHURST, C.R., THAXTON, J.P. and MORGAN, G.W. (1984). Physiological profile of caged layers during one production year, molt and post molt: Egg production, egg shell quality, liver, femur, and blood parameters. *Poultry Science*, **63**, 339–343

GARWOOD, V.A., LOWE, P.C. and HAUGH, C.G. (1979). Method for improving egg-shell strength by selection. *British Poultry Science*, **20**, 289–295

GOULD, R.W. (1972). Non-destructive egg shell thickness measurements using ultrasonic energy. *Poultry Science*, **51**, 1460–1461

GOWE, R.S., BUDDE, H.W. and MCGANN, P.J. (1965). On measuring egg shell colour in poultry breeding and selection programmes. *Poultry Science*, **44**, 264–270

HAMILTON, R.M.G. (1982). Methods and factors that affect the measurement of egg shell quality. *Poultry Science*, **61**, 2022–2039

HAMILTON, R.M.G., HOLLANDS, K.G., VOISEY, P.W. and GRUNDER, A.A. (1979). Relationship between egg shell quality and shell breakage in the field—A review. *World's Poultry Science Journal*, **35**, 177–190

HARTFIEL, W. and SCHMITTEN, F. (1965). Die Bestimmung der Eidotterfarbe. *Archiv für Geflügelkunde*, **29**, 367–386

HEIMAN, V. and CARVER, J.S. (1935). The yolk colour index. *US Egg Poultry Magazine*, **41**, 40–41

HILL, A.T., EISSINGER, R.C., HAMILTON, D.M. and PATKO, J. (1980). Implications of albumen quality decline in sampling and grading eggs from eight commercial stocks. *Canadian Journal of Animal Science*, **60**, 979–989

HILL, A.T. and HALL, J.W. (1980). Effects of various combinations of oil spraying, washing, sanitizing, storage time, strain and age of layer upon albumen quality changes in storage and minimum sample sizes required for their measurement. *Poultry Science*, **59**, 2237–2242

HINTON, C.F., AHMED, E.M., FRY, J.L. and HARMS, R.H. (1970). Reflectance colorimetric evaluation of egg yolk pigmentation. *Poultry Science*, **49**, 1397

HINTON, C.F., FRY, J.L. and HARMS, R.H. (1973). The relationship of yolk pigmentation to candled grade. *Poultry Science*, **52**, 360–364

HUGHES, R.J. (1984). Estimation of shell surface area from measurements of length, breadth and weight of hen eggs. *Poultry Science*, **63**, 2471–2474

HUNTON, P. (1962). Genetics of egg shell colour in a Light Sussex flock. *British Poultry Science,* **3,** 189–193

HUNTON, P. (1969). The measurement of egg shell strength: A comparison of four methods. *British Poultry Science,* **10,** 281–289

HUTT, F.B. (1949). *Genetics of the Fowl.* New York, Toronto, London, McGraw-Hill

JAMES, P.E. and RETZER, H.J. (1967). Measuring egg shell strength by beta backscatter technique. *Poultry Science,* **46,** 1200–1203

KARUNAJEEWA, H., HUGHES, R.J., MCDONALD, M.W. and SHENSTONE, F.S. (1984). A review of factors influencing pigmentation of egg yolk. *World's Poultry Science Journal,* **40,** 52–65

MCREADY, S.T., FRY, J.L., HINTON, C.F. and HARMS, R.H. (1973). Colorimetric characterization of egg yolk and egg yolk products. *Journal of Food Science,* **38,** 175–176

MELEK, O.I. (1977). The lysozyme content of egg protein in fowls and embryo mortality. *Sbornik Nauchnykh Trudov. Moskovskaya Veterinarnaya Akademija,* **92,** 71–74

MISRA, L.K., TRANTHAM, E.C., HAZLEWOOD, C.F., FANGUY, R.C. and GARDNER, F.A. (1980). Nuclear magnetic resonance study of egg quality deterioration. Differences in thick and thin albumen. *Poultry Science,* **59,** 1640–1641

PEARSON, A.W., GREENWOOD, N.M., BUTLER, E.J., FENWICK, G.R. and CURL, C.L. (1983). Fish meal and egg taint. *Journal of the Science of Food and Agriculture,* **34,** 277–285

POVEY, M.J.W. and WILKINSON, J.M. (1980). Application of ultrasonic pulse-echo techniques to egg albumen quality testing: A preliminary report. *British Poultry Science,* **21,** 489–495

ROUSH, W.B. (1981). TI-59 Calculator program for Haugh Unit calculation. *Poultry Science,* **60,** 1086–1088

SCHOORL, P. and BOERSMA, H.Y. (1962). Research on the quality of the egg shell (a new method of determination). *Proceedings of the 12th World's Poultry Congress, Sydney,* pp. 432–435.

SHARP, P.F. and POWELL, C.K. (1931). Increase in the pH of the white and yolk of hen's eggs. *Industrial and Engineering Chemistry,* **23,** 196–199

SIMONS, P.C.M. (1971). *Ultrastructure of the Hen Eggshell and its Physiological Interpretation.* Agricultural Research Report No. 758, Wageningen, Holland

SIMONS, P.C.M. and WIERTZ, G. (1970). Notes on the structure of shell and membranes of the hen's egg: A study with the scanning electron microscope. *Annales de Biologie Animale, Biochimie et Biophysique,* **10,** 31–49

TANABE, H. and OGAWA, N. (1982). Comparative studies on the physical and chemical composition of avian eggs. 10. Electrophoretograms of prealbumins in plasma and yolk of quails. *Japanese Poultry Science,* **19,** 15–19

THOMPSON, B.K., HAMILTON, R.M.G. and GRUNDER, A.A. (1985). The relationship between laboratory measures of egg shell quality and breakage in commercial egg washing and candling equipment. *Poultry Science,* **74,** 901–909

VAN TOLEDO, B., PARSONS, A.H. and COMBS, G.F. JR. (1980). Mammillary structure as a determinant of eggshell strength. *Poultry Science,* **59,** 1667

VAN TOLEDO, B., PARSONS, A.H. and COMBS, G.F. JR. (1982). Role of ultrastructure in determining eggshell strength. *Poultry Science,* **61,** 569–572

VIKRAM, C.S., VEDAM, K. and BUSS, E.G. (1980). Nondestructive evaluation of the strength of eggs by holography. *Poultry Science,* **59,** 2342–2347

VOISEY, P.W. (1975a). Factors affecting the measurement of the shear strength of shell material by the puncture test. *British Poultry Science,* **16,** 209–212

VOISEY, P.W. (1975b). Field comparison of two instruments for measuring shell deformation to estimate egg shell strength. *Poultry Science,* **54,** 190–194

VOISEY, P.W. and FOSTER, W.F. (1970). A non-destructive eggshell strength tester. *Canadian Journal of Animal Science,* **50,** 390–396

VOISEY, P.W. and HAMILTON, R.M.G. (1975). Behaviour of egg shell under compression in relation to deformation measurements. *British Poultry Science,* **16,** 461–470

VOISEY, P.W. and HAMILTON, R.M.G. (1976a). Notes on the measurement of egg specific gravity to estimate egg shell quality. Report 7322-598. Engineering Research Service, Agriculture Canada, Ottawa

VOISEY, P.W. and HAMILTON, R.M.G. (1976b). Factors affecting the non-destructive methods of measuring egg shell strength by the quasi-static compression test. *British Poultry Science,* **17,** 103–124

VOISEY, P.W. and HAMILTON, R.M.G. (1977a). Sources of error in egg specific gravity measurements by the flotation method. *Poultry Science,* **56**, 1457–1462

VOISEY, P.W. and HAMILTON, R.M.G. (1977b). Observations on the relationship between non-destructive egg shell deformation and resistance to fracture by quasi-static compression for measurement of egg shell strength. *Poultry Science,* **56**, 1463–1467

VOISEY, P.W. and HAMILTON, R.M.G. (1977c). The effect of deformation rate and other factors on the force required to fracture egg shells in measuring shell strength. *Poultry Science,* **56**, 1994–2002

VOISEY, P.W. and HUNT, J.R. (1964). A technique for determining approximate fracture propagation rates of egg shells. *Canadian Journal of Animal Science,* **44**, 347–350

VOISEY, P.W. and HUNT, J.R. (1967). Relationship between applied force, deformation of egg shells and fracture force. *Journal of Agricultural Engineering Research,* **12**, 1–4

VOISEY, P.W. and HUNT, J.R. (1973). Apparatus and techniques for measuring eggshell strength and other quality factors. Engineering Specifications 6176. Engineering Research Service, Agriculture Canada, Ottawa

VOISEY, P.W. and HUNT, J.R. (1974). Measurement of eggshell strength. *Journal of Texture Studies,* **5**, 135–182

VOISEY, P.W. and JAMES, P.E. (1970). Factors affecting the performance of the beta-backscatter eggshell measurement. *Canadian Agricultural Engineering,* **12**, 48–51

VOISEY, P.W. and MACDONALD, D.C. (1978). Laboratory measurements of eggshell strength. 1. An instrument for measuring shell strength by quasi-static compression puncture and non-destructive deformation. *Poultry Science,* **57**, 860–869

VOISEY, P.W. and ROBERTSON, G.D. (1969). The rapid measurement of eggshell strength. *Canadian Agricultural Engineering,* **11**, 6–9

VOISEY, P.W., HAMILTON, R.M.G. and THOMPSON, B.K. (1979). Laboratory measurement of eggshell strength. 2. The quasi-static compression, puncture, non-destructive deformation and specific gravity methods applied to the same egg. *Poultry Science,* **58**, 288–294

VOISEY, P.W., HUNT, J.R. and JAMES, P.E. (1969). A comparison of the beta-backscatter and quasi-static compression methods of measuring eggshell strength. *Canadian Journal of Animal Science,* **49**, 157–168

VONDELL, J.H. (1932). Is the production of "off-flavor" eggs an individual characteristic? *Poultry Science,* **11**, 375

VUILLEUMIER, J.P. (1969). The 'Roche Yolk Colour Fan'. An instrument for measuring yolk colour. *Poultry Science,* **48**, 767–779

WELLS, R.G. (1968). The measurement of certain egg quality characteristics: a review. In *Egg Quality: A Study of the Hen's Egg,* (Carter, T.C., ed.), pp. 207–250. Edinburgh, Oliver and Boyd

Part III

Biological basis of egg quality

Chapter 7

Egg quality in individual birds

C.G. Belyavin, K.N. Boorman and J. Volynchook

'Statistically significant differences are not necessarily a good basis on which to build biological hypotheses when individual clutches and individual birds show a large proportion of results which do not agree with the mean result.'

Tyler and Geake (1961a)

Introduction

The concept of egg quality today embraces both internal and external characteristics of the egg. A strong shell of good colour and texture is important as well as a yolk of good colour and albumen that is firm and does not spread far when the egg is broken. One consumer survey (Anon, 1982) revealed that freshness, an uncracked shell, taste, absence of inclusions and deep yolk colour were the top five characteristics perceived as being indicative of quality.

At present, about 7% of eggs are downgraded in commercial packing stations and over 90% of these have shell faults (Goldenlay Eggs, personal communication). What is not clear is the number of eggs lost or downgraded on the farm.

In most cases, the amount of downgrading at the farm or egg packing station is the only indication that producers have of egg quality. Some large production companies and scientists use laboratory measurements to assess egg quality and the scientist tries to take into account the factors important to both producer and consumer. High egg specific gravity, low egg shell deformation value, greater egg shell thickness and egg shell weight are indicative of good egg shell strength but not necessarily the likelihood of a shell cracking. Methods exist for measuring egg shell colour, but assessments of texture are subjective. It is possible that shell structure and chemical composition may also be useful indicators of a shell's ability to withstand insults. Haugh units are a good indication of albumen quality and Roche fan comparisons a good and accepted assessment of yolk colour.

It is clear when considering the data from Goldenlay that shell faults and therefore shell quality appears to be the characteristic of greatest economic significance. Losses to the UK industry amount to at least £8 million a year.

Egg shell quality trends in commercial laying flocks

There is little detailed information, beyond production records for commercial laying flocks, which gives any insight into egg quality traits and trends for the laying

Table 7.1 Trends over the production period for downgrading and indicators of egg shell quality for two flocks of laying hens[a]

		Period[b]														
		1	2	3	4	5	6	7	8	9	10	11	12	13	14	15
Downgrading (%)	Shavers	3.18	2.62	3.47	4.15	5.25	6.95	7.50	9.88	10.69	13.42	14.83	18.11	18.55	19.78	20.84
	ISA	9.50	4.80	5.63	5.67	5.84	6.26	6.41	8.25	8.66	10.37	13.32	13.74	16.09	19.47	20.53
Specific gravity	Shavers	1.091	1.089	1.087	1.084	1.082	1.080	1.079	1.076	1.075	1.074	1.075	1.075	1.074	1.074	1.074
	ISA	1.085	1.086	1.083	1.083	1.083	1.083	1.083	1.083	1.084	1.082	1.082	1.081	1.080	1.080	1.079
Shell deformation (μm)	Shavers	24.1	27.0	27.2	27.5	27.8	27.7	28.7	29.3	28.9	28.6	29.4	30.3	30.5	30.2	30.0
	ISA	27.3	27.1	26.9	27.4	27.5	27.1	26.8	26.0	26.6	27.3	26.9	27.5	28.3	28.4	28.8
Holes (%)	Shavers	57.56	59.19	53.85	58.97	57.95	51.14	56.75	53.47	54.48	40.63	45.90	47.70	42.77	45.10	46.12
	ISA	30.67	34.85	41.29	49.12	49.21	51.24	56.30	65.18	61.30	57.04	52.91	56.72	52.19	46.73	51.73
Star cracks (%)	Shavers	32.27	23.11	32.57	32.75	33.29	38.89	30.11	26.46	21.15	29.46	26.55	29.39	35.98	33.64	32.85
	ISA	4.89	8.55	20.70	20.03	22.16	23.48	21.26	17.40	16.72	15.51	21.16	21.77	18.35	22.41	16.06
Straight cracks (%)	Shavers	10.17	17.70	13.59	8.28	8.77	9.97	13.15	20.07	24.38	29.92	27.56	22.91	21.26	21.26	21.04
	ISA	64.44	56.60	38.01	30.85	28.63	25.28	22.45	17.43	21.98	27.46	25.94	21.51	29.47	30.87	32.22
Severity 1 cracks (%)	Shavers	70.05	78.89	83.31	85.04	86.32	84.10	79.15	75.19	69.14	71.83	57.32	53.49	55.77	49.57	43.32
	ISA	27.33	64.68	72.53	66.35	73.75	65.68	65.91	68.89	64.97	54.56	57.24	51.83	42.91	48.32	43.13
Severity 2 cracks (%)	Shavers	19.63	16.53	13.50	11.34	9.67	11.77	12.17	14.75	16.51	12.61	22.56	20.50	21.09	20.77	27.92
	ISA	54.81	30.44	20.78	24.79	18.79	23.87	22.15	19.39	24.54	25.03	22.68	23.74	24.91	19.97	22.86
Severity 3 cracks (%)	Shavers	10.32	4.59	3.19	3.63	4.01	4.13	8.68	10.07	14.36	15.56	20.13	26.02	23.15	29.66	28.77
	ISA	17.86	4.88	6.70	8.86	7.46	10.46	11.96	11.72	10.49	20.41	20.08	24.43	32.18	31.72	34.02

[a]One flock comprised 10156 white egg laying, light hybrids (Shaver 288) and the other flock comprised 984 brown egg laying, heavy hybrids (ISA Brown). For the Shaver birds, a 25% sample of one day's production was sampled on one day each week and for the ISA birds, one day's complete production was sampled each week. A random subsample (every 10th egg; 10% subsample) of the sampled eggs was marked for subsequent laboratory measurements (egg specific gravity and shell deformation value). Cracked eggs were removed and classified according to type (Elson, 1978) and severity.
[b]Period numbers relate to four-week periods starting from 20 weeks of age.

period. It is assumed that as birds age their ability to produce egg shell decreases and so egg shells produced at the end of lay are thinner and hence weaker than those produced early in lay.

More detailed information has been collected for trends for laying flocks over the laying period (*see* Belyavin, 1979; Belyavin and Boorman, 1982). They monitored in detail two flocks.

Pooled data from this study are shown in *Table 7.1*. Downgrading was due to cracks in most cases confirming the significance of the egg shell as the most important quality characteristic. Belyavin and Boorman (1982) used regression analyses to test changes in measured variables with time for significance and linear correlation coefficients to test the relationship between certain measurements.

Increased downgrading with age was associated with decreased egg specific gravity and increased egg shell deformation values. A classification of cracks according to type showed that in both flocks, holes were the predominant shell fault throughout lay except that straight cracks initially predominated in one flock. The impact cracks i.e. star and straight, increased in the Shaver flock over the laying period and in the ISA flock there was an initial decline, then an increase, before a final decline by the end of lay.

The classification of cracked eggs according to severity showed that the severity of cracking increased after an initial decline as both flocks aged. For all measured variables, with the exception of star cracks for the Shaver flock, the trends for the laying period were significant ($P<0.01$).

Data recorded from three further commercial flocks support the findings above, namely that as a flock ages rate of lay decreases and the incidence of downgrading increases (*see* Belyavin, 1979).

Egg shell quality in individual birds

The data of Belyavin (1979) and Belyavin and Boorman (1982) gave considerable insight into the complexity and development of the problem within a commercial flock. However, what is not clear is whether the decline in egg shell quality over a period of time represented a gradual decline in all birds or whether individuals were abruptly 'breaking down' at different ages distorting the overall flock picture. The curve for a flock, after all, is an integration of the trends for individuals. Belyavin (1979) isolated 48 individuals *in situ* in a flock of about 1000 ISA Brown hens and studied their characteristics over a laying year. Eggs were sampled, as far as possible, on a regular weekly basis. Belyavin attempted to identify trends for individuals for egg shell quality by fitting curves to the data. The results showed that there was considerable variation between individuals when considering their mean performance for the laying period and also when considering their detailed trends, as defined by curves, for any production characteristic. Eggs were only sampled from the individuals at the most on one day each week and had they been sampled more regularly some of the variation may have been removed.

In more general terms the trends for some characteristics were similar for all birds, for example, egg output which increased rapidly and then declined, and egg weight which showed a progressive increase with time.

The mean trend for egg specific gravity for the individuals was downward (Boorman, Volynchook and Belyavin, 1985) but a detailed study involving curves and a reference line showed that the pattern of decline was different for individual birds and that the ability to shell eggs deteriorated suddenly in some birds. Others deteriorated less quickly and the age at which the deterioration started varied (Belyavin, 1979).

Boorman, Volynchook and Belyavin (1985) concluded that although some individuals showed a fair degree of similarity with the mean trend for the flock, others showed sudden large differences or consistent smaller differences. It is evident that the flock curve is not a simple integration of similar curves for individuals or of sudden thresholds in shell quality at different times in individuals. Boorman, Volynchook and Belyavin (1985) also showed that shell quality in an individual may be largely unrelated to the mean of the flock and that an individual's shell quality at one time may or may not be generally characteristic of that bird's relation to the mean. A sudden decline in the middle period is not necessarily irredeemable. These authors also showed that a decline in shell quality with time, using specific gravity as the measure of quality, is inevitable even when considering birds that are superior in terms of production characteristics and shell quality when compared with the rest of their population.

Variation of egg characteristics with position in the sequence (clutch)

A part of the variation in egg characteristics is associated with the position of the egg in the sequence or clutch. There have been several studies of such variation. Most of these were performed 20 or more years ago, although recently there has been some renewed interest in the subject.

Early studies

Romanoff and Romanoff (1949) reviewed many of the early studies (Atwood, 1929; Bennion and Warren, 1933; Wilhelm, 1940; Berg, 1945) and an important study was made by Tyler and Geake (1961a).

All these studies show that variation in mass and shell characteristics among eggs of the same sequence is to be expected. When means of eggs at the same position in the sequence were considered for sequences of particular lengths, a pattern emerged in these means for each sequence length. Details of some of the main studies are shown in *Table 7.2*, which serves to illustrate that the hens used included those typical of contemporary stock and the feeding and lighting, as far as can be judged, were consistent with contemporary practices. Results of those studies involving egg mass and those involving shell thickness are shown in *Figures 7.1a* and *7.1b* respectively. There is some agreement among studies. For short sequences (two and three eggs) there was a decline in mass as the sequence progressed. This tendency also seems to underline the trends among early eggs of longer sequences, but becomes much less clear in later eggs of such sequences and there are some marked exceptions (four and five-egg sequences, Tyler and Geake, 1961a). Nevertheless, the mean of last eggs of the sequence was often found to be the smallest. Similarly for shell strength, as assessed by thickness or mass/unit area, there are some common trends in the means. Thus, while on average the shell of the second egg of a two-egg sequence was thicker than that of the first, that of the second egg of a longer sequence was thinner than that of the first. This decline from the shell thickness of the first egg affected subsequent eggs of sequences of more

Table 7.2 Details of some studies of effect of position in the sequence on egg characteristics

Study	Stock[a]	Number	Age at start	Duration	Management	Lighting	Feeding	Measures[b]
Bennion and Warren (1933)	WL	125	Start of lay	Laying year	Not stated	Not stated	Not stated	M_E
Wilhelm (1940)	WL	40	28 weeks	13 months	Pens with outside access	At least 13 h/d	Mash/grain grit	M_E, M_s T_s, P_s
Berg (1945)	WL	3 × 36	During pullet year	30 d	Batteries	Not stated	Standard layer diets	T_s, S_s
	WL	36	During second year	30 d				
	NH	72						
Tyler and Geake (1961a)	WL	4	Start of lay	Three laying years	Experimental cages	Not stated, assumed artificial, conventional	Standard layer diet	M_E T_s/A_s
	BL	4						
	RIR	4						
	LS	4						

[a]WL, RIR, NH, BL, LS: White Leghorn, Rhode Island Red, New Hampshire, Black Leghorn, Light Sussex, respectively.
[b]M_E: Egg mass; M_s: shell mass; T_s: shell thickness; P_s: shell as a proportion of egg; S_s: shell smoothness; T_s/A_s: shell mass/shell area.

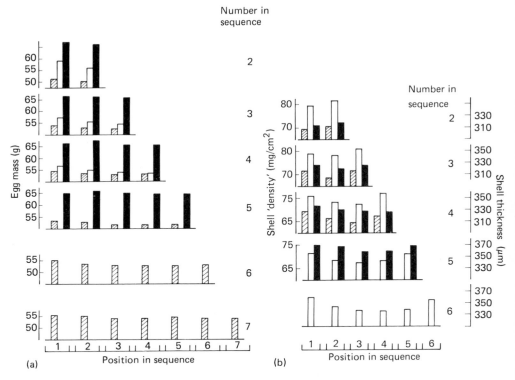

Figure 7.1 Trends found in some studies in means of egg characteristics in relation to position in the sequence for sequences of different lengths. (a) Egg mass: ▨ Bennion and Warren (1933); ☐ Wilhelm (1940); ■ Tyler and Geake (1961a)—means of all seasons and stocks. (b) Shell thickness: ▨ Wilhelm (1940)—thickness in μm; ☐ Berg (1945)—thickness in μm—means of all stocks; ■ Tyler and Geake (1961a)—thickness in mg/cm², means of all seasons and stocks.

than two eggs until the ultimate and penultimate eggs, which showed a recovery of shell thickness culminating in a shell of the last egg similar in thickness to that of the first. These trends were consistent among studies except for the four-egg sequences of Tyler and Geake (1961a). It should be noted that for longer sequences replications tended to be fewer than for shorter sequences, while Tyler and Geake used few individuals (*Table 7.2*) but studied them intensively.

These trends have been commented on by their original reporters and there has been speculation about their cause. However, Tyler and Geake (1961a) drew special attention to the number of sequences and individual birds at variance with those trends. As examples, they noted that despite the consistency among means demonstrating the smaller size of the second egg of a two-egg sequence, in their study this was not true of 33.3% of such sequences studied. This also applied to shell thickness, the second egg having a thinner shell in 37.1% of all such sequences. Similar proportions of sequences contradicted the generality of a thicker shell of the last egg compared with the penultimate egg in three and five-egg sequences.

Recent studies

Choi *et al.* (1981) studied trends in eggs laid by a flock of 860, 50-week-old Babcock B-300 laying hens conventionally fed and, it may be assumed, lit. Their method was to weigh the eggs and shells from those hens which laid on three consecutive days. Thus the first day's collection included an unknown proportion of eggs which were the first of their sequences, while the third day's collection would include such a proportion of last eggs. Oviposition time each day represents the progress of the sequence, eggs laid later on any one day will tend to be later eggs of the sequence. On the first day, egg mass showed a significant decline with oviposition time. This decline was less marked on the second day and was undetectable by the third. These effects are explicable if it is assumed that first eggs are, on average, heavier (*Figure 7.1a*). Thus mass would be high early on the first day, when many first eggs would be laid, and decline during the day. The generally heavier eggs early in the sequence would similarly influence the second day's collection, only the effect would be smaller. By the third day most of the eggs collected would be mid-sequence and later eggs and the relationship would be lost. Shell mass of eggs laid on the first day showed a curvilinear relationship with oviposition time, declining during the morning to increase later in the day. Again, this reflects the expected pattern (*Figure 7.1b*) of a thicker shell of the first egg, followed by a decline and subsequent increase as the sequence progresses, if it is assumed that many eggs were being laid in sequences of more than two. On the subsequent two days increases in shell mass with oviposition time were found but the relationship was generally linear, starting from a lower initial mass, as would be expected if first eggs were missing.

The study of Choi *et al.* (1981) represents the only recent confirmation that the trends identified in sequences in earlier studies continue to exist in modern hybrids. In general though the likely effects on such trends of continued breeding for higher production and, increasingly, of concern over shell quality in breeding programmes are unpredictable. It may be deduced from the study of Choi *et al.* that sequences of three eggs or more were predominating in their birds, because a predominance of two-egg sequences would, presumably, have led to a simple linear increase in shell mass on the first day. It might also be deduced that any progress made towards better shell quality in the stock used had not been made by eliminating the decline in shell mass after the first egg of the sequence. A much earlier study had indicated such a possibility; Taylor and Lerner (1939) showed a decrease in the decline of shell thickness (percentage shell) from first to second egg of the sequence in White Leghorn birds selected for thicker shells.

As part of studies of individual birds isolated among flocks kept in commercial conditions, Belyavin (1979) monitored sequences in 12 ISA Brown (Warren SSL) hens for periods of the laying year. Although no trends were established with statistical significance, there were good indications that the first eggs of sequences were more poorly shelled than subsequent eggs. This was a surprising indicator and a more intensive study was undertaken with 24 individually caged Shaver 585 hens from 57 to 81 weeks of age conventionally fed and lit in an experimental facility (Volynchook, Boorman and Belyavin, 1982). The original analysis of these data was aimed at establishing the uniqueness, or otherwise, of first and last eggs and attempting to describe trends within sequences as simple linear functions. Sequences were not, at that stage, segregated on the basis of length, except that the main analysis excluded sequences of less than three eggs. The results of this analysis

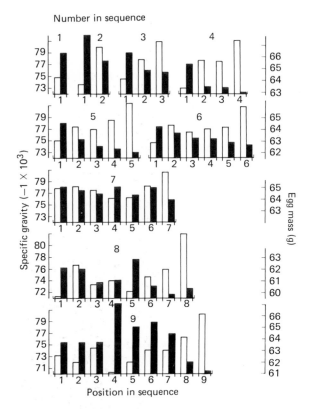

Figure 7.2 Trends in means of egg characteristics in relation to position in the sequence for sequences of different lengths. From data of Volynchook, Boorman and Belyavin (1982) for 24 57–81-week-old Shaver 585 hens. □ Egg specific gravity; ■ egg mass.

were also considered by Boorman, Volynchook and Belyavin (1985). Egg mass was negatively related to position in the sequence, while specific gravity, measured by the hydrometer method (Wells, 1967), was positively related. Separate analyses of means of first and last eggs and the means of their respective sequences, showed first eggs to be larger and of lower specific gravity while last eggs were smaller and of higher specific gravity. These analyses do not entirely resolve the nature of differences between consecutive eggs of the sequence, so the data have also been segregated on the basis of sequence length (*Figure 7.2*). As with other studies, variations among individuals and sequences were numerous and replications for longer clutches few. The trends in the means of shorter sequences for mass were in general agreement with earlier studies (*Figure 7.1a*), although those for longer sequences show tendencies towards mid-sequence increases in mass.

The trends in specific gravity showed a marked difference from those for measures of shell thickness in other studies. In this case for sequences of most lengths, the first eggs were of lower specific gravity than the second eggs, and often considerably so. The relationship between the specific gravity of the second eggs and subsequent eggs of the sequence was similar to the relationship between the first eggs and subsequent eggs described for previous studies (*Figure 7.1b*). As this would suggest, there was in all cases a marked increase in specific gravity in later eggs of the sequences, culminating in the highest specific gravity associated with the means of the final eggs. For longer sequences (10 to 16 eggs, not shown), for which there were very few replicates, trends were generally similar and the tendency emerging in the means of eight- and nine-egg sequences for there to be some means in mid-sequence as low as those of first eggs seemed to be a general phenomenon.

The contrast between these findings for specific gravity of first eggs of sequences of more than two eggs and those reviewed above for shell thickness is puzzling. It may be that the special nature of first eggs renders the usually good relationship between shell thickness and specific gravity (Tyler and Geake, 1961b; Wells, 1967) less reliable or different. The only other measure of shell thickness used in these studies was mass/unit area (Volynchook, Boorman and Belyavin, 1982) and this was calculated from a regression involving specific gravity and mass derived from a random sample (100) of eggs from the same birds. This measure showed the same trends but was not entirely independent of specific gravity. It seems unlikely that use of specific gravity would produce such a misleading pattern of change, although because of the changes in shell thickness and egg mass, use of specific gravity might accentuate some of the differences.

If these different patterns are accepted, they could be interpreted as the intercalation of a poorly shelled first egg at the start of a typical sequence pattern. Whether this pattern is a particular feature, for some reason, of this small flock which was in late lay, or whether such patterns are a feature of contemporary brown egg stocks, as the indications from the earlier study of Belyavin (1979) who used ISA Brown might imply, cannot be resolved. The generality of the effect is, however, of some interest because the increasing irregularity of lay with age will increase the proportion of shorter sequences and therefore of first eggs, and if these are more poorly shelled on average, they will be more likely to crack. Opposing this trend, any shift from longer to shorter sequences would eliminate the occurrence of the weaker shells that tended to occur in the middle of longer sequences. The extent and generality of these trends would therefore influence one of the factors contributing to the decline in shell quality with age.

Mechanism of changes within sequences

Whatever the nature of the patterns in the means and despite their large variances, the existence of such patterns has fostered speculation about possible reasons and mechanisms. It is not relevant to discuss this in great depth here, but some reference to it is necessary in the context of egg quality because it is a matter of importance whether such patterns are inherent or are imposed by conditions under which hens are kept.

Chief among considerations of biological mechanisms has been the relationship between the shell and the interval between ovipositions. Since so much of this interval is spent in the shell gland, it is reasoned that shell deposition, and therefore thickness, should reflect the length of the interval. Berg (1945) showed significant correlations between mean interval length and the mean change in thickness of each shell from the thickness of the shell of the first egg within each sequence length. Choi et al. (1981) showed a correlation between the difference in time of oviposition between two consecutive days and average shell mass among hens. Tyler and Geake (1961a) pointed out that despite the possible validity of the hypothesis, Berg's data based on means could not be used in its support because there were likely to be a great many exceptions from the means. In this context, it is relevant to question whether the variance in intervals is of the same order as that for shell thickness and whether individuals vary to the same extent and in the same direction from the mean for both variates. This cannot be defined, but concordance is not implied by the correlation coefficients quoted.

Of special note in consideration of time of formation is the nature of the shell of the last egg of the sequence and its time of formation. The generally thicker shell has been associated with the longer formation time of this egg and the fact that this is associated with, on average, a smaller size has been taken as evidence that the longer formation time is accounted for by residence in the shell gland rather than elsewhere in the tract (Berg, 1945). Roland (1981) examined positions of eggs in the oviduct by killing hens, concluding that 'although there is individual birds variation .... much of the difference in IBO (interval between ovipositions) of morning and evening eggs is not due to the time the egg spends in the oviduct, but is instead due to a delay in ovulation'. An experiment such as this does not allow the identification of last eggs, so this finding applies to last eggs of sequence only in so far as there will be a relatively high proportion of these among eggs laid in the evening.

Overall, the generally opposed relationships between shell thickness and egg mass during progression of the sequence lead to difficulties in interpretations based on oviposition interval. Ahemeral light–dark cycles of more than 24 h lead to increases in shell and egg mass and there are increases in time of residence throughout the tract. Although association of these phenomena is not necessarily simple (Melek, Morris and Jennings, 1973), mechanisms are easier to envisage. If in sequence effects most of the increase in formation time for later eggs is due to delay in ovulation it is difficult to understand how, on average, their shells tend to be thicker. In any event, discussion about relationships between shell thickness and oviposition interval is of limited value because even if this interval is a determinant of shell thickness, the reason for change of this interval during progression of the sequence remains to be explained.

Explanation, at least of the thicker shells on average of eggs laid later in the sequence, might be more fruitfully sought in consideration of lighting and feeding. In traditional lighting patterns the average specific gravity of eggs laid in the afternoon is greater than that of eggs laid in the morning (Roland, Sloan and Harms, 1973). Since eggs laid in the afternoon will include a greater proportion of last eggs of the sequence, this might be expected. However, Roland, Sloan and Harms pointed out that a greater proportion of the shelling of eggs laid in the afternoon occurs in the light, when the bird feeds. During the dark, much of the calcium for shell formation must be provided from the skeleton and it may be that this process is less effective in some way in such provision than is supply from the diet. Thus eggs laid later in the sequence may have thicker shells because they tend to be laid later in the day. Therefore it is uncertain whether such shells reflect inherent patterns or lighting (feeding) pattern of the birds or both.

Roland (1981) measured shell characteristics and oviposition times of penultimate and ultimate eggs of sequences laid in the morning or in the afternoon. The birds were conventionally lit and, it may be assumed, fed. There were many fewer observations for the morning than for the afternoon, but there was a clear, significant difference between the means of the consecutive eggs in the afternoon, specific gravity and shell mass being greater for last eggs, whereas there was none in the morning. This difference between morning and afternoon eggs was reflected in oviposition interval. The evidence from this study is therefore that the proportion of shell formation in the light is the important factor. This does not address the question of the patterns in other parts of the sequence and the important question of the nature of first eggs. The pattern seen in the means, however, whether of the 'traditional' type (*Figure 7.1b*) or the 'conflicting' type (*Figure 7.2*) is not amenable to explanation by the steady increase in the proportion of shell formation in the light.

The probability that mean trends in sequences are at least in part a reflection of lighting pattern is of some consequence because novel lighting patterns are being investigated and used. However, even if explanations for patterns are found based on consistent biological phenomena or management practices, it still remains to be explained how such large numbers of sequences and individuals on occasions can vary from the mean trends.

Blood ions and shell deposition in individuals

The difficulty in investigating relationships between blood ions and shell quality is the variability in the latter and the fluctuations in the former with time of day and shell formation. Luck and Scanes (1979) pointed out the importance of the ionised ('free') component of plasma calcium in shell formation and the reproductive process in the hen. They demonstrated a sinusoidal pattern in ionised calcium during the period between ovipositions. The maximum was just before shell formation was assumed to begin and the minimum was late in the shell formation process, the concentration increasing again at oviposition. To demonstrate this they used several hens taking samples from each and combining data for samples on the basis of time in relation to oviposition.

Investigation of the relationship between plasma ionised calcium and shell quality would need to take account of this fluctuation, so that birds producing shells of different qualities could be compared at the same point in the plasma calcium cycle. This either involves serial sampling from individuals, a difficult procedure and one likely to affect the process being investigated, or attempting to sample at a point fixed in relation to a known or predictable event in the cycle. In the case of ionised calcium there is another difficulty—that of the method itself and its large variability. Volynchook and Boorman (unpublished) have measured plasma ionised calcium and shell quality in individual hens at maxima and minima of the former expected in relation to estimated oviposition time. The aim of this investigation was to attempt to explain some of the variation in shell quality among individuals in terms of plasma calcium, but no relationship was evident. In view of the uncertainties and difficulties mentioned above, this is not surprising.

Plasma inorganic phosphorus also fluctuates during the day. Miller, Harms and Wilson (1977a, 1977b) and Mongin and Sauveur (1979) have described these fluctuations. As an example, the findings of the latter authors will be used. For conventionally fed and lit birds, for most of the day plasma phosphorus concentration is low. As shell formation starts there is an increase which is rapidly enhanced by the ensuing dark period. The enhancement is thought to be due to skeletal mobilisation necessary to maintain shell formation in the dark period and although the initial increase occurs if a calcium grit is provided, this persistent form of calcium in the intestine apparently obviates the need for skeletal mobilisation and therefore prevents the enhancement during the dark period.

High plasma phosphorus is thought to be associated with thinner shells and Miles and Harms (1982) have shown a clear linear negative correlation between means of egg specific gravity and plasma phosphorus concentration among groups of hens receiving dietary treatments which affect plasma phosphorus. This may be viewed as a direct effect of blood phosphorus on calcification in the shell gland or as an interference with supply of calcium from skeletal mobilisation.

Volynchook (unpublished) measured plasma inorganic phosphorus in ten 60-week-old Hubbard Golden Comet hens conventionally fed and lit. In this study blood was sampled from each hen each day for complete sequences. The time chosen for sampling was about 30 min before the end of the dark period, because it was thought that this time would reflect the time of maximum skeletal contribution and minimum dietary contribution. When all values were considered there was a significant negative regression relationship between shell weight and plasma phosphorus, but when the analysis was limited to first eggs of sequences a clearer relationship emerged (*Figure 7.3*). This is to be expected in that first eggs are those

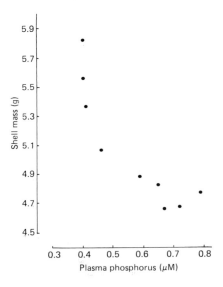

Figure 7.3 Relationship between shell mass of first egg of the sequence and plasma phosphorus concentration at the end of the dark period in Hubbard Golden Comet hens in late lay receiving a diet containing about 4.5 g available P and 38 g Ca/kg.

laid nearest to the time chosen for sampling. It should be stressed that these data are few and one aberrant phosphorus concentration has been omitted, but they do indicate that in some individuals a propensity towards high plasma phosphorus during shell formation in the dark explains some of the variation in shell mass of the first egg of the sequence. These data also indicate that some of the difficulties of individual variation and the complexity of the egg forming process can be overcome in attempts to identify sources of variation in egg quality.

Relationships between egg shell quality in individual birds and other production characteristics

Boorman, Volynchook and Belyavin (1985) showed that there are no simple rules for predicting which individuals are likely to produce poor shells. They presented

Table 7.3 Some production characteristics of ten ISA Brown laying hens having above or below average shell quality (means for 20–80 weeks of age)

| | Above average birds | | | | | | Below average birds | | | | | |
	1	2	3	4	5	Mean	6	7	8	9	10	Mean
Mean food intake (g/bird d)	111	110	123	125	137	121	122	119	141	115	124	124
Eggs produced	341	306	342	314	335	328	294	269	366	314	329	314
Mean egg mass (g)	52.7	52.4	59.3	64.1	69.3	59.6	57.9	63.5	65.6	62.6	65.8	63.1
Total egg mass produced (kg)	18.0	16.0	20.3	20.1	23.2	19.5	17.0	17.1	24.0	19.7	21.6	19.9
Mean egg specific gravity (-1×10^3)	91	89	88	87	86	88	57	73	73	77	77	71
Mean dry shell mass per egg (g)	5.00	5.02	5.51	5.86	6.21	5.52	2.20	4.49	4.41	4.98	5.06	4.23
Total shell produced (kg)	1.71	1.54	1.88	1.84	2.08	1.81	0.647	1.21	1.61	1.56	1.66	1.34
Shell (mg) as proportion of egg mass (g)	97	98	95	94	92	95	40	73	69	82	79	69

Examples of individuals distributed randomly in a commercially-housed flock under conventional feeding (38 g Ca/kg) and lighting (17 h light/24 h) conditions.

data (*Table 7.3*) showing mean characteristics of production and of the eggs of the five best birds and of five which were among the worst. They were unable to conclude that it was the highest egg producers which produce the worst shells and although there are more birds producing heavier eggs among the group producing poor shells, there is no simple relationship between these characteristics.

The data of Belyavin (1979) collected from the 48 individual birds enables relationships between egg specific gravity and other characteristics of the eggs and production to be evaluated. A limitation of the data which must be borne in mind is that by sampling one egg/week the position of the egg in the sequence was ignored and consequently the effects of this (*see* above).

There was a significant correlation ($P<0.01$, $r = 0.378$) between food consumed to 60 weeks of age and shell weight at 60 weeks of age when considering the data for the 48 individuals. Overall means for the entire laying period (20–80 weeks of age) were considered and correlations between egg specific gravity and other characteristics of production and of the eggs (*see Table 7.4*).

Table 7.4 Correlation coefficients between mean egg specific gravity (20–80 weeks of age) and means of other characteristics of production and eggs for 48 individual ISA Brown hens

Characteristics	*Correlation coefficient*	*Significance*[a]
Feed intake	−0.0983	NS
Egg numbers	0.1377	NS
Egg weight	−0.1649	NS
Weight of egg contents	−0.2785	NS
Dry shell weight	0.7448	**
Shell thickness	0.9217	**
Shell deformation value	−0.8413	**

[a]NS denotes not significant; ** denotes $P<0.01$.

For these data there appeared to be no significant relationship between overall egg shell quality, as measured by egg specific gravity, and food consumption, egg numbers or egg weight. However, significant correlations ($P<0.01$) existed between specific gravity and dry shell weight ($r = 0.7448$), shell thickness ($r = 0.9217$) and shell deformation value ($r = 0.8413$). This shows the value of egg specific gravity as a measure of egg shell strength but suggests that there is no relationship between shell strength and other characteristics of production, further supporting views that it is not the high producing birds or those with low food intake which produce weak egg shells.

Because data were collected weekly over the complete production period it is also possible to test for relationships between egg specific gravity at different stages of the period (24, 40, 60 and 80 weeks of age) for the individual birds. For all pairs tested there was a significant ($P<0.05$) correlation. For these data at least it would therefore appear that egg specific gravity measurements made early on are good indicators of subsequent values later in the production period. However, in the majority of cases the correlation coefficient (r) was below 0.5, indicating that it is of little practical value. For two comparisons (40 week with 60 week and 40 week with 80 week) the value was higher ($r = 0.7307$ and 0.5521 respectively) indicating greater reliability, but still questioning the use of early specific gravity values as indicators of possible values at the end of lay.

Implications for improving shell quality

The situation observed as a flock phenomenon is actually a complex interaction of many individuals. Within each individual there is also a complex picture of events. Each egg is a complex structure and is a unique occurrence making a study of egg quality in individuals somewhat difficult. The possibilities for variability in the constituent processes of its formation, their interaction and the interaction of these with environmental factors are likely to be large. Mean trends for eggs within sequences presumably reflect some basic causal agents around which this variability is centred. There are major differences between individuals even when they are derived from the same genetic population.

The existence of vast differences between individuals as shown for egg shell quality is also apparent in all other production characteristics (*see* Belyavin, 1979). This has interesting implications with regard to the management of commercial laying flocks where in modern conditions large numbers of individuals are accommodated together and by necessity have to be managed as one.

In reality, it may be that birds should be managed as individuals but this is obviously unpractical. It has been shown that individual requirements for calcium may vary considerably, particularly as birds age. Volynchook (unpublished) demonstrated varied responses to the feeding of free-choice calcium even to the extent of some birds ceasing to lay rather than 'to eat for calcium'. This illustrates the extent to which individual differences may exist in a population.

There is evidence that the incorporation into the management of the flock of a modified light pattern leads to improvements in egg shell quality (*see* Melek, Morris and Jennings, 1973; Yannakopoulos and Morris, 1979; Sauveur and Mongin, 1983). It may be that these modified light patterns in some way accommodate the inherent variation present in the population and enable birds to find a pattern of production closer to their natural physiological cycle. Certainly the repeat-type pattern of Sauveur and Mongin (1983) does enable the birds to eat during the period of shell formation.

Egg quality has become a more important part of egg layer breeding programmes. Poggenpoel (1982) cited van Tijen and Kuit who estimated an average heritability of 0.39 for shell quality. Most of the estimates included were based on egg specific gravity.

It would seem that selection should ideally be undertaken with individual birds and egg specific gravity is as good a measure as any on which to base the selection. Care is required when sampling the eggs for measurement because of the sequence effects. It is therefore necessary to measure a number of consecutive eggs/bird on each sampling occasion, with knowledge, if possible, of the part of the sequence represented.

Poggenpoel (1982) after six generations of selection of individual birds was able to produce from a base population two lines with significantly different mean egg specific gravities (1.095 and 1.082). The belief that selection for egg quality characteristics in a breeding programme has an adverse effect on other production characteristics was not entirely substantiated by the findings of McPhee, Burton and Fuelling (1982). By selecting for high egg specific gravity in a flock of Australorp hens they reduced the incidence of soft-shelled eggs. There was a reduction in egg weight but no change in egg production despite a reduction in age at first egg. Albumen height was also reduced but the keeping quality of the eggs appeared to be enhanced. Through a reduction in body weight and food intake an

Table 7.5 Hatchability results of eggs from hens selected on the basis of their performance for shell quality

	First setting			Second setting		
	No. eggs	% Fertile	% Hatch[a]	No. eggs	% Fertile	% Hatch[a]
'Good' hens	510	89.2	79.8	658	91.8	84.5
'Bad' hens	457	86.7	67.4	485	89.7	71.3
Commercial	510	92.4	75.9	569	91.0	82.1

[a]All eggs

improvement in the efficiency of egg production resulted. The data of Belyavin (1979) imply also the lack of relationship between egg quality characteristics and other production criteria.

Belyavin (unpublished) monitored parent female stock and ranked the birds according to their performance for production and egg quality. He then divided the population into above average and below average birds and produced hatching eggs from the two groups along with a control group which had undergone no selection. Results for hatchability (*Table 7.5*) show the effects of the selection procedures. It is likely that the data reflect the effect of shell quality on weight loss during incubation and Poggenpoel (1982) also found that significant differences in weight loss over 14 d in an incubator could be produced by selecting for egg specific gravity. The differences in hatchability between hen types in the study of Belyavin were statistically significant ($P<0.01$).

References

ANON (1982). *Influences on Consumer Purchases of Eggs*. An investigation by students of Harper Adams Agricultural College as part of their HND course in Agricultural Marketing and Business Administration, pp. 30–35

ATWOOD, H. (1929). Observations concerning the time factor in egg production. *Poultry Science, 8*, 137–140

BELYAVIN, C.G. (1979). *Egg-shell Quality in the Older Hen*. PhD Thesis, University of Nottingham

BELYAVIN, C.G. and BOORMAN, K.N. (1982). Crack type and severity as indications of shell quality. *Poultry Science, 61*, 591–594

BENNION, N.L. and WARREN, D.C. (1933). Some factors affecting egg size in the domestic fowl. *Poultry Science, 12*, 362–367

BERG, L.R. (1945). The relationship of clutch position and time interval between eggs to eggshell quality. *Poultry Science, 24*, 555–563

BOORMAN, K.N., VOLYNCHOOK, J.G. and BELYAVIN, C.G. (1985). Eggshell formation and quality. In *Recent Advances in Animal Nutrition—1985*, (Haresign, W. and Cole, D.J.A., eds), pp. 181–195. London, Butterworths

CHOI, J.H., MILES, R.D., ARAFA, A.S. and HARMS, R.H. (1981). The influence of oviposition time on egg weight, shell quality, and blood phosphorus. *Poultry Science, 60*, 824–828

ELSON, H.A. (1978). Laying cage floor design and shell damage. In *Gleadthorpe Experimental Husbandry Farm Poultry Booklet 1978*, pp. 52–60. MAFF

LUCK, M.R. and SCANES, C.G. (1979). Plasma levels of ionised calcium in the laying hen (*Gallus domesticus*). *Comparative Biochemistry and Physiology, 63A*, 177–181

MCPHEE, C.P., BURTON, H.W. and FUELLING, D.E. (1982). Selection for high specific gravity of eggs in a flock of Australorp hens. *British Poultry Science, 23*, 215–223

MELEK, O., MORRIS, T.R. and JENNINGS, R.C. (1973). The time factor in egg formation for hens exposed to ahemeral light–dark cycles. *British Poultry Science, 14*, 493–498

MILES, R.D. and HARMS, R.H. (1982). Relationship between egg specific gravity and plasma phosphorus from hens fed different dietary calcium, phosphorus, and sodium levels. *Poultry Science, 61*, 175–177

MILLER, E.R., HARMS, R.H. and WILSON, H.R. (1977a). Cyclic changes in serum phosphorus of laying hens. *Poultry Science, 56*, 586–589

MILLER, E.R., HARMS, R.H. and WILSON, H.R. (1977b). Serum calcium and phosphorus levels in hens relative to the time of oviposition. *Poultry Science, 56*, 1501–1503

MONGIN, P. and SAUVEUR, B. (1979). Plasma inorganic phosphorus concentration during egg-shell formation. Effect of the physical form of the dietary calcium. *British Poultry Science, 20*, 401–412

POGGENPOEL, D.G. (1982). Two-way selection for egg specific gravity. *Zootechnica International, 6*, 33–34

ROLAND, D.A. (1981). Relation of interval between eggs and time of oviposition of egg shell quality. *Poultry Science, 60*, 1066–1070

ROLAND, D.A., SLOAN, D.R. and HARMS, R.H. (1973). Calcium metabolism in the laying hen. 6. Shell quality in relation to time of oviposition. *Poultry Science, 52*, 506–510

ROMANOFF, A.L. and ROMANOFF, A.J. (1949). *The Avian Egg.* New York, Wiley

SAUVEUR, B. and MONGIN, P. (1983). Performance of layers reared and/or kept under different 6-hour light–dark cycles. *British Poultry Science, 24*, 405–416

TAYLOR, L.W. and LERNER, I.M. (1939). Inheritance of eggshell thickness in White Leghorn pullets. *Journal of Agricultural Research, 58*, 383–396

TYLER, C. and GEAKE, F.H. (1961a). Studies on egg shells. XIV–Variations in egg weight, shell thickness and membrane thickness between eggs within a clutch. *Journal of the Science of Food and Agriculture, 12*, 273–280

TYLER, C. and GEAKE, F.H. (1961b). Studies on egg shells. XV–Critical appraisal of various methods of assessing shell thickness. *Journal of the Science of Food and Agriculture, 12*, 281–289

VOLYNCHOOK, J.G., BOORMAN, K.N. and BELYAVIN, C.G. (1982). Shell quality in hens in later lay: trends within sequences. *World's Poultry Science Journal, 38*, 138

WELLS, R.G. (1967). Egg shell strength. 1. The relationship between egg breakage in the field and certain laboratory assessments of shell strength. *British Poultry Science, 8*, 131–139

WILHELM, L.A. (1940). Some factors affecting variations in egg shell quality. *Poultry Science, 19*, 246–253

YANNAKOPOULOS, A.L. and MORRIS, T.R. (1979). Effect of light, vitamin D and dietary phosphorus on egg-shell quality late in the pullet laying year. *British Poultry Science, 20*, 337–342

Chapter 8

Egg shell formation and quality

S.G. Tullett

Structure and formation of the normal egg shell

The first serious studies of egg shell structure were carried out by Wilhelm von Nathusius (1821–1899). His work figures predominantly in the classical treatise *The Avian Egg* by Romanoff and Romanoff (1949) and his most important findings have been translated and published in a single volume by Tyler (1964). Since these first studies, researchers have tended not only to subdivide the structural features of the egg shell differently, but also to give different names to the same structure.

Table 8.1 Structural features of the hen's egg shell[a]

	Cuticle or bloom	
	Surface crystal layer	
Spongy layer · Column layer ·	Palisade layer } Exospherites	} True shell
Mammillary knob layer {	Cone layer	
	Basal caps Eisopherites	
	Outer shell membrane	
	Inner shell membrane	
	Limiting membrane	

[a]This lists the various layers of the egg shell from the outer to innermost layers and gives the majority of the terms encountered in the literature. Based mainly on von Nathusius (*see* Tyler, 1964), Schmidt (1957, 1962a, 1962b) and Tyler (1969).

Table 8.1 considers the true calcitic shell with its associated membranes on the inside and cuticle on the outside and shows the terms most commonly encountered in the literature. *Figure 8.1a* is a schematic representation of the structure of the hen's egg shown by a section through the long axis and *Figure 8.1b* shows a radial section through the egg shell. An outline of the chemical composition of the component parts of the hen's egg shell is given in *Table 8.2*; more details are given below where the components are dealt with in turn and a general overview of shell formation presented.

Shell membranes

The crystalline shell is lined internally by two membranes which adhere to one another to form a compound membrane, except at the blunt pole of the egg where they separate to form the air-space. Each membrane consists of a network of fibres lying parallel to the shell surface. In cross section, each membrane fibre is

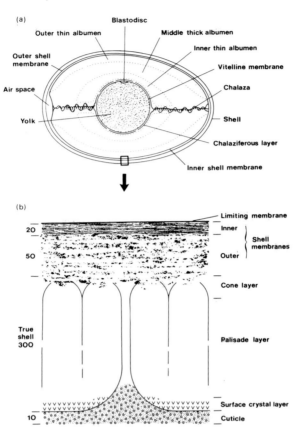

Figure 8.1 (a) Structure of the domestic fowl egg as shown by a section through the long axis. (b) A radial section through the egg shell and underlying membranes. Figures on the left of (b) show the thicknesses of each layer in μm

composed of a proteinaceous core surrounded by a mucopolysaccharide mantle. The mantle is separated from the core by a cleft about 0.1 μm wide and it is in this cleft that the lipid that can be isolated from shell membranes probably occurs (*see* Candlish, 1972).

Fibre cores in the inner shell membrane are up to 23 μm long and the tapering ends of adjoining cores overlap for some 6 μm in a common mantle. Total fibre diameter in the inner shell membrane averages about 0.9 μm with a maximum diameter of 1.5 μm. In the outer membrane the fibre length is up to 15 μm with an average and maximum diameter of 1.3 μm and about 3 μm, respectively (Simons and Wiertz, 1963; Simons, 1971).

The egg shell membranes have about 2% ash, which contains phosphorus, calcium, potassium, magnesium, sodium, zinc, manganese, iron, copper, boron and aluminium (Wedral, Vadehra and Baker, 1974). On an ash-free basis the membranes are about 95% protein, 2% carbohydrate and 3% fat. Although many workers have been of the opinion that the membrane protein was keratin (*Table 8.2*), it is now generally accepted that keratin is not a component (Terepka, 1963;

Table 8.2 Organic components of the shell

			References[a]
Shell membranes			
Protein	Keratin		1–9
	Collagen		10,11
	Elastin		12–16
Carbohydrate	Hexosamines	Glucosamine	7,8,17
		Galactosamine	7,8,17
		Sialic acid	7,8,17,18
	Neutral sugars	Glucose	8,17,18
		Galactose	7,8,17,18
		Mannose	7,8,17,18
		Fucose	8,17
	Aldopentoses	Xylulose	18
Fat	Neutral lipids	Mono-, di- and tri-glyceride	
		Free fatty acids	
		Cholesterol	
		Cholesterol esters	19
	Phospholipids	Lysolecithin	
		Lecithin	
		Cephalin	
		Sphingomyelin	
Mammillary cores		Neutral mucopolysaccharide	17,20
		Sialomucins	
Egg shell matrix			
Protein		Unspecified but non-collagenous	7,21,22
Carbohydrate	Hexosamines	Glucosamine	7,23,24
		Galactosamine	7,23,24
		Sialic acid	21,23,24
	Neutral sugars	Glucose	23
		Galactose	7,23
		Mannose	7,23
		Fucose	7,23
		Xylose	23
	Hexuronic acids	Glucuronic acid	7,24
		Iduronic acid	7
	Muco-polysaccharides	Hyaluronic acid	24
		Chondroitin sulphate A	7
		Chondroitin sulphate B	7
Fat		Unspecified	22
Calcium-binding components		Unspecified except for ovocalcin	25–27

continued on next page

Table 8.2 Continued

Cuticle			
Protein		Unspecified	7,18
	Hexosamines	Glucosamine	17
		Galactosamine	17
		Sialic acid	17,18
Carbohydrate	Neutral sugars	Glucose	17,18
		Galactose	7,17,18
		Mannose	7,17,18
		Fucose	7,17,18
	Pentoses	Xylulose	18
		Unidentified pentose	17
Fat	Neutral lipids	Mono-, di- and tri-glyceride	
		Free fatty acids	
		Cholesterol	
		Cholesterol esters	19
	Phospholipids	Lysolecithin	
		Lecithin	
		Cephalin	
		Sphingomyelin	
Porphyrins			28

[a]Key to references: 1. Lindwall (1881)—cited by Candlish (1972); 2. Calvery (1933); 3. Jones and Mecham (1944); 4. Munks *et al.* (1945); 5. Wolken (1951); 6. Masshoff and Stolpmann (1961); 7. Baker and Balch (1962); 8. Balch and Cooke (1970); 9. Britton and Hale (1977); 10. Candlish and Scougall (1969); 11. Wong *et al.* (1984); 12. Simons (1971); 13. Baumgartner *et al.* (1978); 14. Starcher and King (1980); 15. Leach, Rucker and van Dyke (1981); 16. Crombie *et al.* (1981); 17. Cooke and Balch (1970a); 18. Wedral, Vadehra and Baker (1974); 19. Hasiak, Vadehra and Baker (1970); 20. Robinson and King (1968); 21. Frank, Burger and Swanson (1965); 22. Simkiss and Tyler (1957); 23. Cooke and Balch (1970b); 24. Heaney and Robinson (1976); 25. Abatangelo *et al.* (1978); 26. Krampitz, Meisel and Witt-Krause (1980); 27. Leach (1982); 28. With (1973)

Bellairs and Boyde, 1969; Hoffer, 1971; Candlish, 1972; Wedral, Vadehra and Baker, 1974). The presence of collagen was suggested by the isolation of hydroxylysine in hydrolysates of the protein by Candlish and Scougall (1969). Collagen-like proteins similar to type I (predominantly in the coarser fibres) and type V (predominantly in the finer fibres of the inner shell membrane) collagen have been found in the egg shell membranes of the hen's egg (Wong *et al.*, 1984), although the yield was small. Using a specific orcein stain, Simons (1971) concluded that the protein elastin was present in the fibre mantles but not the cores. Hydroxyproline, desmosine and isodesmosine have been detected in the membrane protein but the amino acid sequence differs from mammalian elastin (Baumgartner *et al.*, 1978; Starcher and King, 1980; Leach, Rucker and van Dyke, 1981; Crombie *et al.*, 1981) and the protein is not readily solubilised by elastase (Starcher and King, 1980; Leach, Rucker and van Dyke, 1981). Thus, although the protein component has cross-links common to the well known fibrous proteins keratin, collagen and elastin, its amino acid composition differs from these proteins which led Leach (1978) to conclude that the major component of the egg shell membranes was a unique protein.

The inner surface of the inner shell membrane appears smooth (Masshoff and Stolpmann, 1961). This is due to the presence of a thin homogeneous layer, 2.7 μm thick (Simons and Wiertz, 1963), that may act to exclude albumen from the spaces between the membrane fibres (von Nathusius, 1868—*see* Tyler, 1964). Bellairs and

Boyde (1969) applied the term 'limiting membrane' to this layer and studies with the electron microscope suggest that it is composed of the same material as the mantles of the membrane fibres, and is in contact with them (Simons and Wiertz, 1963; Bellairs and Boyde, 1969).

Mammillary cores

The mammillary cores are small masses of organic matter attached to the outer surface of the outer shell membrane. They represent the 'seeding sites' on which crystallisation of the shell begins and they subsequently become embedded within the cone layer of the shell.

From histochemical studies, Simkiss and Tyler (1957) suggested that the mammillary cores consisted of a protein–acid mucopolysaccharide complex but a reappraisal of the results (Simkiss and Tyler, 1958—cited by Baker and Balch, 1962) indicated the presence of neutral sugar. Robinson and King (1968) found the mammillary cores to contain neutral mucopolysaccharides surrounded by weakly acidic substances which may be sialomucins. The mucopolysaccharides were firmly bound to the shell membrane fibres and disulphide bonds and hydrogen bonding were thought to be responsible for maintaining the integrity of the cores. Although Robinson and King (1968) were of the opinion that the sialomucins may be part of the organic matrix of the egg shell rather than the mammillary cores, Cooke and Balch (1970a) concluded that the sialic acid-containing material was part of the outer surfaces of the mammillary cores. Robinson and King (1968) suggested that the cores may represent a specialised form of the shell membrane fibres containing intrachain disulphide bonds.

Organic matrix

The true crystalline shell is laid down on a matrix composed of fine fibrils of organic matter. This matrix is distributed unevenly through the shell increasing in concentration from the inside to a maximum concentration two-thirds of the way through the egg shell and then decreasing rapidly to the outside of the shell (Cooke and Balch, 1970b). Simons and Wiertz (1963) and Simons (1971) give details of the matrix; in the bulk of the true shell it has the appearance of a meshwork of fibrils each up to $0.01\,\mu m$ thick and $10\,\mu m$ long running parallel to the surface of the shell. Associated with the fibrils are vesicles (gas filled?) about $0.4\,\mu m$ in diameter.

Simkiss and Tyler (1957) described the matrix as a protein–acid mucopolysaccharide complex. At least 70% of the matrix is protein and about 11% is polysaccharide of which 35% is accounted for by chondroitin sulphate A and B (Baker and Balch, 1962). Approximately 20% of the uronic acid content is present as hyaluronic acid (Heaney and Robinson, 1976). Analysis of the amino acid composition of the matrix has led to the suggestion that it resembles the non-collagenous protein associated with chondroitin sulphate in cartilage (Baker and Balch, 1962). Several components of the matrix are characteristic of calcium-binding systems generally. For example, it has been known for some time that the egg shell matrix is capable of chelating ions due to its mucopolysaccharide content and that mucopolysaccharides occur at most sites of calcification (Simkiss and Tyler, 1958). Abatangelo et al. (1978), studying the calcium-binding protein in the egg shell matrix, found that matrix with free carboxylic groups bound more calcium than matrix in which the carboxylic groups were blocked with carbodiimide. The slight residual binding in matrix with blocked carboxylic groups was attributed to the presence of sulphate groups. In many of the biological proteins that interact with calcium the binding sites are mostly carboxyl side chain groups. Recently, a calcium-binding polypeptide called ovocalcin, containing the carboxylic residue γ-carboxyglutamic acid, has been isolated from the egg shell matrix (Krampitz, Meisel and Witt-Krause, 1980). A similar calcium-binding protein (osteocalcin) containing γ-carboxyglutamic acid residues has been isolated from all the vertebrate bones which have been examined so far, including fossil ones (*see* Krampitz and Witt, 1979).

Cuticle

The cuticular layer on the outer surface of the crystalline shell is composed of spheres of organic material up to 1 μm in diameter. In addition to clothing the shell, the cuticle bridges and plugs the pores thus preventing microbes from gaining entry to the egg contents. Although some pigment is present within the true shell the majority is carried in the cuticular layer.

Baker and Balch (1962) found the composition of the cuticle to be about 90% protein and 10% carbohydrate but they did not assess the cuticle for fat content. Wedral, Vadehra and Baker (1974) give a composition of 85–87% protein, 3.5–4.4% carbohydrate and 2.5–3.5% fat with 3.5% ash.

Observations of the outer surface of the egg with a scanning electron microscope reveal the cuticle is highly fissured—it has the characteristic appearance of dried mud (Becking, 1975). Cuticle is occasionally absent from eggs (Board, 1975). Such eggs are not characteristic of a particular hen, rather they appear to be produced randomly in sequences where the rest of the eggs may be well endowed with cuticle (Tullett and Sparks, unpublished observations).

True shell—its formation and composition

The crystalline shell is composed of calcium carbonate in the form of calcite laid down on the organic matrix, the latter accounting for up to 2% of the weight of the true shell. In order to fully understand how the crystalline shell is assembled by the hen and how egg shell abnormalities arise it is necessary to describe briefly the whole process of egg formation (*Figure 8.2*).

With the exception of the yolk all the components of the egg are produced in or transported across the cells lining the oviduct. Two general cell groups are recognised, the epithelial cells and the tubular gland cells, although within these two groups many cell types have been described. For a detailed review of oviduct fine structure the reader is referred to the exhaustive accounts by Aitken (1971), Hodges (1974), Gilbert (1979) and Solomon (1983) and to the papers by Wyburn *et al.* (1970), Draper *et al.* (1972), Wyburn *et al.* (1973) and Bakst and Howarth (1975). Most of these references also consider egg formation, and the following summary is based on these publications and the references therein.

In a modern high production hen, a mature ovum (the yolky female germ cell) is shed daily from the ovary. The ovum is engulfed by the proximal end of the oviduct, the infundibulum, and spends about 0.5 h travelling through this region, during which time the chalaziferous layer of albumen is added around the yolk. Beginning at the infundibulum the inside surface of the oviduct is ridged, the ridges running in a slight but distinct spiral fashion along the oviduct. This may start the

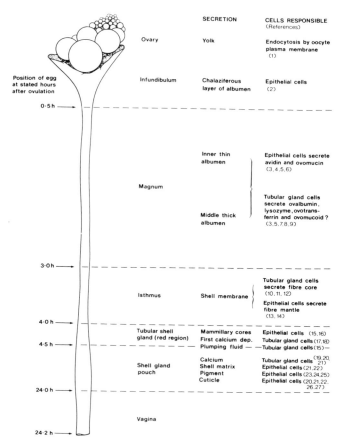

	SECRETION	CELLS RESPONSIBLE (References)
Ovary	Yolk	Endocytosis by oocyte plasma membrane (1)
Infundibulum	Chalaziferous layer of albumen	Epithelial cells (2)
Magnum	Inner thin albumen	Epithelial cells secrete avidin and ovomucin (3,4,5,6)
	Middle thick albumen	Tubular gland cells secrete ovalbumin, lysozyme, ovotrans- ferrin and ovomucoid? (3,5,7,8,9)
Isthmus	Shell membrane	Tubular gland cells secrete fibre core (10,11,12) Epithelial cells secrete fibre mantle (13,14)
Tubular shell gland (red region)	Mammillary cores	Epithelial cells (15,16)
	First calcium dep.	Tubular gland cells (17,18)
	Plumping fluid	Tubular gland cells (15)
Shell gland pouch	Calcium	Tubular gland cells (19,20, 21)
	Shell matrix	Epithelial cells (21,22)
	Pigment	Epithelial cells (23,24,25)
	Cuticle	Epithelial cells (20,21,22, 26,27)
Vagina		

Position of egg at stated hours after ovulation:
0·5 h
3·0 h
4·0 h
4·5 h
24·0 h
24·2 h

Figure 8.2 The process of egg formation. See text for details. Key to references: 1. Perry and Gilbert (1979); 2. Scott and Huang (1941); 3. Kohler, Grimley and O'Malley (1968); 4. O'Malley *et al.* (1969); 5. Wyburn *et al.* (1970); 6. Touhimaa (1975); 7. Oka and Schimke (1969); 8. Palmiter and Gutman (1972); 9. Schimke *et al.* (1977); 10. Khairallah (1966); 11. Hoffer (1971—on quail); 12. Draper *et al.* (1972); 13. Candlish (1972); 14. Solomon (1975); 15. Wyburn *et al.* (1973); 16. Stemberger, Mueller and Leach (1977); 17. Solomon, Fryer and Baird (1975); 18. Davidson (1973); 19. Richardson (1935); 20. Johnston, Aitken and Wyburn (1963); 21. Breen and de Bruyn (1969); 22. Hodges (1974); 23. Baird, Solomon and Tedstone (1975); 24. Tamura *et al.* (1965); 25. Aitken (1971); 26. Tamura and Fujii (1966—on quail); 27. Baird *et al.* (1980).

egg on its rotating course which results eventually in the formation of the chalazae, twisted mucin fibres which appear from the protein in the chalaziferous layer.

During the time spent in the next and longest segment of the oviduct, the magnum, the egg white or albumen is deposited around the yolk. But, at this stage the albumen is in the form of a concentrated protein and represents only half the volume of albumen in the freshly laid egg. Secretion of some of the proteins found in albumen have been positively linked to a specific cell type in the magnum (*Figure 8.2*).

The developing egg passes next through the isthmus where there is a rapid development of two shell membranes around the albumen. Under the pressure of the descending ovum, granules which have coalesced within the tubular gland cells are extruded as a fibre into the lumen of the oviduct (*see Figure 20* in Solomon, 1983). The fibre cores and maybe some mantle material result from the secretions of the tubular gland cells whilst additional mantle material is added from the epithelial cells.

Secretion of the shell membranes is followed by the deposition on the outer surface of the outer shell membrane of the small organic mammillary cores which act as 'seeding' sites upon which shell crystallisation is initiated. The secretion of the cores is completed and calcium deposition begins in the tubular shell gland, a small area of the oviduct which some workers have regarded as part of the isthmus but is now generally treated as part of the shell gland. For a period of about 4 h, initially in the tubular shell gland (Draper, 1966) but mainly in the shell gland pouch, there is only a slow calcification of the shell, the main event being an uptake of water, some salts and glucose from the shell gland fluid by the albumen with the result that its volume increases and approaches that of the egg as laid. This process, known as 'plumping', begins to stretch the shell membranes and results in a distention of the shell gland wall which some workers consider to be the stimulus for the rapid phase of calcification to begin. Plumping also increases the spacing between the 'seeding' sites.

Formation of the true shell begins in the tubular shell gland with the initial deposition of crystallites peripherally around each mammillary core. Crystal growth inwards is largely inhibited by the shell membranes but there is some growth of the developing cones inwards into some of the spaces between the fibres of the outer shell membrane and this produces the basal caps. With continued development the cones eventually begin to fuse along their edges to form the foundation of the palisade layer. Continued deposition completes the true shell. Tyler and Simkiss (1959) suggested that throughout the process of crystallisation plumping fluid continues to pass slowly through the developing shell into the albumen and that this may help keep spaces between some of the crystal columns open to form the pores.

In simple terms, the egg shell derives from the combination of calcium and bicarbonate ions:

$$Ca^{2+} + HCO_3^- \rightarrow CaCO_3 + H^+$$

There is no storage of calcium in the cells of the oviduct, rather it moves from the blood both by passive and, more importantly, active mechanisms. Secretion of bicarbonate depends more on a concentration gradient than calcium but bicarbonate is also actively transported (Eastin and Spaziani, 1978). The passive transport of calcium occurs in association with the transport of other ions such as sodium, potassium, chloride and bicarbonate which poses problems for acid–base balance. Details of the shell gland transport system are still being worked out.. The reader is referred to Mongin and Carter (1977) for a general model, to Mongin (1978) for a consideration of the problem of acidosis caused by the production of excess hydrogen ions in the process, and to the more recent work of Nys and de Laage (1984) and Lundholm (1985) which also considers the calcium-binding proteins found in the shell gland cells.

The bulk of the true shell may be envisaged to be composed of long columns of calcite (Tullett, 1975, 1978). When thin radial sections are examined in polarised light, columns of calcite are indeed observed running radially through the palisade layer (Terepka, 1963; Schmidt, 1957, 1964). In transverse section the separate columns are seen to fit together like a jigsaw puzzle (Becking, 1975). X-ray diffraction analysis, however, suggests that the columns are not monocrystals (Erben, 1970), but there exists no consensus on the diffraction data available from several studies (*see* Perrott, Scott and Board, 1981; Sharp and Silyn-Roberts, 1984). A further stratum, the surface crystal layer, is present above the palisade layer and consists of small rhombohedral crystallites with their greatest dimension perpendicular to the egg shell surface (Simons and Wiertz, 1963; Simons, 1971). Diffraction data support the notion of a preferred orientation of crystallites in this layer (Favejee *et al.*, 1965; Perrott, Scott and Board, 1981; Sharp and Silyn-Roberts, 1984).

Whilst the shell membranes are essential for egg shell formation they do not bind calcium. Rather, they probably just provide a structure on which the 'seeding' sites or mammillary cores can be deposited and held in a favourable configuration for future crystallisation. The mammillary cores were described by Parsons (1982) as the epitactic centres for calcite crystal initiation. This implies that the cores have a suitable arrangement of charged chemical groups which provide a template onto which calcium and carbonate ions may fit to give the calcite crystal lattice. On the other hand, sialic acid which is present on the surfaces of the cores (Cooke and Balch, 1970a), readily complexes with calcium ions (Lura, 1963) and may be involved in nucleation. Once crystallisation is initiated the various calcium-binding components in the organic matrix together with calcium are capable of self-organisation. The action of the enzyme carbonic anhydrase by localising a high concentration of carbonate ions, derived either from bicarbonate or metabolic carbon dioxide, completes the formation of the crystals (Krampitz and Witt, 1979).

Shell structure, strength and quality

There has been much work directed to understanding the strength of egg shells and their behaviour under impact, compression and the like are well documented (*see* Hamilton, 1982). Similarly, there is an extensive literature on mineral metabolism particularly with regard to dietary calcium and phosphorus levels. These aspects will not be discussed in the present chapter. Suffice it to say that despite intensive research in these and other fields, there still exists no consensus on how egg shell strength may be usefully improved or how the production of eggs with shells of low breaking strength may be avoided. Creger, Phillips and Scott (1976) state: 'The only means of attempting to control the egg shell strength of commercial laying birds at present is by the dietary manipulation of the calcium and phosphorus content of the diets. The success has been minimal.' This is a terrible indictment of all the excellent nutritional work that has been done and obviously they could not have taken into account the more recent work on lighting patterns which result in an improved shell thickness (e.g. Yannakopoulos and Morris, 1979). But cracked and broken eggs still represent a serious loss, not only in financial terms to the industry but also in terms of the loss of a high quality food product. Recently, however, there has been some exciting progress made in assessing shell quality in terms of the fine structure of the egg shell which may shape the way we approach our research on egg shells. The next part of the review looks briefly at some current hypotheses concerned generally with egg shell quality, fine structure and the probable causes of specific egg shell abnormalities.

The effects of flock age and moulting on egg shell quality

As commercial layers age, not only does egg production fall, but egg shell quality deteriorates. These changes can be reversed, however, if the birds are moulted. Although our understanding of the reasons for these changes are incomplete there is some evidence that they are connected with alterations in vitamin D_3 metabolism, particularly the production of the metabolite $1,25(OH)_2D_3$ produced in the kidney. This metabolite has a number of effects. It stimulates calcium resorption from bone and helps prevent calcium being excreted in the urine. It also induces the cells lining the intestine to synthesise calcium-binding proteins and increases the calcium absorption from the gut. Abe *et al.* (1982) found that the *in vitro* production of $1,25(OH)_2D_3$ by kidney tissue taken from laying birds during shell calcification was less in old compared with young birds. Further, after a forced moult, egg shell quality, the production of $1,25(OH)_2D_3$ and the accumulation of $1,25(OH)_2D_3$ in the blood plasma and target tissues (intestine and bone) were all restored partially towards the levels found in young hens. Inclusion of $1,25(OH)_2D_3$ in the diet increases shell thickness in hens which have been in lay for 9 months (Morris, Jenkins and Simonite, 1977). These findings imply that the decline in shell quality with increasing flock age is related to a decreasing ability to absorb calcium from the intestine and to mobilise skeletal calcium. Roland, Sloan and Harms (1975) and Roland (1979), however, found that with increasing flock age, the amount of shell deposited did not change or slightly increased. But, because egg weight was increasing with flock age, this resulted in thinner shells on the eggs from older birds and hence a fall in egg shell quality. Forced moulting resulted in an increase in shell weight and an improvement in production by reducing the number of shell-less eggs (Roland and Brake, 1982). These authors suggested that following a forced moult, an improvement in calcium metabolism (either in absorption, transport or deposition) was the major cause of the improved shell quality.

Some aspects of shell structure related to shell strength

Shell thickness is the main but not the only factor that determines shell strength. Tyler (1969) suggested that better correlations should be obtained with the square of shell thickness and later Ar, Rahn and Paganelli (1979) found a highly significant correlation between egg shell strength measured by its yield point (by measuring the snapping strength of a strip of shell loaded at its free end) and the square of shell thickness using eggs from 47 species.

According to Richards and Swanson (1965), shell thickness alone accounts for 56% of the observed differences in strength of domestic fowl egg shells whilst shape accounted for 15–35% of the differences remaining after shell thickness had been considered. Carter (1970) also considered shape to be an important determinant of shell strength but Stewart (1936) had argued that shell strength did not depend on shape.

Carter (1971) found it was the thickness of the outer two-thirds of the shell that was almost entirely responsible for the tensile strength of the egg shell. The models of factors affecting shell strength advanced later by Carter (e.g. Carter, 1976) also took into account the thickness of the weak inner layer. It may be surprising, therefore, that it appears to be the cone layer that is altered in intrinsically weak, low-quality shells (Robinson and King, 1970; King and Robinson, 1972) and in eggs found cracked on supermarket shelves (Solomon, 1985a, 1985b). King and Robinson (1972) found that generally in weak, thin shells the cones were of irregular shape, were very porous and were frequently fragmented and not firmly attached to the outer shell membrane fibres. In these eggs the plane of fracture tended to pass right through the cones and not between the crystal columns as is the case for strong thick shells.

In a good quality shell the membrane fibres penetrate into the cones to a depth of some 20 μm and become associated with the mammillary core embedded within the cone (Simons and Wiertz, 1963). In this way the shell is firmly anchored to the egg shell membranes. It has been argued that the shell to membrane relationship is critical for good shell quality; any lack of establishment between the membrane fibres and the first crystals to 'seed' from solution will produce a potential area of weakness (Bunk and Balloun, 1978; Solomon, 1985a). Bunk and Balloun (1977) commented: 'There is a considerable literature concerning dietary mineral balances for optimal shell thickness and quality, but without a proper foundation for the calcium salts to crystallize upon, poor shell quality would still occur despite an adequate intake.' They also argued that the foundation of the shell (i.e. the cone layer) may be of equal importance to the thickness of the palisade layer in determining shell quality. Later (1978) they identified three categories of cone layer alterations in shells of low puncture strength—a proliferation of round calcified bodies resting upon the outer shell membrane, disorganised multinucleated cones and cones possessing cavernous tips with no mammillary core formation.

The critical early stages of egg shell formation are well documented with scanning electron micrographs being presented by Fujii and Tamura (1970), Erben and Kriesten (1974) and Creger, Phillips and Scott (1976). Recently, an abstract has appeared presenting new evidence clarifying the initiation and development of the cones on the shell membranes (Dieckert, Dieckert and Creger, 1985). They claim that discrete structural components on the outer shell membrane deposited in the isthmus are the sites for the attachment of a distinct, stainable organic material deposited in the red region or tubular shell gland. These individual complexes form the foundations for the growth of the 'rosette-like' clusters of calcium carbonate characteristic of the mature cones. Hopefully, a full paper with more details will follow.

Creger, Phillips and Scott (1976) stated that 'The number of initial calcium deposit sites is probably genetically controlled..... and the subsequent crystalline growth may well determine the future strength of the egg shell.' Simons (1971) observed that good quality egg shells (low deformation values) had a higher density of cones than poor quality egg shells indicating that shell quality was improved by having more compact, smaller cones. He also suggested that the smaller crystal column diameter found in guinea-fowl egg shells may account for their greater strength compared to chicken egg shells. Van der Plas (1966—cited by Simons, 1971) also pointed out that when the diameter of the column is low relative to column length then the shells may be stronger. Toledo, Parsons and Combs (1982), however, investigating eggs with the same shell thickness, but with high or low strength as determined by resistance to quasi-static loading, found the opposite. That is, eggs with low shell strength had smaller cones. Manganese deficiency results in fewer but larger cones probably due to the fusion of several mammillary cores early in shell formation. The shells are also thinner and have translucent areas. These changes have been linked with changes in the organic matrix but little is known of how they affect shell strength (Leach and Gross, 1983).

A positive relationship between shell deformation and shell porosity measured as the weight loss from the egg during a certain time was found by Simons (1971). This is in agreement with the general findings of Quinn, Gordon and Godfrey (1945) who noted that more cracks occurred in eggs from lines of hens selected on the basis of their eggs showing a high weight loss during incubation.

The amount and distribution of the organic matrix in the shell is also implicated in shell strength (Petersen and Tyler, 1967; Simons, 1971). Simons (1971) suggested that the more compact the matrix in the palisade layer the stronger the shell.

Tyler and Thomas (1966) found that shells were strengthened by the presence of the shell membranes when snapped outwards and by the cuticle if snapped inwards. Belyavin and Boorman (1980) found that the influence of the cuticle on shell strength determined as shell deformation did not go beyond a contribution to shell thickness.

Egg shell abnormalities

Several shell abnormalities have been characterised and, although the cause of each will be described under the separate headings, it is clear that most are interrelated. An overall explanation for most abnormalities could be given if our knowledge of oviduct was better. Scanning electron micrographs of many of the shell abnormalities discussed have been presented by Fujii, Watari and Tamura (1980). Eggs with slightly ridged shells can be found from any flock, sometimes in high numbers (*see*, for example, Roland, 1978) and are not discussed in the following account.

The body-checked egg

A body-checked egg is one that breaks in the shell gland and is then partially repaired by additional calcification. This leads to a prominent ridge around the waist of the egg which has been referred to as an equatorial bulge. Roland (1981) suggested that body-checked eggs were one of the major causes of shell problems today. In certain flocks he found 90% of the B grade eggs, and as many as 50% of the cracked eggs, were body-checks. On average, 5% of the eggs laid by flocks investigated by Roland (1978) were body-checked. The same author has published a review summarising current knowledge on this type of egg (Roland, 1984). The incidence of body-checked eggs increases with flock age and with the number of hens per cage. Most body-checked eggs are laid in the early morning and their incidence can be manipulated by alterations in the photoperiod. If they are causing a problem then practical considerations include an elimination of activity in the hen house after approximately 4 pm (i.e. during the critical early phase of calcification when the shell is still fragile and when activity can cause it to break in the shell gland) and a reduction in the photoperiod.

Hughes and Black (1976) found that when birds were subjected to handling stress the proportion of eggs with equatorial bulges increased. They suggested that, under stress, adrenaline is released causing strong shell gland contractions that break the egg.

Translucency

The cracks in body-checked eggs can be seen more easily by candling the eggs because the cracks are translucent. Some eggs, however, have naturally translucent areas, spots or streaks, caused by the local accumulation of moisture in the shell. In the normal egg there appears to be an area of well-calcified matrix that is low in organic matter just above the cone layer and this impedes water movement into the shell. In translucent shells the organic matrix does not dry out because the low organic/high mineral content barrier is not present and water can pass into the shell more easily (Talbot and Tyler, 1974a).

Damage to a shell may not always produce breakage but it may lead to the development of a complex series of cracks within the calcite columns, many of them parallel to the outer surface of the egg, into which water can move to produce a translucent area (Talbot and Tyler, 1974b).

Naturally occurring translucent streaks (i.e. those not produced by damage) represent areas of weakness but the shell does not necesarily crack along these translucent streaks. Rather, cracks originate at the point of impact and proceed round the egg. The crack may then encounter a translucent streak but the number of eggs in which this occurs appears to be no higher than the number expected by chance (Garlich, Parkhurst and Ball, 1975).

Corrugated eggs

Corrugated eggs are produced, for example, when birds suffer infectious bronchitis or can be produced experimentally by feeding a diet deficient in copper or by feeding the lathyrogen beta-aminopropionitrile—BAPN (Barnett, Richey and Morgan, 1957; Baumgartner et al., 1978; Sparks, Board and Tullett, 1985). In the cases of copper deficiency and feeding of BAPN the eggs produced are larger than normal owing to an increased amount of water in the albumen, a finding suggesting an inability of the membranes to create sufficient rigidity to terminate the plumping action (Baumgartner et al., 1978; Sparks, Board and Tullett, 1985). This can be explained because copper is necessary for the action of, and BAPN inhibits, the enzyme lysyl oxidase which is found in the hen's oviduct (Harris, Blount and Leach, 1979). This enzyme is responsible for the production of lysine-derived cross links in the shell membrane protein which give the membrane fibres their tensile strength.

A and B eggs

A and B eggs are formed when one egg (the A egg) is retained in the shell gland beyond the normal length of time and is still there when the next egg (the B egg) reaches the shell gland (van Middlekoop, 1971). Typically an A egg is laid on a day following one on which no egg was laid and its shell is well formed but feels rough. This is due to an additional calcified layer deposited over the cuticle, sometimes over the whole surface but usually as a band over part of it. Typically a B egg is laid on the same day as the A egg and has two forms. In one, the shell is thin and has a flattened area surrounded by a ring of wrinkled shell where it was pressed against the A egg when the latter was in the shell gland. Alternatively, the B egg may be shell-less (Carter, 1977).

Shell-less and soft-shelled eggs

The incidence of shell-less and soft-shelled eggs is difficult to measure because normally most are lost through the cage floor and are uncollected. In one survey, however, shell-less and soft-shelled eggs varied between 2.4% in hens aged 8 months to 16.1% in hens aged 17 months whilst averaging 7.77% of all eggs collected (Roland, 1977).

The production of shell-less and soft-shelled eggs can be induced by a variety of experimental techniques. One of these involves inserting a loop of surgical thread through the wall of the shell gland (Sykes, 1953). This operation causes an alteration in the secretion of shell gland fluid, in particular it causes a rise in the phosphate content (Ogasawara, Koga and Nishiyama, 1974). Hester *et al.* (1980) found that birds which laid soft-shelled and shell-less eggs had higher plasma phosphate levels than those laying eggs with normal shells. Phosphates are known to be poisons of calcification (Simkiss, 1964) and the injection of phosphate solutions into the shell gland about 3 h after an egg has entered the gland causes the expulsion of the soft-shelled egg within about 30 min (Ogasawara, Koga and Nishiyama, 1975).

Ogasawara, Koga and Nishiyama (1974) found a high level of phosphate developed in the shell gland fluid at the end of the shell calcification process. It is possible, therefore, that shell-less eggs are the result of two ovulations within the same day. One egg may receive a normal shell but with an extra-calcified layer (A egg) whilst the second egg enters the shell gland as the phosphate levels are recovering but are still sufficiently high to cause an almost immediate expulsion from the shell gland.

A rise in the phosphate levels in the shell gland has been advanced as the cause of the change from deposition of the true shell to organic cuticle in the domestic fowl and the change in the crystallisation pattern of calcium carbonate from columns of calcite to spheres of vaterite which constitute the 'cover' on the eggs of some seabirds. It is a mixture of calcite and vaterite that is found in the meagre calcified deposits of shell-less and soft-shelled eggs (Tullett *et al.*, 1976). Scanning electron micrographs of shell-less and soft-shelled eggs are presented by Tullett *et al.* (1976) and by Koga, Fujihara and Yoshimura (1982).

Pimpling

Two types of egg shell pimpling were described by Roland *et al.* (1975). In the first type the pimples are attached only to the exterior surface of the shell and are easily removed. In the second type the pimples are attached to the egg at any point between the shell membranes and exterior surface of the egg. If this latter type of pimple is removed a hole may be made in the shell from which the egg contents may leak. The incidence of pimpling increases as a flock ages (Ball *et al.*, 1974; Roland *et al.*, 1975) but is not disease-related (Ball *et al.*, 1974).

Ball *et al.* (1973) suggest that pimpling may arise from masses of albumen-like debris produced in the magnum which become attached to the outer shell membrane prior to the onset of shell secretion. Such an explanation would be in agreement with the work of von Nathusius (1868—*see* Figure 158A in Romanoff and Romanoff (1949) of a radial section through such a pimpled area). Masses of substances other than albumen may also be involved judging from the series of scanning electron micrographs presented by Costello, Meola and Odom (1985).

Roland *et al.* (1975) found that pimpling could be created artificially by the introduction of 1.5 g of calcium carbonate into the uterus at certain times of day. But, despite this and several other studies it is still not clear what factors predispose a bird to lay pimpled eggs.

Coated eggs

Whilst the A egg and pimpled eggs are special cases, superficial coatings applied on top of the normal cuticle are of general occurrence. These coatings can alter both the apparent colour and texture of the shell. Affected eggs have been variously described as having a 'sandpaper' texture, as being white-banded, calcium-splashed, having a chalky deposit or a fine-dusting or being pink or lilac.

Eggs with superficial coatings have been reported under field conditions at an incidence varying from 5% to 20% and can be a serious problem to egg producers, because such eggs are downgraded if their incidence is high or if the changes are particularly marked (Overfield, personal communication). The incidence may be high when hens first come into lay and then again later in the laying cycle. The phenomenon is not confined to brown egg laying hens. It can also be recognised under certain conditions in white eggs, for although there is no colour change the egg's texture is altered (Hughes and Gilbert, unpublished observation).

All these different manifestations are believed to occur because the egg has been retained in the shell gland for a period after it should have been laid (Hughes and Gilbert, 1984). The reason for retention appears to be the imposition of a stress or external disturbance upon the bird. Hens which receive a sufficient dose of adrenaline (1 mg given subcutaneously) retain an egg which is on the point of being laid, and this egg is subsequently laid with an abnormal coating (Hughes and Gilbert, 1984). The following egg is frequently laid soft-shelled or thin-shelled, perhaps because it was prevented from entering the shell gland by the presence there of the retained egg and then was laid before shell formation was complete, because the oviposition time had already been pre-set. These two eggs are those described earlier as Type A and Type B. The hen typically does not return to laying normal eggs once the Type B egg has been laid; the incidence of abnormal eggs remains high for an extended period (Hughes and Gilbert, 1984). Indeed, the production of coated eggs may be due to the hen's shell formation cycle being disturbed because in very few cases is the abnormality only superficial, rather there are indications that the fault may be initiated early in shell formation because the egg shell usually displays an abnormal cone layer (Solomon, personal communication). El-Boushy, Simons and Wiertz (1968) observed irregular, loose and basally rounded cones in egg shells produced by hens subjected to environmental physical stress. Similar effects have occurred after the imposition of behavioural stresses such as the translocation of hens from pens to cages, from a familar cage to one adjacent to a strange bird, or after a nest box has been made inaccessible to a hen normally accustomed to laying in it (Hughes, Gilbert and Brown, 1985), and the exact timing of the stress may influence the shell abnormality produced.

The coatings, after scraping off, have been analysed and shown to consist of calcium carbonate (Martindale, unpublished observation). It can be readily removed by brief immersion of the egg in EDTA (Wells, unpublished observation). Samples of typical coating material generally do not give an X-ray diffraction pattern (Waddell and Board, personal communication) suggesting that the delay in oviposition allows additional calcium carbonate to be deposited on the surface of the cuticle but in an amorphous form. The exact appearance of the coating is believed to depend both upon the length of the retention time and upon other factors so far unknown.

Shell breakage after grading

Many eggs that survive collection and grading subsequently crack before they reach the customer. In a survey of cracked eggs collected from retail outlets, Solomon (1985a) found there was a much higher proportion of structural abnormalities in the

(a)

(b)

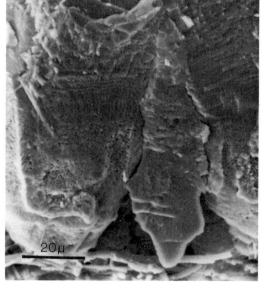

Figure 8.3 (a) Inner surface of a domestic fowl egg shell showing an isolated abnormal cone (A) with no shell membrane fibre tracts and surrounded by otherwise normal cones. The shell membranes were removed by plasma etching. (b) Radial section through cone layer of shell showing an abnormal cone similar to (A) having little contact with the shell membrane fibres. The abnormal cone is also driving a wedge between two otherwise normal cones.

Figure 8.4 (a) High power view of the edge of a cone showing cuffing (C). (b) Inner surface of a domestic fowl egg shell showing severe cuffing around groups of cones resulting in a mosaic pattern.

cone layer associated with the crack line than with other parts of the intact shell. Some of these abnormalities are shown in *Figures 8.3, 8.4* and *8.5*. A process known as plasma-etching (*see* Reid, 1983) was used to remove the shell membranes. Compared with previously used chemical techniques this leaves the crystalline shell intact and helps reveal the intimate relationship which must exist between the shell membrane fibres and the cone layer if the shell is to be structurally sound (Solomon, 1985a, 1985b). The appearance of the cones when the membranes are etched from a good quality egg shell is shown by all the cones in *Figure 8.3a* except that labelled A. The tracts which were taken into the cones by the fibres of the outer shell membrane are left clearly visible. The cone labelled A is abnormal and obviously had little contact with the shell membranes as can be confirmed by the radial section through a similar cone shown in *Figure 8.3b*. Even worse, such a cone drives a wedge between the neighbouring cones. Round calcified bodies in the cone layer of weak thin shells have been mentioned earlier but Solomon recognises two types. In one, rounded bodies are found lying on the membranes but they make no great contribution to or contact with the palisade layer. In the other, smaller bodies appear to grow on the sides of the cones but do not make contact with the shell membranes.

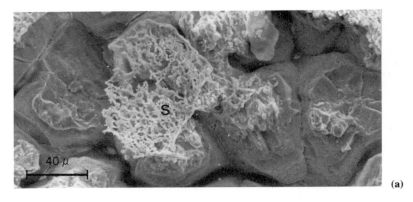

(a)

(b)

Figure 8.5 (a) Inner surface of domestic fowl egg shell showing sulphur-rich shell membranes (S) remaining after the shell had been plasma-etched. (b) Inner surface of egg shell. Sheared mammillae (SM) or cones tend to be associated with the same area of shell exhibiting remnants of shell membranes after plasma etching.

Spicular caps of calcium carbonate on the cones are another common abnormality and in some eggs the cones may develop as needle-shaped crystals of aragonite rather than calcite. Aragonite is more commonly associated with reptilian eggs such as those of turtles. A further abnormality is a cuff of crystalline material around the cones which may also fill the spaces between the cones (*Figure 8.4a*). In addition, further cuffing may occur around whole groups of cones giving a mosaic pattern to the inside surface of the egg shell (*Figure 8.4b*).

All the abnormalities mentioned so far must arise in the oviduct before the egg is laid. Another commonly observed abnormality is the presence on some cones of remnants of shell membranes resistant to plasma etching (*Figure 8.5a*). Such remnants are rich in sulphur and tend to be associated with areas of the shell showing sheared cones (*Figure 8.5b*). It appears that the cones have a line of weakness which fractures with the result that when the membranes are removed by plasma etching the tips of the cones also come away. The sheared cones could be an abnormality associated with a changed membrane composition but the possibility exists that they are the result of repeated insults to the egg shell at or near the same point on the egg, each insult not being sufficient to break the shell but leading to a progressive weakening of the shell and possibly fracturing within the cones, until a final insult breaks the shell. Work is under way to discover whether sheared cones are the result of repeated insults to the shell, or a true abnormality arising during shell formation which makes the egg shell intrinsically weak.

Acknowledgements

It is a pleasure to thank Dr Sally Solomon and Miss Jill Watt of the University of Glasgow's Veterinary School for helpful discussions and for kindly providing the plates for this chapter. Drs Barry Hughes and Alan Gilbert kindly supplied a draft of their work for the section on coated eggs.

References

ABATANGELO, G., DAGA-GORDINI, D., CASTELLANI, I. and CORTIVO, R. (1978). Some observations on the calcium ion binding to the eggshell matrix. *Calcified Tissue Research,* **26**, 247–252

ABE, E., HORIKAWA, H., MASUMURA, T., SUGAHARA, M., KUBOTA, M. and SUDA, T. (1982). Disorders of cholecalciferol metabolism in old egg-laying hens. *Journal of Nutrition,* **112**, 436–446

AITKEN, R.N.C. (1971). The oviduct. In *Physiology and Biochemistry of the Domestic Fowl, Vol. 3,* (Bell, D.J. and Freeman, B.M., eds), pp. 1237–1289. London, Academic Press

AR, A., RAHN, H. and PAGANELLI, C.V. (1979). The avian egg: mass and strength. *Condor,* **81**, 331–337

BAIRD, T., REID, J., KENNEDY, S.H.E. and SOLOMON, S.E. (1980). The effect of mercury ingestion on the avian oviduct. In *Electron Microscopy 1980, Vol. 2,* (Brederoo, P. and De Priester, W., eds), pp. 414–415. Leiden, Electron Microscopy Foundation

BAIRD, T., SOLOMON, S.E. and TEDSTONE, D.R. (1975). Localization and characterization of egg shell porphyrins in several avian species. *British Poultry Science,* **16**, 201–208

BAKER, J.R. and BALCH, D.A. (1962). A study of the organic material of hen's egg-shell. *Biochemical Journal,* **82**, 352–361

BAKST, M. and HOWARTH, B. (1975). SEM preparation and observations of the hen's oviduct. *Anatomical Record,* **181**, 211–226

BALCH, D.A. and COOKE, R.A. (1970). A study of the composition of the hen's egg-shell membranes. *Annales de Biologie Animale, Biochimie et Biophysique,* **10**, 13–25

BALL, R.F., HILL, J.F., MACKIN, R.J. and LOGAN, V. (1974). Evidence that the common rough, or pimply egg condition is not disease related. *Poultry Science,* **53**, 840–842

BALL, R.F., MACKIN, R.J., HILL, J.F. and WYATT, A.J. (1973). The nature and probable cause of rough egg shells laid by two lines of white leghorns. *Poultry Science,* **52**, 500–506

BARNETT, B.D., RICHEY, D.J. and MORGAN, C.L. (1957). Effect of beta-aminopropionitrile on reproduction of chickens. *Proceedings of the Society for Experimental Biology and Medicine,* **95**, 101–104

BAUMGARTNER, S., BROWN, D.J., SALEVSKY, E. and LEACH, M. (1978). Copper deficiency in the laying hen. *Journal of Nutrition,* **108**, 804–811

BECKING, J.H. (1975). The ultrastructure of the avian eggshell. *Ibis,* **117**, 143–151

BELLAIRS, R. and BOYDE, A. (1969). Scanning electron microscopy of the shell membranes of the hen's egg. *Zeitschrift für Zellforschung,* **96**, 237–249

BELYAVIN, C.G. and BOORMAN, K.N. (1980). The influence of the cuticle on egg-shell strength. *British Poultry Science,* **21**, 295–298

BOARD, R.G. (1975). The microstructure of the cuticle-less shell of the eggs of the domestic hen. *British Poultry Science,* **16**, 89–91

BREEN, P.C. and DE BRUYN, P.P.H. (1969). The fine structure of the secretory cells of the uterus (shell gland) of the chicken. *Journal of Morphology,* **128**, 35–66

BRITTON, W.M. and HALE, K.K. (1977). Amino acid analysis of shell membranes of eggs from young and old hens varying in shell quality. *Poultry Science,* **56**, 865–871

BUNK, M.J. and BALLOUN, S.L. (1977). Structure and relationship of the mammillary core to membrane fibres and initial calcification of the avian egg shell. *British Poultry Science,* **18**, 617–621

BUNK, M.J. and BALLOUN, S.L. (1978). Ultrastructure of the mammillary region of low puncture strength avian eggshells. *Poultry Science,* **57**, 639–647

CALVERY, H.O. (1933). Some analyses of eggshell keratin. *Journal of Biological Chemistry,* **100**, 183–186

CANDLISH, J.K. (1972). The role of the shell membranes in the functional integrity of the egg. In *Egg Formation and Production,* (Freeman, B.M. and Lake, P.E., eds), pp. 87–105. Edinburgh, British Poultry Science

CANDLISH, J.K. and SCOUGALL, R.K. (1969). L-5-hydroxylysine as a constituent of the shell membranes of the hen's egg. *International Journal of Protein Research,* **1**, 299–302

CARTER, T.C. (1970). The hen's egg: some factors affecting deformation in statically loaded shells. *British Poultry Science,* **11**, 15–38

CARTER, T.C. (1971). The hen's egg: variation in tensile strength of shell material and its relationship with shearing strength. *British Poultry Science,* **12**, 57–76

CARTER, T.C. (1976). The hen's egg: shell forces at impact and quasi-static compression. *British Poultry Science,* **17**, 199–214

CARTER, T.C. (1977). The hen's egg: incidence and inheritance of some egg abnormalities. *British Poultry Science,* **18**, 309–313

COOKE, A.S. and BALCH, D.A. (1970a). Studies of membrane, mammillary cores and cuticle of the hen egg shell. *British Poultry Science,* **11**, 345–352

COOKE, A.S. and BALCH, D.A. (1970b). The distribution and carbohydrate composition of the organic matrix in hen egg shell. *British Poultry Science,* **11**, 353–365

COSTELLO, D., MEOLA, S.M. and ODOM, T.W. (1985). Observations of the effects of eggshell pimpling on shell ultrastructure. *Poultry Science,* **54**, 1484–1487

CREGER, C.R., PHILLIPS, H. and SCOTT, J.T. (1976). Formation of an eggshell. *Poultry Science,* **55**, 1717–1723

CROMBIE, G., SNIDER, R., FARIS, B. and FRANZBLAU, C. (1981). Lysine-derived cross-links in the egg shell membrane. *Biochimica et Biophysica Acta,* **640**, 365–367

DAVIDSON, M.F. (1973). Staining properties of the luminal epithelium of the isthmus and shell gland of the oviduct of the hen *Gallus domesticus* during the passage of an egg. *British Poultry Science,* **14**, 631–633

DIECKERT, M.C., DIECKERT, J.W. and CREGER, C.R. (1985). Ontogeny of mammillary bodies of the avian shell membrane. *Poultry Science,* **64** (Supplement 1), 90

DRAPER, M.H. (1966). The accumulation of water and electrolytes in the egg of the hen. In *Physiology of the Domestic Fowl,* (Horton-Smith, C. and Amoroso, E.C., eds), pp. 63–74. Edinburgh, Oliver and Boyd

DRAPER, M.H., DAVIDSON, M.F., WYBURN, G.M. and JOHNSTON, H.S. (1972). The fine structure of the fibrous membrane forming region of the isthmus of oviduct of *Gallus domesticus. Quarterly Journal of Experimental Physiology,* **57**, 297–309

EASTIN, W.C. and SPAZIANI, E. (1978). On the mechanism of calcium secretion in the avian shell gland (uterus). *Biology of Reproduction,* **19**, 505–518

EL-BOUSHY, A.R., SIMONS, P.C.M. and WIERTZ, G. (1968). Structure and ultra-structure of the hen's eggshell as influenced by environmental temperature humidity and vitamin C additions. *Poultry Science,* **47**, 456–467

ERBEN, H.K. (1970). Ultrastrukturen und Mineralisation rezenter und fossiler eischalen bei vogeln und reptilien. *Biomineralisation,* **1**, 1–66

ERBEN, H.K. and KRIESTEN, K. (1974). Mikromorphologie der Frühstadien bei der Kristallbildung in normalen und abnormalen Hühner-Eischalen. *Biomineralisation,* **7**, 28–36

FAVEJEE, J.CH.L., VAN DER PLAS, L., SCHOORL, R. and FLOOR, P. (1965). X-ray diffraction of the crystalline structure of the avian eggshell: some critical remarks. *Biophysics Journal,* **5**, 359–361

FRANK, F.R., BURGER, R.E. and SWANSON, M.H. (1965). The relationships among shell membrane, selected chemical properties, and the resistance to shell failure in *Gallus domesticus* eggs. *Poultry Science,* **44**, 63–69

FUJII, S. and TAMURA, T. (1970). Scanning electron microscopy of shell formation in the hen's egg. *Journal of the Faculty of Fisheries and Animal Husbandry, Hiroshima University*, **9**, 65–81

FUJII, S., WATARI, T. and TAMURA, T. (1980). Scanning electron microscopy on the structure of abnormal hen's eggshell. *Journal of the Faculty of Applied Biological Science, Hiroshima University*, **19**, 101–111

GARLICH, J.D., PARKHURST, C.R. and BALL, H.R. (1975). The comparison of rough, normal and translucent eggs with respect to shell strength and calcification. *Poultry Science*, **54**, 1574–1580

GILBERT, A.B. (1979). Female genital organs. In *Form and Function in Birds, Volume 1*, (King, A.S. and McLelland, J., eds), pp. 237–360. London, Academic Press

HAMILTON, R.M.G. (1982). Methods and factors that affect the measurement of eggshell quality. *Poultry Science*, **61**, 2022–2039

HARRIS, E.D., BLOUNT, J.E. and LEACH, R.M. (1979). Localisation of lysyl oxidase in hen oviduct: implications in egg shell membrane formation and composition. *Science*, **208**, 55–56

HASIAK, R.J., VADEHRA, P.V. and BAKER, R.C. (1970). Lipid composition of the egg exteriors of the chicken *Gallus gallus*. *Comparative Biochemistry and Physiology*, **37**, 429–435

HEANEY, R.K. and ROBINSON, D.S. (1976). The isolation and characterisation of hyaluronic acid in egg shell. *Biochimica et Biophysica Acta*, **451**, 133–142

HESTER, P.Y., WILSON, E.K., PIERSON, F.W. and FABIJANSKA, I. (1980). Plasma inorganic phosphate, calcium, and magnesium levels of hens which laid soft-shelled or shell-less eggs. *Poultry Science*, **59**, 2336–2341

HODGES, R.D. (1974). *The Histology of the Fowl*. London, Academic Press

HOFFER, A.P. (1971). The ultrastructure and cytochemistry of the shell membrane-secreting region of the Japanese quail oviduct. *American Journal of Anatomy*, **131**, 253–288

HUGHES, B.O. and BLACK, A.J. (1976). The influence of handling on egg production, egg shell quality and avoidance behaviour of hens. *British Poultry Science*, **17**, 135–144

HUGHES, B.O. and GILBERT, A.B. (1984). Induction of eggshell abnormalities in domestic fowls by administration of adrenaline. *IRCS Medical Science*, **12**, 969–970

HUGHES, B.O., GILBERT, A.B. and BROWN, M.F. (1986). Categorisation and causes of abnormal eggshells: relationship with stress. *British Poultry Science*, **27**, 325–337

JOHNSTON, H.S., AITKEN, R.N.C. and WYBURN, G.M. (1963). The fine structure of the uterus of the domestic fowl. *Journal of Anatomy*, **97**, 333–334

JONES, C.B. and MECHAM, D.K. (1944). Dispersion of keratins. II. Studies on the dispersion of keratins by reduction in neutral solutions of protein denaturants. *Archives of Biochemistry*, **3**, 193–202

KHAIRALLAH, L. (1966). The fine structure of the tubular glands in the isthmus of the oviduct of the hen. PhD Thesis, Boston University Graduate School (cited by Gilbert, 1979)

KING, N.R. and ROBINSON, D.S. (1972). The use of the scanning electron microscope for comparing the structure of weak and strong egg shells. *Journal of Microscopy*, **95**, 437–443

KOGA, O., FUJIHARA, N. and YOSHIMURA, Y. (1982). Scanning electron micrograph of surface structures of soft-shelled eggs by regularly laying hens. *Poultry Science*, **61**, 403–406

KOHLER, P.O., GRIMLEY, P.M. and O'MALLEY, B.W. (1968). Protein synthesis: differential stimulation of cell specific proteins in epithelial cells of the chick oviduct. *Science*, **160**, 86–87

KRAMPITZ, G. and WITT, W. (1979). Biochemical aspects of biomineralisation. *Topics in Current Chemistry*, **78**, 57–144

KRAMPITZ, G., MEISEL, H. and WITT-KRAUSE, W. (1980). Identification of carboxyglutamic acid in ovocalcin. *Naturwissenschaften*, **67**, 38–39

LEACH, R.M. (1978). Studies on the major protein component of eggshell membranes. *Poultry Science*, **57**, 1151

LEACH, R.M. (1982). Biochemistry of the organic matrix of the eggshell. *Poultry Science*, **61**, 2040–2047

LEACH, R.M. and GROSS, J.R. (1983). The effect of manganese deficiency upon the ultrastructure of the eggshell. *Poultry Science*, **62**, 499–504

LEACH, R.M., RUCKER, R.B. and VAN DYKE, G.P. (1981). Eggshell membrane protein: a non-elastin desmosine/isodesmosine-containing protein. *Archives of Biochemistry and Biophysics*, **207**, 353–359

LUNDHOLM, C.E. (1985). Relation between Ca^{2+} uptake and ATPase activity in the particulate fractions of the eggshell gland mucosa of the domestic fowl and duck. *Comparative Biochemistry and Physiology*, **81A**, 787–799

LURA, H.E. (1963). Complex formation of calcium of the tooth. *Advances in Fluoride Research and Dental Caries Prevention*, **2**, 77–83

MASSHOFF, W. and STOLPMANN, H.J. (1961). Licht- und elektronmikroskopishe Untersuchungen an der Schallenhaut und Kalkschale des Huhnereies. *Zeitschrift für Zellforschung*, **55**, 818–832

MONGIN, P. (1978). Acid-base balance during eggshell formation. In *Respiratory Function in Birds, Adult and Embryonic*, (Piiper, J., ed.), pp. 247–259. Berlin, Springer-Verlag

MONGIN, P. and CARTER, N.W. (1977). Studies on the avian shell gland during egg formation: aqueous and electrolytic composition of the mucosa. *British Poultry Science*, **18**, 339–351

MORRIS, K.M.L., JENKINS, S.A. and SIMONITE, J.P. (1977). The effect on eggshell thickness of the inclusion of the calcinogenic plant *Solanum malacoxylan* in the diet of laying hens. *Veterinary Record*, **101**, 502–504

MUNKS, B., ROBINSON, A., BEACH, E.F. and WILLIAMS, H.H. (1945). Amino acids in the production of chicken egg and muscle. *Poultry Science*, **24**, 459–464

NYS, Y. and DE LAAGE, X. (1984). Effects of suppression of eggshell calcification and of $1,25(OH)_2D_3$ on Mg^{2+}, Ca^{2+} and $Mg^{2+}HCO_3^-$ ATPase, alkaline phosphatase, carbonic anhydrase and CaBP levels -1. The laying hen uterus. *Comparative Biochemistry and Physiology*, **78A**, 833–838

OGASAWARA, T., KOGA, O. and NISHIYAMA, H. (1974). Effect of a shell gland irritant on the secretion rate, calcium and inorganic phosphorus levels of the shell gland fluid in the laying hen. *Japanese Journal of Zootechnical Science*, **45**, 668–673

OGASAWARA, T., KOGA, O. and NISHIYAMA, H. (1975). Premature oviposition induced by intrauterine injection of phosphate solution in the laying hen. *Japanese Journal of Zootechnical Science*, **46**, 185–191

OKA, T. and SCHIMKE, R.T. (1969). Progesterone antagonism of oestrogen-induced cytodifferentiation in chick oviduct. *Science*, **163**, 83–85

O'MALLEY, B.W., MCGUIRE, W.L., KOHLER, P.O. and KORENMANN, S.G. (1969). Studies on the mechanism of steroid hormone regulation of synthesis of specific proteins. *Recent Progress in Hormone Research*, **25**, 105–160

PALMITER, R.D. and GUTMAN, G.A. (1972). Fluorescent antibody localisation of ovalbumin, conalbumin, ovomucoid and lysozyme in chick oviduct magnum. *Journal of Biological Chemistry*, **247**, 6459–6464

PARSONS, A.H. (1982). Structure of the eggshell. *Poultry Science*, **61**, 2013–2021

PERROTT, H.R., SCOTT, V.D. and BOARD, R.G. (1981). Crystal orientation in the shell of the domestic fowl: an electron diffraction study. *Calcified Tissue International*, **33**, 119–124

PERRY, M.M. and GILBERT, A.B. (1979). Yolk transport in the ovarian follicle of the hen (*Gallus domesticus*): lipoprotein-like particles at the periphery of the oocyte in the rapid growth phase. *Journal of Cell Science*, **39**, 257–272

PETERSEN, J. and TYLER, C. (1967). The strength of guinea fowl (*Numida meleagris*) eggshells. *British Poultry Science*, **7**, 291–296

QUINN, J.P., GORDON, C.D. and GODFREY, A.B. (1945). Breeding for egg shell quality as indicated by egg weight loss. *Poultry Science*, **24**, 399–403

REID, J. (1983). The use of the plasma chemistry unit as an aid to the scanning electron microscope study of avian egg-shell structure. *British Poultry Science*, **24**, 233–235

RICHARDS, J.F. and SWANSON, M.H. (1965). The relationship of egg shape to shell strength. *Poultry Science*, **44**, 1555–1558

RICHARDSON, K.C. (1935). The secretory phenomenon in the oviduct of the fowl, including the process of shell formation examined by the microincineration technique. *Philosophical Transactions of the Royal Society, Series B*, **225**, 149–195

ROBINSON, D.S. and KING, N.R. (1968). Mucopolysaccharides of an avian egg shell membrane. *Journal of the Royal Microscopical Society*, **88**, 13–22

ROBINSON, D.S. and KING, N.R. (1970). The structure of the organic mammillary cores in some weak eggshells. *British Poultry Science*, **11**, 39–44

ROLAND, D.A. (1977). The extent of uncollected eggs due to inadequate shell. *Poultry Science*, **56**, 1517–1521

ROLAND, D.A. (1978). The incidence of body-checked and misshapen eggs in relation to the number of hens per cage and time of oviposition. *Poultry Science*, **57**, 1705–1709

ROLAND, D.A. (1979). Factors influencing shell quality of aging hens. *Poultry Science*, **58**, 774–777

ROLAND, D.A. (1981). Crack down on cracked eggs. *Poultry International*, **20**, 38–53

ROLAND, D.A. (1984). Eggshell quality 1: the body-checked egg. *World's Poultry Science Journal*, **40**, 250–254

ROLAND, D.A. and BRAKE, J. (1982). Influence of premolt production on postmolt performance with explanation for improvement in egg production due to force molting. *Poultry Science*, **61**, 2473–2481

ROLAND, D.A., SLOAN, D.R. and HARMS, R.H. (1975). The ability of hens to maintain calcium deposition in the eggshell and egg yolk as the hen ages. *Poultry Science*, **54**, 1720–1723

ROLAND, D.A., THOMPSON, J.B., VOITLE, R.A. and HARMS, R.H. (1975). Studies on the cause, prevention and artificial creation of pimpled eggshells. *Poultry Science*, **54**, 1485–1491

ROMANOFF, A.L. and ROMANOFF, A.J. (1949). *The Avian Egg*. New York, Wiley

SCHIMKE, R.T., PENNQUIN, P., ROBINS, D. and MCKNIGHT, G.S. (1977). Hormonal regulation of egg white protein synthesis in chick oviduct. In *Hormones and Cell Regulation, Vol. 1*, (Dumont, J. and Nunez, J., eds), pp. 209–221. Amsterdam, North Holland

SCHMIDT, W.J. (1957). Über den aufbau der schale des vogeleies nebst bemerkungen uber kalkige eischalen andrer. *Tiere Bericht oberhessischen Gesellschaft für Natur-und-Heilkunde*. Giessen (Naturwiss, Abt), **28**, 82–108

SCHMIDT, W.J. (1962a). Leigt der eischalenkalk der vögel als submickroskopische kristallite vor? *Zeitschrift für Zellforschung*, **57**, 848–880

SCHMIDT, W.J. (1962b). Über die basalkalotten der vogeleischale. *Journal of Ornithology, Leipzig*, **103**, 28–37

SCHMIDT, W.J. (1964). Über die strukter einiger abnormer vogel-eischalen nebst bemerkungen zu neueren auffassungen betreffend bau und bildung der kalkschale. *Zeitschrift für Morphologie und Ökologie der Tiere*, **53**, 311–361

SCOTT, H.M. and HUANG, W. (1941). Histological observations on the formation of the chalazae in the hen's egg. *Poultry Science*, **20**, 402–405

SHARP, R.M. and SILYN-ROBERTS, H. (1984). Development of preferred orientation in the eggshell of the domestic fowl. *Biophysics Journal*, **46**, 175–180

SIMKISS, K. (1964). Phosphates as crystal poisons of calcification. *Biological Reviews*, **39**, 487–505

SIMKISS, K. and TYLER, C. (1957). A histochemical study of the organic matrix of hen egg-shells. *Quarterly Journal of Microscopical Science*, **98**, 19–28

SIMKISS, K. and TYLER, C. (1958). Reactions between eggshell matrix and metallic cations. *Quarterly Journal of Microscopical Science*, **99**, 5–13

SIMONS, P.C.M. (1971). *Ultrastructure of the Hen Eggshell and its Physiological Interpretation*. Wageningen, Centre for Agricultural Publishing and Documentation

SIMONS, P.C.M. and WIERTZ, G. (1963). Notes on the structure of membranes and shell in the hen's egg: an electron microscopical study. *Zeitschrift für Zellforschung*, **59**, 555–567

SOLOMON, S.E. (1975). Studies on the isthmus region of the domestic fowl. *British Poultry Science*, **16**, 255–258

SOLOMON, S.E. (1983). Oviduct. In *The Physiology and Biochemistry of the Domestic Fowl, Vol. 4*, (Freeman, B.M., ed.), pp. 379–419. London, Academic Press

SOLOMON, S.E. (1985a). *Structural Evaluation of Eggshell Quality*. Eggs Authority Technical Bulletin No. 18

SOLOMON, S.E. (1985b). Eggshell quality—a structural evaluation. *Poultry International*, October, 58–62

SOLOMON, S.E., FRYER, J.R. and BAIRD, T. (1975). The ultrastructural localisation of calcium in the avian shell gland. *Journal of Microscopy*, **105**, 215–222

SPARKS, N.H.C., BOARD, R.G. and TULLETT, S.G. (1986). The structure of the eggshell membranes in the domestic duck (*Anas platyrhynchos*) and turkey (*Meleagris gallopavo*) eggs and those of hens (*Gallus domesticus*) fed beta-amino propionitrile. In preparation

STARCHER, B.C. and KING, G.S. (1980). The presence of desmosine and isodesmosine in eggshell membrane protein. *Connective Tissue Research*, **8**, 53–55

STEMBERGER, B.H., MUELLER, W.J. and LEACH, R.M. (1977). Microscopic study of the initial stages of egg shell calcification. *Poultry Science*, **56**, 537–543

STEWART, G.F. (1936). Shell characteristics and their relationship to the breaking strength. *Poultry Science*, **13**, 119–124

SYKES, A.H. (1953). Premature oviposition in the hen. *Nature, London*, **172**, 1098

TALBOT, C.J. and TYLER, C. (1974a). A study of the fundamental cause of natural translucent areas in eggshells. *British Poultry Science*, **15**, 197–204

TALBOT, C.J. and TYLER, C. (1974b). A study of the fundamental cause of artificial translucent areas in eggshells. *British Poultry Science*, **15**, 205–215

TAMURA, T. and FUJII, S. (1966). Histological observations on the quail oviduct: on the secretions in the mucous epithelium of the uterus. *Journal of the Faculty of Fisheries and Animal Husbandry, Hiroshima University*, **6**, 357–371

TAMURA, T., FUJII, S., KUNISAKI, H. and YAMANE, M. (1965). Histological observations on the quail oviduct, with reference to pigment (porphyrin) in the uterus. *Journal of the Faculty of Fisheries and Animal Husbandry, Hiroshima University*, **6**, 37–57

TEREPKA, A.R. (1963). Structure and calcification in the avian egg shell. *Experimental Cell Research*, **30**, 171–182

TOLEDO, B. VAN, PARSONS, A.H. and COMBS, G.F. (1982). Role of ultrastructure in determining eggshell strength. *Poultry Science*, **61**, 569–572

TULLETT, S.G. (1975). Regulation of avian eggshell porosity. *Journal of Zoology, London*, **177**, 339–348

TULLETT, S.G. (1978). Pore size versus pore number in avian eggshells. In *Respiratory Function in Birds, Adult and Embryonic*, (Piiper, J., ed.), pp. 217–226. Berlin, Springer-Verlag

TULLETT, S.G., BOARD, R.G., LOVE, G. PERROTT, H.R. and SCOTT, V.D. (1976). Vaterite deposition during eggshell formation in the cormorant, gannet and shag, and in 'shell-less' eggs of the domestic fowl. *Acta Zoologica (Stockholm)*, **57**, 79–87

TUOHIMAA, P. (1975). Immunofluorescence demonstration of avidin in the immature chick oviduct epithelium after progesterone. *Histochemie*, **44**, 95–101

TYLER, C. (1964). *Wilhelm von Nathusius on Avian Eggshells*. Reading, The University

TYLER, C. (1969). Avian egg shells: their structure and characteristics. *International Review of General and Experimental Zoology*, **4**, 81–130

TYLER, C. and SIMKISS, K. (1959). A study of the eggshells of ratite bird. *Proceedings of the Zoological Society, London*, **133**, 201–243

TYLER, C. and THOMAS, H.P. (1966). A study of the snapping strength of eggshells and the effect of various factors on it. *British Poultry Science*, **7**, 227–238

VAN MIDDLEKOOP, J.H. (1971). Shell abnormalities due to the presence of two eggs in the shell gland. *Archiv für Geflügelkunde*, **35**, 122–127

WEDRAL, E.M., VADEHRA, D.V. and BAKER, R.C. (1974). Chemical composition of the cuticle and inner and outer membranes from egg of *Gallus gallus*. *Comparative Biochemistry and Physiology*, **47B**, 631–640

WITH, T.K. (1973). Porphyrins in eggshells. *Biochemical Journal*, **137**, 597–598

WOLKEN, J.J. (1951). Structure of the hen's egg membranes. *Anatomical Record*, **111**, 79–89

WONG, M., HENDRIX, M.J.C., VON DER MARK, K., LITTLE, C. and STERN, R. (1984). Collagen in the eggshell membranes of the hen. *Developmental Biology*, **104**, 28–36

WYBURN, G.M., JOHNSTON, H.S., DRAPER, M.H. and DAVIDSON, M.F. (1970). The fine structure of the infundibulum and magnum of the oviduct of *Gallus domesticus*. *Quarterly Journal of Experimental Physiology*, **15**, 213–232

WYBURN, G.M., JOHNSTON, H.S., DRAPER, M.H. and DAVIDSON, M.F. (1973). The ultrastructure of the shell-forming region of the oviduct and the development of the shell of *Gallus domesticus*. *Quarterly Journal of Experimental Physiology*, **58**, 143–151

YANNAKOPOULOS, A.L. and MORRIS, T.R. (1979). Effect of light, vitamin D and dietary phosphorus on egg shell quality late in the pullet laying year. *British Poultry Science*, **20**, 337–342

Chapter 9

Egg shell pigmentation

Sally E. Solomon

Introduction

In explanation of bright plumage and dark skin, intraspecies attraction and protection against the injurious effect of ultraviolet light meet with general acceptance. The pigments involved in the diverse colouration of feathers are melanins, carotenoids and porphyrins, while skin pigmentation is primarily a function of melanin synthesis and migration of melanocytes from the deeper layers of the epidermis. Since biochromes in those situations do appear to have a functional significance it might be reasonable to assume that the myriad patterns and colours displayed by the eggs of wild birds and to a lesser extent domesticated species are more than just evidence of the off loading of metabolic waste products (*Figures 9.1* and *9.2*).

Porphyrin biosynthesis

Porphyrins are cyclic compounds formed by the linkage of four pyrrole rings through methylene bridges and one of the characteristic properties of porphyrins is

Figure 9.1 Colour contrast. The milk white ostrich egg contrasts sharply with the black egg laid by the emu.

147

Figure 9.2 The eggs of wild birds display a wide variety of colours and patterns.

the formation of complexes with metal ions, e.g. haemoglobin and chlorophyll which have as their central core iron and magnesium respectively. In nature these metaloporphyrins complex with proteins, giving rise to cytochromes, catalases and other such substances. Active succinate and glycine are implicated as starters in the biosynthesis of porphobilinogen which is then transferred through enzymatic action to uroporphyrin. Decarboxylation of uroporphyrinogen produces coproporphyrinogen and decarboxylation of the latter in turn forms protoporphyrinogen which is then auto-oxidised to protoporphyrin. The porphyrinogens are in themselves colourless, whereas the final product, i.e. the porphyrins, are coloured. According to Harper (1963) the double bonds in the porphyrins are responsible for the characteristic absorption and fluorescence of these compounds. In man, elevated levels of coproporphyrin and uroporphyrin in the blood signify the syndrome porphyria.

Significance of shell colour in domestic species

Going on the premise that uniformity of shell colour gives the seller a price advantage, the cost to the egg producer in downgrading because of variability in colour is not insignificant in monetary terms. The aesthetic appeal of the brown egg is understandable but does pigmentation enhance the strength of the shell and therefore its resistance to cracking? Opinions are divided. According to Carter (1975) shell colour has the greatest influence on the incidence of cracks and other shell defects. More recently, Campo and Escudero (1984) showed that the darker brown shelled eggs of the Vasca breed are stronger and thicker than the lighter coloured ones, and Briggs and Williams (1975) have produced data to suggest that egg shell strength, hatchability and egg production of the Japanese quail laying white eggs does not appear to be as good as those laying normally pigmented eggs. The species-specific nature of such an investigation is underlined by the earlier work of Briggs and Teulings (1974) with the Athens Randombred population. Their results indicate that there is no justification for attributing shell strength to shell colour. This opinion is corroborated by Shoffner *et al.* (1982) who conclude that differences in shell strength between brown and white shelled eggs are due to factors other than the presence of pigment, with respect to Rhode Island Red and White Leghorn birds.

The oviduct

It appears that hereditary factors play a role in the transmission of shell colour and pattern (Lucotte, 1975) and that the factor is transmitted through the female of the species. With (1973) comments that because egg shell pigment does not consist

Figure 9.3 The quail shell. The arrow indicates the dense pigment layer associated with the cuticle. Pigment also appears to extend into the crystal matrix. Magnification × 200.

Figure 9.4 A domestic fowl shell—White Leghorn. The shell appears unpigmented. Magnification × 200.

exclusively of protoporphyrin, but comprises an admixture of the latter with uroporphyrin and coproporphyrin, it is unlikely that it is the result of haem degradation. He concludes that the oviduct is the most likely origin of egg shell porphyrin. Stevens *et al.* (1974) demonstrated that the first two enzymes of the porphyrin biosynthetic pathway were present in the glandular tissue of the shell gland pouch region of the oviduct and that the levels varied according to oviduct activity. They hypothesise a link between progesterone levels and the ability of the pouch cells to produce ALA-synthetase. Lucotte, Choussy and Barbier (1975) provided data on the *in vitro* synthesis of porphyrins by uterine extracts after the addition of aminolevulinic acid. The latter is formed by the decarboxylation of amino-ketoadipic acid from succinyl Coenzyme A and glycine. Their results show a threefold increase in the quantity of protoporphyrin in the shell gland pouch with a pigmented egg *in situ*. Similar results were recorded by Baird, Solomon and Tedstone (1975) for the domestic fowl and quail (*Figures 9.3* and *9.4*). They reported an increased concentration of protoporphyrin in the shell gland pouch of white and brown egg laying birds during shell formation. Their results do not, however, indicate whether the values are the result of the active synthetic activity of the oviduct or merely a reflection of the cyclic passage of these pigments across the shell gland pouch during shell formation, at which time this region fluoresces strongly in ultraviolet light.

Histological investigation of the autofluorescence capability of the shell forming region of the oviduct demonstrates the transient reaction in the surface epithelial cells in particular (Baird, Solomon and Tedstone, 1975). The surface cells lining the shell gland pouch comprise a mixed population of ciliated and non-ciliated secretory cells. Their histochemistry and ultrastructural organisation have been described (Solomon, 1983) but no evidence has been presented to suggest unequivocally their involvement in the synthesis and storage of porphyrins (*Figures 9.5* and *9.6*).

The subcellular requirements for porphyrin synthesis are obscure, but presumably involve the mitochondrial fraction of the cell. In this respect the surface epithelial cells are poorly equipped, unlike the tubular gland cells of the pouch region which display a fluctuating population of mitochondria during egg formation (*Figure 9.7*). The absence of autofluorescence in the tubular gland cells might be explained by implicating them in the production of the colourless precursor

Figure 9.5 A scanning micrograph of the surface epithelial cells lining the shell gland pouch. (N) nucleus, (G) protein granules. Magnification × 2500, reduced to 50%.

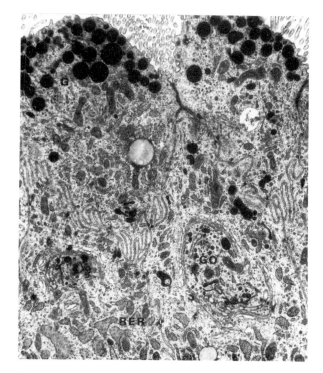

Figure 9.6 A transmission micrograph of the surface epithelial cells of the shell gland pouch. In addition to their content of electron dense protein granules (G), the cells contain a well developed Golgi complex (GO), and rough endoplasmic reticulum (RER). Magnification × 8000, reduced to 65%.

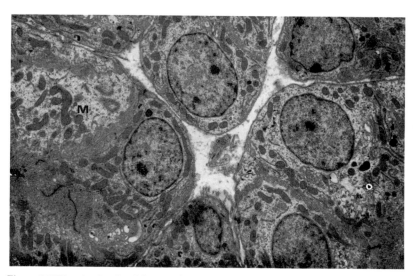

Figure 9.7 The gland cells of the pouch region contain a fluctuating population of mitochondria (M). Magnification × 8000, reduced to 68%.

porphyrinogen. The transfer of the latter across the surface epithelium and the auto-oxidation at this level of porphyrinogen to porphyrin would account for the reaction observed in these cells.

Although the bulk of the pigment is deposited on the cuticular layer of the shell, some deposition does occur within the calcite matrix (Baird, Solomon and Tedstone, 1975). The active transfer of calcium across the surface epithelium is generally considered to involve a protein carrier. The cuticle is a protein and carbohydrate complex which serves as a waterproofing agent and as a barrier to bacterial and fungal invasion, inferred by a process of elimination to be produced by the non-ciliated cells of the surface epithelium in the shell gland pouch (Baird *et al.*, 1980). It would be biologically economic if either one of these proteins also facilitated the transfer of porphyrin to the egg shell.

The egg shell

During the formation of the 'perfect' shell, calcite crystals 'seed' onto preferential nucleation sites on the outer shell membrane which at ultrastructural level

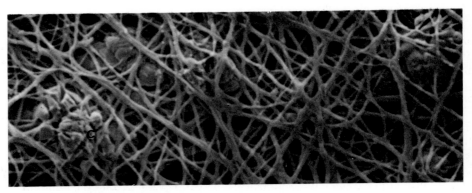

Figure 9.8 During the initial stages of calcification, calcium salts (C) deposit onto the web of membrane fibres. Magnification × 1200, reduced to 80%.

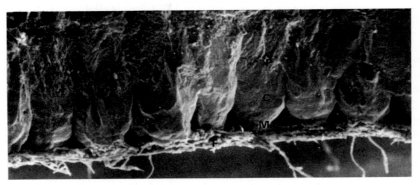

Figure 9.9 A transverse section through a normal shell reveals the membrane fibres (F), mammillary caps (M), cones (C) and palisade layer (P). Magnification × 480, reduced to 72%.

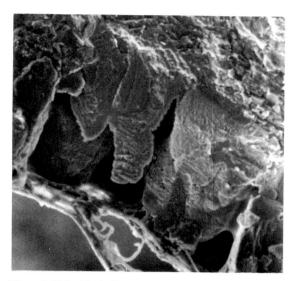

Figure 9.10 In this shell, a lack of establishment exists between the membrane fibres and the true shell. Magnification × 480, reduced to 72%.

comprises a web of interlacing fibres of variable diameter (*Figure 9.8*). From these sites continued crystal growth results in the formation of the cone, palisade, and vertical crystal layer (*Figure 9.9*). The organic framework of the shell ramifies throughout the calcite complex, together with a variable quantity of pigment, and preceding oviposition the cuticular layer is deposited together with the bulk of the shell colour.

The 'perfect' egg shell as such does not exist; the dynamic process of calcification which takes some 20 h to complete witnesses the formation of many aberrant crystal forms, both within and upon the shell, and the magnitude and nature of these defects will exert considerable influence on the physical parameters of the shell. The vast majority of these defects are initiated and localised at the mammillary layer, although some do have a 'knock-on' effect as revealed by examination of transverse sections of 'poor' quality shells (*Figure 9.10*). As commented on previously, both brown and white shells contain pigment within the calcite matrix, although as might be anticipated the quantity present within the white shell is reduced. It is interesting to note however (*Table 9.1*) that the protoporphyrin

Table 9.1 Tissue porphyrin concentrations (mg/g wet weight)

	Tissue	*Uroporphyrin*		*Coproporphyrin*		*Protoporphyrin*	
		Egg in shell gland	*Oviduct empty*	*Egg in shell gland*	*Oviduct empty*	*Egg in shell gland*	*Oviduct empty*
Quail	Isthmus	0	0	0.016	0	0.823	0.222
	Shell gland	0	0	1.18	0.38	4.765	1.765
Brown	Isthmus	0	0	0	0	0.078	0.025
'Ranger hybrid'	Shell gland	0.066	0	0.021	0.06	2.51	0.89
White	Isthmus	0	0	0.064	0.022	0.19	0.06
Leghorn	Shell gland	0	0	1.5	0.49	2.12	1.001

contents in the shell gland pouch of both brown and white layers, expressed as mg/g wet weight, are not significantly different. Shoffner *et al.* (1982) suggest that the tinted shell phenomenon in White Leghorns is the result of the leakage of protoporphyrin into the lumen from shell gland tissue. This accidental leakage hypothesis in white layers implies that under normal conditions some inhibitory factor operates. The findings of Kennedy and Vevers (1973) and Baird, Solomon and Tedstone (1975) do not support this concept since all the white eggs examined by both groups revealed the presence of protoporphyrin as an integral part of shell structure. Assuming, therefore, that the presence of pigment within the shell is a natural and normal occurrence, does it have a function separate to the cuticular pigment?

As revealed by electron diffraction analyses, the individual molecules of protoporphyrin are distributed in an amorphous form within the calcite matrix. During sublimation of the shell under vacuum, these molecules evaporate and can be collected on glass slides as individual crystals (*Figure 9.11*). The flat porphyrin

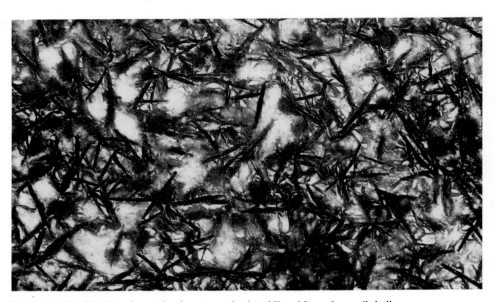

Figure 9.11 Needle-shaped crystals of protoporphyrin sublimed from the quail shell. Magnification × 60000.

molecules are similar in their ring structure to the phthalocyanins used as solid state lubricants in engineering, and so it is tempting to speculate that the insertion of porphyrin molecules into the growing calcite confers a degree of resilience on the shell because of their potential cushioning effect. If this hypothesis is valid, then the earlier porphyrin transfer occurs, the stronger will be the shell.

Shell colour is a variable phenomenon even within hens of the same breed and in general diminishes with age. Shell quality also decreases with age in terms of decreased resistance to cracking. The reduced complement of porphyrin which such eggs experience could explain in part their greater vulnerability at this time, although since older birds also lay larger eggs this must also provide a greater surface area for the insertion of the available pigment.

Reptilian ancestry

Birds do not appear to have inherited the process of pigmentation from their reptilian ancestors, since the eggs of the latter are off-white to white in colour and do not release pigment upon sublimation. The crystal growth mechanism in the eggs of the marine turtle is such that the end product is a soft pliable structure made up of long radiating needles of calcium carbonate in its aragonite configuration (*Figure 9.12*). The primary crystalline layer, i.e. that layer of crystals which nucleates onto the membrane fibres, is eventually overgrown by a secondary layer of randomly orientated widely spaced crystals. As such, it has no need for the cushioning effect of the porphyrins, which could render the shell tougher and therefore more liable to crack upon impact. The turtle will deposit on average 150 eggs in a clutch into a pre-excavated hole in the sand. Incubation proceeds without maternal care for a period of 60 d (Solomon and Baird, 1979). Obviously under these conditions the question of camouflage is irrelevant.

Figure 9.12 The turtle egg shell. The radiating crystals of aragonite are arranged in units (A). Magnification × 1280, reduced to 80%.

The eggs of wild species

So far in the discussion of this subject attention has been drawn in the main to white and brown eggs, but within the class Aves as a whole, egg shell colour ranges from white through blue and green to dark brown and black, accompanied by characteristic patterns of pigment deposition which aid in species recognition. The comprehensive account given by Kennedy and Vevers (1976) of a survey of avian egg shell pigments demonstrates the presence of three major components, namely, protoporphyrin, biliverdin and a zinc biliverdin chelate. They occur usually in combination, although protoporphyrin and biliverdin can occur on their own. According to the authors, the heavy markings are always protoporphyrin deposits. Even in wild birds, however, the pattern of pigmentation varies within any one clutch such that the last egg laid may be virtually unmarked. The Falconiformes will normally lay 2–4 eggs, but rarely rear more than one chick. There is no strong evidence in the literature for a correlation between position of egg in clutch, egg colour and chick survival, but in terms of temperature control, the dark pigmented eggs of these species will be more conducive to embryonic survival since they will tend to lose heat more slowly than lighter coloured eggs and in this respect will be better equipped for prolonged periods of parental absence.

The ease with which the surface pigment is removed reflects the time of deposition. Pigment deposited after the cuticle will be susceptible to streaking during its exit from the oviduct, whereas pigment secreted as part of the cuticular complex will no doubt derive greater stability from this association.

Conclusions

With few exceptions, egg shell pigmentation is ubiquitous throughout the class Aves and no doubt confers that degree of camouflage and hence protection which is essential to an arboreal or campestral habitat. Pigmentation probably does play a role in temperature regulation, but its role as a factor influencing shell strength is still a matter of debate. The potential economic importance of this concept, however, should ensure further investigation into the temporal and spatial relationship between the calcite complex and the porphyrin molecule.

Acknowledgements

I thank the Department of Zoology, Glasgow University, for giving me access to their egg collection and J. Watt for allowing me to include *Figure 9.8* in this chapter. *Figure 9.6* was originally used in *The Oviduct* and I am grateful to Academic Press for permission to re-use this plate. Finally I am indebted to Mrs J. Crawford for typing the manuscript.

References

BAIRD, T., SOLOMON, S.E. and TEDSTONE, D.R. (1975). Localisation and characterisation of eggshell porphyrins in several avian species. *British Poultry Science*, **16**, 201–208

BAIRD, T., REID, J., KENNEDY, S.H.E. and SOLOMON, S.E. (1980). The effect of mercury ingestion on the avian oviduct. In *Proceedings of the Seventh European Congress on Electron Microscopy, Vol. 12*, (Brederoo, P. and de Priester, W., eds), pp. 414–415. Leiden, Seventh European Congress on Electron Microscopy Foundation

BRIGGS, D.M. and TEULINGS, E. (1974). Correlation and repeatability between chicken egg shell color and breaking strength. *Poultry Science*, **53**, 1904

BRIGGS, D.M. and WILLIAMS, C.M. (1975). Shell strength, hatchability, egg production and egg shell pigmentation in the Japanese Quail. *Poultry Science*, **54**, 1738

CAMPO, J.L. and ESCUDERO, J. (1984). Relationship between egg shell colour and two measurements of shell strength in the Vasca Breed. *British Poultry Science*, **25**, 467–476

CARTER, T.C. (1975). The hen's egg: Relationships of seven characteristics of the strain of hen to the incidence of cracks and other shell defects. *British Poultry Science*, **16**, 289–296

HARPER, H.A. (1963). *Review of Physiological Chemistry, 9th Edition*. Los Altos, California, Lange Medical Publications, 437 pp

KENNEDY, G.Y. and VEVERS, H.G. (1973). Eggshell pigments of the Araucano fowl. *Comparative Biochemistry and Physiology*, **44B**, 11–25

KENNEDY, G.Y. and VEVERS, H.G. (1976). A survey of avian eggshell pigments. *Comparative Biochemistry and Physiology*, **55B**, 117–123

LUCOTTE, G. (1975). Polymorphism of egg shell pigmentation in Japanese Quail *Coturnix-Coturnix-japonica*. Part 3. Variability and phenotypic transmission modalities in the dominant form. *Comptes Rendus des Séances de la Société de Biologie*, **168**, 30–33

LUCOTTE, G., CHOUSSY, M. and BARBIER, M. (1975). Polymorphism of egg shell pigmentation in Japanese Quail *Coturnix-Coturnix japonica* Part 4. Porphyrin biosynthesis by uterus phenotypes in the dominant form. *Comptes Rendus des Séances de la Société de Biologie*, **169**, 34–38

SHOFFNER, R.N., SHUMAN, R., OTIS, J.S., BITGOOD, J.J., GARWOOD, V. and LOWE, P. (1982). The effect of a protoporphyrin mutant on some economic traits of the chicken. *Poultry Science*, **61**, 817–820

SOLOMON, S.E. (1983). Oviduct. In *Physiology and Biochemistry of the Domestic Fowl, Vol. 4*, (Freeman, B.M., ed.), pp. 379–419. London and New York, Academic Press

SOLOMON, S.E. and BAIRD, T. (1979). Aspects of the biology of *Chelonia mydas* L. In *Oceanography and Marine Biology, Vol. 17*, (Barnes, M., ed.), pp. 347–363. Aberdeen University Press

STEVENS, E.V., MILLER, L.K., WEINSTEIN, S. and KAPPAS, A. (1974). Biosynthesis of Delta amino levulinic acid and porphobilinogen in the domestic fowl *Gallus domesticus*. *Comparative Biochemistry and Physiology*, **47B**, 779–786

WITH, T.K. (1973). Porphyrins in egg shells. *Biochemical Journal*, **137**, 597–598

Chapter 10

Egg lipids

R.C. Noble

Introduction

The nutritive value of the domestic chicken's egg, both as an overall source of energy and in the provision of a range of macro- and micro-nutrients, is well known. As a complete food the egg has played a major role in the evolution of established patterns between livestock products and the human diet. The major nutritional component of the egg, which has been placed there for the purpose of sustaining and nourishing the developing embryo, is the lipid of the yolk. As a result, the egg of the domestic chicken provides a significant source of fat in many human diets. Although the pattern of fat consumption has always undergone some changes, in the past two decades there have been moves, in Western society in particular, to reduce not only the amount of energy consumed but also the amount of fat. The moves against the consumption of animal fats have been particularly dramatic based on a firm belief, erroneous or otherwise, that some animal foods are very much less beneficial than others. In spite of old and established standards for the part played by the egg in the human diet, its high concentration of fat in the yolk, including its cholesterol content, now mitigates against total acceptability. The belief that a change in dietary lipid patterns, which would include a severe reduction in the intake of egg lipid, provides a key to better health has been a persuasive view avidly embraced by an eager consumer looking for a simple panacea to the ills of modern lifestyle and actively promoted by commercially interested parties. Thus at a time when the poultry industry through technical and scientific developments is able to ensure an efficient and large supply of eggs, consumer demand is dwindling. The case for a reduction in the consumption of eggs may lack scientific substance but to the consumer it has contained persuasive arguments which will prove difficult to dispel. Responses to counter much of the bad publicity are essential and may include a need for a change in the product itself. Achieving these changes may well be possible but may also incur a price to be paid in terms of efficient production.

The present review concerns itself with a description of the lipid content of the egg and the attempts to manipulate the relative proportions of the major components in the light of present consumer preferences.

The nature of lipids

The term lipid is used to cover a wide range of complex and heterogeneous substances that are insoluble in water and soluble in organic solvents. Nowadays the term is restricted to fatty acids and their derivatives or metabolites. The principal classes consist of fatty acid (long chain monocarboxylic acid) moieties linked by an ester bond to an alcohol, in the main the trihydric alcohol glycerol, or by amide bonds to long chain bases. They may also contain other moieties, e.g. phosphoric acid, organic bases, sugars. They can be subdivided into two major groups, simple lipids containing one or two of the above hydrolysis products per molecule (e.g. tri-, di- and monoglycerides, free and esterified cholesterol, free fatty acids) and complex lipids containing three or more of the hydrolysis products per molecule (e.g. phospholipids, sphingolipids); more often these classes are referred to as neutral and polar respectively.

The role of lipids as essential biological constituents with a range of biochemical and structural functions was known long before much meaningful fractionation was possible. The development of a range of chromatographic procedures in the 1960s led to dramatic changes in analytical abilities and an explosion in our knowledge of lipid composition and function. Continuing progress is being made to the procedures and has been accompanied by progress in automation of the analytical manipulations of both samples and data.

The apolar nature of lipids requires some form of soluble complex for their dissolution in the aqueous environment of the plasma and elsewhere. This is achieved through lipid–protein interaction to form complexes known as lipoproteins. By this means the naturally hydrophobic lipids are able to be transported from one body site to another. Although the nature of the lipid–protein binding is poorly understood, methods have been devised for their division into major discrete classes of families which possess both metabolic and compositional distinctions. The common division of the lipoproteins into high density, low density and very low density fractions is indicative of the methods of their isolation based on flotation by ultracentrifugation and electrophoresis.

Lipid analytical methodology has been the subject of several recent review volumes and textbooks to which the reader is referred (Perkins, 1976; Kuksis, 1978; Christie, 1982; Christie and Noble, 1984).

Formation and accumulation of yolk lipid

The average egg weighing 60 g contains approximately 6 g of fat. Almost all the fat is contained within the yolk, an extremely small part occurring within the cuticle of the shell (Romanoff and Romanoff, 1949). The sequential maturation of the ova or yolk occurs within the ovary at approximately 24 h intervals and is achieved through a hierarchical arrangement of maturing follicles with 4–6 large follicles in particular always present (Gilbert, 1971b). Consistent patterns of egg laying are thereby established (Gilbert and Wood-Gush, 1971). Maintenance of egg output necessitates therefore the transport and turnover of enormous quantities of lipid (Gilbert, 1971a) which far exceed that able to be absorbed from the diet. The metabolic effort required to sustain the supply of lipid for yolk formation is thus achieved by a unique and highly organised synthesis and transport system.

With the approach of the onset of egg laying, both the weight and lipid content of the liver undergo dramatic increases. The overall concentration of total lipid increases some 2–3-fold above that found in the immature bird or cockerel and is accounted for, in particular, by an increase in the level of the triglycerides (Lorenz, Chaikoff and Entenman, 1938; Husbands and Brown, 1965). Although similar increases in the levels of phospholipids and free cholesterol are not observed, kinetic studies have suggested that their turnover within the liver is significantly increased (Taurog et al., 1944). The changes in the liver lipid levels are clearly in response to the lipid requirements for egg production and are manifested through the extensive and interrelated hormone changes that are occurring (Taurog et al., 1944; Common, Bolton and Rutledge, 1948; Balnave, 1968; Gilbert, 1971b); the changes therefore may be easily promoted by the administration of oestrogen alone or in the synergistic presence of androgen and progesterone. The gross lipid changes are accompanied also by changes in fatty acid composition (Chung, Ning and Tsao, 1966; Balnave, 1969), the alterations subsequently being reflected in yolk lipid fatty acid composition. The accumulation of lipid in the liver largely occurs through a stimulation of fatty acid and lipid synthesis which, in contrast to mammals, is predominantly associated with the liver rather than the adipose tissue (Leveille et al., 1975).

Table 10.1 Proportions of major lipids (% weight of total) in the plasma of the laying hen

Lipid		Phospholipid	
Cholesteryl esters	3.9	Phosphatidyl ethanolamine	17.7
Triglycerides	62.9	Phosphatidyl inositol	2.2
Free fatty acids	1.0	Phosphatidyl choline	70.9
Free cholesterol	6.8	Sphingomyelin	3.6
Phospholipids	25.4	Lyso-phosphatidyl choline	5.6

Table 10.2 Concentrations and lipid compositions of the lipoprotein fractions in the plasma of non-laying and laying hens (Yu, Campbell and Marquardt, 1976)

	VLDL	LDL	HDL
Non-laying bird:			
Total lipid[a]	61	150	205
Free + esterified cholesterol[b]	13.3	25.9	40.8
Triglycerides[b]	65.0	24.5	4.6
Phospholipids[b]	21.7	49.7	54.7
Laying bird:			
Total lipid[a]	1225	125	100
Free + esterified cholesterol[b]	5.8	11.4	26.5
Triglycerides[b]	64.6	50.4	23.4
Phospholipids[b]	29.5	38.2	50.1

[a] mg lipid/100 ml plasma
[b] % of total lipid
VLDL = very low density lipoprotein; LDL = low density lipoprotein; HDL = high density lipoprotein

The liver lipid changes are in turn accompanied by marked increases in the concentrations of the plasma lipids, in particular triglycerides (*Tables 10.1* and *10.2*), which again can be stimulated by hormonal administrations (Heald and Badman, 1963; Heald et al., 1964; Balnave, 1969). Total plasma lipid concentration increases from 200–500 mg/100 ml in the immature hen to a level which may exceed 2000 mg/100 ml. The range of lipid fractions present in the plasma of the hen is in general very similar to that commonly present in the plasma of other animals (*Table 10.1*). As in other animal species, three distinct lipoproteins (very low density (VLDL), low density (LDL) and high density (HDL) fractions) are identified in the plasma (Gornall and Kuksis, 1973; Yu, Campbell and Marquardt, 1976; Chapman,

1980). The changes in the plasma lipid concentration which precede egg laying are associated almost wholly with a dramatic rise in the concentration of the triglyceride-rich very low density lipoprotein fraction as a result of increased synthesis within the liver (Kudzma, St Claire and Friedberg, 1975) and decreased clearance from the plasma (Bacon, Brown and Musser, 1973). There is little or no change in the concentrations of the low and high density lipoprotein fractions (*Table 10.2*). Although the changes in the proportions of the lipoprotein fractions are accompanied by alterations to the lipid compositions of both the low and high density lipoprotein fractions, the lipid composition of the very low density fraction remains virtually unaltered. Thus the changes in the plasma lipid composition observed at the onset of lay are mainly a reflection of a changing pattern of lipoprotein distribution. Once laying has started, plasma lipid levels diminish slightly due to a reduction in oestrogen secretion by the ovary (Heald and Badman, 1963). Fundamental physical and chemical structural differences have been shown to exist in the very low density lipoproteins synthesised for yolk formation (Kudzma, Swaney and Ellis, 1979; Griffin, 1981), some of which are clearly orientated towards a specific function in the lipid transfer from plasma to yolk and possibly embryonic nutritional requirements.

The development of the ovum can be divided into several distinct phases (Bellairs, 1967; Gilbert, 1971b; Griffin, Perry and Gilbert, 1984). Lipid transfer has been implicated in all the successive developmental phases, the composition and mode of the transfer differing considerably with each. However, most of the yolk lipid is accumulated during the main vitellogenic period of maximum ovum development which takes place during the last 7–11 d of maturation and only ceases about 2–3 h before ovulation (Gilbert, 1971b). Extensive alterations to capillary and membrane structure of the follicle, in conjunction with a specific receptor-mediated process of endocytosis across the ovum basement membrane, allows a massive transfer of the yolk lipid precursors from the plasma (Perry and Gilbert, 1979). Both morphological and chemical evidence exists to indicate that the accumulation of lipid which occurs during the final phase of ovum development proceeds by direct intact transfer and is thus very similar in composition to that of the plasma, in particular the plasma very low density lipoproteins. Therefore, although several suggestions have been made that passage of the plasma lipid is accompanied by hydrolysis and resynthesis before deposition (Budowski, Bottino and Reiser, 1961; Bensadoun and Kompiang, 1979), the vast evidence of opinion is firmly in favour that this does not occur. Extensive similarities in the lipids, their fatty acid compositions and the structural arrangements of the component lipids within the plasma and yolk have been shown (Christie and Moore, 1972; Gornall and Kuksis, 1973); similarities in lipoprotein structure also exist (Griffin, Perry and Gilbert, 1984). Where slight differences between yolk and plasma lipid compositions have been noted (Gornall and Kuksis, 1973), explanations have not been easily forthcoming as both selectivity of uptake of plasma lipid components and reorganisation of the lipid once within the ovum are incompatible with the extensive morphological and biochemical evidence.

Separation of the yolk components

General descriptions of the yolk and its changing relationships with the other major components of the egg over the laying period are covered by the many excellent reviews that have appeared over the years (Romanoff and Romanoff, 1949; Gilbert, 1971c; Griminger, 1976). Simple inspection of the yolk clearly shows that the contents cannot be considered as homogeneous; a simple division into white and yellow components has been recognised for some considerable time. The white yolk, which is associated with the germinal disc and therefore deposited during early ovum maturation, constitutes only about 1–2% of the total yolk mass. The majority of the yolk material exists as an oil–water emulsion in the form of large floating spheres (size 25–150 μm diameter) present in a continuous aqueous–protein phase; its deposition during the later stages of ovum formation determines that it contains the majority of the yolk lipid. Much smaller granules (size up to 2 μm diameter) occur both in the spheres and the continuous phase (Bellairs, 1961; Gilbert, 1971c). Observations of inhomogeneity of the yellow yolk are merely representations of the cyclic rates of deposition. Because of the wide physical differences of the major yolk components, a range of methodology may be used for their separation. The usual separation involves differential flotation based on centrifugation (Cook, 1968; Gornall and Kuksis, 1973). Almost all the lipid is present as lipoprotein complexes, the overall lipid:protein ratio of the yolk as a whole being about 2:1. By low speed centrifugation, sedimentation of the granular fractions occurs which account for about 25% of the total yolk solid and 7% of the total yolk lipid. Further separation of the granular fraction yields two high density lipoprotein fractions (the lipovitellins) and a small amount of a low density triglyceride-rich lipoprotein. Prolonged centrifugation at high speed yields the vast bulk of the yolk lipid (>90%) that is associated with the low density triglyceride-rich fraction found within the large spheres. A very small amount of residual lipid may be recovered from the aqueous infranatant.

Lipid composition of the yolk

Extractable lipid accounts for about 33% of the total weight of the yolk and 60–65% of its dry matter content. The proportions of the major individual lipid fractions found in the yolk of an average egg are listed in *Table 10.3*. These lipid and subsequent fatty acid compositions are from analyses performed in the author's laboratory on eggs obtained under normal standard dietary conditions. In general, they are in agreement with analyses which have been performed elsewhere (Riemenschneider, Ellis and Titus, 1938; Rhodes and Lea, 1957; Privett, Blank and Schmit, 1962; Noble and Moore, 1964, 1965, 1966; Parkinson, 1966; Cook, 1968; Cook and Martin, 1969; Gornall and Kuksis, 1973). However, as can be seen later, under conditions where particular specialised diets have been fed extensive changes can be observed in both the lipid and fatty acid compositions of the yolk. As would be expected from their plasma origin, by far the principal lipid fraction of the yolk

Table 10.3 Proportions of major lipids (% weight of total) in the yolk

Lipid		Phospholipid	
Cholesteryl esters	1.3	Phosphatidyl ethanolamine	23.9
Triglycerides	63.1	Phosphatidyl serine	2.7
Free fatty acids	0.9	Phosphatidyl choline	69.1
Free cholesterol	4.9	Sphingomyelin	1.0
Phospholipids	29.7	Others	3.2

is triglyceride which is accompanied also by substantial quantities of phospholipid; the only other major component is free cholesterol. Cholesteryl esters and free fatty acids, which may constitute a significant proportion of the lipid content of animal tissues, are only minor components. Many other extractable 'lipid-like' substances may be present in the yolk, e.g. pigments, carotenoids, but their overall proportions are negligible. Phosphatidyl choline and phosphatidyl ethanolamine are by far the major phospholipid components. Although there is general agreement on the distribution of the major phospholipids in the yolk, early analyses do display some discrepancies. Thus low proportions of phosphatidyl ethanolamine and high levels of lyso-phosphatidyl choline (Rhodes and Lea, 1957) are questionable and may have arisen through the shortcomings of the analytical methods available.

The fatty acid compositions of the cholesteryl ester, triglyceride and total phospholipid fractions present in the yolk are given in *Table 10.4* and those of the major individual phospholipid fractions in *Table 10.5*. The fatty acids listed account for the majority of the total fatty acids present, the remaining small percentage consists of C14, C15, C17 and C20 acids. In the cholesteryl ester, triglyceride and total phospholipid fractions, oleic acid is the major fatty acid present. Palmitic and stearic acids together account for more than one-third of the fatty acids; substantial levels of linoleic acid are present in each. In the phospholipid fraction a high level of arachidonic acid and other polyunsaturated fatty acids are also present. In the phosphatidyl ethanolamine, phosphatidyl serine and phosphatidyl choline fractions palmitic and stearic acids together account for about 50% of the total fatty acids. This is a feature common to similar phospholipid fractions from most animal tissues and is consistent with the structure of these fractions when isolated from most

Table 10.4 Fatty acid compositions (major fatty acids, % by weight of total) of the cholesteryl esters, triglyceride and total phospholipid fractions of the yolk

	Cholesteryl esters	*Triglycerides*	*Phospholipids*
Palmitic	29.1	24.5	28.4
Palmitoleic	1.0	6.6	1.9
Stearic	9.5	6.4	14.9
Oleic	40.1	46.2	29.5
Linoleic	18.0	14.7	13.8
Linolenic	0.3	1.1	0.3
Arachidonic	0.9	0.3	6.2
Docosahexaenoic	0.5	<0.2	4.1

Table 10.5 Fatty acid compositions (major fatty acids, % by weight of total) of the major phospholipid classes of the yolk

	Phosphatidyl ethanolamine	*Phosphatidyl serine*	*Phosphatidyl choline*	*Sphingomyelin*
Palmitic	21.7	33.6	33.7	41.7
Palmitoleic	1.1	5.4	1.0	6.5
Stearic	30.1	27.3	15.8	17.6
Oleic	15.3	15.9	27.7	23.7
Linoleic	9.2	7.3	14.1	9.1
Linolenic	<0.5	<0.5	<0.5	<0.5
Arachidonic	13.2	8.5	4.4	<0.5
Docosahexaenoic	8.4	1.2	1.8	<0.5

natural sources (Strickland, 1973). There are, however, marked differences in the distribution of the palmitic and stearic acids between these major yolk phospholipids, with the relative level of palmitic acid highest in the phosphatidyl choline and lowest in the phosphatidyl ethanolamine. Again the feature is in common with the distribution of palmitic and stearic acids in the phospholipids of many tissues. The high levels of linoleic and arachidonic acids in the phosphatidyl ethanolamine, phosphatidyl serine and phosphatidyl choline, accompanied by relatively high levels of docosahexaenoic acid in the phosphatidyl ethanolamine, is also characteristic of these fractions in animal tissues. The predominance of palmitic acid in the sphingomyelin is a feature notable to this fraction.

There have been many structural analyses performed on the triglyceride and phospholipid fractions of the yolk. Indeed the phosphatidyl choline fraction of the yolk has been widely used as a convenient standard for comparative tissue lipid structural analyses and evolvement of methodology. The overall positional distribution of the fatty acids in the phosphatidyl ethanolamine and phosphatidyl choline fractions has been established through techniques involving partial enzymic fatty acid release (Christie, 1982). In both the phosphatidyl ethanolamine and phosphatidyl choline the selective distribution of fatty acids (*Table 10.6*) is similar

Table 10.6 Stereospecific analysis of yolk phospholipid and triglyceride: amount of major fatty acid associated with each position (Christie and Moore, 1972)

	Phospholipid		Triglyceride		
	Position 1	Position 2	Position 1	Position 2	Position 3
Palmitic	71.8	2.0	71.5	5.1	6.5
Palmitoleic	—	—	6.0	2.6	5.7
Stearic	18.1	0.5	4.1	1.4	8.7
Oleic	7.3	44.2	14.7	56.0	74.6
Linoleic	0.6	27.8	2.3	33.5	3.5
Linolenic	—	6.9	0.8	1.2	0.6
Arachidonic	—	1.5			
Docosahexaenoic	—	13.8			

to that widely displayed by the phospholipid fractions of most animal tissues in which saturated fatty acids are predominantly associated with position 1 and unsaturated fatty acids with position 2 (Hawke, 1962; Parkinson, 1966; Kuksis and Marai, 1967; Holub and Kuksis, 1969; Christie and Moore, 1972; Strickland, 1973). Through a combination of chromatographic separations and enzymic hydrolyses, details of the main molecular species of the yolk phosphatidyl ethanolamine and phosphatidyl choline have been obtained. 1-palmitoyl-2-oleoyl (some 37%) and 1-palmitoyl-2-linoleoyl (some 20%) are the main molecular species of the phosphatidyl choline (Kuksis and Marai, 1967). Phosphatidyl ethanolamine shows a much lower concentration of these molecular species and high proportions of stearic acid in position 1 in association with oleic and linoleic acids in position 2 (Holub and Kuksis, 1969). There are far greater proportions of C20 and C22 polyunsaturated fatty acid containing species in the phosphatidyl ethanolamine which, in contrast to the phosphatidyl choline fraction, display a preferential association for stearic acid in position 1. Both phosphatidyl ethanolamine and phosphatidyl choline have negligible proportions of disaturated species. Stereospecific analyses of the yolk triglycerides (Christie and Moore, 1970, 1972) show a high degree of asymmetry between the fatty acids associated with positions 1 and 3 (*Table 10.6*).

Over 70% of the fatty acids associated with position 1 is palmitic acid, position 2 is mainly occupied by oleic and linoleic acids whilst position 3 is mainly occupied by oleic acid with a small amount of saturated fatty acid. The differences in the distribution of the fatty acids between positions 1 and 3 of the yolk triglycerides are much greater than is normally found in triglycerides of animal tissues and even those of the chicken itself (Brockerhoff, 1966; Brockerhoff, Hoyle and Wolmark, 1966). Within the yolk triglyceride, therefore, there is a specific non-random combination of fatty acids as displayed by the yolk phosphatidyl ethanolamine and phosphatidyl choline fractions. Although some similarities have been observed between the arrangement of the fatty acids in the yolk triglycerides and phospholipids, e.g. 1-saturated-2-unsaturated species, there were also many notable differences (Christie and Moore, 1970). In particular the triglycerides showed a significant proportion of species with saturated fatty acids in positions 1 and 2. Comparative structural analyses have not been able to provide any substantive evidence of a biosynthetic relationship between the origins of the yolk triglycerides and phospholipids.

Extensive investigations have been made of the distribution and fatty acid profiles of the lipids associated with the specific lipoproteins of the yolk (Evans and Bandemer, 1961; Cook, 1968; Cook and Martin, 1969; Gilbert, 1971c; McIndoe, 1971; Gornall and Kuksis, 1973; Evans et al., 1973; Griffin, Perry and Gilbert, 1984). The structure of the major yolk lipoprotein fraction, the triglyceride-rich low density fraction, is very similar to that of mammalian plasma very low density lipoprotein and consists of a non-polar core of virtually pure triglyceride which is stabilised at the lipid/water interphase by a surrounding coat comprised of a mixture of apoproteins, phospholipids and cholesterol. Various analytical procedures have been able to identify two separate populations, low density fractions 1 and 2, which differ in size and unit protein structure. However their lipid compositions are similar, the high levels of triglyceride being associated with some 25–30% of phospholipid in which the major components are phosphatidyl ethanolamine and phosphatidyl choline (*Table 10.7*). The high density fraction can also be subdivided into two components, the α and β lipovitellins. They also display similar lipid compositions, the major component being the phospholipids containing phosphatidyl ethanolamine and phosphatidyl choline in similar proportions to that displayed by the low density fraction. The lipids of the triglyceride-rich low density fraction in the granules do not appear to have been characterised to any extent but from the evidence available it appears to have a similar composition to the low density fraction of the spheres (Gornall and Kuksis,

Table 10.7 Distribution of major lipid fractions in the yolk lipoprotein fractions

	Low density fraction	High density fraction
Percentage of total lipid	93	7
Triglycerides[a]	69	35
Total cholesterol[a]	4	4
Total phospholipids[a]	27	61
Phosphatidyl ethanolamine[b]	19	18
Phosphatidyl choline[b]	72	75

[a] % of total lipid
[b] % of total phospholipid

1973). The lipid compositions, lipid–protein ratios, density and size of the triglyceride-rich low density fractions vary considerably with changing physiological and dietary states (Evans, Flegal and Bauer, 1975). Detailed comparisons of the molecular species of the triglycerides, phosphatidyl ethanolamine and phosphatidyl choline fractions within each major lipoprotein of the yolk (Gornall and Kuksis, 1973) have shown the existence of a close similarity in the qualitative composition of the individual molecular species for each lipid class.

Yolk lipid composition and human diet

After many years of investigation and discussion, tne role of dietary cholesterol and fatty acid compositional intake in the etiology of cardiovascular disease and other human ailments still remains a controversial issue. However, the general opinion (NACNE, 1983; DHSS, 1984) is that the incidence of such diseases would be reduced and the general health of our society improved by a reduction in the consumption of cholesterol accompanied by a change in the dietary regimen of fatty acids in favour of increased levels of polyunsaturates. With cholesterol being solely derived from animal products, coupled with the epidemiological and experimental observations relating animal fats to cardiovascular disease, the continuing controversy confines itself mainly to a discussion about animal fat consumption. With the egg providing an obvious source of fat in the human diet, its inclusion in the whole controversy of fat intake is inevitable. It is therefore highly relevant to consider the lipid composition of the egg in comparison with other major sources of dietary lipid.

Although basic dietary facts remain irrefutable, much can be made through the mode of their presentation. In this respect egg lipid is no exception. *Table 10.8* compares the basic lipid and overall fatty acid composition of the egg yolk with that of ox liver, a food of undoubted respectability. Whereas the egg displays its obvious content of lipid through its concentration in a single compartment, namely the yolk, the presence of a relatively high lipid content within the liver is not visually apparent. The presence of hidden 'structural' fat as exemplified by the liver contrasts sharply with the more apparent 'depot' fat of animal products such as the egg and presents obvious advantages in certain areas of consumer persuasion. However, although the presence of such lipid may not be readily distinguishable, dietarily its acceptability may be no different and indeed in many instances may be

Table 10.8 Comparative levels of cholesterol, saturated and polyunsaturated fatty acids in egg yolk and ox liver lipid

	Yolk	Ox liver[c]
Cholesteryl esters[a]	1.3	3.3
Free cholesterol[a]	4.9	7.8
Linoleic acid[b]	15.9	7.2
Linolenic acid[b]	1.0	2.0
C20 + C22 polyunsaturates[b]	3.2	4.1
Total saturates[b]	34.2	54.9
P/S ratio	0.55	0.24

[a]% of total lipid
[b]% of total fatty acids
[c]Composite data from Poukka, 1966; Kinsella and Butler, 1970

considerably worse. As can be seen from *Table 10.8*, the free cholesterol content of the yolk lipid is 5% and is accompanied by about 1% of cholesterol in the esterified form. By comparison, the free cholesterol level in the liver lipid is about 8% which, with the addition of that present in the esterified form, gives a proportion of total cholesterol in the lipid of the liver which is nearly twice that of the yolk. Comparisons of the individual and total polyunsaturated fatty acid contents of the yolk and liver also prove to be interesting. The level of linoleic acid in the yolk is about 16% of the total fatty acids which with the addition of other C18, C20 and C22 polyunsaturated fatty acids gives a total polyunsaturated content of some 20%. Unlike most 'depot' fats, the relative concentration of linoleic acid in the triglyceride fraction of the yolk slightly exceeds that of the phospholipid fraction (*see Tables 10.4* and *10.5*). By comparison, the levels of linoleic acid and total polyunsaturated fatty acids in the lipid of the ox liver, some 7% and 13% respectively, are only about one-half those of the egg yolk. Indeed the levels of linoleic and total polyunsaturated fatty acids in the yolk exceed those displayed by a selection of acceptable table margarines (private observation). Of the remainder of the fatty acids in the yolk, mono-unsaturates comprise about 47% and saturates 34%; the yolk can thus be considered as predominantly unsaturated. Currently in the UK the dietary intake of polyunsaturated relative to saturated fatty acid (the P/S ratio) is 0.28 and it is suggested that P/S ratios of 0.32 (NACNE, 1983) and 0.4 (DHSS, 1984) should be aimed for. With a P/S ratio of 0.59 yolk lipid clearly far exceeds the present ratio of the UK diet and is also above the levels that have been suggested in the most recent nutritional guidelines. Ox liver by comparison has a P/S ratio of 0.24.

In spite of the accuracy of compositional data as a measure of lipid quality, nutritional effects are also dependent upon the gross consumption of the particular dietary constituent. Therefore, although from a qualitative point of view the yolk lipid has much in its favour, it must also be judged with respect to the general recommendation for a reduction in total dietary fat intake. It can be calculated that consumption of a single average 60 g egg/day will provide only 4–5% of the total UK recommended daily intake of fat (DHSS, 1984). However, it is with regard to its contribution to total dietary intake of cholesterol that the egg is particularly criticised. Evidence for this is largely based not upon the relative proportion of cholesterol in the yolk lipid, but upon the gross amount of cholesterol within an arbitrary volume or weight. It is interesting to note therefore that the same basic information on the cholesterol content of the egg (Feeley, Criner and Watt, 1972) has been given as 504 mg (Allen and Mackey, 1982) and 1480 mg (Sabine, 1977)/100 g depending upon whether it was based on the whole egg or just the yolk. In both cases the egg was rated very highly as a source of cholesterol when compared with other foods. By contrast, in another selection of comparative figures on the cholesterol content of various foods (Naber, 1976) but based on average daily dietary consumptions, the egg was given a very much better rating by providing less than one-half and one-third respectively of the amount of cholesterol from 3 ounces (85 g) of kidney and liver. These examples of differing interpretations of dietary information are unfortunately not uncommon.

Alteration of yolk lipid composition

Providing that the hen exists in a suitable environment, is of an age of high reproductive capacity and receives a diet that is adequate in all the necessary nutrients, eggs of a relatively uniform size and lipid composition are assured. The major emphasis on hepatic synthesis rather than dietary sources provides a far greater assurance of lipid supply for yolk formation with less vulnerability to temporary dietary and environmental imbalances. However, lipid from the diet and, in extreme circumstances, from adipose tissue stores do make some contribution to lipid supply and are not without some influence on yolk formation. Under nutritional or environmental circumstances that are not suited to egg formation changes in egg production, composition, or both become evident; in extreme circumstances the overall effects may result in the complete cessation of egg production.

An array of factors which affect lipid composition of the yolk have been studied. These range from the practicalities of optimising egg production through to deliberate attempts to implement changes in lipid composition to suit particular consumer requirements. The effects upon yolk lipid composition arising from environmental and nutritional changes vary considerably and depend upon a host of interrelated physiological and biochemical responses by the hen. Indeed, although both the liver and plasma lipids may show extreme changes, these may not necessarily be translated into similar effects on yolk lipid composition (Menge et al., 1974; Wood and Bitman, 1984).

Genetical influence

The ultimate control of egg production is through the genetical potential of the bird; variation in the lipid composition of the egg is merely part of this genetical influence. Thus not only has a wide variation in the total yolk size and its lipid content been observed between strains and breeds (Washburn, 1979), but also specific differences in the cholesterol and fatty acid contents. Attempts to change the cholesterol content of the yolk by genetical selection have met with mixed success. Although significant changes in yolk cholesterol content have been achieved (Washburn and Marks, 1977), their significance was eroded by accompanying changes in overall egg production. Likewise, although significant differences have been observed in the relative proportions of both saturated and polyunsaturated fatty acids (Edwards, 1964), their dietary potential seems very limited (Washburn, 1979).

Changes during the laying period

It is well known that during the laying period a considerable increase occurs in egg size. This in turn is accompanied by significant increases in the percentage content of the egg yolk relative to albumen and an increase in yolk lipid content and certain of its constituents (Menge et al., 1974; Fletcher et al., 1981; Chwalibog, 1985). Recent investigations on the yolk lipid of eggs from broiler birds at 25 weeks and 41 weeks of age have also shown changes in lipid and fatty acid compositions during the laying period (Noble et al., 1986).

Environmental influence

It is generally accepted that environmental factors associated with housing, stock density and temperature do not significantly affect any major lipid compositional changes in the egg (Chwalibog, 1985). However, although no alteration in lipid composition may occur, overall total yolk lipid content may be reduced under conditions of a high environmental temperature (Kampen, 1983).

General dietary influences

Investigations into the effects of nutritional factors on egg lipid composition are extensive. Such investigations have ranged from the effects of very general dietary intake and compositional alterations to specific features implicated directly in lipid metabolic changes. The effects of large scale changes of total dietary energy intake are extensively cushioned by physiological and biochemical adjustments by the hen. Thus, when high energy diets are fed (Gardener and Young, 1972) adjustment through reduced consumption may occur. Even in extreme circumstances of energy intake, over-production of yolk lipid components by the liver merely leads to increased yolk deposition but no effect on composition. Conversely, reduced energy intake is balanced by reduced yolk lipid deposition but again little change in composition. Major changes in the proportions of dietary carbohydrate and protein are also without any great effect on yolk lipid composition although they may alter total lipid content (Gardener and Young, 1972; Babatunde and Fetuga, 1976; Andersson, Elwinger and Pamlenyi, 1978). Changes in total lipid intake are also without any great effect on total yolk lipid content (Reiser, 1950, 1951; Ostrander *et al.*, 1960). However manipulation of the dietary lipid composition can, in many instances, be readily translated into effects on egg lipid composition. The majority of such investigations have involved manipulations of the major naturally occurring lipid constituents of the diet with only a few specific instances of components being investigated which, under normal circumstances, are of negligible dietary importance (Wood and Bitman, 1984).

Alteration of yolk fatty acid composition

Of the major yolk lipid constituents, fatty acid composition is most readily altered by the diet, both by the amount and type of fat included. Increased dietary levels of saturated fatty acids have a minimal effect only on yolk fatty acid composition, but the effects of polyunsaturated fatty acids are substantial. However, although the dietary saturated fatty acids do not increase to any extent the saturated fatty acid levels of the yolk (Cruickshank, 1934; Fisher and Leveille, 1957; Feigenbaum and Fisher, 1959; Summers, Slinger and Anderson, 1966), there is some evidence that they may affect oleic and linoleic acid levels. For instance, whereas initial observations showed no effects upon oleic and linoleic acid levels in the yolk (Cruickshank, 1934; Fisher and Leveille, 1957; Feigenbaum and Fisher, 1959), subsequent feeding of a similar tallow based diet produced increased levels of oleic acid and a decreased level of linoleic acid (Murty and Reiser, 1961; Summers, Slinger and Anderson, 1966), but some doubt has been expressed about the fatty acid compositions, in particular the oleic acid contents, of the respective diets. In contrast to the effects of saturated fatty acids, increased dietary levels of mono- and polyunsaturated fatty acids have a large effect on the unsaturated fatty acid levels of the yolk. Feeding olive oil or increasing the oleic acid level of the diet increased the oleic acid level in the yolk (Donaldson, 1967; Pankey and Stadelman, 1969). Incorporation into the diet of a range of vegetable oils containing either linoleic or linolenic acid resulted in large increases in their concentrations in the yolk lipid (Cruickshank, 1934; Fisher and Leveille, 1957; Wheeler, Peterson and Michaels, 1959; Murty and Reiser, 1961; Summers, Slinger and Anderson, 1966). It is generally concluded that these changes in the levels of the polyunsaturated fatty acids are balanced by proportional changes in the levels of oleic acid. The inclusion in the diet of high levels of C20 and C22 tetra, penta and hexaenoic acids is also reflected in higher levels in the yolk lipids (Reiser, 1951; Navarro *et al.*, 1972; Couch and Saloma, 1973). To increase the polyunsaturated fatty acid content of the yolk is therefore easily accomplished. Although the possible attraction of this in terms of human nutritional benefit has been suggested, many other considerations have to be made, e.g. economic, overall contribution to a changed fatty acid intake, concomitant effects upon other lipid fractions of the yolk (*see* later) and effects upon storage.

Where extensive changes in the fatty acid composition of the yolk have been achieved, their effects have varied between the different lipid fractions. In many instances they have also been associated with changes in lipoprotein patterns, the distribution of fatty acids and protein between the lipoproteins and structural alteration to some of the major lipid fractions (Navarro *et al.*, 1972; Couch and Saloma, 1973; Shenstone and Burley, 1975; Evans *et al.*, 1977).

Two fatty acid components of commonly fed diets have been studied for their indirect effect on yolk lipid composition. The presence of erucic acid (a mono-unsaturated C22 acid) in rapeseed oil increases the proportions of oleic and polyunsaturated fatty acids in the egg at the expense of saturated fatty acid levels (Vogtmann, Clandinin and Hardin, 1974; Vogtmann and Clandinin, 1975); although there was a high dietary intake extremely low levels only of erucic acid were found in the yolk. In spite of the highly unsaturated fatty acid composition of cottonseed oil, its feeding results in increased levels of stearic acid in the yolk associated in turn with extensive lipoprotein distributional changes (Allen *et al.*, 1967; Shenstone and Burley, 1975; Evans *et al.*, 1977). This has been shown to be due to the presence of the cyclopropene fatty acids, sterculic and malvalic acids, which inhibit the stearic desaturase system in the liver and thereby changing considerably the ratio of stearic to oleic acid in the yolk lipid precursors.

Alteration of yolk cholesterol content

Attempts to alter the cholesterol content of the yolk have been widespread and various, ranging from the manipulation of normal dietary components to the inclusion of drugs or other well known hypocholesterolaemic agents (*Table 10.9*). In many cases the outcome, which is dependent upon the balance of the overall effects on cholesterol absorption, endogenous synthesis and partition of excretion between the egg and intestine, is far from predictable. Under normal circumstances commercial diets vary little in their low content of cholesterol. Where the cholesterol content of the diet has been increased an associated increase in the cholesterol content of the yolk has also been observed (Harris and Wilcox, 1963; Weiss, Johnson and Naber, 1967), particularly under conditions where total fat intake has also been increased. In spite of their effect in reducing plasma cholesterol concentration, feeding polyunsaturated fatty acids increases yolk cholesterol levels (Summers, Slinger and Anderson, 1966; Weiss, Naber and Johnson, 1964). Extremes of neither saturated nor unsaturated fatty acids in the

Table 10.9 Effects of various dietary additions on yolk cholesterol levels

Dietary addition	Effect[a]	Dietary addition	Effect[a]
Cholesterol	++	Lecithin	+
Fat	+	Emulsifiers	+
Saturated fatty acids	+	Plant sterols	−
Polyunsaturated fatty acids	+	D-thyroxin	+
plus cholesterol	++	Ethyl p-chloro	
		phenoxyisobutyrate	+
Cellulose	+	Triparanol	− −
Pectin	−	Azasterols	−
Oat hulls	−	Probucol	−

[a] +, −, 0–50% enhancement or reduction; ++, − −, >50% enhancement or reduction

diet are therefore beneficial in maintaining minimum levels of cholesterol in the yolk. The effect of dietary fibrous materials on yolk cholesterol levels is highly variable. Thus, whereas the inclusion of pectin and oat hulls reduced the levels, cellulose increased it (Turk and Barnett, 1972; Menge *et al.*, 1974). The inclusion in the diet of specific components such as lecithin and emulsifiers that promote cholesterol absorption accentuate its deposition in the yolk (Naber, 1976). On the other hand, the inclusion of increased amounts of plant sterols in the diet have been shown to result in a considerable reduction in yolk cholesterol levels through their ability to compete with cholesterol during absorption and subsequent metabolism (Weiss, Johnson and Naber, 1967; Clarenburg, Kim Chung and Wakefield, 1971). A selection of drugs noted for their plasma hypocholesterolaemic effects have been tried with variable effects on yolk cholesterol deposition. D-thyroxin, although reducing the plasma cholesterol level, increased the content in the yolk (Weiss, Johnson and Naber, 1967). Similar effects were obtained following the administration of a selection of hypocholesterolaemic agents. In these cases plasma hypercholesterolaemia is effected through increased cholesterol excretion; unfortunately the egg comprises a major pathway for such excretion. Stimulation of sterol accumulation other than cholesterol within the hen and thus the egg has also been attempted by the administration of drugs such as triparanol, azasterols and probucol (Burgess, Burgess and Wilson, 1962; Singh, Weiss and Naber, 1972; Naber, Elliot and Smith, 1974). Replacement of cholesterol by desmosterol occurred to a large extent, but in some instances there was an eventual cessation of egg laying due to an accompanying reduction in steroidal hormone synthesis. As in the case of fatty acid composition, therefore, extensive changes in yolk cholesterol content can be effected. However, both their short and long term values with respect to egg production and dietetic value require extensive consideration.

Storage and yolk lipid composition

There have been several suggestions that storage of eggs, even under the most ideal conditions, is accompanied by structural and compositional changes. Detailed investigations of lipid and fatty acid compositions of the major lipoprotein classes, together with their relative distribution in the yolk, during storage over many months failed to detect any significant changes (Evans, Bauer and Flegal, 1974a, 1974b).

Summary

Lipid excretion via the egg is the culmination of intensive and coordinated changes in the lipid metabolism of the hen. Although designed to provide adequate nutrition for embryo development, man's intervention has increasingly exploited these changes in order that the egg should provide a regulated and large supply of dietary material for human consumption. To achieve such a constant and substantial lipid output in the egg requires extensive synthesis and mobilisation in the hen. The ability of egg lipid to conform to the nutritional requirements now demanded of it by a lifestyle adopted by much of modern society is being questioned. The lipid composition of the egg has therefore come under much scrutiny, especially with regard to its fatty acid and cholesterol contents. There exists a wide variation in interpretation of the nutritive merit of egg lipid, the interpretations being coloured by a range of commercial and dietetic interests. Undoubtedly though, either the failure to accept the lipid nutritional qualities of the egg for what they are or to manipulate the composition to suit the 'needs' of society, will undermine the historic role that the egg has played in human nutrition.

References

ALLEN, C.E. and MACKEY, M.A. (1982). Compositional characteristics and the potential for change in foods of animal origin. In *Animal Products in Human Nutrition*, (Beitz, D.C. and Hansen, R.G., eds), pp. 199–224. New York, Academic Press

ALLEN, E., JOHNSON, A.R., FOGERTY, A.C., PEARSON, J.A. and SHENSTONE, F.S. (1967). Inhibition by cyclopropene fatty acids of the desaturation of stearic acid in hen liver. *Lipids*, **2**, 419–423

ANDERSSON, K., ELWINGER, K. and PAMLENYI, I. (1978). Restricted feeding and different protein levels to two strains of SCWL hybrids. *Swedish Journal of Agricultural Research*, **8**, 241–247

BABATUNDE, G.M. and FETUGA, B.C. (1976). Effect of protein levels in the diets of layers on the egg production rate and the chemical composition of poultry eggs in the tropics. *Journal of the Science of Food and Agriculture*, **27**, 454–462

BACON, W.L., BROWN, K.I. and MUSSER, M.A. (1973). Low density lipoproteins of chicken, turkey and quail egg yolk. *Poultry Science*, **52**, 1741–1744

BALNAVE, D. (1968). The influence of gonadal hormones on the uptake of [^{14}C] acetate by liver lipid fractions in the immature male chick. *Journal of Endocrinology*, **42**, 119–127

BALNAVE, D. (1969). The effect of certain gonadal hormones on the content and composition of lipids in the blood and liver of immature male chicks. *Comparative Biochemistry and Physiology*, **28**, 709–716

BELLAIRS, R. (1961). The structure of the yolk of the hen's eggs as studied by electron microscopy. *Journal of Biophysical and Biochemical Cytology*, **11**, 207–226

BELLAIRS, R. (1967). Aspects of the development of the yolk spheres in the hen's oocyte studied by electron microscopy. *Journal of Embryology and Experimental Morphology*, **17**, 267–281

BENSADOUN, A. and KOMPIANG, I.P. (1979). Role of lipoprotein lipase in plasma triglyceride removal. *Federation Proceedings: Federation of American Societies for Experimental Biology*, **38**, 2622–2626

BROCKERHOFF, H. (1966). Fatty acid distribution patterns of animal depot fats. *Comparative Biochemistry and Physiology*, **19**, 1–12

BROCKERHOFF, H., HOYLE, R.J. and WOLMARK, N. (1966). Positional distribution of fatty acids in triglycerides of animal depot fats. *Biochimica et Biophysica Acta*, **116**, 67–72

BUDOWSKI, P., BOTTINO, N.R. and REISER, R. (1961). Lipid transport in the laying hen and the incubating egg. *Archives of Biochemistry and Biophysics*, **93**, 483–490

BURGESS, T.L., BURGESS, C.L. and WILSON, J.D. (1962). Effect of MER-29 on egg production in the chicken. *Proceedings of the Society for Experimental Biology and Medicine*, **109**, 218–221

CHAPMAN, M.J. (1980). Animal lipoproteins: chemistry, structure and comparative aspects. *Journal of Lipid Research*, **21**, 789–853

CHRISTIE, W.W. (1982). *Lipid Analysis, 2nd Edition*. Oxford, Pergamon Press

CHRISTIE, W.W. and MOORE, J.H. (1970). The structure of egg yolk triglycerides. *Biochimica et Biophysica Acta*, **218**, 83–88

CHRISTIE, W.W. and MOORE, J.H. (1972). The lipid components of the plasma, liver and ovarian follicles in the domestic chicken (*Gallus gallus*). *Comparative Biochemistry and Physiology*, **41B**, 287–295

CHRISTIE, W.W. and NOBLE, R.C. (1984). Recent developments in lipid analysis. In *Food Constituents and Food Residues*, (Lawrence, J.F., ed.). New York, Marcel Dekker

CHUNG, R.A., NING, J.M.J. and TSAO, Y.C. (1966). Effect of diethylstilbestrol and cholesterol on the fatty acid metabolism of cockerels. *Poultry Science*, **45**, 661–667

CHWALIBOG, A. (1985). *Studies on Energy Metabolism in Laying Hens*. Report of the National Institute of Animal Science No. 578, Copenhagen, Denmark

CLARENBURG, R., KIM CHUNG, I.A. and WAKEFIELD, L.M. (1971). Reducing the egg cholesterol level by including emulsified sitosterol in standard chicken diet. *Journal of Nutrition*, **101**, 289–297

COMMON, R.H., BOLTON, W. and RUTLEDGE, W.A. (1948). The influence of gonadal hormones on the composition of the blood and liver of the domestic fowl. *Journal of Endocrinology*, **5**, 263–273

COOK, W.H. (1968). Macromolecular components of egg yolk. In *Egg Quality: A Study of the Hen's Egg*, (Carter, T.C., ed.), pp. 109–132. Edinburgh, Oliver and Boyd

COOK, W.H. and MARTIN, W.G. (1969). Egg lipoproteins. In *Structural and Functional Aspects of Lipoproteins in Living Systems*, (Tria, E. and Scanu, A.M., eds), pp. 579–615. London, Academic Press

COUCH, J.R. and SALOMA, A.E. (1973). Effect of diet on triglyceride structure and composition of egg yolk lipids. *Lipids*, **8**, 385–392

CRUICKSHANK, E.M. (1934). Studies in fat metabolism in the fowl. 1. The composition of the egg fat and depot fat of the fowl as affected by the ingestion of large amounts of different fats. *Biochemical Journal*, **28**, 965–977

DHSS (1984). *Diet and Cardiovascular Disease*. COMA Report No. 28. London, HMSO

DONALDSON, W.E. (1967). Lipid composition of chick embryo and yolk as affected by stage of incubation and maternal diet. *Poultry Science*, **46**, 693–697

EDWARDS, H.M. Jr. (1964). The influence of breed and/or strain on the fatty acid composition of egg lipids. *Poultry Science*, **43**, 751–754

EVANS, R.J. and BANDEMER, S.L. (1961). Lipide distribution in egg yolk lipoprotein complexes. *Poultry Science*, **40**, 597–603

EVANS, R.J., BAUER, D.H. and FLEGAL, C.J. (1974a). The egg yolk very low density lipoproteins of fresh and stored shell eggs. *Poultry Science*, **53**, 645–652

EVANS, R.J., BAUER, D.H. and FLEGAL, C.J. (1974b). Lipovitellins in fresh and stored shell eggs. *Poultry Science*, **53**, 745–750

EVANS, R.J., FLEGAL, C.J. and BAUER, D.H. (1975). Molecular sizes of egg yolk very low density lipoproteins fractionated by ultracentrifugation. *Poultry Science*, **54**, 889–895

EVANS, R.J., BAUER, D.H., BANDEMER, S.L., VAGHEFI, S.B. and FLEGAL, C.J. (1973). Structure of egg yolk very low density lipoprotein. Polydispersity of the very low density lipoprotein and the role of lipovitellenin in the structure. *Archives of Biochemistry and Biophysics*, **154**, 493–500

EVANS, R.J., FLEGAL, C.J., FOERDER, C.A., BAUER, D.H. and LAVIGNE, M. (1977). The influence of crude cottonseed oil in the feed on the blood and egg yolk lipoproteins of laying hens. *Poultry Science*, **56**, 468–479

FEELEY, R.M., CRINER, P.E. and WATT, B.K. (1972). Cholesterol content of foods. *Journal of the American Dietetic Association*, **61**, 134–149

FEIGENBAUM, A.S. and FISHER, H. (1959). The influence of dietary fat on the incorporation of fatty acids into the body and egg fat of the hen. *Archives of Biochemistry and Biophysics*, **79**, 302–306

FISHER, H. and LEVEILLE, G.A. (1957). Observations on the cholesterol, linoleic and linolenic acid content of eggs as influenced by dietary fats. *Journal of Nutrition*, **63**, 119–129

FLETCHER, D.L., BRITTON, W.M., RAHM, A.P. and SAVAGE, S.I. (1981). The influence of layer flock age on egg component yields and solids content. *Poultry Science*, **60**, 983–987

GARDENER, F.A. and YOUNG, L.L. (1972). The influence of dietary protein and energy levels on the protein and lipid content of the hen's egg. *Poultry Science*, **51**, 994–997

GILBERT, A.B. (1971a). The female reproductive effort. In *Physiology and Biochemistry of the Domestic Fowl, Volume 3*, (Bell, D.J. and Freeman, B.M., eds), pp. 1153–1162. London, Academic Press

References 175

GILBERT, A.B. (1971b). The ovary. In *Physiology and Biochemistry of the Domestic Fowl, Volume 3*, (Bell, D.J. and Freeman, B.M., eds), pp. 1163–1208. London, Academic Press

GILBERT, A.B. (1971c). The egg: its physical and chemical aspects. In *Physiology and Biochemistry of the Domestic Fowl, Volume 3*, (Bell, D.J. and Freeman, B.M., eds), pp. 1379–1399. London, Academic Press

GILBERT, A.B. and WOOD-GUSH, D.G.M. (1971). Ovulatory and oviposatory cycles. In *Physiology and Biochemistry of the Domestic Fowl, Volume 3*, (Bell, D.J. and Freeman, B.M., eds), pp. 1353–1378. London, Academic Press

GORNALL, D.A. and KUKSIS, A. (1973). Alterations in lipid composition of plasma lipoproteins during deposition of egg yolk. *Journal of Lipid Research*, **14**, 197–205

GRIFFIN, H.D. (1981). Plasma very low density lipoproteins (VLDL) in immature and laying hens (*Gallus domesticus*). *Biochemical Society Transactions*, **9**, 155P

GRIFFIN, H.D., PERRY, M.M. and GILBERT, A.B. (1984). Yolk formation. In *Physiology and Biochemistry of the Domestic Fowl, Volume 5*, (Freeman, B.M., ed.), pp. 345–380. London, Academic Press

GRIMINGER, P. (1976). Lipid metabolism. In *Avian Physiology, 3rd Edition*, (Sturkie, P.D., ed.), pp. 252–262. New York, Springer Verlag

HARRIS, P.C. and WILCOX, F.H. (1963). Studies on egg yolk cholesterol. 3. Effect of dietary cholesterol. *Poultry Science*, **42**, 186–189

HAWKE, J.C. (1962). Distribution of fatty acids between the α- and β-positions of egg phosphatidylcholine. *Chemistry and Industry*, **81**, 1761

HEALD, P.J. and BADMAN, H.G. (1963). Lipid metabolism and the laying hen. 1. Plasma-free fatty acids and the onset of laying in the domestic fowl. *Biochimica et Biophysica Acta*, **70**, 381–388

HEALD, P.J., BADMAN, H.G., WHARTON, J., WULWIK, C.M. and HOOPER, P.I. (1964). Lipid metabolism and the laying hen. II. The nature and quantities of the free fatty acids of the plasma during the onset of laying. *Biochimica et Biophysica Acta*, **84**, 1–7

HOLUB, B.J. and KUKSIS, A. (1969). Molecular species of phosphatidyl ethanolamine from egg yolk. *Lipids*, **4**, 466–472

HUSBANDS, D.H.R. and BROWN, W.O. (1965). Sex differences in the composition and acetate incorporation into the liver lipids of the adult fowl. *Comparative Biochemistry and Physiology*, **14**, 445–451

KAMPEN, VAN M. (1983). Heat stress, feed restriction, and the lipid composition of egg yolk. *Poultry Science*, **62**, 819–823

KINSELLA, J.E. and BUTLER, T.F. (1970). Liver lipids of the lactating bovine: fatty acid composition. *Journal of Dairy Science*, **53**, 604–606

KUDZMA, D.J., ST. CLAIRE, F.L. and FRIEDBERG, S.J. (1975). Mechanism of avian estrogen-induced hypertriglyceridemia: evidence for overproduction of triglyceride. *Journal of Lipid Research*, **16**, 123–133

KUDZMA, D.J., SWANEY, J.B. and ELLIS, E.N. (1979). Effect of estrogen administration on the lipoproteins and apoproteins of the chicken. *Biochimica et Biophysica Acta*, **572**, 257–268

KUKSIS, A. (1978). *Handbook of Lipid Research, Volume 1*. New York, Plenum Press

KUKSIS, A. and MARAI, L. (1967). Determination of the complete structure of natural lecithins. *Lipids*, **2**, 217–224

LEVEILLE, G.A., ROMSOS, D.R., YEH, Y.Y. and O'HEA, E.K. (1975). Lipid biosynthesis in the chick. A consideration of site of synthesis, influence of diet and possible regulatory mechanisms. *Poultry Science*, **54**, 1075–1093

LORENZ, F.W., CHAIKOFF, I.L. and ENTENMAN, C. (1938). Liver lipids of the laying and non-laying bird. *Journal of Biological Chemistry*, **123**, 577–585

MCINDOE, W.M. (1971). Yolk synthesis. In *Physiology and Biochemistry of the Domestic Fowl, Volume 3*, (Bell, D.J. and Freeman, B.M., eds), pp. 1209–1223. London, Academic Press

MENGE, H., LITTLEFIELD, L.H., FROBISH, L.T. and WEINLAND, B.T. (1974). Effect of cellulose and cholesterol on blood and yolk lipids and reproductive efficiency of the hen. *Journal of Nutrition*, **104**, 1554–1566

MURTY, N.L. and REISER, R. (1961). Influence of graded levels of dietary linoleic and linolenic acids on the fatty acid composition of hen's eggs. *Journal of Nutrition*, **75**, 287–294

NABER, E.C. (1976). The cholesterol problem, the egg and lipid metabolism in the laying hen. *Poultry Science*, **55**, 14–30

NABER, E.C., ELLIOT, J.F. and SMITH, T.L. (1974). Effect of probucol on reproductive performance and liver lipid metabolism in the laying hen. *Poultry Science*, **53**, 1960

NATIONAL ADVISORY COMMITTEE ON NUTRITION EDUCATION (NACNE) (1983). *Proposals for Nutritional Guidelines for Health Education in Britain*. Discussion paper. London, HMSO

NAVARRO, J.G., SAAVEDRA, J.C., BORIE, F.B. and CAIOZZI, M.M. (1972). Influence of dietary fish meal on egg fatty acid composition. *Journal of the Science of Food and Agriculture*, **23**, 1287–1292

NOBLE, R.C. and MOORE, J.H. (1964). Studies on the lipid metabolism of the chick embryo. *Canadian Journal of Biochemistry*, **42**, 1729–1741

NOBLE, R.C. and MOORE, J.H. (1965). Metabolism of the yolk phospholipids by the developing chick embryo. *Canadian Journal of Biochemistry*, **43**, 1677–1686

NOBLE, R.C. and MOORE, J.H. (1966). Some aspects of the lipid metabolism of the chick embryo. In *Physiology of the Domestic Fowl*, (Horton-Smith, C. and Amaroso, E.C., eds), pp. 87–102. Edinburgh, Oliver and Boyd

NOBLE, R.C., LONSDALE, F., CONNOR, K. and BROWN, D. (1986). Changes in the lipid metabolism of the chick embryo with parental age. *Poultry Science*, **65**, 409–416

OSTRANDER, J.G., JORDAN, R., STADELMAN, W.J., ROGLER, J.C. and VAIL, G.E. (1960). The ether extract of yolks of eggs from hens on feed containing different fats. *Poultry Science*, **39**, 746–750

PANKEY, R.D. and STADELMAN, W.J. (1969). Effect of dietary fats on some chemical and functional properties of eggs. *Journal of Food Science*, **34**, 312–317

PARKINSON, T.L. (1966). The chemical composition of eggs. *Journal of the Science of Food and Agriculture*, **17**, 101–111

PERKINS, E.G. (1976). *Analysis of Lipids and Lipoproteins*. Champaign, Illinois, American Oil Chemists' Society

PERRY, M.M. and GILBERT, A.B. (1979). Yolk transport in the ovarian follicle of the hen (*Gallus domesticus*): Lipoprotein-like particles at the periphery of the oocyte in the rapid growth phase. *Journal of Cell Science*, **39**, 257–272

POUKKA, R. (1966). Tissue lipids in calves suffering from muscular dystrophy. *British Journal of Nutrition*, **20**, 245–256

PRIVETT, O.S., BLANK, M.L. and SCHMIT, J.A. (1962). Studies on the composition of egg lipid. *Journal of Food Science*, **27**, 463–468

REISER, R. (1950). Fatty acid changes in egg yolk of hens on a fat-free and a cottonseed oil ration. *Journal of Nutrition*, **40**, 429–440

REISER, R. (1951). The syntheses and interconversions of polyunsaturated fatty acids by the laying hen. *Journal of Nutrition*, **44**, 159–175

RHODES, D.N. and LEA, C.H. (1957). Phospholipids. 4. On the composition of hen's egg phospholipids. *Biochemical Journal*, **65**, 526–533

RIEMENSCHNEIDER, R.W., ELLIS, N.R. and TITUS, H.W. (1938). The fat acids in the lecithin and glyceride fractions of egg yolk. *Journal of Biological Chemistry*, **126**, 255–263

ROMANOFF, A.L. and ROMANOFF, A.J. (1949). *The Avian Egg*. New York, John Wiley

SABINE, J.R. (1977). *Cholesterol*. New York, Marcel Dekker

SHENSTONE, F.S. and BURLEY, R.W. (1975). Variable effects on egg yolks and yolk lipoprotein fractions of feeding methyl sterculate to hens: periodic changes in lipid composition and gelation temperature. *Journal of the Science of Food and Agriculture*, **26**, 285–294

SINGH, R.A., WEISS, J.F. and NABER, E.C. (1972). Effect of azasterols on sterol metabolism in the laying hen. *Poultry Science*, **51**, 449–457

STRICKLAND, K.P. (1973). The chemistry of phospholipids. In *Form and Function of Phospholipids*, (Ansell, G.B., Dawson, R.M.C. and Hawthorne, J.N., eds), pp. 9–42. Amsterdam, Elsevier

SUMMERS, J.D., SLINGER, S.J. and ANDERSON, W.J. (1966). The effect of feeding various fats and fat by-products on the fatty acid and cholesterol composition of eggs. *British Poultry Science*, **7**, 127–134

TAUROG, A., LORENZ, F.W., ENTENMAN, C. and CHAIKOFF, I.L. (1944). The effect of diethylstilbestrol on the *in vitro* formation of phospholipids in the liver as measured with radioactive phosphorus. *Endocrinology*, **35**, 483–487

TURK, D.E. and BARNETT, B.D. (1972). Diet and egg cholesterol content. *Poultry Science*, **51**, 1881

VOGTMANN, H. and CLANDININ, D.R. (1975). The effect of crude and refined low erucic acid rapeseed oils in diets for laying hens. *British Poultry Science*, **16**, 55–61

VOGTMANN, H., CLANDININ, D.R. and HARDIN, R.T. (1974). The influence of high and low erucic acid rapeseed oils on the reproductive performance of laying hens and on the lipid fraction of egg yolk. *Canadian Journal of Animal Science*, **54**, 403–410

WASHBURN, K.W. (1979). Genetic variation in the chemical composition of the egg. *Poultry Science*, **58**, 529–535

WASHBURN, K.W. and MARKS, H.L. (1977). Changes in fitness traits associated with selection for divergence in yolk cholesterol concentration. *British Poultry Science*, **18**, 189–199

WEISS, J.F., JOHNSON, R.M. and NABER, E.C. (1967). Effect of some dietary factors and drugs on cholesterol concentration in the egg and plasma of the hen. *Journal of Nutrition*, **91**, 119–128

WEISS, J.F., NABER, E.C. and JOHNSON, R.M. (1964). Effect of dietary fat and other factors on egg yolk cholesterol. 1. The 'cholesterol' content of egg yolk as influenced by dietary unsaturated fat and the method of determination. *Archives of Biochemistry and Biophysics*, **105**, 521–526

WHEELER, P., PETERSON, D.W. and MICHAELS, G.D. (1959). Fatty acid distribution in egg yolk as influenced by type and level of dietary fat. *Journal of Nutrition*, **69**, 253–260

WOOD, D.L. and BITMAN, J. (1984). The effect of feeding di-(2-ethylhexyl)phthalate and related compounds on lipids in the laying hen. *Poultry Science*, **63**, 469–477

YU, J.Y.L., CAMPBELL, L.D. and MARQUARDT, R.R. (1976). Immunological and compositional patterns of lipoproteins in chickens (*Gallus domesticus*) plasma. *Poultry Science*, **55**, 1626–1631

Chapter 11

The chemical basis of albumen quality

D.S. Robinson

Introduction

The overall chemical composition and physical structure of the domestic hen's egg has been known for a long time and is now only described here, briefly, for completeness. In the fresh whole egg the yolk is held centrally by the chalazae, which are anchored to the thick white gel; the thick egg white gel itself, as shown in *Figure 11.1*, is also held firmly in position by its attachment to the inner shell membranes of the egg.

For the domestic market such an organised structure of the egg is important. The central position of the yolk, which is a good medium for microbial growth, ensures for the yolk constituents that contact with the inner shell membranes is prevented. Furthermore egg white, which is in contact with the shell membranes, is a relatively poor medium for microbial growth, as a substantial number of the egg white proteins possess antimicrobial properties. These include enzyme inhibitors,

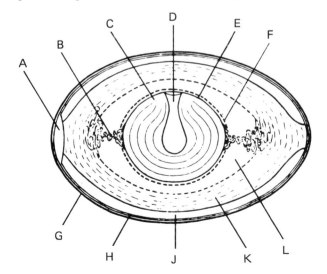

Figure 11.1 The physical structure of the hen's egg. A, air cell; B, chalaza; C, yolk; D, germinal disc and white yolk; E, vitelline membrane; F, film of mucin; G, shell; H, shell membranes; J, outer thin white; K, thick white; L, inner thin white. Reprinted with permission from Brooks and Hale (1959).

Table 11.1 Egg white proteins[a]

Protein	% of total solids	Classification
Ovalbumin	54	Phospho- and glycoprotein
Conalbumin	13	Iron-binding glycoprotein
Ovomucoids	11	Trypsin inhibitor glycoproteins
Lysozyme	3.5	Enzyme
Ovomucins	1.5	Glycoproteins
Ovoglycoprotein	0.5	Glycoprotein
Ovoinhibitors	0.1	Protease inhibitor, glycoproteins
Ovomacroglobulin	0.5	Glycoproteins, immunogenic
Other globulins	4.0	
Flavoprotein	0.8	Binds riboflavin, glycoprotein
Avidin	0.05	Binds biotin, glycoprotein

[a]After Robinson (1972).

immunoglobulins, vitamin binding proteins and the iron binding protein, now known as ovotransferrin (*Table 11.1*). Lysozyme is also present in egg white in very substantial amounts, lysozyme being an enzyme capable of hydrolysing the peptidoglycan component of cell walls of many microorganisms.

For both the domestic and the industrial markets the egg contents afford a valuable source of human food. The yolk contains approximately 50% solids, consisting of almost equal amounts of protein and lipid. Also the yolk contains substantial quantities of vitamin D and vitamin A, which arise from the animal food fed to the hens. The yolk also contains significant amounts of calcium and magnesium, whereas egg white contains greater amounts of sodium and potassium (*Table 11.2*). Egg white contains approximately 12% protein and hence 88% water. However, for both egg white and yolk the amino acid composition of the proteins affords a valuable source of essential amino acids. Indeed because of their high nutritional value, egg proteins have been used widely as a reference protein for nutritional studies in both animals and man. In addition to their important nutritional value egg proteins, and in particular egg white proteins, possess a number of valuable functional properties which include heat-induced gelation, foam enhancement, foam stabilisation and emulsification. It is these properties which determine the still widespread use of whole liquid egg and other egg products by the food industry, and in particular the confectionery industry and the housewife. For example, the main egg protein, ovalbumin, which represents up to 54% of the total dry solids of egg white, exhibits a heat set property and thus egg white solidifies to form a solid and very well recognised gelatinous structure at

Table 11.2 Major inorganic elements in egg components[a]

Element	% of total liquid	
	White	Yolk
Na	0.15	0.055
K	0.14	0.094
Ca	0.013	0.13
Mg	0.01	0.13
S	0.2	0.16
Cl	0.13	0.13

[a]After Shenstone (1968).

approximately 60 °C. This unique property is due to the heat denaturation of ovalbumin at approximately 60 °C. Such commercially valuable characteristics account for the still widespread use of egg white as a constituent of many food products. Commercially, egg albumen is also widely used by the confectionery industry because of its ability to form stable foams. Foam formation and foam stability, in addition to the desirable heat denaturation properties of ovalbumin, are important commercially for the manufacture of meringues, angel cake, sponge cakes and other confectionery products. Various attempts by food manufacturers have been made to replace egg white in some of these foods, but in general terms this has not been successful due to the instability of foams produced by alternative novel protein products, which often lack the precise heat denaturation characteristic of ovalbumin and the foam stabilising role of egg white ovomucins. However, for the continued use of eggs, both commercially and in the home, it is likely to be increasingly important for the poultry industry to supply products of the highest quality, which can be used preferentially because of good foaming and heat set properties. Furthermore such products, as ingredients for many foods, should contain a minimum number of contaminating microorganisms which can produce thermostable enzymes that may impair the desirable functional properties. The procurement of egg products with low microbial counts depends partly on the structural integrity of the whole egg, where the yolk is maintained in a central position by the chalazae and the layer of thick albumen (*Figure 11.1*). Hence the industry should aim to produce eggs of the highest internal quality and readily downgrade inferior products.

The role of ovomucin

The commercially valuable foaming property of egg albumen has been shown by Johnson and Zabic (1981a) to be positively correlated to both the amount of ovomucin and the interaction of ovomucin with other globulin type proteins present in egg white. Using separate egg white proteins, obtained by prior fractionation, Johnson and Zabic (1981a) showed through the application of response surface methodology that increased amounts of ovomucin, lysozyme and ovalbumin increased angel cake volume. Direct correlations between ovomucin and lysozyme levels with foaming index values were also observed; the region of optimum response was defined by low levels of lysozyme and high levels of ovomucin. During the baking process ovomucin–lysozyme complexes also offered a protective effect on foam volume, as ovomucin alone was shown to give rise to foams which collapsed during baking, whereas the addition of small amounts of lysozyme to ovomucin solutions produced a protective effect (Johnson and Zabic, 1981b). Furthermore, ultrastructural studies using electron microscopy (Johnson and Zabic, 1981c) have shown that lysozyme improves the overall foam appearance. This is thought to be due to an association with ovomucin to form an ovomucin–lysozyme complex. Mori, Nakamura and Sato (1974) have also claimed that the decrease in foaming power of egg white during frozen storage at −20 °C is caused by changes in the egg white globulins and ovomucin.

For a long time it has been known that ovomucin is also important for maintaining the structural integrity of the egg, as shown in *Figure 11.1*, where the albumen is separated mainly into layers of thin and thick. The thick albumen in fresh eggs represents approximately 50% of the total egg white. The gelatinous nature of the thick albumen and the integrity of the chalazae are believed to be due to the unique molecular structure of ovomucin glycoproteins. The evidence for the importance of ovomucin resides firstly in the fact that the thick egg white gel fraction contains four times more ovomucin than the thin egg white fractions. Moreover, it was shown by Brooks and Hale (1961), and Robinson and Monsey (1972a), that thick egg albumen contains the greatest amount of ovomucin, and that the concentration of ovomucin declines in association with the natural liquefaction of egg white during the storage of whole shell eggs. Furthermore, fresh eggs which differ in albumen firmness also differ in their content of ovomucin; those eggs which possess the thickest albumen contained the most ovomucin. It has been claimed by Butler *et al.* (1972) that disease impairs synthesis of albumen proteins in the magnum of the hen, which ultimately affects the internal quality of the laid eggs.

Austic (1977) has shown that eggs removed from laying hens prior to their entry to the shell gland contained a greater proportion of thick egg white and a higher concentration of ovomucin. After plumping in the shell gland, which involves the absorption of water and minerals and probably many other substances, the amount of thick egg white and ovomucin decreases (Solomon, 1976). Austic (1977) also showed that the variation of ovomucin in the proportion of thick egg white of eggs obtained at oviposition seemed to be related to the events of plumping occurring in the shell gland of the laying hen. Sauveur (1973) has demonstrated using oviducal eggs, that albumen height and viscosity are influenced by the composition of external solutions within which the albumen is bathed. Thus, it appears that during the plumping of eggs in the shell gland substances are introduced into the thick egg white which bring about a simultaneous contraction of the thick egg white gel and a decrease in the content of ovomucin. However, for high quality newly laid eggs this contraction of the thick egg white gel is limited, whereas for poor quality newly laid eggs the contraction of the thick egg white gel may be excessive during the plumping of the egg in the shell gland of the laying hen. Such observations may ultimately provide clues to the molecular mechanism of the natural liquefaction of the thick egg white gel.

The chemical composition of ovomucin

In order to understand how ovomucin determines the gelatinous properties of thick egg white and enhances foam stability, it is necessary to determine the chemical composition of ovomucin, its heterogeneity and the molecular structure of the ovomucin macromolecules. To the protein chemist ovomucin, as obtained after dilution of egg white with four volumes of water, was until 1964 an intractable substance due to its gross insolubility in aqueous solution. Reduction of the disulphide bonds of ovomucin by mercaptoethanol in the presence of 8 M urea as a denaturing agent (Robinson and Monsey, 1964) yielded reduced ovomucins, which were eventually fractionated into two components by preparative ultracentrifugation in density gradients. A full description of these components designated α- and β-ovomucins was given by Robinson and Monsey (1971). The two α- and β-ovomucins clearly exist before reduction with thiol reagents, as the complex insoluble and intractable copolymer linked covalently by disulphide bonds. It has since been shown that the carbohydrate-rich and carbohydrate-poor components initially described by Kato and Sato (1971) are chemically similar to the α- and β-ovomucins. Analytical ultracentrifugation of the reduced ovomucins, in the presence of 5 M guanidinium chloride (GuCl), showed the presence of the more

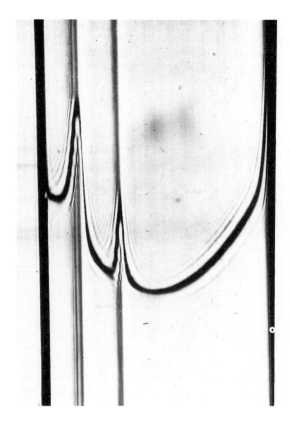

Figure 11.2 Schileren picture of reduced α- and β-ovomucins separated for the analytical ultracentrifuge. Reprinted with permission from Robinson and Monsey (1975).

rapidly sedimenting β-ovomucin component and the slower sedimenting α-ovomucin component (*Figure 11.2*). The molecular weight of the reduced α-ovomucin has been calculated to be 210 000 (Robinson and Monsey, 1971), whereas reduced β-ovomucin is an aggregate (MW 720 000) of a smaller monomer (MW 112 000) (Robinson and Monsey, 1975). However, analytical ultracentrifugation in the presence of urea only showed the presence of one sedimenting component which demonstrates even in the presence of 8 M urea, the existence of a non-covalently bonded intermolecular complex of reduced α- and β-ovomucins (Robinson and Monsey, 1966). The methods used by Kato and Sato (1972) for the fractionation of ovomucin into carbohydrate-rich and carbohydrate-poor components also require the presence of reducing reagents:

$$\text{Ovomucin complex} + \text{HS—CH}_2\text{—CH}_2\text{—OH} \xrightarrow[\text{GuCl}]{5\,\text{M}} \underset{\substack{\uparrow \\ \text{SH}}}{\alpha\text{-ovomucin}} + \underset{\substack{\uparrow \\ \text{SH}}}{\beta\text{-ovomucin}}$$

$$\text{mercaptoethanol}$$

Although Hayakawa and Sato (1976, 1978) have used ultrasonic methods for dispersing ovomucin, it also seems possible that depolymerisation during such treatment may have occurred due to the action of free radicals, which can arise during the ultrasonic treatment of cellular material. The solubilisation of ovomucin by sodium dodecyl sulphate (Adachi et al., 1973) in the absence of reducing agent only produces large aggregates (30S and 35S).

Table 11.3 The carbohydrates of egg white glycoproteins[a]

	Glucosamine (g/100 g)	Galactosamine (g/100 g)	Galactose (g/100 g)	Mannose (g/100 g)	Sialic acid (g/100 g)
Ovalbumin	1.2	–	–	1.7–2.0	–
Ovotransferrin	1.7	–	–	0.9	–
Ovomucoids	9.5–17.7	–	0.53–4.07	6.4–8.6	0.03–2.23
α-ovomucin	5.4	0.5	1.8	4.6	1.0
β-ovomucins	12.3	8.9	22.00	0.7	13.8
Flavoprotein	8.7	–	1.1	3.9	0.86
Ovoglycoprotein	13.8	–	4.5	9.0	3.0
Ovomacroglobulin	5.5	–	(0.3)	–
Ovoinhibitors	2.8–5.6	–	–	2.1–3.7	0.1–0.3
Avidin	4.1			4.6	

[a]Reprinted with permission from Robinson (1972).

Like the other egg white proteins, with the exception of lysozyme, the α- and β-ovomucins are glycoproteins (*Table 11.3*). During the isolation and purification of the ovomucin complex, lysozyme is also coprecipitated, lysozyme itself being a cationic protein with a high isoelectric point (pI approximately 10.2) and hence with an overall positive charge at acidic, neutral and slightly alkaline pH values. The α- and β-ovomucins clearly have different chemical compositions (Robinson and Monsey, 1971, 1975). The β-ovomucin, in view of its high content of carbohydrate, could perhaps be considered to be mainly a polysaccharide. The composition of β-ovomucin is unusual, insofar as it contains large quantities of N–acetylgalactosamine, galactose and sialic acid (N–acetylneuraminic acid). These monosaccharides are not present in the other egg white glycoproteins, which on the contrary contain small amounts of the other aldoses, N–acetylglucosamine and mannose. As during the storage of eggs the content of β-ovomucin decreases (*Table 11.4*), it is clear that the β-ovomucin component is substantially responsible for the

Table 11.4 Relative amounts of α- and β-reduced ovomucins present in the preparations

Sample[a]	% of total peak area	
	α-reduced	β-reduced
(1)	65.9	34.0
(2)	73.7	26.2
(3)	86.0	13.9
(4)	91.2	8.7

[a]Sample (1): ovomucin complex from newly laid thick egg white; Sample (2): ovomucin complex from thick egg white which contained magnesium acetate (I = 0.03) held at 37 °C for 20 h; Sample (3): ovomucin complex from thick egg white which contained sodium chloride (I = 0.03) held at 37 °C for 20 h; Sample (4): ovomucin complex from thick egg white without additive held at 37 °C for 20 h.
Reprinted with permission from Robinson and Monsey (1972b)

Table 11.5 Chemical composition of S–carboxymethyl-β-ovomucin (amino acids were determined by using anhydrous molecular weights).

	Content of dry sample (g/100 g)	Content of total protein (mol/10^5 g)
Lysine	1.73	50.9
Ammonia	1.60	
Histidine	0.63	17.3
Arginine	0.92	22.2
Aspartic acid	1.41	46.4
Threonine[a]	4.35	162.8
Serine[a]	3.73	162.0
Glutamic acid	2.30	67.4
Proline	2.22	86.6
Glycine	0.54	35.6
Alanine	0.94	50.0
Valine	1.22	46.6
Cysteine (half)[b]	0.92	33.9
Methionine	0.50	14.4
Isoleucine	1.06	35.4
Leucine	2.00	66.7
Tyrosine	0.99	23.0
Phenylalanine	0.99	25.4
Total protein	28.05	
Glucosamine	12.30	244.9
Galactosamine	8.86	176.5
Galactose	22.00	435.3
Mannose	0.70	13.9
Total Sialic acid	10.59	122.3
Sulphate	4.24	157.6
Total	86.74	

[a]Corrected for destruction (threonine 5.7% loss; serine 9.2% loss)
[b]Determined as S–carboxymethylcysteine
Reprinted with permission from Robinson and Monsey (1975).

gelatinous properties of the thick egg white gel (Robinson and Monsey, 1972a; Kato et al., 1979). Chemical analysis has also shown that the high carbohydrate content of β-ovomucin is closely associated with a high content of the hydroxy amino acids, serine and threonine (*Table 11.5*). These amino acids are often found as the linkage points for oligosaccharide residues to polypeptide chains. The linkage point between hydroxy amino acids and hexosamines in such glycoproteins is normally a glycosidic bond between the hydroxyl group of the amino acid and the anomeric carbon atom of a N–acetylhexosamine residue. Degradative studies on isolated β-ovomucin, using proteolytic enzymes to hydrolyse the peptide moieties (Kato, Hirata and Kobayashi, 1978) have shown that at least some of the carbohydrate exists as trisaccharide units linked to serine or threonine residues (*Figure 11.3*). The oligosaccharide isolated was enriched with hydroxy amino acids (*Table 11.6*). The trisaccharide isolated was sulphated and contained equimolar amounts of N–acetylgalactosamine, galactose, sialic acid and sulphate. The β-glycosidically linked oligosaccharide is relatively linear and contains a high density of negative charges which are provided by sialic acid and a sulphonic acid group. Clearly such oligosaccharide chains are likely to associate through ionic bonds with both mineral cations, like magnesium and sodium, or cationic proteins, such as lysozyme. Thus the β-ovomucin component may be responsible at the

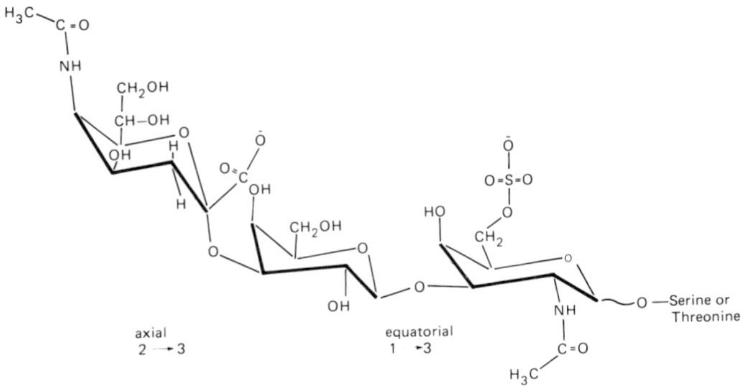

Figure 11.3 Possible structure of β-ovomucin trisaccharide. Compiled from Kato, Hirata and Kobayashi (1978).

Table 11.6 Amino acid composition of sulphated glycopeptides in ovomucin

Amino acids	Contents (mol/100 mol)
Lys	3.6
His	1.0
Arg	1.7
Asp	trace
Thr	24.8
Ser	24.0
Glu	4.0
Pro	16.3
Gly	trace
Ala	6.6
Cys	0
Val	4.4
Met	0.9
Ile	2.7
Leu	8.0
Tyr	trace
Phe	trace
Trp	0

Reprinted with permission from Kato *et al.* (1982).

molecular level for both the gelatinous properties of thick egg white, through either self association and entanglement or the previously proposed interaction with lysozyme (Brooks and Hale, 1961). However, the other type of oligosaccharide detected by Kato, Hirata and Kobayashi (1978) and named oligosaccharide (1), which has not yet been characterised, might be equally important for the maintenance of the thick egg white gel.

Support for the proposal that such oligosaccharides have an important role for the formation and stability of gels can be obtained from consideration of the molecular structure of other gelling agents, such as carageenans and alginates (*Figure 11.4*) often used in the food industry. Alginates contain blocks of L-guluronic acid (*Figure 11.4*) that are believed to be responsible for the formation of a polymer network resulting in restricted molecular movement in solution, and hence gelation. The carageenans contain sulphated polysaccharide chains which

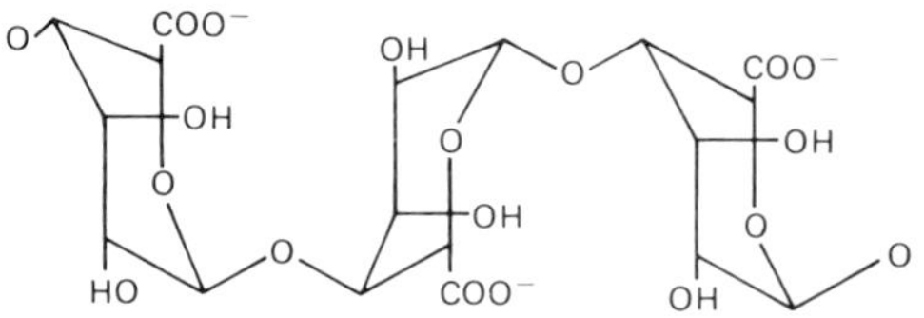

Figure 11.4 The twisted molecular structure for blocks of guluronic acid residues in alginic acid. Reprinted with permission from Sime (1983).

may associate through ionic salt-like links with metal ions. Other gelling agents used in foods are agar, guar gum and carob gum, which are also polysaccharides. On the other hand, some proteins like gelatin can form gels at ambient temperature due to localised intermolecular interactions between the unusual helical chains present in degraded collagen. Soybean gels are formed due to the presence of high polymers which arise from extensive disulphide bonding between different glycinin subunits. Thus compositional similarities exist between the ovomucins, other polysaccharide gelling agents and the disulphide bonded soybean proteins. However, unlike some of the other food gels, thick egg white exhibits shear thinning (Robinson and Monsey, 1972a). This thixotropic property suggests that entanglement of polymer chains, rather than the existence of knots and localised junctions, is responsible for the semi-solid nature of the thick egg white gel. However, while it is clear that β-ovomucin is solubilised, and probably degraded, during the natural liquefaction of the thick egg white gel, the mechanism by which the solubilisation occurs remains unknown.

Liquefaction of thick egg white

Various suggestions for the mechanism of thick egg white liquefaction have included the hydrolysis by protease enzymes, the depolymerisation by hydroxyl ion at increasing pH values, the reduction by thiol type reducing agents and the interaction with lysozyme. Given the chemical composition of native ovomucin as a disulphide bonded glycoprotein complex, it is clear that proteolytic enzymes and disulphide bond reducing agents will all depolymerise ovomucin and hence bring about the associated liquefaction of thick egg white. Hydroxyl ion would also be expected to cause the depolymerisation of ovomucin and liquefaction of thick egg white gels. However, such a demonstration of liquefaction induced by chemical additives (Donovan, Davis and Wiele, 1972; Tomimatsu and Donovan, 1972; Beveridge and Nakai, 1975) does not establish that these substances are themselves solely responsible for the natural liquefaction of the egg white gel or the natural depolymerisation of ovomucin. Additionally, it may now be suggested, in view of the existence of O-glycosidically linked trisaccharides, specifically in β-ovomucin, that enzymatic hydrolysis of this glycosidic link may also be responsible for the liquefaction of the thick egg white gel. However, such enzymes have not yet been detected in samples of fresh egg white or shell gland plumping fluid. Although chemical cleavage of the O-glycosidically linked trisaccharide has been observed in the presence of hydroxyl ion by Kato *et al.* (1979), it is not known whether such a chemical reaction takes place during the natural liquefaction of thick egg white gel at the relatively low pH value of 9.2 in native egg white.

Ovomucin–lysozyme interaction

Just as it is not yet possible to define the mechanism by which ovomucins are depolymerised during egg white liquefaction, likewise it is not yet possible to describe how the α- and β-ovomucin components give rise to a gelatinous structure at the molecular level. Due to the acidic nature of ovomucins, and in particular the cationic nature of lysozyme, it has frequently been suggested (Brooks and Hale, 1961; Kato and Sato, 1972; Robinson, 1972) that the gelatinous nature of egg white is due to the interaction between ovomucin and lysozyme. Alternatively, it has also been suggested that the destruction of the gelatinous nature of thick egg white is due to an enhanced interaction with ovomucin and lysozyme as the natural pH of the egg white changes after oviposition (Hawthorne, 1950; Robinson, 1972). However, these two hypotheses are not necessarily mutually exclusive. The evidence for these hypotheses is based on the long known observation of lysozyme coprecipitating with ovomucins during their isolation and purification. Such aggregation arises from the increased electrostatic interactions between the positively charged lysozyme molecules and the negatively charged ovomucins, as the ionic strength of the solution is decreased by dilution with water. Further evidence for the association between ovomucins and lysozyme has been obtained by Robinson and Monsey (1972b) and Miller, Kato and Nakai (1982). It has been shown that the aggregation from solution between lysozyme and reduced carboxylated ovomucins increases as the pH value changes from 7 to 9, which corresponds with the changing pH value of egg white at the oviposition. However, such aggregation, as evidenced by precipitation, does not seem to occur during the natural thinning of egg white. Recently it has been claimed by Hayakawa *et al.* (1983) that β-ovomucin inhibits the formation of α-ovomucin–lysozyme complexes. The methods of Hayakawa *et al.* (1983) are novel insofar as measurements of both protein and carbohydrate are used in conjunction with simultaneous equations to determine the concentrations of the individual α- and β-ovomucin components in solutions. Such a hypothesis is compatible with the findings of Robinson and Monsey (1972a) and Kato *et al.* (1981), where it was shown that only α-ovomucin was isolated as a lysozyme complex from stored egg albumen. Additionally, self-association and interaction of reduced α- and β-ovomucin has also been observed during ultracentrifugation (Miller, Kato and Nakai, 1982), even in the presence of 6 M urea as a denaturing reagent (Robinson and Monsey, 1966, 1971). Furthermore, as α- and β-ovomucins are in reality reduced ovomucins, and have only been isolated and separated after reduction of disulphide bonds or ultrasonic disintegration, it seems likely that the self-association and interaction of α- and β-ovomucins (Miller, Kato and Nakai, 1982) in egg white is greater than previously recognised, as the α- and β-ovomucins are combined and exist as one ovomucin complex in native egg white. Now it seems unlikely that the formation of an ovomucin–lysozyme complex is the sole cause of egg white thinning, and more likely that β-ovomucin is specifically degraded during egg white liquefaction.

It has been found that the separate addition of magnesium ion to thick egg white gel results in stabilisation of the thick egg white gel (Robinson and Monsey, 1972b) and inhibits the natural liquefaction reaction (Monsey and Robinson, 1974).

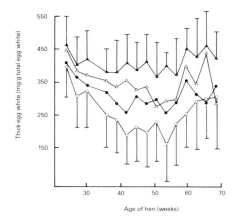

Figure 11.5 The effect of dietary magnesium and age of hen on the proportion of thick egg white of eggs stored at 20 °C for 20 d. (○) diet containing 1.6 g Mg/kg given from 1 d old; (●) diet containing 4.1 g Mg/kg given from 1 d old; (△) diet containing 8.1 g Mg/kg given from 1 d old; (▲) diet containing 4.3 g Mg/kg given from 21 weeks of age. Reprinted with permission from Monsey *et al.* (1977).

Furthermore, dietary additions of magnesium ion to the food of laying hens results in stabilisation of the thick egg white gel (*Figure 11.5*) coupled to incorporation of greater amounts of magnesium ion into egg albumen (Monsey *et al.*, 1977). As β-ovomucins in particular are acidic glycoproteins containing sialic acid and ester sulphate, and as the natural liquefaction of egg white is inhibited in the presence of magnesium ion, and as magnesium ion also inhibits ovomucin–lysozyme interactions (*Figure 11.6*), it is tempting to speculate that Mg^{2+}, due to its small size and high charge density, replaces lysozyme in ovomucin complexes and gives rise to a more stable magnesium–ovomucin complex in egg albumen.

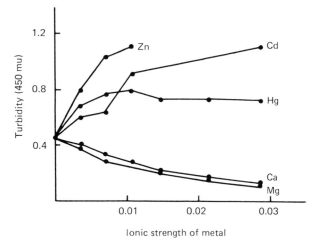

Figure 11.6 The effect of cations on the aggregation of reduced ovomucins with lysozyme. Reprinted with permission from Robinson (1972).

Forward view

In the future further information gained for the chemical composition and the unique molecular structure of β-ovomucins may ultimately allow the application of non-destructive physical methods for the determination of egg white quality in whole shell eggs. Nuclear magnetic resonance spectroscopy might ultimately afford such a non-destructive technique capable of detecting the presence of identifiable glycoproteins in egg white.

Other studies concerned with elucidating the mechanism of glycoprotein biosynthesis have indicated that the glycosylation of ribosomal synthesised proteins occurs in the endoplasmic reticulum of cells as a post-ribosomal event. Therefore, it seems likely that for the biosynthesis of ovomucin in the magnum tissues of the hen, the synthesis of a single homogenous pro-ovomucin protein moiety would be controlled genetically, whereas the subsequent glycosylation reactions would primarily be controlled by the presence of glycosylating enzymes and carrier substances within the oviduct secreting cells. An example of the biosynthesis of a single homogeneous precursor protein can be found in the case of legume proteins, where post-ribosomal glycosylation, and proteolysis, are responsible for the formation of subunits which are linked through disulphide bonds (Gatehouse, Croy and Boulter, 1984).

References

ADACHI, N., AZUMA, J., JANADO, M. and ONODERA, K. (1973). Solubilisation and characterisation of ovomucin without chemical modification. *Agricultural and Biological Chemistry.*, **37**, 2175–2180

AUSTIC, R.E. (1977). Role of the shell gland in determination of albumen quality. *Poultry Science*, **56**, 202–210

BEVERIDGE, T. and NAKAI, S. (1975). Effect of sulphydryl blocking on the thinning of egg white. *Journal of Food Science*, **40**, 864–868

BROOKS, J. and HALE, H.P. (1959). The mechanical properties of the thick white of the hen's egg. *Biochimica et Biophysica Acta*, **32**, 237–250

BROOKS, J. and HALE, H.P. (1961). The mechanical properties of the thick white of the hen's egg II. The relation between rigidity and composition. *Biochimica et Biophysica Acta*, **46**, 289–301

BUTLER, E.J., CURTIS, M.J., PEARSON, A.W. and MCDOUGALL, J.S. (1972). Effect of infectious bronchitis on the structure and composition of egg albumen. *Journal of the Science of Food and Agriculture*, **23**, 359–369

DONOVAN, J.W., DAVIS, J.G. and WIELE, M.B. (1973). Viscometric studies of alkaline degradation of ovomucin. *Journal of Agricultural and Food Chemistry*, **20**, 223–228

GATEHOUSE, J.A., CROY, R.R.D. and BOULTER, D. (1984). The synthesis and structure of pea storage proteins. *CRC Critical Reviews in Plant Sciences*, **1**, 287–314

HAWTHORNE, J.R. (1950). The action of egg white lysozyme on ovomucoid and ovomucin. *Biochimica et Biophysica Acta*, **6**, 28–35

HAYAKAWA, S. and SATO, Y. (1976). Studies on the dissociation of the soluble ovomucin by sonication. *Agricultural and Biological Chemistry*, **40**, 2397–2404

HAYAKAWA, S. and SATO, Y. (1978). Subunit structures of sonicated α- and β-ovomucin and their molecular weights estimated by sedimentation equilibrium. *Agricultural and Biological Chemistry*, **42**, 957–961

HAYAKAWA, S., KONDO, H., NAKAMURA, R. and SATO, Y. (1983). Effect of β-ovomucin on the solubility of α-ovomucin and further inspection of the structure of ovomucin complex in thick egg white. *Agricultural and Biological Chemistry.*, **47**, 815–820

JOHNSON, T.M. and ZABIC, M.E. (1981a). Response surface methodology for analysis of protein interactions in angel food cakes. *Journal of Food Science*, **46**, 1226–1230

JOHNSON, T.M. and ZABIC, M.E. (1981b). Egg albumen proteins interaction in an angel food cake system. *Journal of Food Science*, **46**, 1231–1236

JOHNSON, T.M. and ZABIC, M.E. (1981c). Ultrastructural examination of egg albumen protein foams. *Journal of Food Science*, **46**, 1237–1240

KATO, A. and SATO, Y. (1971). The separation and characterisation of carbohydrate rich component from ovomucin in chicken eggs. *Agricultural and Biological Chemistry*, **35**, 439–440

KATO, A. and SATO, Y. (1972). The release of carbohydrate rich component from ovomucin gel during storage. *Agricultural and Biological Chemistry*, **36**, 831–836

KATO, A., HIRATA, S. and KOBAYASHI, K. (1978). Structure of the sulphated oligosaccharide chain of ovomucin. *Agricultural and Biological Chemistry*, **42**, 1025–1029

KATO, A., OGINO, K., KURAMOTO, Y. and KOBAYASHI, K. (1979). Degradation of the O-glycosidically linked carbohydrate units of ovomucin during egg white thinning. *Journal of Food Science*, **44**, 1341–1344

KATO, A., OGATA, S., MATSUDOMI, N. and KOBAYASHI, K. (1981). Comparative study of aggregated and disaggregated ovomucin during egg white thinning. *Journal of Agricultural and Food Chemistry*, **29**, 821–823

KATO, A., MIYOSHI, Y., SUGA, M. and KOBAYASHI, K. (1982). Separation and characterisation of sulphated glycopeptides from ovomucin, chalazae and yolk membrane in chicken eggs. *Agricultural and Biological Chemistry*, **46**, 1285–1290

MILLER, S.M., KATO, A. and NAKAI, S. (1982). Sedimentation equilibrium study of the interaction between egg white lysozyme and ovomucin. *Journal of Agricultural and Food Chemistry*, **30**, 1127–1132

MONSEY, J.B. and ROBINSON, D.S. (1974). The relationship between the concentration of metals and the rate of liquefaction of thick egg white. *British Poultry Science*, **15**, 369–373

MONSEY, J.B., ROBINSON, D.S., MILLER, W.S. and ELLIS, M. (1977). The effect of feeding magnesium-enriched diets on the quality of albumen of stored eggs. *British Journal of Nutrition*, **37**, 35–44

MORI, T., NAKAMURA, R. and SATO, Y. (1974). Frozen storage of eggs III. Changes in the foaming power of frozen egg white. *Journal of Food Science and Technology*, **21**, 228–233

ROBINSON, D.S. (1972). Egg white glycoproteins and the physical properties of egg white. In *Egg Formation and Production*, (Freeman, B.M. and Lake, P.E., eds), pp. 65–86. Edinburgh, British Poultry Science Ltd

ROBINSON, D.S. and MONSEY, J.B. (1964). Reduction of ovomucin by mercaptoethanol. *Biochimica et Biophysica Acta*, **83**, 368–370

ROBINSON, D.S. and MONSEY, J.B. (1966). The composition of ovomucin. *Biochemical Journal*, **100**, 61P

ROBINSON, D.S. and MONSEY, J.B. (1971). Studies on the composition of egg-white ovomucin. *Biochemical Journal*, **121**, 537–547

ROBINSON, D.S. and MONSEY, J.B. (1972a). Changes in the composition of ovomucin during liquefaction of thick egg white. *Journal of the Science of Food and Agriculture*, **23**, 29–38

ROBINSON, D.S. and MONSEY, J.B. (1972b). Changes in the composition of ovomucin during liquefaction of thick egg white: the effect of ionic strength and magnesium salts. *Journal of the Science of Food and Agriculture*, **23**, 893–904

ROBINSON, D.S. and MONSEY, J.B. (1975). The composition and proposed subunit structure of egg-white β-ovomucin: the isolation of an unreduced soluble ovomucin. *Biochemical Journal*, **147**, 55–62

SAUVEUR, B. (1973). Reconstitution in vitro de determinimes des proprietes physiques de l'albumen de l'oeuf. *Journal des Recherches Avicoles*, 317–321

SHENSTONE, F.S. (1968). The gross composition, chemistry and physico-chemical basis of organisation of the yolk and white. In *Egg Quality. A Study of the Hen's Egg*, (Carter, T.C., ed.), pp. 26–58. Edinburgh. Oliver and Boyd

SIME, W.J. (1983). The practical utilisation of alginates in food gelling systems. In *Gums and Stabilisers for the Food Industry 2—Applications of Hydrocolloids*, (Phillips, G.O., Wedlock, D.J. and Williams, P.A., eds), pp. 177–188. Oxford, Pergamon Press

SOLOMON, S.E. (1976). The thinning of thick egg white—an ultrastructural and histochemical evaluation. *Anatomia, Histologica Embryologic*, **5**, 96

TOMIMATSU, Y. and DONOVAN, J.W. (1972). Light scattering study of ovomucin. *Journal of Agricultural and Food Chemistry*, **20**, 1067–1073

Part IV

Control of egg quality

Chapter 12

Genetic manipulation of egg quality

Grahame Bulfield and J.C. McKay

Introduction

Any trait that can be measured and exhibits variation in a population of animals can in principle be subjected to genetic analysis and genetic improvement. Most traits of commercial importance in farm animals show continuous variation and have been improved by applying the techniques of quantitative genetics; improvement may continue for many (30+) generations. There are also a number of single gene mutations that have been important in animal breeding; these can be handled by classical Mendelian genetics and the characteristics either fixed or completely removed in a few generations. Recently the application of recombinant DNA methodology to farm animals has added to the more classical breeding techniques. It is now possible to clone and insert single foreign genes into the germline of an animal, referred to as genetic engineering or genetic manipulation.

Each of these approaches and their application to genetic improvement will be discussed in turn.

Animal breeding techniques

Quantitative genetics

The full range of quantitative genetic techniques listed below has been applied with success to the improvement of all aspects of egg production, including egg quality:

(a) selection between strains and strain replacement;
(b) formation and screening of new synthetic strains;
(c) selection within strains.

The initial screening of strains and testing of new synthetic strains has been particularly important in establishing modern brown egg laying strains. Although these strains have a broad genetic base, it may be necessary to screen exotic and unimproved strains again if egg quality criteria are redefined (*cf.* Simmons and Somes, 1985).

Traditional selection within strains has been as dramatically successful when applied to egg quality traits as for other poultry production traits. Not only have population means been improved for traits like egg shell colour, albumen quality and shell strength but birds produce high quality eggs more consistently and do so for a higher proportion of the laying cycle. The number of egg quality traits under selection may be extended as consumer demands require and prospects are good for improvement in these traits. For example, aspects of composition such as cholesterol and fat content or ratio of yolk to white have heritabilities in the range of 0.3–0.5 (Kinney, 1969; Marks and Washburn, 1977; Washburn and Marks, 1977). These data suggest that almost any aspect of egg quality which can be expressed in quantitative terms (Wells, 1968) can be altered by conventional animal breeding techniques. However, there may be limits to progress such as low hatchability of eggs in populations selected for low cholesterol or fat content (Washburn and Marks, 1977).

Changing the frequency of alleles of large effect

The fixation of favourable alleles

Where polymorphism exists for single genes of large effect, schemes to remove deleterious alleles will make the population more uniform and improve the mean. For example, most commercial brown egg layer populations are polymorphic for an allele causing low amine oxidase activity in the liver. When fed precursors of trimethylamine (e.g. rapeseed meal) birds with low oxidase activity lay eggs with a fishy taint. The development of a simple test to detect these individuals (McKay and Paton, 1984) will allow commercial breeders to remove susceptible animals in a few generations of selection.

Introduction of a gene of major effect by backcrossing

This procedure is very familiar in poultry breeding where there has been a recurrent need to introduce alleles from exotic or unimproved populations into commercial strains. Examples would include the introduction of the dwarfing genes into broiler stocks and, for egg production, specific disease resistance alleles at the B locus and egg colour genes. These are expensive programmes but there may be a need for more in the future as more genes are identified with effects on general performance or specific aspects of egg quality.

Gene transfer by irradiated semen

Pandey and Patchell (1982) have suggested that irradiated male gametes can be used to transfer single genes or blocks of genes between strains or even between species. The technique is being developed in a number of plant species, but our experiments with poultry (McKay and Wishart, 1984) have failed to demonstrate stable genetic transformation of strains by various genes affecting egg quality and other traits. Further investigation of the technique is necessary because it may offer an immediate and inexpensive alternative to backcrossing and because it may allow the transfer of genes between strains or even species without knowledge of the molecular basis of the genetic differences.

Molecular genetic techniques

There are four stages in achieving genetic manipulation of farm animals (Bulfield, 1985). All of them present some technical problems:

(1) The identification of the genes to clone;
(2) The cloning and manipulation of the genes;
(3) Injection of the cloned DNA into a recipient embryo so as to transform the germline;
(4) Ensuring that the injected foreign DNA is expressed in the right amount in the right tissue at the right developmental time.

Gene identification

The possibility of using genetic manipulation to improve egg quality will focus much more attention on defining accepted quality characteristics in biochemical terms. In particular, it now requires a detailed understanding of the importance of individual gene products in affecting quality. Until these gene products are identified individual genes cannot be cloned nor genetic manipulation effected. For example, what gene products (such as enzymes, hormones, cell surface receptors) are operating in the shell gland and convert the white shell of the Leghorn to the deep uniform chocolate brown of the Maran? In fact, further detail to the simple identification of a gene product might be required. Knowledge of how the gene is regulated or how its product is modified after synthesis could be essential. For example, many egg white proteins are glycosylated and this affects albumen quality; in the case of ovalbumin (*see* Robinson, Chapter 11 of this volume) its gel properties and hence quality characteristics are influenced by ovomucin. Ovomucin stability itself is under further enzymatic control. It is exactly the nature of and interaction between gene products such as these that will provide the basic information which is necessary in deciding which genes to clone and how they should be manipulated in such a way that they produce their product in a form and manner that will improve quality.

It is apparent from the above discussion that we are a considerable distance from understanding what makes up various aspects of egg quality at the level of individual gene products. The fact that genetic manipulation of poultry will be achieved very shortly and become routine in a few years makes it important to define egg quality in biochemical terms. The success of the application of these new techniques, in the medium term, will depend entirely on identifying and understanding the role of individual gene products in egg quality.

Gene cloning and embryo transformation

As previously discussed (Bulfield, 1985), techniques have been developed to allow cloning of almost any gene for which a purified protein product is available. Both the egg white (Baker, 1968; Gilbert, 1971; Sippel, 1984) and egg yolk (McIndoe, 1971; Ryffel and Wahli, 1984) contain small numbers of proteins that are present in large amounts (Shenstone, 1968). Several of the genes coding for these proteins have been cloned (Ryffel and Wahli, 1984; Sippel, 1984); in particular a considerable amount of information is available on the structure and the regulation of expression of the ovalbumin gene (O'Malley, Tsai and Schrader, 1983). It should also be possible to clone and characterise the gene coding for the major gene products of the shell gland (after Costanzo *et al.*, 1983).

Although the analysis of the structure and expression of the egg white and yolk protein genes has led to a substantial body of data of value to molecular geneticists, this information is not available in a form in which it could be used to modify egg quality characteristics. Once a quality trait has been defined in the biochemical terms discussed above, the fact that many of the genes have been cloned or should be relatively easy to clone, should enable rapid progress to be made.

DNA-mediated transformation of embryos producing 'transgenic' animals containing and expressing foreign genes has been achieved for mice (Palmiter *et al.*, 1982) and for rabbits, pigs and sheep (Hammer *et al.*, 1985). For these mammalian species, newly fertilised single cell embryos are flushed out of the oviduct and multiple copies of a single cloned gene injected into the male pronucleus. The manipulated embryos are then returned to a pseudopregnant foster mother. About 3% of embryos injected survive and are transgenic (or about 25% of animals born; Palmiter and Brinster, 1985). The important experiment is that of Palmiter *et al.* (1982) where about 600 copies of a hybrid DNA construct made from part of a metallothionein gene and a growth hormone gene was injected into mice. Six of the seven resultant transgenic animals produced large amounts of growth hormone in their liver and grew up to twice as big as their littermates (Evans, Swanson and Rosenfield, 1985). Therefore a characteristic of commercial importance, growth rate, has been altered by genetic engineering techniques.

The ovum of a chicken is considerably different to that of a mammal (Bell and Freeman, 1971) and therefore modified techniques of inserting the foreign DNA have had to be developed (e.g. Souza *et al.*, 1984). It is, however, likely that the first successful germline manipulation experiments will be achieved soon and will become routine in a few years.

Regulation of gene expression

The long-term aim of the genetic manipulation of farm animals will be to introduce copies of foreign genes into a host's germline and have them expressed at the correct level in the correct tissue (or in response to hormones) at the correct developmental time. In the hen's egg, for example, proteins are secreted into the egg white from the oviduct or transported from the liver to the egg yolk in response to oestrogen and progesterone. The proteins are often extensively modified after synthesis: e.g. in egg white, ovalbumin and other proteins are glycosylated; in the yolk, vitellogenin is split into lipovitellin and phosphovitin. Where it is necessary to modify these processes by genetic manipulation, detailed information on regulation of the gene's expression will be required. A lot is now known about the structure, organisation and sequence of genes in higher organisms but little is known about the regulation of their expression. DNA sequences surrounding the coding sequences for a gene (especially the 5' or upstream regions) do appear to have a regulatory function (Davidson, Jacobs and Britten, 1983) and these putative regulatory domains may stretch a considerable distance from the gene. For example, O'Malley, Tsai and Schrader (1983) consider the ovalbumin gene domain containing all the sequences which affect ovalbumin expression in some way, to be as large as 100 kilobases (kb) of DNA, whereas the ovalbumin gene itself only occupies 7.5 kb and the mature message containing the amino acid sequence, 1.87 kb. The molecular nature of the controls or 'switches' operating in this region is, to a large extent, unknown.

Using the ovalbumin gene as the best understood example, the details of some of the regulatory mechanisms controlling gene expression have recently been investigated by two approaches, reviewed by O'Malley, Tsai and Schrader (1983).

First a recombinant DNA construct was made between sequences from 753 nucleotides before the start of the ovalbumin gene and the structural (amino acid coding) part of the chicken β-globin gene. This novel hybrid 'ovalglobin' gene was then transfected into HeLa tissue culture cells. In these cells the hybrid gene did not respond to oestrogen or progesterone but did produce protein at a basal level. Next, six further ovalglobin constructs were made with differing numbers of nucleotides of the sequences preceding the ovalbumin gene (a) −753 (b) −222 (c) −95 (d) −77 (e) −48 and (f) −24. The approximate percentage expression of these constructs was: 100, 100, 100, 20, 2, 0, therefore indicating that the regions −77 to −48 and −48 to −24 must contain some regulatory sequences. In fact both these regions contain conserved sequences found preceding most eukaryotic genes, the −77 to −48 region a sequence resembling GGTCAATCT (the 'CAAT' box) and the −48 to −24 region a sequence like TATATAT (the 'TATA' box); both are putative promoter regulatory sequences.

A similar experiment was performed by transfecting the same ovalglobin DNA constructs into oviduct tubular gland cells. In these cells the constructs can be induced by progesterone, oestrogen and glucocorticoids. This time although removal of sequences from −753 to −222 still permitted progesterone induction, the removal of sequences from −222 to −95 abolished it. This applied to regulation by all three steroid hormones. Therefore, the sequences preceding the ovalbumin gene which regulate hormone induction are in the region −222 to −95 whereas those for constitutive regulation of expression (the promoter sequences) are in two other regions (−77 to −48 and −48 to −22).

This problem of gene regulation has been approached in a second way by O'Malley, Tsai and Schrader (1983). The affinity of short pieces of DNA preceding the ovalbumin gene for purified progesterone receptor was tested. A region −150 to −200 was shown to have a much greater affinity than any other region. A computer search for conserved sequences preceding six chicken oviduct genes which are all oestrogen-regulated showed that they all have a common nine base pair sequence at about −140 whereas three other chicken genes (not regulated by oestrogen) did not have this sequence.

These putative regulatory sequences can now be investigated directly. The DNA sequence can be mutated specifically by recombinant DNA techniques and the effect of the altered sequence on gene expression determined by transfecting hybrid constructs into tissue culture cells (as previously described). Once the DNA sequence of the various regulatory elements is known, these can be used to confer specific regulatory properties on novel gene constructs to be used in genetic manipulation experiments. For example, it would then be possible to put the oestrogen-sensitive sequences and sequences controlling oviduct expression from the ovalbumin gene onto *any* foreign gene and get the resulting protein produced at high levels in the oviduct and exported into the egg white. It will also be possible to modify the primary amino acid sequence of existing egg proteins to, for example, make them resistant to glycosylation or degradation.

Conclusions

The various genetic techniques available for improving egg quality have been discussed. It has been stressed that with both the classical techniques and genetic engineering techniques it is extremely important to define egg quality in repeatable measurable terms. For genetic manipulation it is further necessary to understand egg quality in biochemical terms, especially the gene and gene products involved. Once this essential biochemical and genetical information is available the genetic manipulation of egg quality will be possible.

References

BAKER, C.M.A. (1968). The proteins of egg white. In *Egg Quality. A Study of the Hen's Egg*, (Carter, T.C., ed.), pp. 67–108. Edinburgh, Oliver and Boyd

BELL, D.J. and FREEMAN, B.M. (Eds) (1971). *Physiology and Biochemistry of the Domestic Fowl, Volume 3*, London, Academic Press

BULFIELD, G. (1985). The potential for improvement of commercial poultry by genetic engineering techniques. In *Poultry Genetics and Breeding*, (Hill, W.G., Manson, J.M. and Hewitt, D., eds), pp. 37–46. Poultry Science Symposium Number 18, Harlow, Longmans/British Poultry Science Ltd

COSTANZO, F., CASTAGNOLI, L., DENTE, L., ARCARI, P., SMITH, M., COSTANZO, P., RAUGEI, G., IZZO, P., PIETROPAOLO, T.C., BOUGUELERET, L., CIMINO, F., SALVATORE, F. and CORTESE, R. (1983). Cloning of several cDNA segments coding for human liver proteins. *EMBO Journal*, **12**, 57–61

DAVIDSON, E.H., JACOBS, H.T. and BRITTEN, R.J. (1983). Very short repeats and coordinate induction of genes. *Nature*, **301**, 468–469

EVANS, R.M., SWANSON, L. and ROSENFIELD, M.G. (1985). Creation of transgenic animals to study development and as models of human disease. *Recent Progress in Hormone Research*, **41**, 317–337

GILBERT, A.B. (1971). The ovary. In *Physiology and Biochemistry of the Domestic Fowl, Volume 3*, (Bell, D.J. and Freeman, B.M., eds), pp. 1163–1235. London, Academic Press

HAMMER, R.E., PURSEL, V.G., REXROAD, C.E. JR., WALL, R.J., BOLT, D.J., EBERT, K.M., PALMITER, R.D. and BRINSTER, R.L. (1985). Production of transgenic rabbits, sheep and pigs by microinjection. *Nature*, **315**, 680–683

KINNEY, T.B. (1969). A summary of reported heritabilities and of genetic and phenotypic correlations for traits of chickens. *USDA Agriculture Handbook*, No. 363

MARKS, H.L. and WASHBURN, K.W. (1977). Divergent selection for yolk lipid and reproduction efficiency of the hen. *British Poultry Science*, **18**, 179–188

MCINDOE, W.W. (1971). Yolk synthesis. In *Physiology and Biochemistry of the Domestic Fowl, Volume 3*, (Bell, D.J. and Freeman, B.M., eds), pp. 1209–1223. London, Academic Press

MCKAY, J.C. and PATON, I.R. (1984). Genetics of egg tainting. In *Proceedings of the 17th World's Poultry Congress, Helsinki*, pp. 157–158

MCKAY, J.C. and WISHART, G.J.H. (1984). Genetic and physiological effects of irradiation of fowl semen. In *Proceedings of the 26th British Poultry Breeders' Round Table*, pp. 1–7

O'MALLEY, B.W., TSAI, M.J. and SCHRADER, W.T. (1983). Structural considerations for the action of steroid hormones in eukaryotic cells. In *Steroid Hormone Receptors: Structure and Function*, (Eriksson, H. and Gustafsson, J.A., eds), pp. 307–328. Cambridge, Elsevier

PALMITER, R.D. and BRINSTER, R.L. (1985). Transgenic mice. *Cell*, **41**, 343–345

PALMITER, R.D., BRINSTER, R.L., HAMMER, R.E., TRUMBAUER, M.E., ROSENFELD, M.G., BIRNBERG, N.C. and EVANS, R.G. (1982). Dramatic growth of mice that develop from eggs microinjected with metallothionein–growth hormone fusion genes. *Nature*, **300**, 611–615

PANDEY, K.K. and PATCHELL, M.R. (1982). Genetic transformation in chicken by the use of irradiated male gametes. *Molecular and General Genetics*, **185**, 305–308

RYFFEL, G.U. and WAHLI, W. (1984). Regulation and structure of the vitellogenin genes. In *Eukaryotic Genes: their Structure, Activity and Regulation*, (MacLean, N., Gregory, F.P. and Flavell, R.A., eds), pp. 329–331. London, Butterworths

SHENSTONE, F.S. (1968). The gross composition, chemistry and physiochemical basis of organisation of the yolk and white. In *Egg Quality. A Study of the Hen's Egg*, (Carter, T.C., ed.), pp. 26–58. Edinburgh, Oliver and Boyd

SIMMONS, R.W. and SOMES, R.G. (1985). Chemical characteristics of Araucana eggs. *Poultry Science*, **64**, 1264–1268

SIPPEL, A.E. (1984). The egg white protein genes. In *Eukaryotic Genes: their Structure, Activity and Regulation*, (MacLean, N., Gregory, F.P. and Flavell, R.A., eds), pp. 315–327. London, Butterworths

SOUZA, L.M., BOONE, T.C., MURDOCK, D., LANGLEY, K., WYPYCH, J., FENTON, D., JOHNSON, S., LAI, P.H., EVERETT, R., HSU, R-J. and BOSSELMAN, R. (1984). Application of recombinant DNA technologies to studies on chicken growth hormone. *Journal of Experimental Zoology*, **232**, 456–473

WASHBURN, K.W. and MARKS, H.L. (1977). Changes in fitness traits associated with selection for divergence in yolk cholesterol. *British Poultry Science*, **18**, 189–199

WELLS, R.G. (1968). The measurements of certain egg quality characteristics: a review. In *Egg Quality. A Study of the Hen's Egg*, (Carter, T.C., ed.), pp. 207–250. Edinburgh, Oliver and Boyd

Chapter 13

Effect of induced moulting on egg quality

E. Decuypere, G. Huyghebaert and G. Verheyen

Introduction

Egg production and egg quality decrease after 12–14 months of laying and natural moult occurs in many birds. One of the aims, in biological terms, for artificial egg laying pause, besides restoring the egg production level for a new production period, is an increase in egg quality compared to the end of the pullet production cycle. Egg quality, however, comprises several aspects such as egg weight, internal quality and shell quality which are considered in the first section. All these aspects, together with production levels, are changed by moulting procedures but not always in the same way or to the same extent. In a second section, different moulting procedures are compared as to their influence on egg quality parameters. The interacting effects of external factors on egg quality, such as light, season and nutrition before, during or after the moulting period, are discussed in a third section. Finally, some hypotheses on how artificial egg laying pause could improve egg quality are put forward, based on relationships of egg quality parameters with endocrinological and physiological parameters.

Age-related changes in egg quality and effect of artificial moulting

Internal quality

The progressive decline in egg albumen quality (Haugh units) during the hen's first laying year is well known (Pope *et al.*, 1960; Snyder and Orr, 1960; Hansen, 1966a; Noles and Tindell, 1967). Data on the rate of decline in albumen are not consistent and the relationship with egg production levels is not well defined (May, Schmidt and Stadelman, 1957; Pope *et al.*, 1960; Noles and Tindell, 1967). It is reported that the variability in albumen quality increases with flock age, but after a moult, in general, Haugh unit scores increase and show reduced variation (Noles, 1966; Huyghebaert, Fontaine and De Groote, 1977; Lee, 1982). The data of Huyghebaert, Fontaine and De Groote are shown in *Table 13.1*.

Since intensity of production and egg weight are both changing during the first production year and after an artificial moult, it may be asked how these factors act upon interior egg quality. However, intensity of production and egg weight did not seem to affect the internal quality measured as Haugh units (Pope *et al.*, 1960;

Table 13.1 Egg quality parameters during the first and second production year

First year			Second year		
Age (weeks)	Haugh units	Non-destructive deformation (1/1000 mm)	Age (weeks)	Haugh units	Non-destructive deformation (1/1000 mm)
20–24	–	–	97–101	89.9	22.1
25–28	93.1	20.9	102–105	88.7	22.4
29–32	–	–	106–109	86.9	22.9
33–36	89.1	20.5	110–113	85.9	23.1
37–40	–	–	114–117	85.6	23.4
41–44	–	–	118–121	85.6	24.1
45–48	88.4	23.5	122–125	84.9	24.2
49–52	–	–	126–129	82.7	24.5
53–56	88.2	25.4	130–133	79.8	25.6

Courtesy of Huyghebaert, Fontaine and De Groote (1977).

Noles and Tindell, 1967). When flocks were moulted every 6 or 9 months, the improvement in albumen quality expressed as Haugh units, as well as the increase in egg production was greater than in flocks moulted every 12 months (Hansen, 1966a). In the eggs laid during the moult period itself, appearing as early as the second day after food withdrawal, Haugh units were much higher than in eggs laid prior to or following the moult, although in eggs laid following the moult, albumen quality was better than that observed just prior to moult induction (Nordstrom, 1980).

Another point concerning the interior quality of eggs after moulting which could be of importance to egg breakers and that must be considered is the albumen/yolk ratio. Since yolk is worth considerably more than albumen, the purchase of eggs for breaking should be based upon maximising yolk yield. Fletcher *et al.* (1981) pointed out that the adjusted percent yolk [(Yolk weight/(initial whole egg weight — dry shell weight)) × 100] increased significantly from 29 weeks to 62 weeks of age, while the adjusted percent albumen [(initial whole egg weight — (yolk + dry shell weight)/(initial whole egg weight — dry shell weight)) × 100] decreased significantly over the same period. Since all analyses were conducted using egg weight as a covariant, the authors attributed these differences to the direct effect of hen age and not through the effect of hen age on egg weight. Comparing force-moulted hens to natural moulting hens over a period of 9 months during the second laying year, Horst and Peterson (1968) found, as expected, an increase in shell breaking strength and in albumen height (mm) in force-moulted hens, but the respective proportions of yolk and albumen were significantly higher and lower in the force-moulted birds. The decrease in albumen/yolk ratio with age (Cunningham, Cotterill and Funk, 1960; Jenkins and Tyler, 1960; Kline, Meehan and Sugehara, 1965) was not reversed after artificial moulting as was the decrease in albumen quality or shell strength, but rather reinforced. Since large numbers of hens are moulted each year, such information on interior quality of eggs would be useful in making decisions for routing these eggs through marketing channels (table eggs or egg products).

The incidence of meat and blood spots in eggs was not significantly influenced by forced moulting (Horst and Peterson, 1968).

Shell quality

Many reports associate the decline in shell quality primarily with the ageing process (Pope *et al.*, 1960; Petersen, 1964; Noles and Tindell, 1967; Fletcher *et al.*, 1981). The variability in shell quality among individual birds and the effects of the rate of production on shell quality are not clearly understood.

Although in most studies true shell strength has not been measured, related parameters such as egg shell thickness, egg shell weight and egg specific gravity have been correlated with crack incidence (e.g. Hammerle, 1969). Most authors agree on the restoring effect of a forced moult on egg shell strength (Berg and Bearse, 1947; Hansen, 1966a; Horst and Peterson, 1968; Huyghebaert, Fontaine and De Groote, 1977; Lee, 1982; Roland and Brake, 1982; Berry and Brake, 1983), as shown, for example, in *Table 13.1*. The improvement of specific gravity was more pronounced when flocks were moulted after six or nine months of lay compared to flocks moulted after 12 months' laying (Hansen, 1966a).

In a study concerning egg shell quality parameters of Single Comb White Leghorn (SCWL) hens, Garlich *et al.* (1984) found that shell thickness (expressed as mg shell/cm² shell surface area) was greatest at 31 weeks of age and declined throughout the first year. Shell weight was greater immediately post-moult than at

Table 13.2 Comparison between different fasting periods, low sodium and low calcium on performance during egg laying pause and post-moult

	Fasting			Low Na	Low Ca	Least significant differences at P = 0.05 level
	O_1	O_2	O_3			
Moult procedure						
fasting (days)	4	6	8	–	–	
treatment (days)				28	28	
wheatbran (days)						
50 g/day	10	10	10	–	–	
65 g	–	–	10	–	–	
80 g	–	10	10	–	–	
Performances during egg laying pause						
duration of the total production stops (days)	18	29	43	–	–	
second egg laying maturity—time from start of moult to 50% level						
of production (days)	61	61	61	63	63	
production rate (%)	15.2	13.1	7.7	21.7	14.4	
Post-moult performance						
production rate (%)	66.4[a]	69.1[a]	69.3[a]	59.5[b]	64.7[a]	3.08
no. eggs per hen present	167[a]	174[a]	175[a]	150[b]	163[a]	13.1
egg weight (g)	66.8[bc]	67.8[abc]	66.5[c]	68.1[ab]	68.3[a]	1.36
egg mass (g/hen-day)	44.4[a]	46.9[a]	46.1[a]	40.5[b]	44.3[a]	3.70
Haugh units	85.9	86.0	87.3	84.0	86.1	–
non-destructive deformation ($\bigcirc$m)	23.2	23.5	23.5	24.3	23.5	–
% shell-less or broken eggs	5.9[ab]	5.3[ab]	4.6[b]	7.2[a]	6.0[ab]	2.32
% cracked eggs	9.8	9.6	8.3	8.9	8.5	–

Different superscripts in the same row indicate significant differences at the *P* = 0.05 level.
Courtesy of Huyghebaert, Fontaine and De Groote (1977).

any other time. After moulting at 71 weeks of age, percent shell and shell thickness were improved when compared to values immediately pre-moult. These post-moult values were similar to values observed at 43 weeks of age.

Although it is stated that body weight should be reduced through fasting to remove the fat that has accumulated in the shell gland, with a 30% reduction necessary to rejuvenate egg shell quality, Baker, Brake and McDaniel (1983) found no consistent changes in specific gravity between groups in two experimental trials with a range of body weight loss during induced moult from 20% to 35%. However, since it is clear from the work of Thompson, Hamilton and Grunder (1985) that the shell strength measurements commonly used will fail to predict a substantial proportion of breakage in the commercial process of egg handling, perhaps more attention should be given in moult studies to direct observation of cracked or shell-less eggs in the poultry house. Related to this, it may be mentioned that Huyghebaert, Fontaine and De Groote (1977) found differences in the percentage of shell-less and broken eggs due to different moulting procedures, although no differences in non-destructive deformation were observed (*Table 13.2* and *Figure 13.1*).

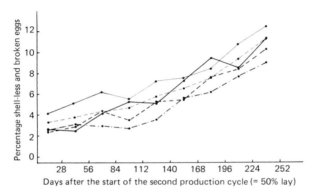

Figure 13.1 Influence of different moulting methods on the evolution of percentage shell-less and broken eggs during the second production cycle. —— 4 days fasting: – – – – 6 days fasting; –·–·– 8 days fasting; ————— low sodium; ---- low calcium. Courtesy of Huyghebaert, Fontaine and De Groote (1977).

Force moulting may also be successfully used to reduce egg shell pimpling, thereby averting losses that egg producers often incur because of this problem in older hens. An egg shell texture condition, pimpling consists of calcium 'bumps' or deposits adhering to or protruding through shell surfaces. The latter are potential leakers. The problem increases as the hen ages, probably because of the continuous use of the oviduct, with an increased fragmentation and sloughing of cells, which then adhere to the shell membrane or shell during calcification (Farmer, Roland and McGuire, 1982). These authors found that pimpling decreased in the first six months after moult, although it gradually increased during post-moult similar to that which would be seen during a hen's first year of lay.

Egg weight

During the first laying year, egg size increases with age followed by a levelling off. After moulting there is an initial decrease in egg size followed by an increase and a

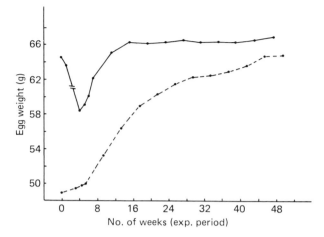

Figure 13.2 Egg weight curves from first and second production cycles of White Leghorn hens. ——— first laying cycle; ——— second laying cycle (after moult). Courtesy of Fontaine, Moermans and De Groote (1978).

levelling off at a slightly higher weight, as shown in *Figure 13.2* (Fontaine, Moermans and De Groote, 1978). This trend was continued in a second moult cycle and moulting policy in general will result in an increased average egg weight or proportion of large grade (Wakeling, 1977; Hamilton and Thompson, 1984; Cunningham and McCormick, 1985). Therefore, some strains are more suitable for moulting than others because particular strain characteristics, such as a predisposition to lay a larger number of small eggs, will increase the economic advantage of moulting (Wakeling, 1985).

Effect of different moulting procedures on egg quality characteristics

Fasting

Many reports have stated that the longer the birds are out of production, the higher the peak in the post-moult period (Len, Abplanalp and Johnson, 1964; Noles, 1966; Huyghebaert, Fontaine and De Groote, 1977). Comparing seven degrees of feed- and/or water-restriction imposed on 17-month-old SCWL hens, Noles (1966) found that the increase in Haugh unit values was small and not consistent with treatments. The differences in interior quality two months after moulting had disappeared by four months of subsequent production. Egg shell quality tended to improve with the severity of the treatment. There was an overall decline in shell quality again four months after moult, while treatment differences remained significant.

Low sodium or calcium

The results using these methods are to a large extent dose-dependent (Begin and Johnson, 1976; Whitehead and Sharp, 1976). The post-moult performances using low sodium diets are as variable among the studies using this method as for the low calcium method (Nevalainen, 1969; Douglas, Harms and Wilson, 1972; Campos and Baiao, 1979; Gilbert *et al.*, 1981; Ross and Herrick, 1981).

In a study to determine the length of time for which the low sodium (0.04–0.05%) should be administered, Naber (1983) found an equal post-moult production performance for the six or eight week low sodium treatment, equivalent to the conventional fasting methods. The four week low sodium treatment as well as all combinations of low sodium/low protein were inferior in production rate, but all treatments showed a similar increase in Haugh units. The improvement in average specific gravity appeared to be related to the length of time the hens were fed the low sodium or the low sodium/low protein diet. There was also a difference in the timing of the generally significant improvements in egg production, egg shell specific gravity and albumen thickness observed from the moulting treatments:

(a) egg production improvement was present over the entire 32 week period following re-establishment of egg laying after treatment;
(b) specific gravity improvement lasted for 24 weeks and then was no longer present;
(c) albumen thickness improvement lasted for 20 weeks before it tended to disappear.

Hence the egg quality advantages for moulting of hens tended to diminish with time, although increased egg production continued to the end of the study.

In an experiment designed to determine the degree of sodium deficiency required to moult hens successfully and also to define the limits of diet sodium content affecting various reproductive characteristics, Naber, Latshaw and Marsh (1984) found that reduction in dietary sodium level produced a nearly linear reduction in egg output and food intake. The post-moult reproductive performance over 32 weeks of hens force moulted with different sodium levels was comparable (not statistically different) with a conventional procedure that involved food and water withdrawal, for egg production increase at 0.03–0.08% sodium, for egg specific gravity increase at 0.03–0.12% sodium and for egg albumen thickness increase at all levels tested (up to 0.16% sodium).

Improvement in egg production is critical to recycling of hens, and this aspect of reproductive performance determines the rather narrow range of dietary sodium levels that can be recommended for recycling. Said *et al.* (1984) also found no differences during 10 subsequent 28 d post-moult periods for egg production rate, egg size, Haugh units and shell quality (measured by non-destructive deformation) between a food and water restriction procedure and a low sodium diet consisting of no added salt for 42 d (0.08% Na). Huyghebaert, Fontaine and De Groote (1977) however found a lower post-moult production level and a higher mean egg weight for hens moulted with a low sodium diet (28 d low sodium, calculated at 0.03%) compared with different food withdrawal methods (*Table 13.2*). The results of the low calcium method (calculated at 0.056%) were somewhat intermediary, but it has to be stated that the real sodium and calcium contents in the food and drinking water in these experiments were not measured. For all moult procedures, however, no differences in Haugh units or shell quality, measured by non-destructive deformation, could be found (*Table 13.2*). All information so far indicates that the limiting factor concerning the choice between the numerous moulting programmes is egg production itself and not egg quality parameters, since every method that gives a satisfactory improvement in post-moult production rate is accompanied by an improved internal egg quality and shell quality, but not vice versa.

When low sodium and fasting were combined by removing the sodium and phosphorus sources from the diet of hens during the first 4 d of the resting period, the post-moult egg production, egg weight and specific gravity were equal to a 10 d food withdrawal moulting procedure (Harms, 1983a). Moreover, the combination of low sodium and a restricted fasting period resulted in a prolonged egg production when compared with hens receiving no food and in this way shortening the length of the resting period without affecting the post-moult performance.

High zinc or copper

Production results after moulting with high zinc diets were comparable to the fasting method (Shippee et al., 1979; McCormick and Cunningham, 1983; Verheyen et al., 1983) or even in favour of zinc when fed up to 8 d (Scott et al., 1976). The level of zinc was 10 000 to 25 000 ppm administered as zinc oxide or zinc acetate (Shippee et al., 1979). Specific gravity and percentage shell were significantly in favour of the zinc treatments while the birds were being brought out of production in the experiments of Scott et al. (1976). However, shell quality differences were not present within 14 d of the zinc treatments or thereafter.

Comparing 10 d fasting with 4 d feeding 10 000 or 20 000 ppm zinc, or 8 d feeding 20 000 ppm zinc as moulting procedures on 64-week-old SCWL hens, McCormick and Cunningham (1984) found similar results as far as egg quality was concerned. Egg quality variables, breaking strength, and egg weight were not significantly different among the various force-moulting procedures over the entire experiment. Percentage shell was also measured and observed not to be affected by the moulting method.

Cunningham and McCormick (1985) found that different strains responded differently to moulting with high zinc or fasting in terms of mean egg weight and Stevenson and Jackson (1984) found differences between Shaver and Warren hybrids in the improvement of Haugh units in response to different moulting programmes. They used food withdrawal or diets containing copper sulphate or zinc oxide at different levels and for varying durations.

Comparing 4 d or 10 d moult programmes with zinc (20 000 ppm) or fasting, Cunningham and McCormick (1985) found that hens on the 10 d moult programmes took longer to return to 50% egg production than hens on the 4 d programmes, but they achieved significantly higher peak egg production. This resulted in similar total egg yields during the first moult cycle, and no differences in egg weights or grades were observed, confirming earlier results. However, fewer but larger eggs were found with the 4 d programmes (zinc oxide and fasting) compared to the 10 d programmes during the second moult cycle (Table 13.3).

All these data suggest that feeding high zinc diets may be useful as a practical method of inducing a pause in egg production. However, Palafox and Ho-a (1980) found a decreased fertility and hatchability for 14–28 d in the subsequent production period after moulting breeder hens with a high zinc (20 000 ppm) diet for 5 d, and this indicates an elevated zinc content in the egg during or shortly after this moulting procedure. Stevenson and Jackson (1984) indeed found a significant increase in egg zinc concentration shortly after feeding a 10 000 or 20 000 ppm zinc diet for 14 d. The zinc diet decreased the egg copper concentration. However, when comparing fasting with different zinc treatments, Scott et al. (1976) found no

Table 13.3 Effect of 4 d or 10 d moulting programmes for a first and second moult cycle

	Moulting programme			
	ZnO 4 d	Food removal 4 d	ZnO 10 d	Food removal 10 d
First moult cycle (60–85 weeks)				
Peak production (%)	72[a]	73[a]	78[b]	76[b]
Weeks to 50% production	4	4	5.5	5
Eggs/hen housed	100[a]	101[a]	99[a]	98[a]
Egg weight (g)	66.1[a]	65.7[a]	65.5[a]	65.7[a]
Extra large (%)	73.4[a]	65.7[a]	67.1[a]	65.4[a]
Large (%)	23.9[a]	31.2[a]	30.2[a]	31.1[a]
Undergrades (%)	12.5[a]	15.2[a]	11.5[a]	14.2[a]
Second moult cycle (86–112 weeks)				
Pre-moult production	58[a]	55[a]	63[b]	62[b]
Peak production	59[a]	54[a]	68[b]	65[b]
Weeks to 50% production	4	4	5.5	5
Eggs/hen housed	71[a]	70[a]	80[b]	82[b]
Egg weight (g)	67.3[a]	66.5[a]	65.1[b]	65.5[b]
Extra large eggs (%)	68.5[a]	62.7[b]	58.6[b]	61.9[b]
Large eggs (%)	28.5[a]	34.4[b]	33.2[b]	31.9[b]
Undergrade eggs (%)	22.5[a]	24.8[a]	20.6[a]	20.4[a]

Different superscripts in the same row indicate significant differences at the $P = 0.05$ level.
After Cunningham and McCormick (1985).

significant differences in zinc content of yolk and albumen during or after the treatment, even when a 20 000 ppm zinc diet was fed for 16 d.

The use of a diet containing copper sulphate (2 g added Cu/kg for 7 d) seemed to be as effective as one containing zinc oxide (20 g added Zn/kg for 14 d) in terms of subsequent egg numbers, egg weight, shell thickness or Haugh units and no increase in egg copper concentration was found (Stevenson and Jackson, 1984).

Effect of external factors interacting with artificial moulting programmes on egg quality

Light

Restriction of the length of the photoperiod is in most cases part of the moulting procedure. Hansen (1966b) found that a light reduction from 16 h L:8 h D to 6 h L:18 h D or 8 h L:16 h D for 39 d or more before food and water restriction increased the rate of lay afterwards by 5–6%. Egg production remained above 50% during the weeks that light was reduced before food withdrawal, and then stopped within 7 d. Hembree, Adams and Craig (1980) found that forced moulting by total light restriction (10 d) plus a diet of cracked corn for 28 d was equally effective as 10 d fasting. The improvement in percentage hen-day production and Haugh units was similar, but the post-moult increase in specific gravity was less in the light restricted group ($P < 0.05$), while the eggs were significantly heavier.

Light restriction (6 h L vs 13 h L) showed little interaction with conventional or low sodium moulting programmes (Naber, Latshaw and Marsh, 1984) as far as egg production and egg quality was concerned. Similar results on the light/low sodium interaction were reported by Berry and Brake (1983). They found, however, a positive interaction between light reduction (8 h L vs 17 h L) and the fasting or high zinc moulting method. Egg weight was reduced and specific gravity increased by the photoperiod reduction during the moulting treatment (Berry and Brake, 1983). It is unclear if the opposite effects of total darkness (Hembree, Adams and Craig, 1980) in comparison to photoperiod reduction (Berry and Brake, 1983) on post-moult egg weight and shell quality are due to strain differences (both experiments were carried out on White Leghorns of 68 or 65 weeks of age), previous treatments or to differences in the treatment itself. Farmers wishing to induce an egg production pause in part of a multiple age flock should take the light/moulting treatment interaction into consideration. Since the low sodium moulting programmes apparently showed no such interactions, adequate low sodium treatment would be beneficial in these circumstances.

Nutrition

Effect of variations in pre-moult nutrition on post-moult performance

Hens that had food rationed during the growing period had consistently higher percentage hen-day egg production during most of the post-moult period than did the full-fed control groups (Hollands and Gowe, 1961; Lee, 1984), but albumen height and shell thickness were not influenced (Lee, 1984).

Restricted or time-limited feeding of birds during the first laying cycle instead of full-feeding also gave higher egg production during the post-moult period—68.4% or 66.6% versus 61.9% respectively (Summers and Leeson, 1977). A severe moult procedure (8 d fasting + 30 d rationed wheat bran), however, was more advisable following *ad libitum* feeding as opposed to restricted feeding during the first production period according to Huyghebaert, Fontaine and De Groote (1977). In all cases, however, egg quality parameters were not affected by the treatments.

Effect of variations in diet during the moult or during the pre-lay phase of an induced moult on post-moult performance

Protein supplementation during the recovery period after a moult should have a positive influence on subsequent production (Brake and Thaxton, 1977), but Hembree, Adams and Craig (1980) reported the failure of an amino acid supplemented recovery diet to affect production performance or egg quality parameters (Haugh units, specific gravity, egg weight) of force-moulted hens. A low protein diet (8.6% vs 16.2%) during the resting period, after 10 d fasting, was reported to give a lower initial production rate and a lower post-moult egg weight, but no influence on post-moult specific gravity (Harms, 1983b).

Supplemented particulate calcium or extra limestone given in advance of the moult, or during the initial stages of a moulting programme, prevents hypocalcaemia, decreases the rate of decline in egg production and results in fewer poor shelled eggs (Garlich and Parkhurst, 1982; Wakeling, 1985). These data support the hypothesis that in the fasting hen a cellular calcium deficiency becomes the first limiting nutrient for ovulation (Nevalainen, 1969; Garlich and Parkhurst, 1982; Luck and Scanes, 1979, 1982). However, it may be questioned what the production level will be after resuming egg laying when total production pause is shortened or eliminated by calcium supplementation before and/or during the initial moulting stages. Brake, Garlich and Carter (1984) found no adverse effect from additional calcium, up to 3.5%, in the diet during the post-fast period prior to the resumption of egg laying.

Effect of variations in post-moult nutrition on second cycle performance

According to Wolford (1984) there is a need for information on the nutritional requirements of the moulted hen during the latter stage of the moult and during the post-moult period in order to reduce the decline in both production and egg quality.

The discussion about protein level or amino acid supplementation during the recovery period and its effect on subsequent performance was mentioned earlier. Even though body weight was depleted and considerable feather growth had to be accomplished during the post-moult period, Christmas and Harms (1983) found that hens (moulting age of 62 weeks) maintained for the entire post-rest period on a diet designed for feeding late in the production year had performance values comparable to hens fed a young pullet-type diet*. These results indicate that significant economic benefits can be obtained, without loss of egg production, egg weight or specific gravity, by the utilisation of less expensive diets which have been designed for birds in the latter stages of lay.

Since the post-moult egg size tends to be excessive, quantitative food restriction during the second laying period may be considered in order to reduce egg weight (Casey, 1974; Wakeling, 1977). The use of ammonium sulphate (AS) as a method of restricting the voluntary food intake of laying hens had no effect on production or egg quality parameters during the pullet year, but in contrast to pullets, the force-moulted SCWL hens compensated for the diluting effect of the AS by a proportional increase in their intake of the AS-containing diets (Hamilton and Sibbald, 1980). These workers found no influence of AS-containing diets on post-moult shell quality (percentage shell or specific gravity), but Haugh units were improved.

As a concluding remark on the effect of different moulting procedures and interacting external factors upon post-moult performance characteristics, it may be stated that, in general, egg quality characteristics seem to be less sensitive to different methods or interactions between factors than the production level itself. This may be related to the fact that the phenotypical variation in egg production vs egg weight, egg shell quality and egg internal quality due to environmental/management influences is estimated respectively at about 80% vs 55%, 70% and 60% respectively.

Relation of egg quality changes during or after forced moult to physiological parameters

Internal quality

In eggs laid following the moult, albumen quality (Haugh units, albumen height) was better than that observed just prior to moult induction, but was not as good as that seen in eggs laid actually during moult induction (Nordstrom, 1980). The

---

*The pullet-type diet differed mainly in Ca:P ratio and contained 6.74% limestone, 1.75% dicalciumphosphate and 0.50% microingredients vs. respectively 8.40%, 0.65% and 0.40% for the late production year laying hen diet.

Table 13.4 Progesterone levels (ng/ml) during the first week of moult induction and in control hens fed *ad libitum* (mean ± SE)

Treatment	Progesterone levels (ng/ml)						
	Prior to treatment	Day 2	Day 3	Day 5	Day 8	Day 10	Day 12
Control group	0.940 ± 0.090^a (12)	0.747 ± 0.071^a (12)	0.748 ± 0.095^a (12)	0.762 ± 0.097^a (11)	0.797 ± 0.136^a (10)	0.817 ± 0.091^a (12)	0.851 ± 0.141^a (12)
Low Ca diet (28 d)	0.900 ± 0.105^{abc} (11)	1.051 ± 0.154^{ab} (11)	1.111 ± 0.280^a (11)	0.729 ± 0.098^{abc} (11)	0.676 ± 0.086^{bc} (11)	0.842 ± 0.127^{abc} (12)	0.525 ± 0.038^c (11)
Fasting (8 d + 20 d wheat bran)	1.391 ± 0.320^a (23)	0.869 ± 0.182^b (22)	0.382 ± 0.033^c (23)	0.282 ± 0.039^c (23)	0.376 ± 0.102^c (22)	0.262 ± 0.011^c (21)	0.311 ± 0.033^c (23)

[a,b,c]Means within a row with different letters are significantly different ($P<0.05$).
Numbers in parentheses indicate number of hens in each group.
Courtesy of Verheyen (unpublished results).

author ascribed the dramatic increase in albumen quality of eggs laid during moult induction, appearing as early as the second day after food withdrawal, to decreased plumping as a result of water conservation by the hen due to decreased water intake during food withdrawal. During the moult treatment (7 d food withdrawal + 21 d ground corn or whole wheat) egg weight, as expected, was reduced, but this persisted for at least 20 d while the very high albumen quality values lasted for only a few days. Perhaps, therefore, this could be related also to hormonal changes occurring during moult induction.

Although the biosynthesis of egg white proteins in oviducal tissues has been extensively studied, little is known regarding their excretion into the lumen of the magnum during the passage of a developing egg. It is known that direct mechanical stimulation plays an important role in the release of albumen. Brant and Nalbandov (1956) were able to induce albumen release by simultaneous administration of an oestrogen and progesterone or oestrogen and androgen. They found that lower progesterone dosages were required for an effect similar to that accomplished by higher doses of androgen. In quails, albumen secretion could be moderated by sex hormones which induced either a facilitation (progesterone) or an inhibition (oestradiol benzoate), probably by modifying the secretory granules making them more or less excretable (Laugier and Brard, 1980). Oestradiol levels decreased after only 1 d of fasting (Tanabe, Ogawa and Nakamura, 1981; Etches, Williams and Rzasa, 1984), while progesterone levels remained rather high for a few days after the start of the moult treatment (*Table 13.4*). Since progesterone facilitates albumen secretion, probably by modifying the secretory granules making them more excretable, and oestrogens have the reverse effect (Laugier and Brard, 1980), these data together with the changing levels of both hormones may in part be responsible for the exceptional albumen quality at the beginning of moult induction. It may be asked if post moult improvement in albumen quality could be related to possible changes in the progesterone/oestradiol secretion ratio compared with values prior to moult induction.

External quality

The exact mechanisms by which forced moulting procedures produce their beneficial responses upon shell quality are still unknown. Roland and Brake (1982) put forward the following three possible explanations.

1. Egg weight could be less for a short period after moult, thus requiring less shell deposition for a given thickness. However, they found no differences in egg weight between any groups in their experiments comparing force-moulted hens (food withdrawal method) with controls.
2. Force-moulted hens may have consumed more food, and thus more calcium, for the increased production. However, dietary calcium level (3.5% or 4.5%) had no significant influence on shell weight and specific gravity in force-moulted hens, but significantly increased both shell quality parameters of controls.
3. They concluded that an improvement in calcium metabolism either in absorption, transport or deposition occurred as a result of forced moulting.

It is known that although increases in calcium intake will improve shell quality in ageing hens, high intakes will not entirely prevent this decline associated with age. In a review of factors influencing egg shell quality, Petersen (1964) suggested a decreased calcium retention with increasing age; decreased absorption, increased excretion and an incomplete replacement of calcium mobilised from the skeleton. All these factors could be altered by a moulting programme. Based upon work with mice, Draper (1964) suggested that the tendency of aged animals towards a negative calcium balance is not due to a decreased absorption rate from the intestine, but is due to an incomplete replacement of calcium eroded from the skeleton.

Femur density (g dry weight/ml femur volume), which could be greatly influenced by the extent of deposits of medullary bone (Simkiss, 1967), increased from 19 to 43 weeks of age and then reached a plateau (Garlich *et al.*, 1984). An equally high density was found in the post-moult laying period (83 weeks), while these workers also found similar post-moult serum calcium at 83 and 49 weeks (29.2% and 29.9%).

The relationships between blood ionised calcium or plasma total calcium and egg shell quality parameters such as specific gravity, non-destructive deformation, shell thickness, quasi-static compression and fracture strength are, however, very weak (Hamilton *et al.*, 1981). Harms (1982) suggested that if a high build-up of phosphorus in the blood could be avoided, the hen would be able to withdraw more of the calcium from the bone and improve egg shell quality. Garlich *et al.* (1984), however, found no differences either in pre- or post-moult serum phosphorus levels or in serum alkaline phosphatase activity, while Roland and Brake (1982) found identical serum phosphorus levels in non-moulted and moulted hens at the end of the food deprivation period.

These results indicate that a post-moult improvement in egg shell quality compared to values prior to moulting is probably not related to changes in calcium metabolism at the skeletal level. A possible improvement or rejuvenation of calcium metabolism at the level of the alimentary tract or shell gland as a consequence of forced moulting requires further research.

Although the influence of exogenous steroids on egg shell characteristics is not consistent (Brahmak-Shatriya, Snetsinger and Waibel, 1969), an effect of possible changes in sex steroid secretion rate or ratio compared to pre-moult values on egg shell characteristics may not be excluded.

Acknowledgement

ED gratefully acknowledges the support of the National Fund for Scientific Research (NFWO).

References

BAKER, M., BRAKE, J. and MCDANIEL, G.R. (1983). The relationship between body weight loss during induced molt and postmolt egg production, egg weight, and shell quality in caged layers. *Poultry Science*, **62**, 409–413

BEGIN, J.J. and JOHNSON, T.H. (1976). Effect of dietary salt on the performance of laying hens. *Poultry Science*, **55**, 2395–2404

BERG, L.R. and BEARSE, G.G. (1947). The changes in egg quality resulting from force moulting White Leghorn yearling hens. *Poultry Science*, **26**, 414–418

BERRY, W.D. and BRAKE, J. (1983). Effect of three induced molting regimes with photoperiod on egg production and shell quality of SCWL-hens. *Poultry Science*, **62**, 1382

BRAHMAK-SHATRIYA, R.D., SNETSINGER, D.C. and WAIBEL, P.E. (1969). Effects of exogenous estrogen and/or androgen on performance, egg shell characteristics and blood plasma changes on laying hens. *Poultry Science*, **48**, 444–451

BRAKE, J. and THAXTON, P. (1977). Post-moult effect of high protein vs low protein diets during a force molt. *Poultry Science*, **56**, 1347

BRAKE, J., GARLICH, J.D. and CARTER, T.A. (1984). Relationship of dietary calcium level during the prelay phase of an induced molt to postmolt performance. *Poultry Science*, **63**, 2497–2500

BRANT, J.W. and NALBANDOV, A.V. (1956). Role of sex hormones in albumen secretion by the oviduct of chickens. *Poultry Science*, **35**, 692–700

CAMPOS, E.J. and BAIAO, N.C. (1979). The effects of methods of forced molting on performance of commercial layers. *Poultry Science*, **58**, 1040

CASEY, J.M. (1974). Effects of restricted feeding on performance of moulted SCWL females. *Poultry Science*, **53**, 1903

CHRISTMAS, R.B. and HARMS, R.H. (1983). The performance of four strains of laying hens subjected to various postrest combinations of calcium and phosphorus after forced rest in winter or summer. *Poultry Science*, **62**, 1816–1822

CUNNINGHAM, D.L. and MCCORMICK, C.C. (1985). A multiple comparison of dietary zinc and feed removal molting procedures: production and income performance. *Poultry Science*, **64**, 253–260

CUNNINGHAM, F.E., COTTERILL, O.J. and FUNK, E.M. (1960). The effect of season and age of bird. 1. On egg size, quality and yield. *Poultry Science*, **39**, 289–299

DOUGLAS, C.R., HARMS, R.H. and WILSON, H.R. (1972). The use of extremely low dietary calcium to alter the production pattern of laying hens. *Poultry Science*, **51**, 2015–2020

DRAPER, H.H. (1964). Physiological aspects of aging. I. Calcium and magnesium metabolism in senescent mice. *Journal of Nutrition*, **83**, 65–72

ETCHES, R.Y., WILLIAMS, J.B. and RZASA, J. (1984). Effects of corticosterone and dietary changes in the hen ovarian function, plasma LH and steroids and the response to exogenous LHRH. *Journal of Reproduction and Fertility*, **70**, 121–130

FARMER, M., ROLAND, D.A. and MCGUIRE, J.A. (1982). Force molting may reduce eggshell pimpling problem. *Feedstuffs*, **54** (September 10), 22

FLETCHER, D.L., BRITTON, W.M., RAHN, A.P. and SAVAGE, S.I. (1981). The influence of layer flock age on egg component yields and solids content. *Poultry Science*, **60**, 983–987

FONTAINE, G., MOERMANS, R.J. and DE GROOTE, G. (1978). Produktiecapaciteit en rentabiliteit van in kunstmatige rui gebrachte WL hennen. *Landbouwtijdschrift*, **31**, 1127–1140

GARLICH, J.D. and PARKHURST, C.R. (1982). Increased egg production by calcium supplementation during the initial fasting period of a forced molt. *Poultry Science*, **61**, 955–961

GARLICH, J., BRAKE, J., PARKHURST, C.R., THAXTON, J.P. and MORGAN, G.W. (1984). Physiological profile of caged layers during one production year, molt and postmolt: egg production, eggshell quality, liver, femur and blood parameters. *Poultry Science*, **63**, 339–343

GILBERT, A.B., PEDDIE, J., MITCHELL, G.G. and TEAGUE, P.W. (1981). The egg-laying response of the domestic hen to variation in dietary calcium. *British Poultry Science*, **22**, 537–548

HAMILTON, R.M.C. and SIBBALD, C.R. (1980). The effects of level and source of ammonium sulphate on feed intake, egg production, and egg quality in White Leghorn pullets and force molted hens. *Poultry Science*, **59**, 119–127

HAMILTON, R.M.C. and THOMPSON, B.K. (1984). Observations on daily variations in feed intake and shell strength of eggs from White Leghorn pullets and force molted hens. *Poultry Science*, **63**, 2335–2344

HAMILTON, R.M.C., GRUNDER, A.A., THOMPSON, B.K. and HOLLANDS, K.G. (1981). Relationship between blood ionized calcium levels and shell strength of eggs laid by White Leghorn hens. *Poultry Science*, **60**, 2380–2384

HAMMERLE, J.R. (1969). An engineering appraisal of egg shell strength evaluation techniques. *Poultry Science*, **48**, 1708–1717

HANSEN, R.S. (1966a). The effect of frequency of rests (forced molts) on hen performance and egg quality. *Poultry Science*, **45**, 1089

HANSEN, R.S. (1966b). Reducing light to facilitate induced rest (forced molt). *Poultry Science*, **45**, 1089 (abstract)

HARMS, R.H. (1982). The influence of nutrition on eggshell quality. Part 2: Phosphorus. *Feedstuffs*, **54** (May 10), 25–26

HARMS, R.H. (1983a). Benefits of low sodium in the diets of laying hens during the period prior to forced rest. *Poultry Science*, **62**, 1107–1109

HARMS, R.H. (1983b). Influence of protein level in the resting diet upon performance of force rested hens. *Poultry Science*, **62**, 273–276

HEMBREE, D.Y., ADAMS, A.W. and CRAIG, J.W. (1980). Effects of force-molting by conventional and experimental light restriction methods on performance and agonistic behavior of hens. *Poultry Science*, **59**, 215–223

HOLLANDS, K.G. and GOWE, R.S. (1961). The effect of restricted and full feeding during confinement rearing on first and second year laying house performance. *Poultry Science*, **40**, 574–583

HORST, P. and PETERSON, J. (1968). Investigations on the influence of forced moulting of hens on performance and egg quality. *World's Poultry Science Journal*, **24**, 283

HUYGHEBAERT, G., FONTAINE, G. and DE GROOTE, G. (1977). Vergelijkende studie van enkele kunstmatige ruimethoden bij W.L. hennen. *Landbouwtijdschrift*, **30**, 957–977

JENKINS, N.K. and TYLER, C. (1960). Changes in egg shell thickness and white and yolk weight and composition over a period of a year. *Journal of Agricultural Science*, **55**, 323–331

KLINE, L., MEEHAN, J.J. and SUGEHARA, T.F. (1965). Relation between layer age and egg-product yields and quality. *Food Technology*, **19**, 1296–1301

LAUGIER, C. and BRARD, E. (1980). Effects of estradiol benzoate and progesterone on egg white proteins secretion. *Poultry Science*, **59**, 643–646

LEE, K. (1982). Effects of forced molt period on postmolt performance of leghorn hens. *Poultry Science*, **61**, 1594–1598

LEE, K. (1984). Feed restriction during the growing period, forced molt, and egg production. *Poultry Science*, **63**, 1895–1897

LEN, R.E., ABPLANALP, H. and JOHNSON, E.A. (1964). Second year production of forced molted hens in the California sample test. *Poultry Science*, **43**, 638–646

LUCK, M.R. and SCANES, C.G. (1979). The relationship between reproductive activity and blood calcium in the calcium-deficient hen. *British Poultry Science*, **20**, 559–564

LUCK, M.R. and SCANES, C.G. (1982). Calcium-homeostasis and the control of ovulation. Aspects of Avian Endocrinology: practical and theoretical implications. *Graduate Studies, Texas Technical University*, **26**, 1–411

MAY, K.N., SCHMIDT, F.J. and STADELMAN, W.J. (1957). Strain variation in albumen quality decline on hen's eggs. *Poultry Science*, **36**, 1376–1379

MCCORMICK, C.C. and CUNNINGHAM, D.L. (1983). Induced molt with dietary zinc oxide. *Proceedings of the Cornell Nutrition Conference, November 1983*, pp. 69–74

MCCORMICK, C.C. and CUNNINGHAM, D.L. (1984). High dietary zinc and fasting as methods of forced resting: a performance comparison. *Poultry Science*, **63**, 1201–1206

NABER, E.C. (1983). Use of low sodium diets and low sodium–low protein diets for recycling of laying hens fed for intervals of 4, 6 or 8 weeks in a low light environment. *Proceedings of the Maryland Nutrition Conference, March 1983*, pp. 7–12

NABER, E.C., LATSHAW, J.D. and MARSH, G.A. (1984). Effectiveness of low sodium diets for recycling of egg production type hens. *Poultry Science*, **63**, 2419–2429

NEVALAINEN, T.J. (1969). The effect of calcium-deficient diet on the reproductive organs of the hen. *Poultry Science*, **48**, 653–659

NOLES, R.K. (1966). Subsequent production and egg quality of forced molted hens. *Poultry Science*, **45**, 50–57

NOLES, R.K. and TINDELL, D. (1967). Observations on the inter-relationships of egg quality traits and their association with season, age, and strain of bird. *Poultry Science*, **46**, 943–952

NORDSTROM, J.O. (1980). Albumen quality of eggs laid during molt induction. *Poultry Science*, **59**, 1711–1714

PALAFOX, A.L. and HO-A, E. (1980). Effect of zinc toxicity in laying White Leghorn pullets and hens. *Poultry Science*, **59**, 2024–2028

PETERSEN, C.F. (1964). Factors influencing egg shell quality. A review. *Idaho Agricultural Experimental Station Research Paper, No. 635*, 110–138

POPE, C.W., WATTS, A.B., WILLIAMS, E. and BRUNSON, C.C. (1960). The effect of the length of time in production and stage of egg formation on certain egg quality measurements and blood constituents of laying hens. *Poultry Science*, **39**, 1427–1431

ROLAND, D.A. and BRAKE, J. (1982). Influence of premoult production on postmoult performance with explanation for improvement in egg production due to force molting. *Poultry Science*, **51**, 2473–2481

ROSS, E. and HERRICK, R.B. (1981). Forced rest induced by molt or low-salt diet and subsequent hen performance. *Poultry Science*, **60**, 63–67

SAID, N.W., SULLIVAN, T.W., BIRD, H.R. and SUNDE, M.L. (1984). A comparison of the effect of two force molting methods on performance of two commercial strains of laying hens. *Poultry Science*, **63**, 2399–2403

SCOTT, J.T., CREGER, C.R., LINTON, S.S. and FARR, F.M. (1976). Molting the white leghorn hen with zinc. *Proceedings of the Texas Nutrition Conference, 1976*, pp. 41–51

SHIPPEE, R.L., STAKE, P.E., KOEHN, V., LAMBERT, J.L. and SIMMONS, R.W. (1979). High dietary zinc or magnesium as forced-resting agents for laying hens. *Poultry Science*, **58**, 949–954

SIMKISS, K. (ed.) (1967). *Calcium Metabolism in Laying Birds. Calcium in Reproductive Physiology*. New York, Reinhold Publishing Company

SNYDER, E.S. and ORR, H.L. (1960). The effect of length of lay, holding temperature, holding time and forced molting on egg quality. *Poultry Science*, **39**, 1297

STEVENSON, M.H. and JACKSON, N. (1984). Comparison of dietary hydrated copper sulphate, dietary zinc oxide and a direct method for inducing moult in laying hens. *British Poultry Science*, **25**, 505–517

SUMMERS, J.D. and LEESON, S. (1977). Sequential effects of restricted feeding and force-molting on laying hen performance. *Poultry Science*, **56**, 600–604

TANABE, Y., OGAWA, T. and NAKAMURA, T. (1981). The effect of short-term starvation on pituitary and plasma LH, plasma estradiol and progesterone, and on pituitary response to LH-RH in the laying hen (*Gallus domesticus*). *General and Comparative Endocrinology*, **43**, 392–398

THOMPSON, B.K., HAMILTON, R.M.G. and GRUNDER, A.A. (1985). The relationship between laboratory measures of egg shell quality and breakage in commercial egg washing and candling equipment. *Poultry Science*, **64**, 901–909

VERHEYEN, G., DECUYPERE, E., KÜHN, E.R., FONTAINE, G. and DE GROOTE, G. (1983). Arrêt de la ponte par induction chez la poule. Effet de différentes méthodes sur certains paramètres de production et sur les concentrations en hormones thyroidiennes, en prolactine, en Ca, P, Na et en protèines dans le sérum sanguin. *Revue de d'Agriculture*, **36**, 1535–1559

WAKELING, D.E. (1977). Induced moulting. A review of the literature, current practice and areas for further research. *World's Poultry Science Journal*, **33**, 12–20

WAKELING, D.E. (1985). New moulting programme keeps water on and adds limestone. *Poultry World*, **25**, 8–10

WHITEHEAD, C.C. and SHARP, P.J. (1976). An assessment of the optimal range of dietary sodium for inducing a pause in laying. *British Poultry Science*, **17**, 601–611

WOLFORD, J.H. (1984). Induced moulting in laying fowls. *World's Poultry Science Journal*, **40**, 66–73

Chapter 14

Environmental effects on egg quality

B. Sauveur and M. Picard

Introduction

The environment of the laying hen is composed of some well known parameters
such as temperature, relative humidity and lighting. However, it also includes other
characteristics, such as the housing condition (deep litter or cages), the shape and
dimensions of the cages, the system of food distribution and the bird density—all
parameters which may act on egg production rate and egg quality. This review tries
to gather results published or recently obtained on several of these topics without
claiming to be exhaustive.

It must also be remembered that the environment of the hen is also the
environment of the egg for the time which is spent between oviposition and
collection. When this environment is unfavourable (e.g. high temperature), the
direct effect on the egg (thinning of egg white or weakening of egg shell) must
evidently not be attributed to the hen.

High environmental temperatures

Studies conducted to determine the effects of high environmental temperatures
(ET) on egg quality are numerous and sometimes out-dated.

In reviewing some publications it is intended to focus successively on: first, a
short description of 'what happens', then an attempt to find which possible
explanations may be involved, before considering a few suggested techniques to
prevent this deterioration of egg quality.

Effect on the weight of the egg and its components

An increase of ET reduces egg weight as indicated by the work undertaken by
Ahvar *et al.* (1982) shown in *Figure 14.1*. This reduction of the egg weight varies
from 0.17–0.98 g/°C of increase of ET with an average value close to 0.4 g/°C. This
response has a curvilinear shape and is particularly noticeable above 25 °C.
According to Smith and Oliver (1972b), the effect of ET on egg weight might be
described by the following function:

$$Y = 59.6 - 1.34(0.2T - 16) - 0.313(0.2T - 16)^2$$

where Y is the egg weight (g) and T is ET in °F.

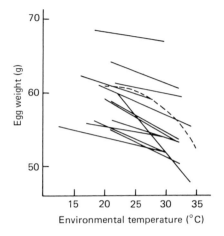

Figure 14.1 Effect of environmental temperature on egg weight. After Ahvar *et al.* (1982).

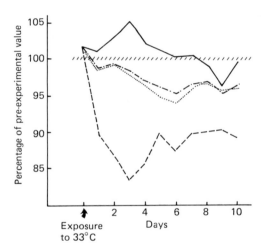

Figure 14.2 Changes in egg weight and egg components during the first 10 d after exposure to 33 °C. ——— vitellus; –·–·– egg; ····· albumen; – – – – shell. (Picard, Antoine and Sauveur, 1984, unpublished results).

In some studies, the relative proportions of yolk and albumen are not modified by high ET (Gee, Mulkey and Huston, 1964; Carmon and Huston, 1965; Smith and Oliver, 1972b) while in other cases the yolk and albumen weight are respectively more and less affected than the average egg weight (Miller and Sunde, 1975; El Jack and Blum, 1978; Ahvar *et al.*, 1982). The shell weight is always proportionally more affected than the other parts.

The dry matter concentration in yolk and albumen is generally not modified (Gee, Mulkey and Huston, 1964; Carmon and Huston, 1965) when temperature is lower than 35 °C. It may be reduced beyond that temperature (Smith and Oliver, 1972a; El-Gammal, Abo-Elkasem and Hassan, 1978). A small decrease in yolk lipid content was noticed by Van Kampen (1983) after a very early heat stress of pullets exposed to 36 °C between three and five weeks of age.

The depressive effects of high ET on shell weight and albumen weight are immediate as indicated by *Figure 14.2* (Picard, Antoine and Sauveur, 1984, unpublished results). In contrast, the weight of vitellus is not affected for four or five days but decreases thereafter. Hence, the decrease in albumen volume is not directly linked to the reduction of the vitellus size.

Effect on albumen quality

Contrary to a widely held view, the initial albumen quality expressed as Haugh units is very little, if any, affected by high ET (Hall and Helbacka, 1959; Clark and Amin, 1965; Daniel and Balnave, 1981; Ahvar *et al.*, 1982). However, the albumen height is rapidly reduced after laying if the egg is not immediately withdrawn from a poultry house with high ET.

Effect on shell quality

It is well established that elevated ET is associated with a decrease in shell quality (*see* reviews of Wolford and Tanaka, 1970; Smith, 1974). Smith and Oliver (1972b) reported that the relationship between ET and shell weight is curvilinear within the range 26.5–35 °C and may be represented by the expression:

$$Y = 6.8 - 0.25(0.2T - 16) - 0.07(0.2T - 16)^2$$

where Y is the shell weight (g) and T is ET in °F. The work of El-Boushy, Simons and Wiertz (1968) demonstrated that all the layers of the shell except the membranes are affected (*Figure 14.3*).

Various physiological mechanisms have been considered in relation to high temperature exposures. Nordstrom (1973) has shown that the developing egg spends a slightly *longer* period of time (about 2 h) in the shell gland at 32 °C than at

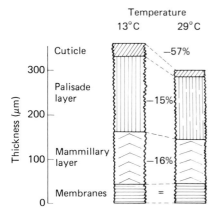

Figure 14.3 Effect of high environmental temperature on the different layers of egg shell (after El-Boushy, Simons and Wiertz, 1968).

21 °C. So factors other than time must be responsible for the decreased deposition of shell at 32 °C. A possibly important factor is a lowered blood flow (-30 to 40%) through ovarian follicles and shell gland due to peripheral vasodilation (Wolfenson *et al.*, 1981).

The most recognised effect of hyperthermia in birds is panting and progressive respiratory alkalosis (Richards, 1970). In this situation, the carbon dioxide content of the blood first decreases and is then followed by an extrarenal elimination of bicarbonate ions which restores the blood pH near to the normal value. This correction effect limits the ionic exchanges in the shell gland (Mongin, 1978) which is consistent with the observed immediate decrease in egg shell thickness (*Figure 14.2*).

The lower intake of calcium due to the effect of high ET on food intake does not necessarily result in a shortage of calcium at the metabolic level. Mueller (1959) reported that calcium retention was increased; however, several authors have observed a decrease in total blood calcium level (de Andrade, Rogler and Featherston, 1974; Kohne and Jones, 1975; El Jack, Blum and Sauveur, 1978) under high ET. More specifically, Odom *et al.* (1982) reported a decrease in blood ionic calcium content which may be due to its binding with organic acids (lactate and pyruvate) or with proteins. It has also been observed that high ET resulted in a lowered carbonic anhydrase activity in the shell gland and kidneys (Goto, Harris and Waldroup, 1979), and in an increase in parathyroid gland weight, duodenal CaBP activity, percentage tibia bone ash (Odom *et al.*, 1983) and 25-hydroxycholecalciferol-1-hydroxylase activity (Bailey and Creger, 1982). So it is likely that, during a thermal stress, the contribution of calcium from bone stores to calcium homeostasis might be limited by an unknown mechanism; this awaits further clarification.

Possible techniques for reducing the effect on shell quality

It is difficult to prevent effects which are not still completely understood. However, various techniques to correct the disorders of the acid-base balance, to compensate for the lowered food intake by manipulation of the diet concentration and to adjust temperature cycles may be discussed here.

Several correction methods of the effects of lowered blood levels in bicarbonate and carbon dioxide have been suggested. Sodium bicarbonate addition to the food was found to be ineffective (El-Boushy, 1966; Cox and Balloun, 1968) or no more effective than under normal ET (Howes, 1967). Only Ernst *et al.* (1975) observed that hens receiving 0.3% of sodium bicarbonate (and 0.05% of sodium chloride) in their diet produced fewer rough-shelled eggs than controls (0.25% sodium chloride diet) during summer. A positive effect of carbonated water was also demonstrated at 35 °C by Odom, Harrison and Darre (1981).

The positive effect on egg shell quality of chronic exposition to carbon dioxide-enriched atmosphere was demonstrated 20 years ago (Frank and Burger, 1965; Mongin, 1968). It may be explained by the fact that the buffer capacity of the blood increases during a chronic respiratory acidosis (Sauveur and Mongin, 1972). Simultaneously, the albumen quality tends to decline (Sauveur, 1974). However, the use of carbon dioxide-enriched atmosphere cannot be suggested as a practical solution against the effects of high ET as long as it involves a lowered ventilation rate. The carbon dioxide concentration in the air is only worthy of control

Table 14.1 Direct vs food intake-mediated effects of high environmental temperatures. After Smith and Oliver (1972a): paired feeding experiments at 21 °C and 38 °C.

	Direct effect (%)	Indirect effect (food intake-mediated) (%)
Laying rate	−23	−26
Egg weight	−10	−7
Dry yolk	−12	−5
Dry albumen	−10	−8
Dry egg shell	−33	−2
Shell thickness	−27	−1
Shell strength	−39	0

experimentally because it may sometimes explain low responses to high ET (Daniel and Balnave, 1981).

Feeding a food more concentrated in some nutrients is a common approach to correct the detrimental effect of heat on food and energy intake. However, the paired feeding experiments conducted by Smith and Oliver (1972a), which show that the harmful effect of heat can be split into a direct and an indirect (food intake-mediated) effect suggest that this may not be worthwhile (*Table 14.1*). Clearly from their data, egg shell quality is mainly affected by heat *per se*, while 40–50% of the heat effect on egg weight and laying rate may be attributed to the food intake reduction. This result is confirmed by several authors and when better performances are observed with a more concentrated food, the improvement is sometimes similar in normal and high ET (Daghir, 1973; Olomu and Offiong, 1983).

In other cases the increase in food concentration is without any effect (El Jack and Blum, 1978) or even unfavourable to egg shell quality on a short-term basis (Tanor, Leeson and Summers, 1984). So an increase in food concentration does not seem to be a substantial tool to fight the effects of heat stress on egg quality.

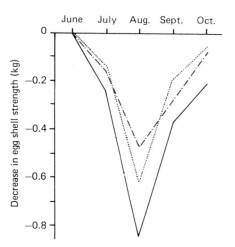

Figure 14.4 Effect of dietary oyster shell and season on egg shell strength. ——— Control; ····· ¼ fossil shell; –·–·–·– ¾ fossil shell. After Mekada *et al.* (1976).

Table 14.2 Combined effects on egg shell of an abrupt increase in environmental temperature (20 °C to 33 °C) and of dietary calcium source (pulverised limestone in the diet vs oyster shells offered separately). After Picard, Antoine and Sauveur, unpublished results (1985)

Diet[a]		End of control period (20 °C)	2nd day at 33 °C	24th–28th days at 33 °C
Control	Egg weight (g)	61.1	60.0	57.7
(pulverised	Egg shell weight (g)	5.84	4.47	5.22
limestone)	SWUSA[b]	8.04	6.26	7.48
Oyster	Egg weight (g)	62.2	60.0	58.9
shell	Egg shell weight (g)	5.82	4.96	5.42
	SWUSA[b]	7.93	6.90	7.67

[a]24 ISA Brown hens per treatment.
[b]Shell weight per unit of surface area (g/100 cm²).

Another possible way of action is the introduction into the diet of oyster shells or other 'hen-sized' sources of calcium which enables the hen to consume calcium independently from other nutrients. The original work of Scott and Mullenhoff (1970) showing a favourable effect of hen-sized oyster shells on egg shell quality was in fact conducted during the hottest part of summer. Later, Roland and Harms (1973) and Mekada *et al.* (1976) confirmed that oyster shell is much more efficient during summer than during winter (*Figure 14.4*) and the same trend is shown in the short-term experiment conducted by Picard, Antoine and Sauveur (unpublished results, 1985) reported in *Table 14.2*.

It has been demonstrated by Bhatti and Morris (1977) that, under continuous lighting, ET can be a phase setting signal for oviposition, egg shell formation taking place during the cool period. Under commercial conditions during summer, Deaton *et al.* (1981) have shown that, if the house ET at night is decreased to that of the outside temperature (21 °C), shell strength will be improved. So 'night cooling' might sometimes be an effective solution even though the economics of such a technique remain to be evaluated.

In conclusion, the detrimental effects of high ET on egg quality (mainly egg shell quality) are not easily corrected; the most effective solutions seem to be to use a 'hen-sized' source of calcium and maybe 'night cooling'.

When high humidity is added to high ET it seems that the depression of egg weight and egg shell quality is even more pronounced. This trend appears in the results of Picard and Bouchot (unpublished results, 1985; *see Table 14.3*), although

Table 14.3 Combined effects of high environmental temperature and relative humidity on egg composition. Picard and Bouchot, unpublished results (1985)[a]

	Temperature (°C)			
	20	33	33	20
	Relative humidity (%)			
	50	30	85	50
Egg weight (g)	58.1	56.2	54.2	59.0
Egg shell weight (g)	5.72	5.47	4.89	5.85
Yolk weight (g)	15.0	14.3	13.9	15.2
Albumen weight (g)	37.5	36.4	35.3	38.0
Yolk dry matter (%)	52.7	51.0	50.9	51.5
Albumen dry matter (%)	12.8	12.4	12.0	12.2

[a]36 ISA Brown hens studied during four successive 28 d periods. Egg measurements taken during the last week of each period.

it is difficult to separate in their experiment the genuine effect of humidity from that of a prolonged exposure to 33 °C.

Lighting programmes

The lighting programmes used during the rearing period of the young pullet control its sexual precocity and subsequently some egg characteristics, such as egg weight and/or egg shell weight. However, this effect is only an indirect one and will not be considered here.

Effect of length of photoperiod with traditional lighting

When laying hens are lighted by only one photoperiod/d (the usual situation) the length of this photoperiod may affect egg shell quality in terms of body-checked eggs and misshapen eggs. Roland and Moore (1980) suggested that body-checked eggs are produced when egg shells are broken in the shell gland during the first hours of calcification. It is important to keep the birds as quiet as possible during this period and that can be achieved by reducing the day length; providing a 15 h instead of an 18 h photoperiod reduced the number of body-checked eggs by at least 50% without any adverse effect on production (Roland, 1982).

Effect of intermittent lighting and ahemeral light–dark cycles

Important modifications to egg quality (egg weight and shell quality) may be obtained by two different manipulations of lighting programmes: intermittent lighting and ahemeral light–dark cycles.

Interest in intermittent lighting (IL) has been revived during the last 10 years because this technique permits a saving in electrical energy and food. The effects on the egg may also be important, but they depend on the type of IL used. According to the reviews by Sauveur (1982) and Rowland (1985) all the schedules of IL reported in the literature may be classified into two categories.

Type 1 intermittent lighting

Type 1 IL consists of a light and dark sequence which is repeated more than once during a 24 h period (e.g. 3L:3D or 1L:3D). It may be regarded as a very short nycthemere of 6 h or 4 h duration. With this situation, each light extinction has a similar effect on the flock and a desynchronisation of ovipositions inside the 24 h period is observed.

Since the first study of Wilson and Abplanalp (1956), numerous authors have described the effects of such very short nycthemeres (Bell and Moreng, 1973; Cooper and Johnston, 1974; Cooper and Barnett, 1977; Bougon et al., 1980; Duplaix, 1980; Nys and Mongin, 1981; Torges, Rauch and Wegner, 1981; Bougon, Protais and L'Hospitalier, 1982; Sauveur and Mongin, 1983). All these studies (Table 14.4 and Figure 14.5) reported a decrease in egg production and food consumption and an increase in egg weight and shell quality (shell weight and shell strength). In the field experiment of Bougon, Protais and L'Hospitalier (1982) the

Table 14.4 Effects of Type 1 intermittent lighting on egg quality (variations in percentage of control values)

Ref.	Lighting pro-gramme	Strain[c]	Age (weeks)	Laying rate	Egg weight	Percentage of shell SG or SWUSA[a]	Shell weight or thickness	Shell breaking strength	Haugh units
1	⅙L:3⅚D	W	20–48	−5.5	+2.7*				
		W	24–76	−5.2	+3.2*		+1.0		+3.0
2	2L:2D	W	20–72	−5.7	+2.5		+6.0*		−2.5*
	2L:4D	W	20–72	−4.1	+0.7		+5.4*		−1.9*
	2L:6D	W	20–72	−2.0	0		+4.2*		−1.7*
3	3L:3D	B	49–65	−1.6	+1.5*			+2.3	−2.8
4	3L:3D	B	24–66	−4.4*	+2.8*			+3.9*	
5	3L:3D	B	39–42	−6.4*	+5.7*	+7.9*		+7.0*	
	4L:4D	B	39–42	−5.3*	+5.7*	+8.1*		+12.5*	
6	2.5L:2.5D	B	29–61		+5.2*	+1.8	+7.2*		
7	4L:2D	W	20–36	−11.0	+3.8*	+5.6*	+9.7*	+7.8*	−1.5
	4L:2D	W	28–72	−11.0*	+3.8*	+3.0*	+7.5*	+1.1	0
	8L:4D	W	28–72	−6.8*	+2.8*	+4.3*	+7.5*	+3.7*	−1.5
8	1.5L:4.5D	B	25–60	−6.5*	+6.8*	+6.7*	+9.6*	+13.6*	
	3L:3D[b]	B	25–60	−5.5*	+5.3*	+4.3*	+7.7*	+11.0*	

[a]SG = specific gravity; SWUSA = shell weight per unit of surface area.
[b]Then evolving to 1.5L:4.5D
[c]W: White-shelled eggs; B: Brown-shelled eggs.
*Significant variation relative to the control group ($P < 0.05$).
Refs. (1) Bell and Moreng, 1973; (2) Cooper and Barnett, 1977; (3) Bougon et al., 1980; (4) Bougon, Protais and L'Hospitalier, 1982; (5) Nys and Mongin, 1981; (6) Duplaix, 1980; (7) Torges, Rauch and Wegner, 1981; (8) Sauveur and Mongin, 1983.

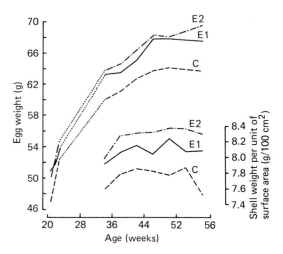

Figure 14.5 Time-scale of egg weight and egg shell weight under control and Type 1 intermittent lighting programmes: C = control 14L:10D; E1 = 8L:16D up to 18 weeks of age then 3L:3D; E2 = 1.5L:4.5D after 4 weeks of age. After Sauveur and Mongin (1983).

average proportion of cracked eggs was reduced from 7.2% down to 5.9%. During the last part of lay the figures were 13.0% and 8.6% respectively.

This increase in shell deposition under very short nycthemeres may be partly due to lengthening of shell deposition in the shell gland as indicated by the observed longest time intervals between ovipositions (Duplaix, Williams and Mongin, 1981; Sauveur and Mongin, 1983) and by the observed better colouration of brown shells (Bougon, Protais and L'Hospitalier, 1982). It is also likely that the chronology of calcium ingestion is better because Type 1 IL is the only situation permitting a correct food intake during shell calcification (Nys and Mongin, 1981; Torges, Rauch and Wegner, 1981).

The increase in egg weight observed with Type 1 IL is not only due to the shell weight increase but also to increases in yolk and albumen depositions without any modification of their normal ratio (Bell and Moreng, 1973; Duplaix, 1980). This may be related to the slowing down of the ovulatory rhythm of the hen.

A slight decrease in Haugh unit value of eggs (between 2 and 4 units) in response to Type 1 IL was reported by Cooper and Barnett (1977) and Bougon, Protais and L'Hospitalier (1982), but not by Bell and Moreng (1973) or Torges, Rauch and Wegner (1981). On the other hand, a significant increase in albumen dry matter content (12.1% vs 11.6%) was recorded by Bougon et al. (1980) using a 3L:3D programme during the last part of the laying period.

Numerous field trials conducted in France confirm the effects of Type 1 IL on egg weight and egg shell strength (Crochon, 1979; Dromigny, 1980; Trémolières, 1983). The size of the response depends on the degree of desynchronisation between the birds, itself depending on the isolation of the poultry house. In experimental conditions (references 5, 6 and 8 of *Table 14.4*) with an excellent desynchronisation, the variations in laying rate and egg weight are large (between 5 and 10%), while in field conditions both are smaller (between 3 and 5%). However, the reduction in cracked eggs is always significant.

Type 2 intermittent lighting

The Type 2 IL is characterised by asymmetrical or non-repeating light patterns; a main dark period can always be distinguished and the hens remain synchronised. The birds choose their waking up and sleeping times in order to obtain a 'subjective day' of no longer than 15 h (Mongin, 1980). The best known example of this Type 2 IL is 2L:8D:2L:12D. Such treatments do not generally alter either egg production or egg weight and shell quality, as shown by Van Tienhoven and Ostrander (1973, 1976) using light layers as well as by Skoglund and Whittaker (1980) with medium-weight strains. Similarly, interruption of a normal night by a 1 or 2 h light period does not increase egg shell deposition (Brake, 1980; Torges, Rauch and Wegner, 1981), probably because the hens ignore this secondary light period (Sauveur, 1982). In addition, a 'Bio-mittent' programme splitting each of 16 successive hours of light into 15 min light and 45 min dark (Engster, Snetsinger and Ragland, 1979) may induce a slight decrease in egg weight (0.5–1.0%), associated with increased shell strength (1–1.5%).

Ahemeral light–dark cycles

The effects of ahemeral light–dark cycles on egg weight and shell quality have been reviewed by Morris (1981) and Shanawany (1982). As shown in *Figure 14.6*, the

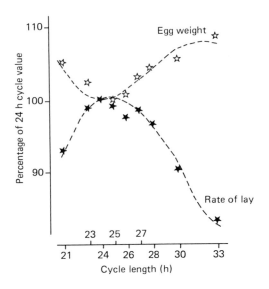

Figure 14.6 Relationship of rate of lay and egg weight to the length of an ahemeral light–dark cycle. After Shanawany (1982).

rate of lay declines linearly as the cycle length increases from 24 h to 33 h. In the same conditions, egg size increases in association with the extra time spent in the oviduct (Melek, Morris and Jennings, 1973). Both yolk weight and albumen weight are increased (Morris, 1973; Leeson, Summers and Etches, 1979). A very marked effect of long ahemeral cycles is the increase of egg shell weight by 4–5% for 26 h cycles, 6–8% for 27 h and up to 11% for 28 h cycles (Fox, Morris and Jennings, 1971; Lacassagne and Sauveur, 1973; Leeson, Summers and Etches, 1979; Yannakopoulos and Morris, 1979).

Cooper and Barnett (1976) and Nordstrom (1982) reported that increased cycle length may be associated with a small, non-significant reduction of the Haugh unit values of the eggs laid (−2%). However, this may be explained by the fact that eggs were collected at different times in the control and in the experimental poultry houses.

A disadvantage of long ahemeral cycles is the lack of any electrical energy saving. This could be corrected by splitting the light period as earlier explained for a 24 h cycle (Type 2 IL), since Van Tienhoven, Ostrander and Gehle (1984), using a 2L:6D:2L:18D, observed increases in egg weight and egg shell strength equal to 8% and 10% respectively.

In conclusion, ahemeral light–dark cycles longer than 24 h and Type 1 IL act partly in the same way. By lengthening the time interval between two successive ovipositions, they permit an increase in yolk, albumen and shell deposition. If they are used when the laying rate is no longer maximal (second half of lay) their detrimental effect on laying rate is small. They are a good means of reducing the problems of shell fragility at the end of lay.

Housing conditions

During the last ten years, several studies have been conducted in order to determine whether the housing conditions of laying hens (free range, deep litter or cages) affect egg composition and/or egg quality. The results are summarised in *Tables 14.5* and *14.6*.

It is evident that such comparisons are not easy because many factors may vary simultaneously. So, although the diets are usually kept constant within the

Table 14.5 Effects of housing conditions on gross egg composition. Variations (%) relative to eggs produced in cages.

Reference	Egg weight	% of each part			Dry matter content			Lipids	Proteins
		Yolk	Albumen	Shell	Yolk	Albumen	Total		
Deep litter									
1								+2.3/+4.1*	
2[a]	+1		−0.7						
2[b]	+4*		−1.0						
4								−3.3*	+2.5*
6	−3.1*								
7					+1.0		−1.2	−1.7	−1.2
8	−0.1	−2.6*	+1.0	+2.3*	+0.6*			−1.2*	
8	−0.3	−0.3	+0.3	−1.1					
9							−1.6	−1.8	−0.8
10	−3.2							0	
Free range									
1								+2.3/+3.8*	
5	+3.1	−4.2*							
9							0	+1.8	+0.8
10	+1.6							0	

*Significant variation relative to eggs produced in cages (P < 0.05).
Refs (1) Bergami *et al.*, 1978; (2) Chand and Razdan, 1977; (4) Mäkinen *et al.*, 1985; (5) Pavlovski, Masic and Apostolov, 1982; (6) Prasad *et al.*, 1981; (7) Ristic and Freudenreich, 1984; (8) Scholtyssek, 1975; (9) Tolan *et al.*, 1974; (10) Torges, Matthes and Harnish, 1976.
[a]0.28 m²/♀.
[b]0.14 m²/♀.

Table 14.6 Effects of housing conditions on some egg quality traits. Variations (%) relative to eggs produced in cages.

Reference[c]	Yolk colour	Albumen height	Egg shell strength	Blood and meat spot incidence
Deep litter				
2[a]		+11*	0	−5
2[b]		+6*	0	+87*
6	0	0		
7	−2.3			
8			−0.3	
8	+1.5*	−4.8*	+5.6	
10	−4.9	−3.2	+3.0	
Free range				
5	+45*	+12*	+9*	
10	−27*	−11*	−6*	

*Significant variation relative to eggs produced in cages (P < 0.05).
[a]0.28 m²/♀.
[b]0.14 m²/♀.
[c]See *Table 14.5* for references.

comparisons between deep litter and cages, they are often hard to control in free range conditions. It is therefore possible that the egg content of some compounds, such as fatty acids or trace elements, are modified in response to feeding rather than by a direct effet of the housing condition.

As shown in *Table 14.5*, most of the observed differences for egg weight and gross egg composition are non-significant. Compared to that recorded in cages, egg weight is not always reduced by deep litter systems, but the yolk percentage might be slightly reduced by 2–4%. Also, the lipid content of the yolk tends to increase both on deep litter and in free range conditions.

Effect on chemical composition of the eggs

Small modifications in the chemical composition of the eggs have been observed by some workers and not by others. Tolan *et al*. (1974) found no significant variation in the amino acid composition of proteins, while Scholtyssek (1975) showed that the relative parts of sulphur amino acids and lysine could be reduced in eggs produced in deep litter and free range as compared with cage conditions. Similarly an increase in palmitic acid content was noted by Bergami *et al*. (1978) and Mäkinen *et al*. (1985), but not by Tolan *et al*. (1974). On the contrary, four available results indicate an increase in linoleic acid (6–15%) and a decrease in stearic (3–6%) and oleic acid (1–4%) contents of the egg with deep litter and free range housing conditions (Tolan *et al*., 1974; Bergami *et al*., 1978). In the same conditions, the cholesterol content increases by between 3 and 25% (Tolan *et al*., 1974; Scholtyssek, 1975; Torges, Matthes and Harnish, 1976; Ristic and Freudenreich, 1984) and the vitamin A content decreases some 0.4–8% (Scholtyssek, 1975; Ristic and Freudenreich, 1984). Other significant variations observed by Tolan *et al*. (1974) were increases in folic acid and vitamin B_{12} contents (40–70%) and decreases in calcium (7%) and iron (6%) contents for eggs produced on deep litter or free range compared with cages.

Effect on egg quality traits

The observed variations for egg quality traits are also small and variable (*Table 14.6*). In deep litter conditions as opposed to cages, albumen and egg shell qualities are not consistently changed. A sharp increase in the blood and meat spot incidence was observed by Chand and Razdan (1977) when the litter floor space was limited to $0.14\,m^2$/bird. The two observations done in free range conditions gave totally opposite results for the three recorded criteria (*Table 14.6*), which probably illustrates the variability of eggs produced in such conditions.

Effect on organoleptic traits of eggs

Organoleptic traits of eggs (odour and flavour) have been studied by three groups of authors (Torges, Matthes and Harnish, 1976; Colas and Sauvageot, 1979; Mäkinen *et al*., 1985). In the first study, eggs produced in cages or on deep litter were classified as better than eggs produced in free range conditions. In the second study, comparing seven free range situations to one deep litter and one cage condition, eggs laid in cages were classified as the best and eggs obtained on deep litter as the worst, all free range eggs occupying an intermediate rank. In the third study, all expressed judgements were satisfactory. So free range eggs present organoleptic traits potentially more variable (and not necessarily better) than eggs produced in more controlled housing conditions.

Moreover, the studies of Torges, Matthes and Harnish (1976) and Matthes (1979) clearly demonstrated that eggs produced in free range conditions showed a higher degree of internal contamination (on yolk and inner shell membrane) by bacteria (*Streptococcus*, *Staphylococcus* and especially *E. coli*), due to the dirtiness of the egg shell.

In conclusion, eggs produced on deep litter or in free range conditions do not present objective advantages for the consumer. Their composition and physical properties are practically unchanged while their bacteriological state is degraded. Thus, modifications of the egg characteristics are not the arguments which might be used to change the usual system of cage housing of hens.

References

AHVAR, F., PETERSEN, J., HORST, P. and THEIN, H. (1982). Veranderungen der Eibeschaffenheit in der 1. Legeperiode unter dem Einfluss hoher Umwelttemperaturen. *Archiv für Geflügelkunde*, **46**, 1–8

BAILEY, C.A. and CREGER, C.R. (1982). 25-hydroxycholecalciferol-1-hydroxylase activity in heat stressed laying hens. *Poultry Science*, **61**, 586–588

BELL, D.D. and MORENG, R.E. (1973). Intermittent feeding and lighting of mature Leghorn hens. *Poultry Science*, **52**, 982–991

BERGAMI, W., GIAVARINI, I., MINOCCHERI, F. and NEGRINI, F. (1978). Compozione delle uova e technica di allevamento. *Rivista de Avicoltura*, **47**, 35–38

BHATTI, B.M. and MORRIS, T.R. (1977). The relative importance of light and temperature as phase setting signals for oviposition in the fowl. *British Poultry Science*, **18**, 391–395

BOUGON, M., PROTAIS, J. and L'HOSPITALIER, R. (1982). Etude des performances et de la qualité des oeufs chez des pondeuses soumises à un éclairement discontinu par périodes de trois heures (2è essai). *Bulletin d'Information de la Station de Ploufragan*, **22**, 155–161

BOUGON, M., LE ROUX, J.L., PROTAIS, J. and L'HOSPITALIER, R. (1980). Etude des performances et de la qualité des oeufs chez des pondeuses soumises à un éclairement discontinu par périodes de trois heures. *Bulletin d'Information de la Station de Ploufragan*, **20**, 69–72, 77

BRAKE, J. (1980). Relationship of intermittent dark or lighted periods to performance of hens. *Poultry Science*, **59**, 1586

CARMON, L.G. and HUSTON, T.M. (1965). The influence of environmental temperature upon egg components of domestic fowl. *Poultry Science*, **44**, 1237–1240

CHAND, D. and RAZDAN, M.N. (1977). Incidence of blood spots and/or meat spots in eggs from White Leghorn hens maintained under different housing conditions during their pullet year production. *Indian Poultry Gazette*, **61**, 151–152

CLARK, C.E. and AMIN, M. (1965). The adaptability of chickens to various temperatures. *Poultry Science*, **44**, 1003–1009

COLAS, B. and SAUVAGEOT, F. (1979). L'opinion favorable dont jouit l'oeuf de ferme est-elle justifiée? Une première approche. *Courrier Avicole*, **765**, 38–41

COOPER, J.B. and BARNETT, B.D. (1976). Ahemeral photoperiods for chicken hens. *Poultry Science*, **55**, 1183–1187

COOPER, J.B. and BARNETT, B.D. (1977). Photoperiod study with chicken hens. *Poultry Science*, **56**, 1832–1835

COOPER, J.B. and JOHNSTON, W.E. (1974). Albumen quality and shell thickness as affected by time of egg gathering. *Poultry Science*, **53**, 1519–1521

COX, A.C. and BALLOUN, S.L. (1968). Lack of effect of sodium bicarbonate on shell characteristics. *Poultry Science*, **47**, 1370–1371

CROCHON, C. (1979). Peut-on réduire le prix de revient de l'oeuf? *Courrier Avicole, Suppl.* **725**, 23–27

DAGHIR, N.J. (1973). Energy requirements of laying hens in a semi-arid continental climate. *British Poultry Science*, **14**, 451–461

DANIEL, M. and BALNAVE, D. (1981). Responses of laying hens to gradual and abrupt increases in ambient temperature and humidity. *Australian Journal of Experimental Agriculture and Animal Husbandry*, **21**, 189–195

DE ANDRADE, A.N., ROGLER, J.C. and FEATHERSTON, W.R. (1974). Effects of heat stress and diet on shell quality and performance of laying hens. *Poultry Science*, **53**, 1916–1917

DEATON, J.W., REECE, F.N., MCNAUGHTON, J.L. and LOTT, B.D. (1981). Effect of differing temperature cycles on egg shell quality and layer performance. *Poultry Science*, **60**, 733–737

DROMIGNY, J.C. (1980). Le point sur les techniques de rationnement. *Courrier Avicole*, **776**, 8–10

DUPLAIX, M. (1980). Effets d'un éclairement discontinu sur la ponte, la qualité des oeufs et le niveau de LH chez *Gallus. Mémoire de DEA, ENSA de Rennes*, 57pp.

DUPLAIX, M., WILLIAMS, J. and MONGIN, P. (1981). Effects of an intermittent lighting schedule on the time of egg-laying and the levels of luteinizing hormone, progesterone and corticosterone in the plasma of the domestic hen. *Journal of Endocrinology*, **91**, 375–383

EL-BOUSHY, A.R. (1966). Egg shell quality and microstructure as affected by vitamin C, other feed additives and high environmental temperatures. *Mededelingen van de Landbouwhoogeschool te Wageningen*, **66**, 1–79

EL-BOUSHY, A.R., SIMONS, P.C.M. and WIERTZ, G. (1968). Structure and ultra-structure of the hen's egg shell as influenced by environmental temperature, humidity and vitamin C additions. *Mededelingen van de Landbouwhoogeschool te Wageningen*, **66**, 456–467

EL-GAMMAL, A.M., ABO-ELKASEM, M. and HASSAN, G.M. (1978). Chemical composition of chicken egg as influenced by crossing, hatching time and season. *Alexandria Journal of Agricultural Research*, **26**, 537–543

EL JACK, M.H. and BLUM, J.C. (1978). The influence of high constant environmental temperature and energy level in the diet on the performance of the laying hen. *Archiv für Geflügelkunde*, **42**, 216–220

EL JACK, M.H., BLUM, J.C. and SAUVEUR, B. (1978). The effect of high constant and fluctuating temperatures on blood acid-base balance and some plasma components of the laying hen. *Archiv für Geflügelkunde*, **42**, 123–127

ENGSTER, H.M., SNETSINGER, D.C. and RAGLAND, W.W. (1979). Biomittent lighting for pullets and layers. *Poultry Digest*, **38**, 604–610

ERNST, R.A., FRANK, F.R., PRICE, F.C., BURGER, R.E. and HALLORAN, H.R. (1975). The effect of feeding low chloride diets with added sodium bicarbonate on egg shell quality and other economic traits. *Poultry Science*, **54**, 270–274

FOX, S., MORRIS, T.R. and JENNINGS, R.C. (1971). The use of non-24-hour cycles to manipulate egg weight in pullets. *World's Poultry Science Journal*, **27**, 159

FRANK, F.R. and BURGER, R.E. (1965). The effect of carbon dioxide inhalation and sodium bicarbonate ingestion on eggshell deposition. *Poultry Science*, **44**, 1604–1606

GEE, G., MULKEY, J. and HUSTON, T. (1964). The influence of environmental temperature upon egg components. *Poultry Science*, **43**, 1321–1322

GOTO, K., HARRIS, G.C., JR. and WALDROUP, P.W. (1979). Relationship between pimpling of egg shells, environmental temperature and carbonic anhydrase activity of certain body tissues. *Poultry Science*, **58**, 1014

HALL, K.N. and HELBACKA, N.V. (1959). Improving albumen quality. *Poultry Science*, **38**, 111–114

HOWES, J.R. (1967). Acid–base relationships and calcium deposition in the egg shell. *Distillers Feed Research Council Proceedings*, **22**, 32–39

KOHNE, H.J. and JONES, J.E. (1975). Acid–base balance, plasma electrolytes and production performances of adult turkey hens under conditions of increasing ambient temperature. *Poultry Science*, **54**, 2038–2045

LACASSAGNE, L. and SAUVEUR, B. (1973). Nycthémères de 26 et 28 heures et dépôt de la coquille chez la poule domestique. *Annales de Zootechnie*, **22**, 103–109

LEESON, S., SUMMERS, J.D. and ETCHES, R.J. (1979). Effect of a 28 hour light:dark cycle on egg shell quality of end-of-lay birds. *Poultry Science*, **58**, 285–287

MÄKINEN, S.M., KAHARI, K., LUMIAHO, L. and UUSI-RAUVA, E. (1985). Contents and flavour of Finnish eggs. *World Poultry*, **48**, 30

MATTHES, S. (1979). Einfluss der Faktoren Gewinnung und Lagerung auf die lebensmittelhygienische Qualität von Hünereiern. *Wiener Terärztliche Monatsschrift*, **66**, 154–156

MEKADA, H., HAYASHI, N., OKUMURA, J.I. and YOKOTA, H.O. (1976). Effect of dietary fossil shell on the quality of hen's egg shell in summer. *Japanese Poultry Science*, **13**, 65–69

MELEK, O., MORRIS, T.R. and JENNINGS, R.C. (1973). The time factor in egg formation for hens exposed to ahemeral light–dark cycles. *British Poultry Science*, **14**, 493–498

MILLER, P.C. and SUNDE, M.L. (1975). The effects of precise constant and cyclic environments on shell quality and other lay performance factors with Leghorn pullets. *Poultry Science*, **54**, 36–46

MONGIN, P. (1968). Keeping laying hens in CO_2 enriched atmosphere. *Proceedings of IIIrd European Poultry Congress, Jerusalem*, Work Group No. 7, p. 565

MONGIN, P. (1978). Acid–base balance during eggshell formation. In *Respiratory Function in Birds, Adult and Embryonic*, (Piiper, J., ed.), pp. 247–259. Berlin, Springer Verlag

MONGIN, P. (1980). Food intake and oviposition by domestic fowl under symmetric skeleton photoperiods. *British Poultry Science*, **21**, 389–394

MORRIS, T.R. (1973). The effects of ahemeral light and dark cycles on egg production in the fowl. *Poultry Science*, **52**, 423–445

MORRIS, T.R. (1981). Using lights to manipulate egg size and pattern of lay in pullet flocks. *Proceedings of Maryland Nutrition Conference for Feed Manufacturers*, pp. 95–101

MUELLER, W.J. (1959). The effect of environmental temperature and humidity on the calcium balance and serum calcium of laying pullets. *Poultry Science*, **38**, 1296–1301

NORDSTROM, J.O. (1973). Duration of egg formation in chickens during heat stress. *Poultry Science*, **52**, 1687–1690

NORDSTROM, J.O. (1982). Shell quality of eggs from hens exposed to 26- and 27-hour light–dark cycles from 56 to 76 weeks of age. *Poultry Science*, **61**, 804–812

NYS, Y. and MONGIN, P. (1981). The effect of 6- and 8-hour light–dark cycles on egg production and pattern of ovipositions. *British Poultry Science*, **22**, 391–397

ODOM, T.W., HARRISON, P.C. and DARRE, M.J. (1981). The effects of carbonated drinking water on egg shell quality during high environmental temperature. *Poultry Science*, **60**, 1704

ODOM, T.W., HARRISON, P.C., MAIN, B. and BOTTJE, W.G. (1982). Changes in the blood acid–base balance and blood ionized calcium concentration of SCWL hens during an acute heat stress. *Poultry Science*, **61**, 1519–1520

ODOM, T.W., CREGER, C.R., CAIN, J.R., COSTELLO, D. and BAILEY, C.A. (1983). The effect of thermal stress on parathyroid gland weight, duodenal calcium-binding protein activity and bone mineral in SCWL hens. *Poultry Science*, **62**, 1476

OLOMU, J.M. and OFFIONG, S.A. (1983). The performance of brown egg-type layers fed different protein and energy levels in the Tropics. *Poultry Science*, **62**, 345–352

PAVLOVSKI, Z., MASIC, B. and APOSTOLOV, N. (1982). Quality of eggs laid by hens kept on free range and in cages. In *Quality of Eggs*, (Beuving, G., Sheele, C.W. and Simons, P.C.M., eds), pp. 231–235. Beekbergen, Spelderholt Institute

PRASAD, A.J., KOTHANDARAMAN, P., KADIRVEL, R. and KRISHNAN, A.R. (1981). Influence of strain, housing and season on egg quality traits in White Leghorn pullets. *Cheiron*, **10**, 63–66

RICHARDS, S.A. (1970). Physiology of thermal panting. *Annales de Biologie Animale, Biochimie et Biophysique*, **10**, 151–168

RISTIC, M. and FREUDENREICH, P. (1984). Einfluss des Haltungs-systems auf die Eiqualität. *Proceedings of the XVIIth World Poultry Congress, Helsinki*, pp. 696–698

ROLAND, D.A., SR (1982) Relationship of body-checked eggs to photoperiod and breaking strength. *Poultry Science*, **61**, 2338–2343

ROLAND, D.A., SR and HARMS, R.H. (1973). Calcium metabolism in the laying hen. 5. Effect of various sources and sizes of calcium carbonate on egg shell quality. *Poultry Science*, **52**, 369–372

ROLAND, D.A. SR and MOORE, C.H. (1980). Effect of photoperiod on the incidence of body-checked and misshapen eggs. *Poultry Science*, **59**, 2703–2707

ROWLAND, K.W. (1985). Intermittent lighting for laying fowls: a review. *World's Poultry Science Journal*, **41**, 5–19

SAUVEUR, B. (1974). Recherches sur la fraction hydro-minérale de l'albumen de l'oeuf de poule. Influence de certaines variations de l'équilibre acido–basique. Thèse de Doctorat d'Etat, Tours.

SAUVEUR, B. (1982). Effets du fractionnement de la photopériode sur la poule en phase d'élevage et de production. In *Fertilité et Alimentation des Volailles*, pp. 1–35. Versailles, INRA

SAUVEUR, B. and MONGIN, P. (1972). Contribution à l'étude de l'hypercapnie aiguë et chronique chez la poule. *Comparative Biochemistry and Physiology*, **41A**, 869–875

SAUVEUR, B. and MONGIN, P. (1983). Performance of layers reared and/or kept under different 6-hour light–dark cycles. *British Poultry Science*, **24**, 405–416

SCHOLTYSSEK, S. (1975). Die Qualität von Eirn aus Käfig-und Bodenhaltung. *Archiv für Geflügelkunde*, **39**, 59–62

SCOTT, M.L. and MULLENHOFF, P.A. (1970). Dietary oyster shell and eggshell quality. *Proceedings of Cornell Nutrition Conference for Feed Manufacturers*, pp. 24–28

SHANAWANY, M.M. (1982). The effect of ahemeral light and dark cycles on the performnance of laying hens (a review). *World's Poultry Science Journal*, **38**, 120–126

SKOGLUND, W.C. and WHITTAKER, D. (1980). Interrupted lighting programs for brown egg breeds. *Poultry Science*, **59**, 2397–2399

SMITH, A.J. (1974). Changes in the average weight and shell thickness of eggs produced by hens exposed to high environmental temperatures. A review. *Tropical Animal Health and Production*, **6**, 237

SMITH, A.J. and OLIVER, J. (1972a). Some nutritional problems associated with egg production at high environmental temperatures. 1. The effect of environmental temperature and rationing treatments on the productivity of pullets fed on diets of different energy content. *Rhodesian Journal of Agricultural Research*, **10**, 3–21

SMITH, A.J. and OLIVER, J. (1972b). Some nutritional problems associated with egg production at high environmental temperatures. 4. The effect of prolonged exposure to high environmental temperatures on the productivity of pullets fed on high-energy diets. *Rhodesian Journal of Agricultural Research*, **10**, 43–60

TANOR, M.A., LEESON, S. and SUMMERS, J.D. (1984). Effect of heat stress and diet composition on performance of White Leghorn hens. *Poultry Science*, **63**, 304–310

TOLAN, A., ROBERTSON, J., ORTON, C.R., HEAD, M.J., CHRISTIE, A.A. and MILBURN, B.A. (1974). Studies on the composition of food. 5. The chemical composition of eggs produced under battery, deep litter and free range conditions. *British Journal of Nutrition*, **31**, 185–200

TORGES, H.G., MATTHES, S. and HARNISH, S. (1976). Vergleichen de Qualitätsuntersuchungen an Eiern aus Kommerziellen Legehennenbeständen in Freiland-, Boden- und Käfighaltung. *Archiv für Lebensmittel-Hygiene*, **27**, 107–112

TORGES, H.G., RAUCH, H.W. and WEGNER, R.M. (1981). Intermittieren de Beleuchtung von Legehennen und ihr Einfluss auf Legeleistung, Eiqualität, Eiablage- und Futteraufnahmerhythmik. *Archiv für Geflügelkunde*, **45**, 76–82

TRÉMOLIÈRES, E. (1983). Programme lumineux et maîtrise de la consommation chez la pondeuse. *Documents Éleveur UFAC*, **80**, 9–12

VAN KAMPEN, M. (1983). Heat stress, feed restriction and the lipid composition of egg yolk. *Poultry Science*, **62**, 819–823

VAN TIENHOVEN, A. and OSTRANDER, C.E. (1973). The effect of interruption of the dark period at different intervals on egg production and shell breaking strength. *Poultry Science*, **52**, 998–1001

VAN TIENHOVEN, A. and OSTRANDER, C.E. (1976). Short total photoperiods and egg production of White Leghorns. *Poultry Science*, **55**, 1361–1364

VAN TIENHOVEN, A., OSTRANDER, C.E. and GEHLE, M. (1984). Response of different commercial strains of laying hens to short total photoperiods in interrupted light experiments during days of 24 and 28 hours. *Poultry Science*, **63**, 2318–2330

WILSON, W.O. and ABPLANALP, H. (1956). Intermittent light stimuli in egg production of chickens. *Poultry Science*, **35**, 532–538

WOLFENSON, D., FREI, Y.F., SNAPIR, N. and BERMAN, A. (1981). Heat stress effects on capillary blood flow and its redistribution in the laying hen. *Pflügers Archiv*, **390**, 86–93

WOLFORD, J.H. and TANAKA, K. (1970). Factors influencing egg shell quality—a review. *World's Poultry Science Journal*, **26**, 763–780

YANNAKOPOULOS, A.L. and MORRIS, T.R. (1979). Effect of light, vitamin D and dietary phosphorus on egg shell quality late in the pullet laying year. *British Poultry Science*, **20**, 337–342

Chapter 15

Effect of nutrition on egg quality

S. Hurwitz

Introduction

Nutritional factors can modify egg quality by virtue of their transfer into the egg, by inducing metabolic changes that result in synthesis of compounds which find their way into the egg, or by changing transport characteristics of the membranes involved in formation of egg components.

The transfer of nutrients into the egg was reviewed by Naber (1979) and will not be dealt with here in detail. It is of importance to note that the egg white composition is hardly modified by the diet and several futile efforts have been made to induce changes in it. However, many nutrients and non-nutrients find their way from food to the yolk. This difference between the two parts of the egg may be related to the fact that egg white components are mostly synthesised by the secreting epithelium, whereas those of the egg yolk are synthesised elsewhere, mostly in the liver. The follicle acts as a transporting membrane, but with distinct permeability characteristics which result in selectivity and discrimination in the transport from blood plasma to the egg yolk.

In the uterus, the organic moiety of the shell is synthesised by the glands, while calcium, which is the shell's major component, is transported from blood. The egg shell is sensitive to the dietary availability of calcium, while its carbonate moiety is influenced, to some extent, by dietary factors which affect the acid–base balance. The organic matrix contains specific proteins, the synthesis of which involves enzymes associated with trace elements. Thus, some effect of nutrition on the organic matrix of the shell is to be expected.

In the present review, one aspect of internal egg quality will be discussed—that of tainting, which has been considered in relative detail during the last two decades. Egg shell formation will be discussed at the metabolic-physiological level.

Egg tainting

'Fishy' taints were described in the early 1930s by Vondell (1932). More than 40 years later, Hobson-Frohock *et al.* (1973) identified the tainting substance as trimethylamine (TMA), and proceeded to show a hyperbolic relationship between the content of TMA and the taint rating (Griffiths, Land and Hobson-Frohock, 1979).

Source of trimethylamine

'Fishy' taints associated with TMA have been described in hens fed either fish meals (Wakeling, 1982) or rapeseed meal (Hobson-Frohock *et al.*, 1975; Overfield and Elson, 1975). These ingredients, however, contain very little, if any, TMA. Therefore, they could either stimulate synthesis or inhibit the catabolism or excretion of TMA. March and MacMillan (1979) theorised that TMA is a normal breakdown product of choline. In the human, De la Huerga and Popper (1951) found that two-thirds of a dose of choline was excreted as TMA and trimethylamine oxide. March and MacMillan (1979) mention that high dietary choline in laying hen diets resulted in fishy flavours in eggs. Their data indicate that TMA is synthesised in the small intestine and especially in the caeca of normal chickens by the resident microflora, and that TMA appears regularly in excreta. The TMA content in the caeca increased significantly when the diet was supplemented with choline, or when rapeseed meal supplied the dietary protein. Hobson-Frohock *et al.* (1977) identified the choline ester sinapine as the active compound in rapeseed meal and suggested that it could be the precursor for TMA.

Genetic variations

In his early work, Vondell (1932) noted that the offensive taints appeared in eggs laid by Rhode Island Reds but not by White Leghorns. This strain difference was later confirmed in many studies and Bolton, Carter and Morley Jones (1976) demonstrated the high degree of heritability of tainting. March and MacMillan (1979) found no difference in caecal synthesis of TMA between hens which produced tainted eggs and those which did not. Furthermore, these authors found no correlation between the intestinal and the egg TMA content, thus eliminating TMA synthesis as a source of the genetic variation.

It has been established that TMA is oxidised in the liver (Baker and Chaykin, 1962). Since a defect in this oxidation occurred in the human (Humbert *et al.*, 1970), Hobson-Frohock *et al.* (1975) suggested that defects in the liver enzymes may be the source of the genetic variation in egg tainting. This suggestion was confirmed by Pearson *et al.* (1979).

Practical solutions

It is obvious that feeding high choline diets, or using rapeseed meals and a high concentration of fishmeal in diets of sensitive strains of hens, should be avoided. However, Fenwick *et al.* (1979) were able to reduce the sinapine content of rapeseed meal by wet treatment with calcium hydroxide to levels lower than required to produce tainting.

Egg shell quality

The egg shell contains approximately 90% mineral, almost all of which (98%) is calcium carbonate. During shell formation the turnover of plasma calcium in the hen is extremely rapid, with a half-life of about 1 min. It is therefore not surprising that calcium metabolism of the laying hen has been the subject of both fascination and intensive research. Some information exists on the relationship between the dietary monovalent ions and the carbonate of the egg shell. Other information also exists on the importance of trace minerals in proper shell formation. The mechanism of the latter is probably by participation in the process of organic matrix synthesis, since trace minerals are known to influence bone matrix synthesis, which is similar in composition to the egg shell matrix (Leach and Muenster, 1962). This possibility was suggested by Longstaff and Hill (1972) but has not apparently been followed up.

Calcium metabolism in birds

Calcium metabolism in birds was reviewed by Simkiss (1961) and later by Hurwitz (1978). In this chapter, calcium metabolism will be discussed briefly in the light of new developments in order to lay a sufficient foundation for an understanding of the more recent findings on its relationship to egg shell quality.

Plasma calcium

Plasma calcium concentration is one of the most regulated components of biological fluids. In higher animals plasma calcium is maintained at 10 mg/dl, with the exception of female reptiles and birds during reproduction, in which plasma calcium may reach 30 mg/dl due to the appearance of vitellogenin. This lipophosphoprotein has a molecular weight of approximately 480 000 (Deely et al., 1975), and a high calcium-binding capacity; it is the main precursor of yolk protein. The appearance of this protein fraction in the plasma of the female about two weeks prior to the onset of egg production does not involve any change in the concentration of ionic calcium, which remains around 1.4–1.5 mM, although the total plasma calcium triples. The maintenance of plasma ionic calcium concentration, termed calcium homeostasis, takes priority over other processes such as bone and egg shell calcification. Calcium homeostasis is essential in view of the utmost importance of this ionic species in the regulation of important biological processes, including cellular information transfer, and its involvement in hormone biosynthesis and release, cellular replication and differentiation, cellular membrane properties and other activities. Several important calcium-binding proteins involved in intracellular regulation, such as Ca–ATPases and calmodulin, have been discovered.

The controlling system

The regulation of plasma calcium may be viewed as a control system with three controlling sub-systems—bone, intestine and kidney, and three regulating hormones—parathyroid hormone (PTH), calcitonin (CT) and 1,25-dihydroxycholecalciferol [1,25(OH)$_2$D] (Hurwitz, 1978; Hurwitz et al., 1983). Bone calcium flow is the sum of its component flows: bone formation and bone resorption. There is little information on the control of bone formation, but most probably it is modulated by plasma phosphate concentration and one or more of the vitamin D hormones. Some evidence also links PTH to this process. In birds, medullary bone formation is controlled by oestrogen (Simkiss, 1961; Kushuara and Schraer, 1982). Bone resorption is stimulated by PTH and depressed by CT. It is also influenced by several non-calcium hormones such as prostaglandins. Intestinal calcium absorption is regulated by 1,25(OH)₂D, but in the laying hen also by some unknown factor. Renal calcium excretion is regulated by plasma calcium itself, and possibly also by PTH and 1,25(OH)₂D.

Properties, synthesis and secretion of the regulating hormones

Parathyroid hormone (PTH)

PTH, a polypeptide hormone with a molecular weight of about 8000, is synthesised by the parathyroid glands situated in the lower neck region. Avian PTH has been isolated recently by Pines, Bar and Hurwitz (1984). However, a radioimmunoassay for the avian hormone does not exist, since it does not crossreact with antibodies against the mammalian hormone. The lack of a radioimmunoassay hinders much of the research possibilities in calcium metabolism of the chicken. Recently, however, Van de Velde, Loveridge and Vermeiden (1984) measured PTH concentration in plasma of laying hens by a cytochemical bioassay.

The secretion of PTH is inversely, but not linearly, proportional to the concentration of plasma calcium (Hurwitz *et al.*, 1983). Other hormones, such as epinephrine, may act as PTH secretagogues (Brown, Hurwitz and Aurbach, 1977). The hormone is catabolised rapidly with a half-life of several minutes.

Calcitonin (CT)

CT is also a polypeptide hormone, with a molecular weight of about 3000. It is synthesised by the ultimobranchial glands which are just distal to the parathyroids. The avian hormone was isolated several years ago (Nieto, Moya and Candella, 1973), and crossreacts with available antibody produced against salmon calcitonin (Cutler, Habener and Potts, 1974). In turkeys, Copp *et al.* (1972) found an increase in the concentration of CT of the venous blood draining the ultimobranchial gland during perfusion with hypercalcaemic blood. In the laying quail, Dacke *et al.* (1972) observed lower serum CT levels during shell formation than during uterine inactivity.

Vitamin D

The relationship between vitamin D and calcium metabolism was recognised years ago when its antirachitic activity in the chick was discovered. The availability of synthetic vitamin D appears to have been the most important factor in the intensification of the poultry industry, since it permitted the change from outdoor rearing to confinement. Vitamin D is synthesised from dehydrocholesterol in the skin, through the action of ultraviolet irradiation, or has to be provided in the food.

A major breakthrough in vitamin D research occurred with the discovery of vitamin D₃ (cholecalciferol) hydroxylation to 25-hydroxycholecalciferol [25(OH)D] in the liver (Blunt, Tanaka and DeLuca, 1968). This process is probably product-inhibited, but Nicholson, Akhtar and Taylor (1979) showed that, in chickens, the activity of the liver enzyme responsible for this hydroxylation is stimulated by oestradiol.

25(OH)D is further hydroxylated into the hormonal form, 1,25-dihydroxycholecalciferol [1,25(OH)₂D] in the kidney (Fraser and Kodicek, 1970; Holick *et al.*, 1971; Norman *et al.*, 1971). The activity of the enzyme which catalyses this synthesis, 25-hydroxycholecalciferol-1-hydroxylase (1-hydroxylase), is regulated by PTH (Fraser and Kodicek, 1973; Henry, Midgett and Norman, 1974). The kidney also produces other hydroxylated vitamin D metabolites such as 24,25-dihydroxycholecalciferol, implicated in bone formation, and some other metabolites. The biological significance of many of these metabolites remains to be elucidated.

The 1,25(OH)$_2$D is secreted into the circulation and is taken up by the intestinal cells where it binds to specific chromatin receptors (Brumbaugh and Haussler, 1974). In the intestinal cell the hormone modifies the membrane lipid composition and stimulates the synthesis of several proteins, such as actin (Wilson and Lawson, 1978), alkaline phosphatase and Ca–ATPase (Bikle *et al.*, 1980; Grunder and Tsang, 1984). Wasserman and Taylor (1966) also found that as a result of vitamin D action in the intestine, a unique calcium-binding protein is synthesised. The concentration of this protein in the intestine is proportional to calcium absorption (Bàr, Maoz and Hurwitz, 1979). This protein, with a molecular weight of 28 000, appears also in other avian tissues such as the shell gland (Bar and Hurwitz, 1973) and kidney (Bar, Hurwitz and Edelstein, 1975). The biochemical changes in the intestinal mucosa have been considered as instrumental in mediating the effect of vitamin D on intestinal calcium absorption. However, the molecular basis for this functional action is still poorly understood. Schachter, Dowdle and Schenker (1960) suggested that vitamin D is responsible for active transport of calcium in the intestine. On the other hand, Harrison and Harrison (1961) found that vitamin D increased the permeability of the intestinal mucosa for calcium in the rat intestine *in vitro*. Hurwitz and Bar (1972), on the basis of *in vivo* work with chicks also concluded that vitamin D modified the intestinal permeability. Furthermore, vitamin D stimulates phosphorus absorption independently of its effect on calcium (Hurwitz and Bar, 1972; Wasserman and Taylor, 1973).

Deficiencies in calcium, phosphorus and vitamin D have been implicated in disorders such as rickets and poor shell quality. Defects in vitamin D metabolism or in the processes leading to its expression, could be responsible for some of the problems encountered in the field. Hurwitz, Bar and Meshorer (1973) suggested that some forms of field rickets in turkeys could be caused by a defect in vitamin D hydroxylation. This suggestion has been confirmed in recent work (Bar and Hurwitz, in preparation).

Regulation of plasma calcium

Work with laying hens which were provided with an unlimited supply of calcium indicated some regulation of calcium intake according to needs. This was achieved by changes in food intake or in oyster shell intake, when this supplement was offered on a free choice basis, in response to shell formation (Griminger and Lutz, 1964; Hughes and Wood-Gush, 1971; Sauveur and Mongin, 1974). This mode of regulation is, however, inaccurate due to the extreme individual variations.

A decrease in ionic calcium during shell formation was observed by Luck and Scanes (1979) and Luck, Sommerville and Scanes (1980). Such a decrease causes stimulation of PTH secretion. The increase in circulating PTH results in an almost immediate increase in bone resorption, supplying the calcium needed in circulation. At the same time, PTH also stimulates synthesis of the kidney 1-hydroxylase, resulting in an increased production of 1,25(OH)$_2$D. This hormone, upon reaching the intestinal mucosa, stimulates calcium absorption. Thus, an immediate but uneconomical homeostatic response of increased bone resorption is replaced by a more efficient but delayed increase in calcium absorption. An increase in plasma calcium leads to opposite changes. CT secretion is stimulated by the hypercalcaemia, resulting, together with the decrease in PTH production, in a diminished bone resorption. The regulatory system has been mathematically described in a simulation model (Hurwitz *et al.*, 1983, 1984).

Calcium homeostasis in the laying hen

The increase in plasma calcium, typical to the laying hen, is unrelated to shell formation since it results from the appearance in the plasma of the precursor of yolk protein—vitellogenin, without any change in ionic calcium. In effect, total plasma calcium is proportional to the rate of egg production and is highly correlated with the plasma concentration of oestrogens (Bar *et al.*, 1978a).

In addition to the general mechanisms described above, specific systems develop in the pullet in preparation for the enormous stress of egg shell formation. The long-term adaptation involves metabolism of vitamin D.

The pre-laying period

About 2–3 weeks prior to the onset of egg production an increase in plasma oestrogen and testosterone results in the formation of medullary bone and an increase in calcium absorption (Simkiss, 1961). The induction of medullary bone formation is a primary action of gonadal hormones (Kushuara and Schraer, 1982), rather than a result of the increased accumulation of calcium in the body due to increased absorption. In effect, the diaphyses and the cortex are quantitatively more important than medullary bone as storage sites of calcium during this pre-laying period (Hurwitz, 1964a; Hurwitz and Bar, 1971).

The increase in calcium absorption during the pre-laying period follows the increase in plasma concentration of $1,25(OH)_2D$ which results from stimulation of the kidney 1-hydroxylase enzyme. Earlier work suggested that this increase in kidney 1-hydroxylase was due to the direct stimulatory action of oestrogen (Castillo *et al.*, 1977; Pike *et al.*, 1978) or prolactin (Spanos *et al.*, 1976). Baksi and Kenny (1977, 1978) stated that the increase in 1-hydroxylase by oestrogen was either direct or indirect, while Sedrani and Taylor (1977) and Montecuccoli *et al.* (1978) suggested that the action was indirect. Additional evidence for an indirect action of oestrogen on the 1-hydroxylase was provided by Bar and Hurwitz (1979) and by Kaetzel and Soares (1984). A lack of correlation between plasma oestrogen and kidney 1-hydroxylase was demonstrated by Bar *et al.* (1978b). The indirect action of oestrogen on the 1-hydroxylase system may follow the primary induction of medullary bone formation and vitellogenin synthesis, both drawing calcium out of the pool, and could thus induce an increase in PTH secretion. Indeed, Castillo *et al.* (1979) found in the maturing pullet that medullary bone formation preceded the increase in 1-hydroxylase. Nicholson, Akhtar and Taylor (1979) found that oestrogens stimulated liver hydroxylase activity, which is responsible for the synthesis of $25(OH)D$. This increase in availability of the precursor could be also partially responsible for the increase in plasma $1,25(OH)_2D$. Thus, the long-term changes in calcium metabolism in the pullet in preparation for egg laying are, to a large extent, vitamin D-dependent.

Shell formation and calcium absorption

Hurwitz and Bar (1965) and Hurwitz, Bar and Cohen (1973) showed that fractional calcium absorption increased in chickens from approximately 30% to over 70% between periods of uterine inactivity and periods of shell formation. Similar changes were noted in laying quails (Bar et al., 1976a,1976b). Taylor and Kirkley (1967) also found, by balance techniques, an increase in calcium retention during 'egg forming' days. It was tempting to explain this modulation of calcium absorption by corresponding changes in the production of 1,25(OH)$_2$D. Kenny (1976) and Abe et al. (1979) observed higher kidney 1-hydroxylase activity in the shell-forming compared with the non-shell-forming quail. However, no changes in the 1-hydroxylase enzyme or in plasma 1,25(OH)$_2$D could be found during a normal egg laying cycle when the time of uterine inactivity was shorter than 6 h (Bar et al., 1976a; Bar, Rosenberg and Hurwitz, 1984), while large changes in calcium absorption occurred. Furthermore, the regulation of calcium absorption during shell formation was maintained even when the vitamin D–intestine regulatory axis was bypassed by feeding the synthetic 1-alpha-hydroxycholecalciferol [1(OH)D] (Bar et al., 1976b), and calcium absorption increased in laying hens without any changes in 1,25(OH)$_2$D (Nys, N'Guyen and Garabedian, 1984). Thus, changes in calcium absorption during the laying cycle could not be explained on the basis of the 1,25(OH)$_2$D–intestine interaction. Furthermore, Hurwitz, Bar and Cohen (1973) could not demonstrate any effect of shell formation on the permeability of the intestine to calcium. Bar and Hurwitz (1975) found no change in intestinal CaBP during the laying cycle, indicating no change in the calcium absorption capacity. One possible explanation for the regulation of calcium absorption in the laying hen was given by Sauveur and Mongin (1983), who found an increase in the concentration of soluble calcium in the intestine during shell formation. This increase in the intestinal lumen/circulation calcium gradient could enhance the transepithelial movement of calcium.

Taylor (1961) calculated the average hourly calcium absorption from the results of the balance experiment of Hurwitz and Griminger (1960), and proceeded to show that the absorbed calcium provided only about 60% of the calcium needed during shell formation. Therefore, the hen had to withdraw the extra needed calcium from its skeleton. This conclusion is supported by recent findings of a decrease in plasma ionic calcium (Luck and Scanes, 1979; Luck, Sommerville and Scanes, 1980), an increase in plasma PTH (Van de Velde, Loveridge and Vermeiden, 1984) and an increase in osteoclast activity of medullary bone during shell formation (Miller, 1977, 1981). In view of this evidence, it seemed surprising that no significant changes in bone calcium were recorded during shell formation (Hurwitz, 1964b). Furthermore, it should be noted that Taylor's calculation assumed that the rate of calcium absorption remained constant at least on a daily basis. If the increase in calcium absorption during shell formation is taken into account and if the calcium supply is uninterrupted during shell formation, the increased calcium absorption during shell formation can supply most of the calcium needed, minimising the need for a net removal of calcium from bone. However, this does not exclude the possibility of the appearance of 'bone calcium' in the egg shell. This appearance is due to the high turnover of bone calcium, especially of medullary bone, and the mixing of this calcium in the plasma pool (Hurwitz, 1965).

The existence of an uninterrupted supply of calcium during shell formation was questioned by Scott, Hull and Mullendorf (1971), who theorised that since shell formation occurred mostly during the night when no food was consumed, the supply of calcium may be exhausted early during this period. However, the results of Sauveur and Mongin (1974) showed a large increase in the rate of intake of food or of oyster shell during the late afternoon hours. This pattern may ensure a sufficient supply of food calcium during the nocturnal shell formation. In fact, Hurwitz and Bar (1965) found in the crop of laying hens killed at 10.00 p.m. the equivalent of approximately 40% of the daily food intake.

It could be theorised that one of the possible bottlenecks with regard to calcium transfer into the shell could be calcium absorption. As explained above, calcium absorption is feedback-regulated through the action of the kidney 1-hydroxylase. Therefore, in the past it had been impossible to determine whether the low calcium absorption exhibited by poor shell producers was the cause or effect (Hurwitz and Bar, 1967). With the availability of a synthetic calcium hormone, 1-alpha(OH)D, the feedback loop could be bypassed. When this compound is fed, the production of the endogenous hormone is suppressed, and calcium absorption becomes completely dependent on the exogenous supply of the hormone. Results indicated that calcium absorption was stimulated to super-natural levels (Bar et al., 1976b, 1978a) and bone calcium increased markedly by the feeding of this compound. However, no change was noted in egg shell quality (Cohen et al., 1978). It can therefore be concluded that under normal conditions, calcium absorption is not the limiting process along the path of transfer of calcium from the intestine to the egg shell.

Shell formation and bone

As mentioned above, the need for net bone breakdown to supply the calcium during shell formation is minimal provided that calcium intake is not interrupted. However, it was shown years ago by Morgan and Mitchell (1938) and confirmed later by Hurwitz and Griminger (1959) that birds were in a negative calcium balance during the onset of egg production, requiring the presence of ample stores of calcium in the skeleton. The ability of the birds to withstand periods of insufficient calcium intake is proportional to the amount of calcium stored in the skeleton (Hurwitz and Bar, 1969). However, population differences in egg shell quality could not be explained on the basis of bone turnover which was found to be the same in high and low shell producers (Hurwitz and Bar, 1967; Buss and Guyer, 1984). The filling of bone stores by dietary feeding of 1(OH)D (Cohen et al., 1978) resulted in no improvement of egg shell quality. This evidence suggests that bone metabolism is also not limiting under normal conditions.

During calcium depletion, medullary bone calcium is maintained despite the exhaustion of calcium from structural bone (Hurwitz, 1964b), indicating that medullary bone is not a simple reservoir of calcium. Due to its extremely high turnover rate relative to structural bone and its lability (Hurwitz, 1965), this bone segment may serve to buffer acute interruptions in calcium absorption, preventing hypo- or hypercalcaemic catastrophies, since its response to PTH occurs within minutes (Candlish and Taylor, 1970; Miller, Bowman and Myers, 1984).

Calcium transfer in the shell gland

Since in a normal population of hens neither the intestine nor the bone has been found to be responsible for variation in egg shell quality, the shell gland remains the logical site to be examined. Several investigators have attempted to study calcium transfer in the uterus *in vitro*. Ehrenspeck, Schraer and Schraer (1971) found that calcium was transported actively by the shell gland. However, calcium transport *in vitro* as measured by these workers and others (Pearson and Goldner, 1973; Easten and Spaziani, 1978) was several orders of magnitude lower than the *in vivo* transport.

The vitamin D-dependent calcium-binding protein was found in the shell glands of birds (Bar and Hurwitz, 1973) at high concentrations. The protein appeared in the uterine mucosa during the calcification of the first egg shell, and disappeared a few days after the arrest of egg production (Bar and Hurwitz, 1973). A significant correlation was found between the calcium-binding protein and shell calcium (Bar, Rosenberg and Hurwitz, 1984). Furthermore, receptors to $1,25(OH)_2D$ were found in the shell gland mucosa (Coty, 1980; Takahashi *et al.*, 1980). It therefore appeared feasible that the calcium transfer in the shell gland was regulated by the vitamin D hormone. In the intestine, a high correlation was found between its $1,25(OH)_2D$ content, calcium-binding protein and calcium absorption (Hurwitz *et al.*, 1983). A significant correlation was found between the $1,25(OH)_2D$ concentration of the shell gland and that in plasma. However, there was no correlation between the hormone content in the shell gland and calcium-binding protein or shell calcium (Bar, Rosenberg and Hurwitz, 1984). Thus, there is no evidence to link the control of calcium transfer in the shell gland to the vitamin D hormone. Supporting evidence for this conclusion was provided by Nys and De Laage (1984).

Calcium intake

An insufficient intake of calcium during the pre-laying period results in reduced calcium stores at the onset of production (Hurwitz and Bar, 1971; Hurwitz, 1976). The overall ability of the hen to direct calcium from its stores to the egg shell depends on the size of the calcium stores (Hurwitz and Bar, 1969). During early egg production the absorption mechanism is not fully developed and the hen is in negative calcium balance. It is therefore of importance to ensure optimal calcium stores. Supplementation of the diet with calcium (2%) during the pre-laying period resulted in an increase in bone calcium storage (Hurwitz, 1976).

The earliest reaction to an insufficient calcium intake during production is a reduction in shell calcium. This is followed by a decrease in egg production (Gilbert *et al.*, 1981; Gilbert, 1983). The correct supply of calcium depends on the inclusion of a proper calcium concentration in the diet, and on the availability of calcium when needed during shell formation. As mentioned, it was suggested by Scott, Hull and Mullendorf (1971) that calcium flow into the intestine may be reduced at night while the shell is being formed, and that this deficiency could be ameliorated by the inclusion of oyster shell in the diet. The longer residence time of this coarse calcium supplement in the stomach may ensure a supply of calcium during the hours of darkness. The value of added oyster shell to egg shell quality was confirmed by some (Roland and Harms, 1973), but others found no benefit (Potts and Washburn, 1977; Hurwitz, S., unpublished results). Possibly, factors related to day length and feeding practices may determine the response to supplementary oyster shell. It is recommended that in practice food should not be limiting during the late afternoon, so that the hens can accumulate sufficient amounts of food in their crop. In cases of food restriction, such as that practised with heavy breeders, food should be provided during the afternoon hours. This practice resulted in improved shell quality (Farmer and Roland, 1981).

Years ago, an equation was formulated to calculate the calcium needs of laying hens, based on egg production rate (P, in fraction), egg calcium (2.2 g) and food intake (F_i, g/d). The calculation also assumed a 50% retention of calcium at the point of a balanced requirement level. A new approach is suggested at present which takes into account the physiological findings outlined above. It also assumes that any excess of calcium within the practical range is not absorbed and is therefore of little physiological consequence. The equation assumes that all calcium transferred to the egg shell should be supplied by the diet. It further assumes a 75% calcium absorption during shell formation and an hourly calcium deposition of 0.130 g Ca as a target function.

The requirement for dietary calcium of the laying hen, Ca_f, in g/kg, is then:

$$Ca_f = \frac{[\text{shell Ca (g)}]/17 \; . \; 1000}{0.75 \; . \; F_i/24}$$

Calcium requirements thus calculated agree with empirical determinations (Summers, Grandhi and Leeson, 1976).

Vitamin D intake and metabolism

The necessity of vitamin D for normal reproduction in the laying hen is well documented. Vitamin D deficiency results, within days, in a reduction in egg shell quality and arrest of egg production (Vohra, Scopes and Wilson, 1979; Takahashi *et al.*, 1983). Despite its importance, Shen, Summers and Leeson (1981) were surprised to find little information on the amount of vitamin D needed to optimise shell quality. A level of 500 IU/kg of vitamin D_3 has been recommended by the National Research Council (1977). This requirement level is in agreement with the studies of Scott, Hull and Mullendorf (1971) and Yannakopoulus and Morris (1979). Shen, Summers and Leeson (1981) also found the minimum requirement level to be between 250 and 500 IU/kg (62.5–125 mg/kg). Kramer and Waibel (1978) found that 7.5–10◯g/kg was needed for egg production in turkey hens, but levels of 10–60◯g were needed for the optimal development of the progeny.

The discovery of vitamin D metabolites raised many hopes for a possible remedy for poor shell calcification. As mentioned earlier, $1,25(OH)_2D$ is not directly involved in egg shell formation, nor is calcium absorption limiting, under normal conditions. However, it has been suggested that defects in the metabolism of vitamin D may be a cause of reduced shell quality. Abe *et al.* (1982) found a decrease in the kidney 1-hydroxylase in old birds, and suggested this as a cause of the reduced shell quality. However, in their study the reduced 1-hydroxylase could have been secondary to the reduced shell deposition, rather than its cause. Their conclusion of the reduced accumulation of the hormone with age in the intestine cannot be fully evaluated due to the lack of kinetic analysis. This study also provided evidence that the potential for production of the hormone did not diminish since the activity increased after moult together with the increase in shell quality. The increase in shell quality after moult was recorded by Hurwitz, Bornstein and Lev (1975). Baksi and Kenny (1981) found reduced 1-hydroxylase in old quails. Their study showed that the ability of the kidney to hydroxylate 25(OH)D was not lost with age, since the birds responded normally to the challenge of low calcium intake. Old birds also exhibited a normal parathyroid response, since Roland, Putman and Hilburn (1978) found in such birds an unhindered ability to withstand the challenge of low calcium intake. It therefore appears that any reduction in shell quality with age cannot be attributed to disturbances in the PTH–1-hydroxylase–intestinal calcium absorption axis.

Whereas there is general agreement that hydroxylated vitamin D metabolites may substitute for vitamin D_3, few researchers could obtain any actual benefit from supplementation of the diets with any of the metabolites. An improvement in shell quality following addition to the diet of *Solanum malacoxylon* (which supplies $1,25(OH)_2D_3$) was reported by Morris, Jenkins and Simonite (1977). Rambeck and Zucker (1985) observed a synergistic effect between $1,25(OH)_2D$ and $24,25(OH)_2D$ in stimulating shell calcium secretion. Some benefit from supplementation with 25(OH)D was reported by McLoughlin and Soares (1976) and Polin and Ringer (1977). On the other hand, no improvement in shell quality by 25(OH)D could be found by Waldroup, Bussell and Cobb (1977), Cohen *et al.* (1978) or Hamilton (1980). Kaetzel, Soares and Swerdel (1978), and Kaetzel and Soares (1979) found that 1(OH)D improved egg breaking strength in old quail. On the other hand, Cohen *et al.* (1978) did not obtain any benefit from supplementation with 1(OH)D on shell quality, and egg production rate was depressed. Abdulrahim, Patel and McGinnin (1979) also found no effect on shell quality of $1,25(OH)_2D$. It may be concluded that any future benefit from vitamin D metabolites would depend on a better identification of defects in vitamin D metabolism.

The profile of vitamin D metabolites in the yolk has not been determined due to technical problems in analysing this fatty material (Koshy and Van der Silk, 1979). It is, however, interesting to note that although any one of the dihydroxylated metabolites was able to sustain production and shell quality, a combination of the two metabolites in the food was essential for normal embryonic development and hatchability (Henry and Norman, 1978; Sunde, Turk and DeLuca, 1978; Soares, Swerdel and Ottinger, 1979; Norman, Leathers and Bishop, 1983).

Shell formation and phosphate

In contrast to plasma calcium, plasma phosphorus is poorly regulated; its level may be varied by dietary means over a wide range. Plasma phosphate may also change in response to various physiological stimuli. PTH activated by the calcium system, depresses plasma phosphate and increases phosphate excretion by the kidney (Wideman and Youtz, 1985) through cAMP-mediated processes (Pines, Polin and Hurwitz, 1983). An increase in plasma inorganic phosphate occurred during shell formation (Mongin and Sauveur, 1979), despite the increase in PTH activity (Van der Velde, Loveridge and Vermeiden, 1984). However, the increase in PTH levels can account for the phosphaturia observed during shell formation. According to Sauveur and Mongin (1983), the increase in plasma phosphorus was related to bone mobilisation during shell formation. Miles and Harms (1982) and Miles, Costa and Harms (1983) demonstrated an inverse linear relationship between egg specific gravity and plasma inorganic phosphorus, and theorised that the high plasma phosphorus concentration which resulted from the high phosphorus content of food, depressed bone mobilisation and thereby reduced egg specific gravity. However, there is no existing evidence linking phosphorus to bone resorption or its regulating hormone, PTH. On the other hand, Sauveur and Mongin (1983) observed an inverse relationship between plasma inorganic phosphorus and the concentration of soluble calcium in the duodenum. Thus, the inverse relationship observed by Miles and Harms (1982) could be an indirect result of a decrease in soluble calcium, calcium absorption and shell quality. These studies, however, confirm earlier results showing that dietary phosphate depressed shell thickness (Taylor, 1965; Hunt and Cheency, 1970), and provide some physiological basis for those observations. The depression of shell quality by dietary phosphorus was confirmed more recently by Yannakopoulus and Morris (1979), Ousterhout (1980), Said *et al.* (1984), and Rodrigues, Owings and Sell (1984). Furthermore, Holcombe, Roland and Harms (1976) observed that laying hens avoided high phosphate diets on a free choice basis. It should be pointed out, however, that egg shell quality actually declines when dietary phosphorus levels are markedly deficient (Bar and Hurwitz, 1984). Thus, a bell-shaped response curve can be reconstructed with regard to the response of shell quality to dietary phosphate (Choi, Miles and Harms, 1980; Harms, 1982), with an optimal level of 0.4–0.5% of total phosphorus in a regular grain-soy diet (Edwards and Suso, 1981).

Egg shell formation and acid–base balance

Frank and Burger (1965) found that supplementation of the laying hen's diet with sodium bicarbonate improved shell formation. It was rationalised at that time that this was caused by the contributed bicarbonate. However, it could be shown that in comparison with the carbonate supplied by calcium carbonate this supplementation was negligible. Furthermore, Loercher, Scheile and Bronsch (1970) showed, in elegant isotope infusion experiments, that plasma bicarbonate or carbon dioxide was not the precursor of egg shell carbonate, which was probably derived from the intermediary metabolism of the uterine mucosa. Furthermore, Mongin and Lacassagne (1964) showed that hens were in metabolic acidosis during shell formation. The acid–base balance of the hen was thoroughly reviewed by Mongin (1968). Acidosis during shell formation, which was also reflected in the uterine cells, was also observed by Cohen and Hurwitz (1974b), but not confirmed by Mongin and Carter (1978). The acidosis could be counteracted by sodium bicarbonate supplementation, which operates by reducing the cation deficit or by increasing the dietary cation/chloride ratio (Cohen and Hurwitz, 1974a). Harms (1982) presented evidence that sodium bicarbonate improved egg shell quality by causing an excretion of some of the excess phosphorus. Thus the previous cation–anion balance which included Na, K and Cl (Cohen and Hurwitz, 1974a) was expanded to contain also phosphorus.

As mentioned, the initial metabolic findings of Mongin could be confirmed. However, various workers reported no benefit of sodium bicarbonate supplementation in the diet (Pepper, Summers and McConachie, 1968; Hamilton and Thompson, 1980; Odiba, Sunde and Bird, 1981; Junqueira, Miles and Harms, 1983). Results obtained by the author (unpublished) also showed no benefit of sodium bicarbonate supplementation for egg shell quality.

Effects of dietary non-nutrients

Several dietary contaminants have been reported to reduce shell quality. Nyholm (1981) reported the involvement of aluminium in defective formation of egg shells in passerine birds. Some years ago, environmental research was concerned with the reasons for the reduced reproductive capacity of wild birds. Eventually this was traced to poor shell quality induced by chlorinated hydrocarbons which contaminated the birds' food. There is agreement that these compounds inhibit shell deposition at the uterine level. The exact mechanism of action is, however, not known. Bird, Peakall and Miller (1983) found that DDE inhibited Ca-ATPase and carbonic anhydrase. Khan and Cutkomp (1982) reported a decrease in Ca-ATPase or in the oligomycine-sensitive ATPase by DDT and DDE. The decrease in the oligomycine-sensitive ATPase correlated well with the decrease in shell thickness, as affected by species (kestrel, mallard duck or chicken), and pesticide (DDT or DDE). Lundholm (1984a,b,c) showed that DDE treatment reduced the intrauterine calcium concentration and inhibited the decrease in the calcium content of the uterine wall during shell formation, through an increase in calcium binding by the microsomes. These disagreements emphasise the need for a more thorough understanding of the mechanism of shell formation before practical problems of shell quality can be solved.

References

ABDULRAHIM, S.M., PATEL, M.B. and MCGINNIN, J. (1979). Effects of vitamin D_3 and D_3 metabolites on production parameters and hatchability. *Poultry Science, 58*, 858–863

ABE, E., TANABE, R., SUDA, T. and YOSHIKI, S. (1979). Circadian rhythms of 1,25-dihydroxyvitamin D_3 production in egg-laying hens. *Biochemical and Biophysical Research Communications, 88*, 500–507

ABE, E., HORIKAWA, H., MASDUMURA, T., SUGAHARA, M., KUBOTA, N. and SUDA, T. (1982). Disorders of cholecalciferol metabolism in old egg-laying hens. *Journal of Nutrition, 112*, 436–446

BAKER, J.R. and CHAYKIN, S. (1962). The biosynthesis of trimethyl amine-N-oxide. *Journal of Biological Chemistry, 237*, 1309–1313

BAKSI, S.N. and KENNY, A.D. (1977). Vitamin D_3 metabolism in immature Japanese quail: effects of ovarian hormones. *Endocrinology, 101*, 1216–1220

BAKSI, S.N. and KENNY, A.D. (1978). Acute effects of estradiol on the renal vitamin D hydroxylases in Japanese quail. *Biochemical Pharmacology, 25*, 2765–2768

BAKSI, S.N. and KENNY, A.D. (1981). Vitamin D metabolism in aged Japanese quail: dietary calcium and estrogen effects. *American Journal of Physiology, 241*, E275–E280

BAR, A. and HURWITZ, S. (1973). Uterine calcium-binding protein in the laying fowl. *Comparative Biochemistry and Physiology, 45A*, 579–586

BAR, A. and HURWITZ, S. (1975). Intestinal and uterine calcium-binding protein in laying hens during different stages of egg formation. *Poultry Science, 54*, 1325–1327

BAR, A. and HURWITZ, S. (1979). The interaction between dietary calcium and gonadal hormones in their effect on plasma calcium, bone, 25-hydroxycholecalciferol-1-hydroxylase and duodenal calcium-binding protein measured by a radioimmunoassay in chicks. *Endocrinology, 104*, 1455–1460

BAR, A. and HURWITZ, S. (1984). Egg shell quality, medullary bone ash, intestinal calcium and phosphorus absorption and calcium-binding protein in phosphate-deficient hens. *Poultry Science, 63*, 1975–1979

BAR, A., HURWITZ, S. and EDELSTEIN, S. (1975). Response of renal calcium-binding protein: independence of kidney hydroxylation. *Biochimica et Biophysica Acta, 411*, 106–112

BAR, A., MAOZ, A. and HURWITZ, S. (1979). Relationship of intestinal and plasma calcium-binding protein to intestinal calcium absorption. *FEBS Letters, 102*, 79–81

BAR, A., ROSENBERG, J. and HURWITZ, S. (1984). The lack of relationship between vitamin D_3 metabolites and calcium-binding protein in the eggshell gland of laying birds. *Comparative Biochemistry and Physiology, 78B*, 75–79

BAR, A., DUBROV, D., EISNER, U. and HURWITZ, S. (1976a). Calcium-binding protein and calcium absorption in the laying quail (*Coturnix coturnix japonica*). *Poultry Science*, **55**, 622–628

BAR, A., EISNER, U., MONTECUCCOLI, G. and HURWITZ, S. (1976b). Regulation of intestinal calcium absorption in the laying quail independent of kidney vitamin D hydroxylation. *Journal of Nutrition*, **106**, 1336–1342

BAR, A., COHEN, A., EISNER, U., RISENFELD, G. and HURWITZ, S. (1978a). Differential response of calcium transport systems in laying hens to exogenous and endogenous changes in vitamin D status. *Journal of Nutrition*, **108**, 1322–1328

BAR, A., COHEN, A., EDELSTEIN, S., SHEMESH, M., MONTECUCCOLI, G. and HURWITZ, S. (1978b). Involvement of cholecalciferol metabolism in birds in the adaptation of calcium absorption to the needs during reproduction. *Comparative Biochemistry and Physiology*, **59B**, 245–249

BIKLE, D.D., EMPSON, R.N., MORRISSEY, R.L., ZOLOK, D.T., BUCCI, T.J., HERMAN, R.H. and PECHET, M.M. (1980). Effect of 1-alpha-hydroxy vitamin D_3 on the rachitic chick intestine: A comparison of the effects of 1,25-dihydroxyvitamin D_3. *Calcified Tissue International*, **32**, 9–17

BIRD, D.M., PEAKALL, D.B. and MILLER, D.S. (1983). Enzymatic changes in the oviduct associated with DDE-induced eggshell thinning in the kestrel, *Falco sparverius*. *Bulletin of Environmental Contamination and Toxicology*, **31**, 11–24

BLUNT, J.W., TANAKA, Y. and DELUCA, H.F. (1968). 25-hydroxycholecalciferol. A biologically active metabolite of vitamin D_3. *Biochemistry*, **7**, 3317–3322

BOLTON, W., CARTER, T.C. and MORLEY JONES, R. (1976). The hen's egg: genetics of taints in eggs from hens fed on rapeseed meal. *British Poultry Science*, **17**, 313–320

BROWN, E.M., HURWITZ, S. and AURBACH, G.D. (1977). Beta adrenergic stimulation of cyclic AMP and parathyroid hormone release from isolated bovine parathyroid cells. *Endocrinology*, **100**, 1696–1702

BRUMBAUGH, P.F. and HAUSSLER, M.R. (1974). 1,25-dihydroxycholecalciferol receptors in the intestine. I. Association of 1,25-dihydroxycholecalciferol with intestinal mucosa chromatin. *Journal of Biological Chemistry*, **249**, 1251–1257

BUSS, E.G. and GUYER, R.B. (1984). Bone parameters of thick and thin eggshell lines of chickens. *Comparative Biochemistry and Physiology*, **78A**, 449–452

CANDLISH, J.K. and TAYLOR, T.G. (1970). The response time to the parathyroid hormone in the laying fowl. *Journal of Endocrinology*, **48**, 143–144

CASTILLO, L., TANAKA, Y., DELUCA, H.F. and SUNDE, M.L. (1977). The stimulation of 25-hydroxyvitamin D_3-1-hydroxylase by estrogen. *Archives of Biochemistry and Biophysics*, **179**, 211–217

CASTILLO, L., TANAKA, Y., WINELAND, M.J., JOWSEY, J.O. and DELUCA, H.F. (1979). Production of 1,25-dihydroxyvitamin D_3 and formation of medullary bone in the egg-laying hen. *Endocrinology*, **104**, 1598–1601

CHOI, J.H., MILES, R.D. and HARMS, R.H. (1980). Interaction of dietary phosphorus and sodium chloride levels on blood phosphorus and egg production of hens. *Poultry Science*, **59**, 1897–1900

COHEN, I. and HURWITZ, S. (1974a). The response of plasma ionic constituents and acid–base balance to dietary sodium, potassium and chloride in laying hens. *Poultry Science*, **52**, 2340–2342

COHEN, I. and HURWITZ, S. (1974b). Intracellular pH and electrolyte concentration in uterine wall of the fowl in relation to shell formation and dietary minerals. *Comparative Biochemistry and Physiology*, **49A**, 689–696

COHEN, I., BAR, A., EISNER, U. and HURWITZ, S. (1978). Calcium absorption, calcium-binding protein, and egg shell quality in laying hens fed hydroxylated vitamin D derivatives. *Poultry Science*, **57**, 1646–1651

COPP, D.H., BYFIELD, P.G.H., KERR, C.R., NEWSOME, F., WALKER, V. and WATTS, E. (1972). Calcitonin and ultimobranchial function in birds and fishes. In *Calcium, Parathyroid Hormone and the Calcitonins*, (Talmage, R.V. and Munson, P., eds), pp. 12–20. Amsterdam, Excerpta Medica

COTY, W.A. (1980). A specific high affinity binding protein for 1,25-dihydroxyvitamin D in chick oviduct shell gland. *Biochemical and Biophysical Research Communications*, **93**, 285–292

CUTLER, G.B. JR, HABENER, J.F. and POTTS, J.T. JR (1974). Comparative immunochemical studies of chicken ultimobrachial calcitonin. *General and Comparative Endocrinology*, **24**, 183–190

DACKE, C.G., BOELKINS, J.N., SMITH, W.K. and KENNY, A.D. (1972). Plasma calcitonin levels in birds during the ovulation cycle. *Journal of Endocrinology*, **54**, 369–370

DE LA HUERGA, J. and POPPER, H. (1951). Urinary excretion of choline metabolites following choline administration in normal patients with hepatobiliary diseases. *Journal of Clinical Investigation*, **30**, 463–470

DEELY, R.G., MULLNIX, K.P., WETKAM, W., KRONENBERG, H.H., MEYERS, M., ELDRIDGE, J.D. and GOLDBERGER, R.F. (1975). Vitellogenin synthesis in the avian liver. Vitellogenin is the precursor of the egg yolk phosphoproteins. *Journal of Biological Chemistry*, **250**, 9060–9066

EASTEN, W.C. JR and SPAZIANI, E. (1978). On the control of calcium secretion in the avian shell gland (uterus). *Biology of Reproduction*, **19**, 493–504

EDWARDS, H.M. JR and SUSO, F.A. (1981). Phosphorus requirement of six strains of caged laying hens. *Poultry Science*, **60**, 2346–2348

EHRENSPECK, G., SCHRAER, H. and SCHRAER, R. (1971). Calcium transfer across isolated avian shell gland. *American Journal of Physiology*, **220**, 967–972

FARMER, M. and ROLAND, D.A., SR (1981). The influence of the time of feeding on calcium status of the digestive system and egg shell quality in broiler-breeder hens. *Poultry Science*, **60**, 1600

FENWICK, G.R., HOBSON-FROHOCK, A., LAND, D.G. and CURTIS, R.F. (1979). Rapeseed meal and egg taint: treatment of rapeseed meal to reduce tainting potential. *British Poultry Science*, **20**, 323–329

FRANK, F.R. and BURGER, R.E. (1965). The effect of carbon dioxide inhalation and sodium bicarbonate ingestion on egg shell deposition. *Poultry Science*, **44**, 1604–1606

FRASER, D.R. and KODICEK, E. (1970). Unique biosynthesis by kidney of a biologically active vitamin D metabolite. *Nature*, **228**, 764–766

FRASER, D.R. and KODICEK, E. (1973). Regulation of 25-hydroxycholecalciferol-1-hydroxylase activity in the kidney by parathyroid hormone. *Nature (New Biology)*, **24**, 163–166

GILBERT, A.B. (1983). Calcium and reproductive function in the hen. *Proceedings of the Nutrition Society*, **42**, 195–212

GILBERT, A.B., PEDDIE, J., MITCHELL, G.G. and TEAGUE, P.W. (1981). The egg laying response of the domestic hen to variation in dietary calcium. *British Poultry Science*, **22**, 537–548

GRIFFITHS, N.M., LAND, D.G. and HOBSON-FROHOCK, A. (1979). Trimethyl amine and egg taint. *British Poultry Science*, **20**, 555–558

GRIMINGER, P. and LUTZ, H. (1964). Observations on the voluntary intake of calcium by the laying hen. *Poultry Science*, **43**, 710–716

GRUNDER, A.A. and TSANG, P.W. (1984). Effects of vitamin D_3 deficiency on adenosine triphosphatase activity of jejunum from White Leghorn hens. *Poultry Science*, **63**, 1073–1075

HAMILTON, R.M.G. (1980). The effects of dietary phosphorus, vitamin D_3, and 25-hydroxy vitamin D_3 levels on feed intake, productive performance, and egg shell quality in two strains of force-molted White Leghorns. *Poultry Science*, **59**, 598–604

HAMILTON, R.M.G. and THOMPSON, B.K. (1980). Effect of sodium plus potassium to chloride ratio in practical-type diets on blood gas levels in three strains of White Leghorn hens and the relationship between acid-base balance and egg shell strength. *Poultry Science*, **59**, 1294–1298

HARMS, R.H. (1982). The influence of nutrition on egg shell quality Part III. Electrolyte balance. *Feedstuffs*, **54**, 25–27

HARRISON, H.E. and HARRISON, H.C. (1961). Transfer of Ca-45 across intestinal wall *in vitro* in relation to action of vitamin D and cortisol. *American Journal of Physiology*, **190**, 265–271

HENRY, H.L. and NORMAN, A.W. (1978). Vitamin D: Two dihydroxylated metabolites are required for normal chicken hatchability. *Science*, **201**, 835–837

HENRY, H.L., MIDGETT, R.J. and NORMAN, A.W. (1974). Regulation of 25-hydroxyvitamin D_3-1-hydroxylase *in vivo*. *Journal of Biological Chemistry*, **249**, 7584–7592

HOBSON-FROHOCK, A., LAND, D.G., GRIFFITHS, M.M. and CURTIS, R.F. (1973). Egg taints: association with trimethylamine. *Nature*, **243**, 304–305

HOBSON-FROHOCK, A., FENWICK, G.R., HEANLEY, R.K., LAND, D.G. and CURTIS, R.F. (1977). Rapeseed meal and egg taint: association with sinapine. *British Poultry Science*, **18**, 539–541

HOBSON-FROHOCK, A., FENWICK, R.G., LAND, D.G., CURTIS, R.F. and GULLIVER, A.L. (1975). Rapeseed meal and egg taint. *British Poultry Science*, **16**, 219–222

HOLCOMBE, D.J., ROLAND, D.A. SR and HARMS, R.H. (1976). The ability of hens to regulate phosphorus intake when offered diets containing different levels of phosphorus. *Poultry Science*, **55**, 308–317

HOLICK, M.F., SCHNOES, H.K., DELUCA, H.F., SUDA, T. and COUSINS, R.J. (1971). Isolation and identification of 1,25-dihydroxycholecalciferol. A metabolite of vitamin D active in the intestine. *Biochemistry*, **10**, 2799–2804

HUGHES, B.O. and WOOD-GUSH, D.G.M. (1971). A specific appetite for calcium in domestic chickens. *Animal Behaviour*, **19**, 490–499

HUMBERT, J.R., HAMMOND, K.B., HATHAWAY, W.E., MARCOUX, J.G. and O'BRIEN, D. (1970). Trimethylaminuria: the fish-odor syndrome. *Lancet*, **i**, 770–771

HUNT, J.R. and CHEENCY, H.W.R. (1970). Influence of dietary phosphorus on shell quality. *British Poultry Science*, **11**, 259–267

HURWITZ, S. (1964a). Calcium metabolism at the onset of egg production as influenced by dietary calcium level. *Poultry Science*, **48**, 1462–1472

HURWITZ, S. (1964b). Bone composition and ^{45}Ca retention in fowl as influenced by shell formation. *American Journal of Physiology*, **206**, 198–204

HURWITZ, S. (1965). Calcium turnover in different bone segments of laying fowl. *American Journal of Physiology*, **208**, 203–207

HURWITZ, S. (1976). Mineral and trace element requirements for replacement pullets. In *Proceedings of 4th Nutrition Conference*, (Swan, H. and Lewis, D., eds), pp. 92–107. London, J & A Churchill

HURWITZ, S. (1978). Calcium metabolism in birds. In *Chemical Zoology, Vol. X, Aves*, (Brush, A.H., ed.), pp. 273–306. New York, Academic Press

HURWITZ, S. and BAR, A. (1965). Absorption of calcium and phosphorus along the gastrointestinal tract of the laying hen, as influenced by dietary calcium and shell formation. *Journal of Nutrition*, **86**, 433–438

HURWITZ, S. and BAR, A. (1967). Calcium metabolism of hens secreting heavy or light egg shells. *Poultry Science*, **46**, 1522–1527

HURWITZ, S. and BAR, A. (1969). Calcium reserves in bones of laying hens: their presence and utilization. *Poultry Science*, **48**, 1391–1396

HURWITZ, S. and BAR, A. (1971). The effect of prelaying mineral nutrition on the development, performance and mineral metabolism of pullets. *Poultry Science*, **50**, 1044–1055

HURWITZ, S. and BAR, A. (1972). Site of vitamin D action in chick intestine. *American Journal of Physiology*, **222**, 761–767

HURWITZ, S. and GRIMINGER, P. (1959). Observations on the calcium balance of laying hens. *Journal of Agricultural Science*, **54**, 373–377

HURWITZ, S. and GRIMINGER, P. (1960). Partition of calcium and phosphorus excretion in the laying hen. *Nature*, **189**, 759–760

HURWITZ, S., BAR, A. and COHEN, I. (1973). Regulation of calcium absorption by fowl intestine. *American Journal of Physiology*, **225**, 150–157

HURWITZ, S., BAR, A. and MESHORER, A. (1973). Field rickets in turkey poults: plasma and bone chemistry, bone histology and intestinal calcium-binding protein. *Poultry Science*, **52**, 1370–1374

HURWITZ, S., BORNSTEIN, S. and LEV, Y. (1975). Some responses of laying hens to induced arrest of egg production. *Poultry Science*, **54**, 415–422

HURWITZ, S., FISHMAN, S., BAR, A. and TALPAZ, H. (1984). Calcium metabolism in birds: computer simulation of response to 1,25-dihydroxycholecalciferol. *American Journal of Physiology*, **246**, R684–R687

HURWITZ, S., FISHMAN, S., BAR, A., PINES, M., RIESENFELD, G. and TALPAZ, H. (1983). Simulation of calcium homeostasis: modeling and parameter estimation. *American Journal of Physiology*, **245**, R664–R672

JUNQUEIRA, O.M., MILES, R.D. and HARMS, R.H. (1983). The inability of sodium bicarbonate to induce an improvement in eggshell quality in the presence of sulfanilamide. *Poultry Science*, **62**, 2062–2064

KAETZEL, D.M. JR and SOARES, J.H. JR (1979). Effects of cholecalciferol steroids on bone and egg shell calcification in Japanese quail. *Journal of Nutrition*, **109**, 1601–1608

KAETZEL, D.M. JR and SOARES, J.H. JR (1984). The effect of dietary cholecalciferol steroids and gonadal hormone implantation on plasma 1,25-dihydroxycholecalciferol and bone calcification in preovulatory and senescent female Japanese quail. *Nutrition Research*, **1**, 621–632

KAETZEL, D.M. JR., SOARES, J.H. JR and SWERDEL, M.R. (1978). Effects of vitamin D_3 metabolites on the bones and egg shells of aged quail and chickens. *Proceedings of the Maryland Nutrition Conference*, pp. 50–54

KENNY, A.D. (1976). Vitamin D metabolism: physiological regulation in egg-laying Japanese quail. *American Journal of Physiology*, **230**, 1609–1615

KHAN, H.M. and CUTKOMP, L.K. (1982). *In vitro* studies on DDT, DDE, and ATPase related to avian eggshell thinning. *Archives of Environmental Contamination and Toxicology*, **11**, 627–633

KOSHY, K. and VAN DER SILK, A.L. (1979). High-performance liquid chromatographic method for the determination of 25-hydroxycholecalciferol in chicken egg yolks. *Journal of Agricultural and Food Chemistry*, **27**, 180–183

KRAMER, S.C. and WAIBEL, P.E. (1978). The vitamin D requirement of the turkey breeder hens in cages. *Minnesota Turkey Research*, pp. 119–123

KUSHUARA, S. and SCHRAER, H. (1982). Cytology and autoradiography of estrogen-induced differentiation of avian endosteal cells. *Calcified Tissue International*, **34**, 352–358

LEACH, R.M. and MUENSTER, A. (1962). Studies on the role of manganese in bone formation. I. Effect on mucopolysaccharide content of chick bone. *Journal of Nutrition*, **28**, 51–62

LOERCHER, K., SCHEILE, C.Z. and BRONSCH, K. (1970). Transfer of continuously infused NaHC^{14} CO$_3$ and Ca^{47}Cl$_2$ to the hen's egg shell. *Annales de Biologie Animale, Biochimie et Biophysique*, **10**(Suppl. 2), 193–198

LONGSTAFF, M. and HILL, R. (1972). The hexose amine and uronic acid contents of the matrix of shells of eggs from pullets fed on diets with different manganese content. *British Poultry Science*, **13**, 377–385

LUCK, M.R. and SCANES, C.G. (1979). Plasma levels of ionized calcium in the laying hen (*Gallus domesticus*). *Comparative Biochemistry and Physiology*, **63A**, 177–191

LUCK, M.R., SOMMERVILLE, B.A. and SCANES, C.G. (1980). The effect of egg shell calcification on the response of plasma calcium to parathyroid hormone and calcium in the domestic fowl (*Gallus domesticus*). *Comparative Biochemistry and Physiology*, **65A**, 151–154

LUNDHOLM, C.E. (1984a). Comparison of the effect of DDE on Ca metabolism and its subcellular fractions in the duck and the domestic fowl. *Acta Pharmacologica et Toxicologica*, **54**, 400–407

LUNDHOLM, C.E. (1984b). Effect of DDE on the Ca metabolism of the duck eggshell gland and its subcellular fractions: relations to the functional stage. *Comparative Biochemistry and Physiology*, **78C**, 5–12

LUNDHOLM, C.E. (1984c). Ca content of duck egg shell gland mucosa homogenate and the rate of Ca^{2+} binding to subcellular fractions during and after the formation of the egg shell. *Comparative Biochemistry and Physiology*, **77B**, 655–663

MARCH, B.E. and MACMILLAN, C. (1979). Trimethylamine production in the ceca and small intestine as a cause of fishy taints in eggs. *Poultry Science*, **58**, 93–98

MCLOUGHLIN, C.P. and SOARES, J.H. JR (1976). A study of the effects of 25-hydroxycholecalciferol and calcium source on egg shell quality. *Poultry Science*, **55**, 1400–1410

MILES, R.D., COSTA, P.T. and HARMS, R.H. (1983). The influence of dietary phosphorus levels on laying hen performance, egg shell quality and various blood parameters. *Poultry Science*, **62**, 1033–1037

MILES, R.D. and HARMS, R.H. (1982). Relationship between egg specific gravity and plasma phosphorus from hens fed different dietary calcium, phosphorus and sodium levels. *Poultry Science*, **61**, 175–177

MILLER, S.C. (1977). Osteoclast cell-surface changes during the egg laying cycle in Japanese quail. *Journal of Cell Biology*, **75**, 101–118

MILLER, S.C. (1981). Osteoclast cell-surface specializations during egg laying in Japanese quail. *American Journal of Anatomy*, **162**, 35–43

MILLER, S.C., BOWMAN, B. and MYERS, R.L. (1984). Morphological aspects of the activation of avian medullary bone osteoclasts by parathyroid hormone. *Anatomical Record*, **208**, 223–231

MONGIN, P. (1968). Role of acid–base balance in physiology of egg shell formation. *World's Poultry Science Journal*, **24**, 200–211

MONGIN, P. and CARTER, N.W. (1978). Studies on the avian shell gland during egg formation: mucosal intracellular pH. *British Poultry Science*, **19**, 93–96

MONGIN, P. and LACASSAGNE, L. (1964). Physiologie de la formation de la coquille de l'oeuf et equilibre acid–basique. *Compte Rendu hebdomadaire des Scéances de l'Académié des Sciences, Paris*, **258**, 3093–3094

MONGIN, P. and SAUVEUR, B. (1979). Plasma inorganic phosphorus concentration during egg-shell formation. *British Poultry Science*, **20**, 401–412

MONTECUCCOLI, G., HURWITZ, S., COHEN, A. and BAR, A. (1978). The role of 25-hydroxycholecalciferol-1-hydroxylase in the response of calcium absorption to the reproductive activity in birds. *Comparative Biochemistry and Physiology*, **57A**, 335–339

MORGAN, C.L. and MITCHELL, J.H. (1938). The calcium and phosphorus balance of laying hens. *Poultry Science*, **17**, 99–104

MORRIS, K.M.L., JENKINS, S.A. and SIMONITE, J.P. (1977). The effect on shell thickness of the inclusion of the calcinogenic plant *Solanum malacoxylon* in the diet of laying hens. *Veterinary Record*, **101**, 502–504

NABER, E.C. (1979). The effect of nutrition on the composition of eggs. *Poultry Science*, **58**, 518–528

NATIONAL RESEARCH COUNCIL (NRC) (1977). *Nutrient Requirements of Poultry, Seventh Edition.* Washington, DC, National Academy of Sciences

NICHOLSON, R.A., AKHTAR, M. and TAYLOR, T.G. (1979). The metabolism of cholecalciferol in the liver of Japanese quail (*Coturnix coturnix japonica*) with particular reference to the effects of oestrogen. *Biochemical Journal*, **182**, 745–750

NIETO, A., MOYA, F. and CANDELLA, J.L. (1973). Isolation and properties of two calcitonins from chicken ultimobranchial glands. *Biochimica et Biophysica Acta*, **322**, 383–391

NORMAN, A.W., LEATHERS, V. and BISHOP, J.E. (1983). Normal egg hatchability requires the simultaneous administration of 1,25-dihydroxycholecalciferol and 24R,25-dihydroxycholecalciferol. *Journal of Nutrition*, **113**, 2505–2515

NORMAN, A.W., MYRTLE, J.F., MIDGETT, R.J., NORWICKI, H.G., WILLIAMS, V. and POPJAK, G. (1971). 1,25-dihydroxycholecalciferol: identification of the proposed active form of vitamin D_3 in the intestine. *Science*, **173**, 51–54

NYHOLM, N.E.I. (1981). Evidence of involvement of aluminium in causation of defective formation of egg shells and of impaired breeding in wild passerine birds. *Environmental Research*, **26**, 363–371

NYS, Y. and DE LAAGE, X. (1984). Effects of suppression of eggshell calcification and of $1,25(OH)_2D_3$ on Mg^{2+}, Ca^{2+} and $Mg^{2+}HCO_3$-ATPase, alkaline phosphatase, carbonic, anhydrase and CaBP levels. I. The laying hen uterus. *Comparative Biochemistry and Physiology*, **78A**, 833–838

NYS, Y., N'GUYEN, T.M. and GARABEDIAN, M. (1984). Involvement of 1,25-dihydroxycholecalciferol in the short- and long-term increase in intestinal calcium absorption in laying hens: stimulation by gonadal hormones is partly independent of 1,25-dihydroxycholecalciferol. *Comparative Biochemistry and Physiology*, **53**, 54–59

ODIBA, J.Y., SUNDE, M.L. and BIRD, H.R. (1981). The effects of dietary levels of chloride and bicarbonate on egg production. *Proceedings of the Society for Experimental Biology and Medicine*, **166**, 532–535

OUSTERHOUT, L.E. (1980). Effects of calcium and phosphorus levels on egg weight and egg shell quality. *Poultry Science*, **59**, 1480–1484

OVERFIELD, N.D. and ELSON, H.A. (1975). Dietary rapeseed meal and the incidence of tainted eggs. *British Poultry Science*, **16**, 213–217

PEARSON, A.W., BUTLER, E.J., CURTIS, R.F., FENWICK, G.R., HOBSON-FROHOCK, A. and LAND, D.G. (1979). Effect of rapeseed meal on hepatic trimethylamine oxidase activity in *Gallus domesticus* in relation to egg taint. *Journal of the Science of Food and Agriculture*, **30**, 291–298

PEARSON, T.W. and GOLDNER, A.M. (1973). Calcium transport across avian uterus. I. Effect of electrolyte substitution. *American Journal of Physiology*, **225**, 1508–1512

PEPPER, W.F., SUMMERS, J.D. and MCCONACHIE, J.D. (1968). The effect of high levels of calcium and sodium bicarbonate on egg shell quality. *Poultry Science*, **47**, 224–229

PIKE, J.W., SPANOS, E., COLSTON, K.W., MACINTYRE, I. and HAUSSLER, M.R. (1978). Influence of estrogen in renal vitamin D hydroxylases and serum $1,25\text{-}(OH)_2D_3$ in chicks. *American Journal of Physiology*, **235**, E338–E343

PINES, M., BAR, A. and HURWITZ, S. (1984).Isolation and purification of avian parathyroid hormone using high performance liquid chromatography and some of its properties. *General and Comparative Endocrinology*, **53**, 224–231

PINES, M., POLIN, D. and HURWITZ, S. (1983). Urinary cyclic AMP excretion in birds: dependence on parathyroid hormone activity. *General and Comparative Endocrinology*, **119**, 90–96

POLIN, D. and RINGER, R.K. (1977). 25-hydroxy-D_3, vitamin D_3 and graded levels of phosphorus: effect on egg production and shell quality. *Feedstuffs*, **49**, 18–19

POTTS, P. and WASHBURN, K.W. (1977). The effect of supplemental calcium and vitamin D_3 and strain differences in egg shell strength. *Poultry Science,* **56**, 1067–1072

RAMBECK, W.A. and ZUCKER, H. (1985). Synergistic effects of $1,25(OH)_2D_3$ and $24,25(OH)_2D_3$ on duodenal CaBP in rachitic chicks and on egg shell weight in Japanese quail. *Biochemical and Biophysical Research Communications,* **126**, 799–804

RODRIGUES, M., OWINGS, W.J. and SELL, J.L. (1984). Influence of phase feeding available phosphorus on egg production characteristics, carcass phosphorus content and serum inorganic phosphorus levels in three commercial layer strains. *Poultry Science,* **63**, 1553–1562

ROLAND, D.A. SR and HARMS, R.H. (1973). Calcium metabolism of hens. 5. Effects of various sources and sizes of calcium carbonate on egg shell quality. *Poultry Science,* **52**, 369–372

ROLAND, D.A. SR, PUTMAN, C.E. and HILBURN, R.L. (1978). The relationship of age on ability of hens to maintain egg shell calcification when stressed with inadequate dietary calcium. *Poultry Science,* **57**, 1616–1621

SAID, N.W., SULLIVAN, T.W., SUNDE, M.C. and BIRD, H.R. (1984). Effect of dietary phosphorus levels and source on productive performance and egg quality of two commercial strains of laying hens. *Poultry Science,* **63**, 2007–2019

SAUVEUR, B. and MONGIN, P. (1974). Effects of time-limited calcium meal upon food and calcium ingestion and egg quality. *British Poultry Science,* **15**, 305–313

SAUVEUR, B. and MONGIN, P. (1983). Plasma inorganic phosphorus concentration during egg shell formation. II. Inverse relationship with intestinal calcium content and shell weight. *Reproduction, Nutrition et Développement,* **23**, 755–764

SCHACHTER, D., DOWDLE, E.B. and SCHENKER, H. (1960). Active transport of calcium by the small intestine of the rat. *American Journal of Physiology,* **198**, 263–268

SCOTT, M.L., HULL, S.J. and MULLENDORF, P.A. (1971). The calcium requirements of laying hens and effects of dietary oyster shell upon egg shell quality. *Poultry Science,* **50**, 1055–1063

SEDRANI, S. and TAYLOR, T.G. (1977). Metabolism of 25-hydroxycholecalciferol in Japanese quail in relation to reproduction. *Journal of Endocrinology,* **72**, 405–406

SHEN, H., SUMMERS, J.D. and LEESON, S. (1981). Egg production and shell quality of layers fed various levels of vitamin D. *Poultry Science,* **60**, 1485–1490

SIMKISS, K. (1961). Calcium metabolism and avian reproduction. *Biological Reviews,* **36**, 321–367

SOARES, J.H. JR, SWERDEL, M.R. and OTTINGER, M.A. (1979). The effectiveness of vitamin D analog 1α-OH-D_3 in promoting fertility and hatchability in the laying hen. *Poultry Science,* **58**, 1004–1006

SPANOS, E., PIKE, J.W., HAUSSLER, M.R., COLSTON, K.W., EVANS, I.M.A., GOLDNER, A.M., MCCAIN, T.A. and MACINTYRE, I. (1976). Circulating 1,25-dihydroxyvitamin D in the chicken: Enhancement by injection of prolactin and during egg laying. *Life Sciences,* **19**, 1751–1756

SUMMERS, J.D., GRANDHI, R. and LEESON, S. (1976). Calcium and phosphorus requirements of the laying hen. *Poultry Science,* **55**, 402–413

SUNDE, M.L., TURK, C.M. and DELUCA, H.F. (1978). The essentiality of vitamin D metabolites for embryonic chick development. *Science,* **200**, 1067–1069

TAKAHASHI, N., ABE, E., TANABE, R. and SUDA, T. (1980). A high-affinity cytosol binding protein for 1,25-dihydroxycholecalciferol in the uterus of Japanese quail. *Biochemical Journal,* **190**, 513–518

TAKAHASHI, N., SHINKI, T., ABE, E., HORIUCHI, N., YAMAGUCHI, A., YOSHIKI, S. and SUDA, T. (1983). The role of vitamin D in medullary bone formation in egg laying Japanese quail and immature male chicks treated with sex hormones. *Calcified Tissue International,* **35**, 465–471

TAYLOR, T.G. (1961). Calcium absorption and metabolism in the laying hen. In *Nutrition of Pigs and Poultry,* (Morgan, J.T. and Lewis, D., eds), pp. 148–157. London, Butterworths

TAYLOR, T.G. (1965). Dietary phosphorus and egg shell thickness in the domestic fowl. *British Poultry Science,* **6**, 70–87

TAYLOR, T.G. and KIRKLEY, J. (1967). The absorption and excretion of minerals in laying hens in relation to egg shell formation. *British Poultry Science,* **8**, 289–295

VAN DE VELDE, A.-P., LOVERIDGE, N. and VERMEIDEN, J.P.W. (1984). Parathyroid hormone response to calcium stress during eggshell calcification. *Endocrinology,* **115**, 1901–1904

VOHRA, P., SCOPES, T.D. and WILSON, W.O. (1979). Egg production and body weight changes of Japanese quail and Leghorn hens following deprivation of either supplementary calcium or vitamin D_3. *Poultry Science,* **58**, 432–440

VONDELL, J.H. (1932). Is the production of "off-flavor" eggs an individual characteristic? *Poultry Science*, **11**, 375

WAKELING, D.E. (1982). A fishy taint in eggs: interaction between fishmeal diets and strain of birds. *British Poultry Science*, **23**, 89–93

WALDROUP, P.W., BUSSELL, W.D. and COBB, A. (1977). Response of laying hens to a new metabolite of vitamin D. *Arkansas Farm Research*, **26**, 2

WASSERMAN, R.H. and TAYLOR, A.N. (1966). Vitamin D-induced calcium-binding protein in chick intestinal mucosa. *Science*, **152**, 791–793

WASSERMANN, R.H. and TAYLOR, A.N. (1973). Intestinal absorption of phosphate in the chick: effect of vitamin D_3 and other parameters. *Journal of Nutrition*, **103**, 586–599

WIDEMAN, R.F. JR and YOUTZ, S.L. (1985). Comparisons of avian renal responses to bovine parathyroid extract, synthetic bovine (1–34)parathyroid hormone, and synthetic human (1–34)parathyroid hormone. *General and Comparative Endocrinology*, **57**, 480–490

WILSON, P.W. and LAWSON, D.E.M. (1978). Incorporation of [3H] leucine into actin-like protein in response to 1,25-dihydroxycholecalciferol in chick intestinal brush borders. *Biochemical Journal*, **173**, 627–631

YANNAKOPOULOS, A.L. and MORRIS, T.R. (1979). Effect of light, vitamin D and dietary phosphorus on egg-shell quality late in the pullet laying year. *British Poultry Science*, **20**, 337–342

Chapter 16

The effect of disease on egg quality

D. Spackman

Introduction

The Oxford English Dictionary defines 'quality' as 'the degree of excellence' of an item. When applied to eggs we must consider the degree of excellence of that package for the purpose for which it is intended, either eating or hatching.

This can apply to the internal quality as it is laid, the keeping quality, the way in which it is capable of supporting embryonic growth, the viability of the neonate as influenced by the egg from which it came, and indeed the ability of the next generation to reproduce if altered in any way by factors connected with its egg of origin. It is therefore not an immediate judgement on the degree of excellence of the new-laid egg as perceived at first sight.

That factors connected with the egg can have long-term and far reaching effects on the next generation has been clearly shown by Spencer Gavora and Gowe (1979), who demonstrated that selection of hens for high egg production characteristics resulted in lower egg transmission of lymphoid leucosis virus and gs antigen into the eggs, thus effecting a reduction in the incidence of the disease in the next generation. This lowered egg transmission represents a facet of improved egg quality in terms of disease.

General aspects of egg quality

In the commercial field poor egg quality is expressed as the lowering of either shell and/or internal quality of the new-laid egg below accepted levels, thus changing the profitability of the enterprise. Few recent assessments of either the degree of lowered quality or the economic consequences have been made. Sherwood (1958) offered a general review of egg quality. Hanson (1968) at the last of these symposia devoted to egg quality in September 1967, put the annual loss from downgrading in the United Kingdom at that time at more than £4–5 million. Maddison (1970) put downgrading at a level of 5.54% with some 82% of that amount being due to cracks. Current estimates, from details supplied by various packing enterprises would seem to suggest a level of 6–7% of all eggs being downgraded, with 90–95% of these being cracked shells. These figures do not take into account eggs removed at the production unit.

The degree to which disease contributes to this situation, directly or indirectly, is almost impossible to calculate. Gordon (1977) put a total loss of potential eating eggs, including those not laid at all because of lowered production potential, at £25–39 million. Sapra and Chabra (1972) offered a general survey of the disease effects on egg quality but put no cost to it.

A more detailed appraisal was offered by Meurier (1972), who divided the total loss due to disease into the part contributed by rearing and that during laying. In France at that time he estimated that 11 eggs/bird potential was being lost through mortality during lay, a further 12 eggs due to lowered production performance through morbidity, and between 1 and 8 eggs/bird through disease factors encountered during rearing, a total of some 24–31 eggs/bird lost. The additional loss through lowered quality he could not assess, though stating it to be considerable. This is likely to be so since 68% of all birds were calculated to be affected by morbidity in addition to 10.5% which died during the laying year.

Miscellaneous factors

As stated earlier, most of the loss of quality can be attributed to below average shell condition, and factors influencing this, with the exception of disease, have been reviewed by Roland (1979) and Hamilton et al. (1979). Wilhelm (1940) also outlined some of the variability in shell quality and pointed out that there was little relationship between total number of eggs laid by a hen in the year and shell quality.

Since, when birds are clinically affected by disease, total production is usually influenced as well as quality, it suggests that high producing hens laying eggs with inferior shell quality are doing so for reasons other than disease. This adds to the difficulty in assessing the importance of disease to total inferior egg quality.

Increasingly, attention is now being paid to internal quality for adjustment of returns to producers, and this also has numerous factors other than disease involved in the variability (Knox and Godfrey, 1934; Lorenz, Taylor and Almquist, 1934; Hunter, Van Wagenen and Hall, 1936).

Some surveys have been conducted which attempt to correlate egg quality with geographic area, and these link the observed effects to density of poultry population within these areas (Buckland, Allen and Bjerring, 1971). Other surveys have shown equally convincing evidence for differences in egg quality, both shell and internal, linked to geographic area (Coles, 1936), but here the highest quality was frequently found in those areas known to have a high poultry population, and low quality found where poultry density was low. As most of the eggs produced at that time were laid by hens kept on range systems, Coles (1936) hypothesised that soil type and relative humidity of the area had significant effects on shell quality; eggs produced on high silica-containing soils and in areas of lower relative humidity having better shell structure, this in turn being capable of sustaining higher internal quality. With the increasing return to extensive methods of egg production in some areas of Europe, these findings merit further investigation, especially with regard to the effect of poultry density in these situations.

Whilst not entering into an extensive review of the effects of environment on egg quality, it is worth noting that Helbacka, Casterline and Smith (1963) found decreased shell calcification in birds maintained in 5% carbon dioxide for 24–48 h. This work was substantiated by Frank and Burger (1965), while McKerley et al. (1967) further found changes in Haugh unit measurements.

Although in these experiments the effects were direct, it may be hypothesised that similar effects may be obtained indirectly through the conditioning of the bird's respiratory system, by higher than normal levels of carbon dioxide and ammonia in the poultry house, to facilitate invasion by pathogens, which themselves may have detrimental effects on egg quality. Some other conditions which can have effects on egg production such as 'bluecomb' disease of pullets, have been shown to be mimicked by certain environmental mismanagement factors, as, for example, water deprivation (Fisher *et al.*,1961).

Alteration in component parts of the egg

The most severe alterations in the yolk come about in carrier birds as the result of infection with *Salmonella pullorum*. Egg production, fertility and hatchability are sometimes affected, but more usually the effects are seen in the poor viability of the neonate and as lesions in the reproductive tract. These consist of misshapen ova, alterations in the consistency of the contents and blood staining. These ova may detach and be incorporated into an egg, clearly of lower quality, but may also fall into the abdominal cavity and result in egg peritonitis. Similar chronic disease situations may result in multiple ovulations, though these are more usually of genetic or interactive origin (Lowry, Dobbs and Abplanalp, 1979). Blood spots or streaks are frequently associated with the vitelline membrane of the yolk. These have a high correlation with genetics and season (Jeffrey, 1945; Lerner,Taylor and Lowry, 1951; Amer, 1961).

Nalbandov and Card (1947) suggested that access to range lowered the incidence of ovarian haemorrages, though it was not clear if this was the result of nutrition or lowered stress factors. Range suffering drought did not lower the incidence. The influence of grass in reducing the incidence of blood and meat spots was not supported by the work of Denton (1947), whose results also could not confirm the theories of Nalbandov and Card (1944) and other workers that meat spots were altered blood spots.

Recent work by the author (Spackman, unpublished data) substantiates that the two are distinct entities, meat spots being pigmented or non-pigmented albumen deposits incorporated into the egg, principally in the chalazae or thick albumen. This work reveals that individual hens produce eggs with approximately the same percentage affected over several months of lay, with neither increase nor decrease in incidence with time. Low incidence birds placed alongside high incidence birds in laying cages do not alter their rate of inclusion incidence (*Table 16.1*). It is unlikely that disease effects are involved at the time the eggs are being laid, although the differing percentage rates found in flocks of the same premises at different times does not preclude the possibility of damage to the oviduct during rearing.

Fowler (1982) has, however, suggested an increased incidence in flocks for one month following an episode of Avian Encephalomyelitis (Epidemic Tremors), and Mercer (1985, personal communication) informed the author of increased incidence following an outbreak of Infectious Bronchitis (IB) in range layers. Such increased incidence has not been seen by the author in flocks being monitored following several known and confirmed disease situations.

That blood spots and meat spots are separate entities is further borne out by the findings of Helbacka and Swanson (1958), who noted that 100% of blood spots were associated with the yolk and 90% of meat spots were in the chalazae or thick

Table 16.1 Initial and rolling average percentage meat spots

	Bird[a]								
	A	B	C	D	E	F	G	H	J
Initial (week 1) (%)	60	60	100	71	69	60	0	14	14
5 week average (%)	66	67	95	72	68	60	5	29	7
10 week average (%)	64	66	87	57	65	59	9	25	7
15 week average (%)	69	58	91	60	64	62	11	18	8

[a]Birds 74 weeks old at start, housed in individual cages in one block thus in intimate contact for pathogen transfer if involved.

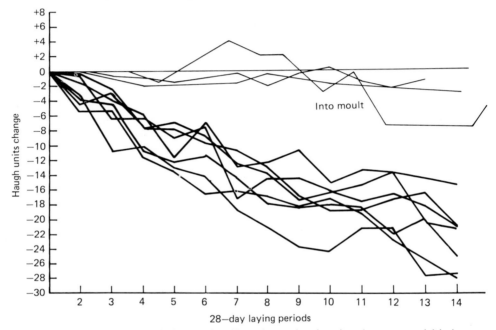

Figure 16.1 Change in Haugh units by age. Specific pathogen-free (——) against commercial (━) conditions. Specific pathogen-free (SPF) stocks: 2 White Leghorn, 1 Rhode Island Red cross. Commercial hybrids: 2 White Leghorn, 5 Rhode Island Red type

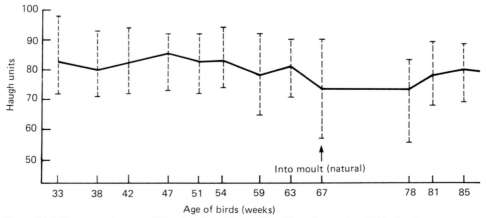

Figure 16.2 Change and range of Haugh units with age. Specific pathogen-free White Leghorn stock in sterile conditions

albumen. Jeffrey (1945) noted that the incidence of blood spots reduced from 10.6% to 4.5% following a moult, but no mention of meat spots was made. The cause of the two kinds of inclusion may thus be completely different in origin.

Though detailed histological description has been given on the oviduct (Smith *et al.*, 1957b) and the formation of the chalazae (Scott and Wai-Lan Huang, 1941), there is little noted about the cause of chalazae which are extra large or broken, which may be due to genetic, environmental, handling or disease factors, and the reason for their appearance is at present not clarified.

Similarly, although known differences are evident between the quality of thick and thin albumen components, some work suggests that absolute amounts of each do not alter (Van Wagenen and Wilgus, 1934). The laminated appearance of the envelope of thick albumen noticed by Schaible, Moore and Davidson (1935) suggesting that it was laid down in sheets, is partially confirmed by the appearance of meat spots under the scanning electron microscope, where this author noticed a similar laminated structure to these albumen-like inclusions (Spackman 1985, unpublished data).

Internal quality, on storage, is known to deteriorate, though this can be further increased following disease (Parnell, 1950). After deterioration in storage, conditions visible on candling such as free-floating bubbles and yolks are noticeable, though these can also be a feature of new-laid eggs (Platt, 1936). Anderson (1935), when describing watery whites, failed to notice the mobile nature of the yolk described by Platt (1936). Histological examinations of the oviduct of birds laying 'watery white' eggs by the author confirm the findings of Coles (1938) and Wyburn *et al.* (1970), that there were less goblet cells throughout the albumen-secreting area, and an abscence of PAS or Alcian Blue staining in epithelial cells in the magnum region, suggesting a relative reduction in ovomucin production.

Stout and Buss (1980) found little relationship between egg production rate and shell thickness in individual birds, and the similarities in *in utero* times suggest a real difference in shell deposition rate in different birds. This work confirmed the findings of Roland, Holcombe and Harms (1977) who concluded that some hens were at times unable to utilise calcium at the site of shell formation, or expelled the egg prematurely, Disease processes were not ruled out as the cause of these individual and intermittent shell-less or partially calcified eggs. In earlier work, Roland (1976) found 2.4%, 5.1% and 10.6% of eggs were being laid without shells and falling through the cage floor in 6, 10 and 13 month old birds respectively. Again it was not clarified if the differences were due simply to increasing age of the birds, or if exposure to disease factors with time were involved.

Although shell quality was not examined, recent experiments by the author have shown that Haugh unit measurement does not decline significantly over a year's lay in several flocks of Specific Antibody Negative (SAN) birds of differing breeds, whilst commercial hybrids in the field decline by about 1.5–2 Haugh units/month throughout a laying cycle. This is suggestive of sub-clinical effects of pathogens in the commercial situation, food, caging and temperature being similar with all groups, filtered air being the main difference in the SAN flocks (Spackman, previously unpublished data, *see Figures 16.1 and 16.2*).

Britton (1977) found that shell membrane weight was less in older birds than young birds and less in eggs with poor shells than in those with good shells. Shell membrane nitrogen and shell magnesium were also less in these poor eggs, indicating a more extensive oviduct involvement than simply the calcium secreting cells of the shell gland. These same findings were observed by Cooke (1970) when investigating corrugated egg shells. The normal incorporation rates of magnesium and phosphorus in the shell have been described by Itoh and Hatano (1964).

Whilst addition of β-aminoproprionitrile to the diet or deficiency of copper in the diet (Barnett, Richey and Morgan, 1957) increase the incidence of corrugated egg shells, two hens in the author's collection persistently lay this type of shell, without additions or subtractions from the diet. This may indicate an earlier disease effect on the oviduct, or an inherited factor might also be involved. That this latter might be the case could be supported by observations on other birds which the author hatched from SAN eggs which had slightly folded lines on the shells. Females from these eggs themselves laid eggs with lines in the shell, and this has continued to the F_3 generation. Male offspring from such eggs, when mated to hens laying normal shells, do not appear to pass on the fault. In none of the foregoing experiments were records kept of temperatures prevailing, which may have had a profound effect on shell quality as noted by Miller and Sunde (1975). Albumen-like masses, similar to meat spots, have been described in the shells of rough-surfaced eggs (Ball et al., 1973), and if associated with an increased incidence of meat spots could be due to the same cause, as yet unclarified. Almquist and Burmester (1934) describe a condition of the shell referred to as 'glassy', which appears thinner and more fragile than ordinary shells, but which, on storage, proves to preserve internal quality better than normal shells. It is therefore unwise to observe all candling abnormalities as detrimental, and even more dangerous to link them all with disease.

A recent abnormality of egg shells in the United Kingdom, described variously as 'splashed shell', 'spotted eggs', 'pinks' or 'whitewash splashed' (also mentioned in Chapter 8), is frequently associated with air spaces in the palisade layer and reduced resistance to deformation and cracking (Spackman, unpublished data). These eggs occur in the early lay period in most birds, but some persist throughout lay in individuals. No direct association with disease has yet been found.

McCallion (1953) could find no significant differences between the histological appearance of the oviducts of hens laying thick or thin-shelled eggs, and concluded that differences must lie at the biochemical level. This is supported by Gutowska and Mitchell (1945) who found two or three times the activity of carbonic anhydrase in the shell glands of good shelled egg layers. Hirakata, Hetsuka and Ohashi (1977) also found higher carbonic anhydrase activity in the shell glands of young layers than in older birds, though no disease history was given.

The rate of peristalsis of the oviduct is subject to changes due to the irritability of foreign matter or oedema from infection in the wall, and there is also the possibility of reverse peristalsis. This author has seen cases similar to those described by Curtis (1916), of membranous or soft-shelled eggs in the abdominal cavity, which could only have got there by reverse peristalsis. This often follows an episode of infection with respiratory viruses, and accompanies production of soft-shelled eggs to the exterior as well.

Erratic oviposition and egg defects have been noted in the broiler breeder pullet (Jaap and Muir, 1968). They estimate some 82–90% of broiler breeders may produce defective eggs, which obviously are lowered in quality both for hatching or eating purposes.

Hughes and Parker (1971) noted that 45% of Delaware egg-type pullets laying shell-less eggs also produced a hard-shelled egg on the same day. When laid close together, the hard-shelled egg had a rough texture. Steggerda and Hollander (1944) also observed a chalky-white deposit on some eggs but made no mention of soft-shelled eggs. Their description, however, matches that of Hughes and Parker (1971) and from their illustrations, is shown to be identical to the type of egg investigated by the author in a variety of situations. They have been noted in increased incidence after Infectious Avian Encephalomyelitis (Epidemic Tremors), Infectious Laryngotracheitis (ILT), water deprivation, interruption of power supply, defective time clock functioning and other general stress situations. Like the eggs of Steggerda and Hollander (1944), one area of the shell is often flattened and does not have the rough texture of much of the remainder. It is conjectured that this is where the egg is in contact with its soft-shelled companion. Hughes and Parker (1971), on the other hand, theorise that the entry of the soft-shelled egg into the uterus causes premature expulsion of both. This does not explain the flattened, non-rough circular area on the hard-shelled egg, although this feature was not noted by them. They did, however, state that most of these eggs, and the shell-less eggs, were laid in the last two hours of the light period, which correspond with findings in the UK (Belyavin, personal communication), and which suggest retention for an extended period in the oviduct rather than premature expulsion.

Cain and Heyn (1964) used X-ray diffraction techniques to analyse the crystalline structure of the normal egg shell. Using this same technique it has been found that the rough-shelled eggs described above, found in association with soft-shelled eggs, have a covering of vaterite, an alternative crystal form of calcium, which has been found previously on soft-shelled eggs (Tullett *et al.*, 1976). The shell of these eggs is paler and specific gravity is often below normal, although the shell is thicker than that of unaffected eggs laid by the same flock. Specific gravity has been accepted as a good measure for likelihood to crack (Holder and Bradford, 1979) and shell colour has also been associated with shell strength (Godfrey, 1949).

Effects of bacteria on egg quality

Shell quality has a direct bearing on the ability of bacteria to penetrate into the interior of eggs, and the resulting infection can have severe consequences on both the hatchability and keeping quality of eggs (Board, 1966). Of particular importance are *Salmonella* species and Sauter and Petersen (1974) have shown that different serotypes of *Salmonellae* have varying abilities to penetrate even good egg shells. In trials, eggs of low shell quality (1.070 specific gravity) were penetrated 14.3% of the time by *S. orienburg* and 82.1% by *S. typhimurium*. The corresponding figures for good shell quality (1.090 specific gravity) were 3.8% and 21.5%. Exotic species commonly found in breeder flocks, such as *S. derby*, *S. senftenburg* and *S. worthington* also penetrated over 50% of eggs of poor shell quality. This has potentially serious implications both for public health aspects of eating eggs, and for hatching egg production, particularly in litter and range systems. Vielitz (1976) implicates salmonellosis in lowered egg shell quality.

Reid *et al.* (1961) found total mortality in the first nine days after hatching was increased from 1.8% in controls to 8.2% in offspring of hens whose eggs were contaminated by *Escherichia coli*. Affected chicks also weighed significantly less at hatching and after 80 d growth. Though Grewal *et al.* (1977) indicate that 10–15% of intestinal coliforms belong to pathogenic serotypes, and claim disruption of egg production accompanied by misshapen ova in cases examined by them from the field, they make no mention of other pathogens which may have precipitated the proliferation of *E. coli* within these birds. The invasion of the ovary and oviduct via the airsacs is a probability in some of these cases without interference of other organisms and resulting in salpingitis.

The role of Mycoplasmata in egg production and quality is somewhat controversial. Whether they act directly or only in combination with other pathogens is not clarified in all cases in the field. Lott *et al.*(1978) found a loss of egg production after challenge with *M. synoviae* in broiler breeders, amounting to some 25% two weeks later. But no change in either shell strength or Haugh unit measurements was found. However, because of climatic changes and a sudden exposure to cold weather, the control group also had a production loss of 19% and it is unclear whether the extra loss of production in the *M. synoviae* affected birds was simply a similar reaction to the temperature change in a relatively small experimental group size of 68 birds. Frazier (1972) states that mycoplasmosis lowers shell quality and it is felt by workers in the field generally that falls in production early in lay are often accompanied by positive seroconversion to *M. synoviae*. Most of these flocks, however, also have high titres to IB, either from field challenge or live vaccination, and it is difficult to determine in most cases if the production fall would have been as great if *M. synoviae* alone was involved. A similar situation was found by Timms (1972) in dual infections of *M. gallisepticum* and IB. Production falls and rough-surfaced shells were only a feature of the IB alone or dual infection, and not of *M. gallisepticum* challenge alone. Gentry (1978), however, points to benefits of as much as 10% extra production where immunisation against *M. gallisepticum* has been carried out on multi-aged sites. Domermuth, Gross and DuBose (1967) have shown salpingitis and the laying of soft-shelled eggs in birds challenged with *M. gallisepticum* which were negative for antibodies for both Newcastle Disease (ND) and IB. The oviducts of these birds had frequent small areas of lymphoid tissue, follicular in nature. The same lesions were found in turkeys similarly affected with *M. gallisepticum*. Ball, Singh and Pomeroy (1969) found a similar three-fold increase in lymphoid foci in the oviducts of turkey hens challenged with *M. meleagridis*, but considered this, like the changes induced by *M. gallisepticum*, not to be the cause of lowered fertility in the field.

Lerner, Taylor and Beach (1950) making investigations on the effect of respiratory disease on reproduction, diagnosed a typical infectious coryza caused by uncomplicated *Haemophilus gallinarum* infection, but later observations by Taylor *et al.* (1953) called into question the purity of one of the antigens used in the original diagnosis and stated that IB could not be ruled out. They do, however, describe the presence of coagulated white spots in the albumen of these eggs. If these were unpigmented meat spots (since the flock involved was composed of White Leghorns), then the appearance of these following a disease outbreak is different to the usual findings described earlier, but confirms the observations of Sevoian and Levine (1957) with IB.

Effect of viruses on egg quality

The same flock of White Leghorns worked on by Lerner, Taylor and Beach (1950) formed part of a series examined by Hill and Lorenz (1956) when analysing the diseases associated with egg changes. They state that the inability to repeat the changes with *Haemophilus gallinarum* in this, and in further cases where ND vaccine was used at the height of the production change, rule out *H. gallinarum* as the causative agent. In neither case is it clarified, however, if the viruses mentioned were themselves directly involved in the changes seen, or were only complicating entities in proper diagnosis. Hill and Lorenz (1956) do make the point that egg damage usually follows some time after cessation of active disease symptoms, and may persist for a considerable time thereafter.

Although Brandly (1934) states that carrier birds from an outbreak of ILT lay eggs with a lower hatchability than non-carrier sister birds, no explanation is offered as to the means by which this is brought about. It may be that a portion of the flock was laying the 'sandpaper' shells noted earlier as often following an episode of ILT, and which exhibit low hatchability. Generally ILT has an effect only on total number of eggs produced and unless complicated by other agents little effect on shell or internal quality. This has also been found to be the case following the use of live vaccine on birds already in lay (Kerr, personal communication). Hinshaw, Jones and Graybill (1931) noted that production starts to fall 4 d after challenge and has returned to normal 30 d after onset. Suprisingly, in examining 25 outbreaks involving almost 15000 layers, and with production drops of up to 12%, the total overall loss amounted to 1.6 eggs/bird alive at the start of the outbreak, with no further loss in downgrading.

Raggi, Brownell and Stewart (1961) did note a decline in shell thickness in flocks affected with ILT, but this may have been a secondary effect of the lowered food consumption experienced by their birds.

General descriptions of the effects of ND on egg production and quality have been given by Lorenz and Newlon (1944), Berg, Bearse and Hamilton (1947), Knox (1950) and Quinn (1950) in chickens, and by Gale, McCartney and Sanger (1961) in turkeys.

Lorenz and Newlon (1944) describe 6.4% of eggs being produced in an outbreak as 'bubbly', these being produced by 21.7% of the flock on resumption of lay. Before cessation of lay, quality had been characterised by soft-shelled eggs, but these did not appear when laying recommenced. A considerable number of shells of these post-clinical eggs were abnormal in shape and texture, however. There was no correlation between abnormal shells and bubbly air cells. Almost all eggs had lowered thick albumen quality.

Berg, Bearse and Hamilton (1947) also found a lowered albumen quality of some 23% from pre-outbreak levels compared to only 9% decline in non-affected birds over the same period of time. The loss of quality persisted for four months in affected groups. Shell thickness decreased by about 9% at the same time, compared to 0.6% in non-affected groups, but this quickly returned to normal. Roughness of the surface did, however, remain a feature. Examination of individual birds revealed that not all birds which had been clinically affected produced abnormal eggs, but where abnormal shells existed, abnormal albumen quality was permanent. The birds worst affected in subsequent quality were those which had paused the least number of days in production during the outbreak.

Knox (1950) noted a considerable difference in the reaction of outbred, crossbred and incrossbred pullets to challenge at the same time. He also found production to be affected adversely for up to 12 weeks following challenge with ND with a significant decline in egg size during this period.

Gale, McCartney and Sanger (1961) noted a fall in egg production three days following onset of respiratory symptoms in turkeys, accompanied by soft-shelled eggs, depigmentation of the shell, alterations in shell deformation and appearance and watery whites. These changes were also seen in other birds on the site in which no respiratory signs were evident. The keeping quality of eggs laid by hens recovered from ND is adversely affected (Parnell, 1950; Quinn, 1950; Quinn, Brant and Thompson, 1956). Parnell (1950) found some hens able to recover their ability to secrete thick albumen, whilst others did not. Quinn (1950) and Quinn, Brant and Thompson (1956) also found that the albumen of eggs laid by pullets recovered from ND declined 20% more than that of similar unaffected birds when held at 25°C for 7 d.

The thinning of the shell following ND is not caused by alterations in calcium metabolism during the outbreak (Clegg and Mueller, 1951), but rather a failure of the shell gland to utilise the calcium efficiently. The pathology of the reproductive tract of birds infected with ND has been described by Biswal and Morrill (1954), and effects on fertility in turkeys by Rosenwald et al. (1966). The dangers of transfer of the disease due to inter-farm trade in eggs laid by hens in the recovery period, particularly if of poor shell quality and so more liable to breakage, is illustrated by the findings of DeLay (1947), who isolated ND virus from such eggs and embryos, and from the yolk sac of 4–6-day-old chicks from this type of egg.

Depigmented eggs were found in the clinical stages of an outbreak of paramyxovirus-1 infection in chickens in the UK in 1984. This virus, which initially affected pigeons widely in Europe, is closely related to classical ND (Alexander et al., 1985). Bankowski, Almquist and Dombrucki (1981) found a significant decrease in hatchability and yield of viable poults in turkeys affected by paramyxovirus Yucaipa. The effects were short-lived in the flocks.

The effects of field challenge of laying hens with IB virus has been described by Gordeuk and Bressler (1950), Box (1964), Garside (1967), McDougall (1968) and Pradhan (1979).

Infected birds lost 44% of production during an 11-week period following infection in the trials of Gordeuk and Bressler (1950) and only 52% of those eggs laid during that period were suitable for commercial handling. On average, albumen quality was one commercial grade lower than control eggs as judged by the USDA recommendations.

Garside (1967) noted that egg production fell over 10–14 d following challenge, with or without respiratory signs. Subsequently eggs became smaller, misshapen, with weak and rough shells, longitudinal ridges and hair cracks. Bleaching of the shell and poor calcification were also noted, and the albumen became thin and watery. Production rose again after 3–4 weeks, shell strength improved, but poor texture, malformations and poor albumen quality persisted. Although loss of production was immediate, the increase in downgrading did not start commercially until two weeks later, and then rose for a further 12 weeks from a low of 10% to a peak of 60% before slowly falling to 50% downgrading of all eggs submitted. This did not include eggs already removed at the farm because of severe abnormalities.

McMartin (1968) recorded the effect on egg production of 22 individual hens vaccinated or not against IB during rearing, and challenged or not with Mycoplasma gallisepticum 31 days prior to IB challenge. He found the reproductive tract more resistant to IB challenge than the respiratory tract. The percentage of abnormal eggs laid by unvaccinated birds averaged 32% compared to 20% in vaccinated birds. These results indicate that in the case of IB, vaccination may either not be successful in some cases, or that quality changes may be expected even with vaccination.

Sevoian and Levine (1957) in the most complete investigations into the effects of IB on eggs and the reproductive tract, found birds going out of lay 5 d post-challenge. Water and food consumption decreased by 30% and 50% respectively at this time. Only 30% of birds came back into production by five weeks post-challenge and the average time out of production was 35 d. At this time egg weight was 1 g less than before infection and internal quality decline was reflected in a loss of 3–5 Haugh units. Misshapen eggs were produced by 17% of the group, and soft-shelled eggs were laid consistently by 25% of birds. Thin-shelled eggs were produced by 12% of birds and eggs with calcareous deposits on them by 10% of birds.

Oviduct size regressed during infection and may be compared to the normal regression which takes place during a moult as described by Smith et al. (1957a). The epithelial lining of the oviduct of challenged birds was slightly reduced in height and took on a cuboidal shape, especially goblet cells. In moulted birds there is a similar height reduction but no distortion of shape of the cell. The loss of cilia in the tracts of challenged birds is also not a feature of moulted birds. Two-thirds of affected birds had oedema and lymphocytic infiltration of the lamina propria. These changes in oviduct architecture inevitably will result in alterations to the structure of the albumen and shell produced by the affected tracts. The use of the scanning electron microscope to study egg shells (King and Robinson, 1972) can be a valuable tool when searching for the cause of shell weakness in these post-infection eggs. The fracture planes found through the mammillae of weak egg shells by King and Robinson (1972) are identical to the pictures obtained by this author in the shells of eggs of hens, vaccinated with H120 and H52 IB vaccines, then challenged in lay with H52 vaccine (Spackman, previously unpublished data, see Figures 16.3 and 16.4). These changes occurred in the absence of production drops, the birds having a haemagglutinating inhibition titre of log 2^8, normally accepted in the field as a protective level against production falls. Further observations of the mammillary area of weak egg shells have been made by Bunk and Balloun (1978).

The effect of IB on egg production and quality is not confined to challenge of birds already in lay, but has been shown to be significantly correlated to challenge during the first week of life (Broadfoot and Smith, 1954; Broadfoot, Pomeroy and Smith, 1956; Jones and Jordan, 1970; Crinion, Ball and Hofstad, 1971a, 1971b; Crinion, 1972; McMartin and MacLeod, 1972).

In the survey of Broadfoot and Smith (1954), mention is made of normal nesting behaviour in such chickens together with normal depigmentation of the skin associated with laying, yet a high proportion of these birds did not produce eggs, and many others produced misshapen eggs with poor internal quality. An interesting finding in this report is that false layers, as evidenced by the numerous ova in the body cavity, were about 43% of a hybrid flock but only 10.5% of a crossbred flock on the same site.

Broadfoot, Pomeroy and Smith (1956) calculated that the incidence of false layers may be as high as 25% if exposed at one-day-old, reducing to 6% if exposure is not until 14 d of age. This is in chicks with low or nil maternal antibodies. Cystic, non-patent oviducts were found in many of these birds, but ovaries were fully active. Patent oviducts were frequently of abnormal length, size and glandular development, and many had cysts in the wall, thus interfering with normal secretion and formation of egg material.

Jones and Jordan (1970) found the anterior portion of the oviduct to be most severely affected. Crinion, Ball and Hofstad (1971a, 1971b) described the histological changes in oviducts of birds infected at one-day-old, together with the correlation with abnormal egg quality. They found that where the oviduct was patent, but a degree of glandular hyperplasia existed, then eggs laid by these hens had inferior quality of shell and/or albumen.

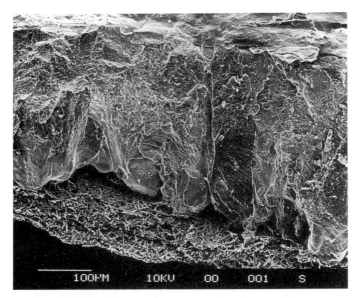

Figure 16.3 Transverse section of egg shell of hen four days post challenge with H52 infectious bronchitis vaccine showing loose arrangement of cones and disruption of membrane attachment. (Magnification ×480, reduced by one-half in reproduction)

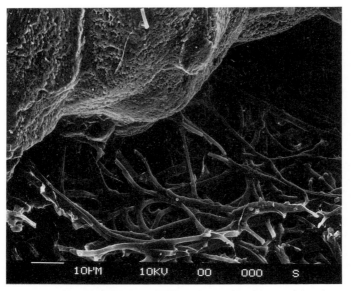

Figure 16.4 Porous type of mammilla and poor attachment of membrane fibres. Egg laid by hen four days post aerosol with H52 infectious bronchitis vaccine. (Magnification ×2700, reduced by one-half in reproduction)

Crinion (1972) showed that having omitted the false layers from an infected group, because their eggs could not have quality measurements made upon them, the remaining birds also laid eggs of lower Haugh unit measurement, with a wider variation than control birds. There was also a highly significant decrease in shell thickness and egg specific gravity from affected birds. Exposed birds laid eggs of which 14% had calcareous deposits on the shell, 14% had ridges on the shells, 2% had a faulty shape index, 15% had yolks which separated from the thick albumen on breaking out and 19% had albumen which adhered to the shell. This compared with levels of less than 0.5% for all those parameters in the eggs of control birds.

With widespread inter-farm trading of eggs, it is important to know the extent of the carrier status for IB, and the possibility of spread by this route.

Jones and Jordan (1970) recovered virus from the reproductive tract of pullets infected at one-day-old during days 5–11 post-infection only. No virus could be isolated from these birds after they were in lay, even those showing evidence of internal laying.

Cook (1968), infecting birds at various ages from 6 to 17 weeks, found a normal period of recovery of virus from 5–10 weeks post-inoculation, and up to 18 weeks in one group, but in this latter case suspected re-infection from an outside source. The isolations were from cloaca and trachea with little apparent difference between the sites.

Fabricant and Levine (1951) recovered the virus from the yolks of eggs as early as two days post-inoculation and the last isolation was made 43 d after exposure. This compared with the last successful isolation from the trachea 28 d after exposure.

Transfer of maternal antibody to IB at the same time as active infection with the virus takes place is not a fully protective mechanism, as shown by Hofstad and Kenzy (1950).

Cumming (1970) presented evidence of airborne transmission of virus over a distance of 1100 m in Australia, but the involvement of faeces, fomites or man (Spackman and Cameron, 1983) or wild birds (Alexander et al., 1979) must also be considered. The possibility of subsequent problems caused by so-called 'variant' strains of Massachusetts strain of IB virus (Krasselt, 1981), following apparently effective vaccination with conventional Massachusetts-type vaccines, has yet to be clarified.

Bisgaard (1976) demonstrated that not only did IB produce misshapen eggs with rough, thin and bleached shells and watery albumen, preventing their being selected for incubation, but also fertility rates were affected, with falls of 2–22% (average 7.4%) and hatchability decreased from 3–44% (average 13.7%) in those eggs which were selected. Both these factors were influenced for about four weeks, shorter than the visible effects on egg quality. Similarly, Broadfoot and Smith (1954) showed that IB could result in a high proportion of eggs not being selected for incubation, and with an apparent trend for differences between family groups.

The role of adenoviruses in egg production and quality changes is less clear. Berry (1971b) showed that adenovirus inoculation was capable of producing a 10% drop in egg production, but no change in quality was mentioned. Winterfield, Fadly and Gallina (1973) described the isolation of an adenovirus in Indiana from a flock exhibiting a sudden increase in misshapen and ridged eggs, with little decline in egg numbers. Shell thickness was normal. Conversely Cowen et al. (1978) found no change in shell quality with four adenoviruses they tested, including that isolated by Winterfield, Fadly and Gallina (1973).

The appearance in the Netherlands in the early 1970s (Van Eck et al., 1976) and later in other areas (McFerran *et al.*, 1977; Anon, 1978; Baxendale, 1978) of soft-shelled eggs and shell-less eggs associated with precipitins to adenovirus, which were subsequently shown (McFerran *et al.*, 1977) to be associated with a haemagglutinating adenovirus Egg Drop Syndrome (EDS-76) is more conclusive evidence for the involvement of this class of virus in egg quality changes. The severe drops in production which were seen appear to be the result mainly of the production of shell-less eggs which are lost through the cage floor, rather than being the failure of hens to produce the eggs at all. It differs in this respect from both ND and IB where numbers produced are also drastically reduced. Outbreaks generally appear about the time of peak production and may show no more clinical signs than transient diarrhoea and lowered food consumption, other than the egg changes. Horizontal spread is slow and so may leave a multi-age site with significant downgrading of eggs for several weeks or months. Downgrading for dirty eggs often rises to above 10%. Extensive atrophy of the glandular tissue of the shell gland, together with oedema and lymphocyte infiltration, are the main histological features. The virus, which can be isolated from the oviduct, appears to limit its effects to the shell gland, again a feature different from the other viruses exerting an influence on the oviduct.

Darbyshire and Peters (1980) infected birds of varying ages with an isolate of the EDS-76 adenovirus and found all produced eggs with abnormal shells, but no change in internal quality, confirming field observations. Fertility and hatchability in eggs suitable for setting were unaffected. Infection of chickens already in lay (33 weeks of age) produced a higher number of abnormal shells than infection pre-lay. Eggs laid by hens 7–11 d following infection yielded chicks from whose livers the virus could be recovered, thus indicating a possibility of vertical transmission. McCracken and McFerran (1978) also reproduced the disease in adult birds, resulting in depigmentation and shell-less eggs, first seen 7 d post-inoculation, when the depigmented eggs first appeared, and returning to normal 25 d after exposure. Thinning of the shell followed one day after colour loss and soft-shelled eggs were almost back to normal levels by 24 d after challenge. The overall daily egg production remained at 80% throughout. This short-term duration of soft-shelled eggs is probably due to simultaneous exposure of all the birds in the group compared to the slow horizontal spread within a flock in the field, where such eggs can be a feature for up to nine weeks after challenge.

Cook and Darbyshire (1981) challenged one-day-old pullet chicks with EDS-76 adenovirus and at commencement of lay found egg production and shell quality to be unaffected, but egg weight reduced and internal quality poorer than controls. There is no explanation for this effect on internal quality, but the group size was small and, as pointed out by the authors, should be viewed with caution.

Kralj and Mazija (1978) studied 112 000 breeding birds and 17 000 laying birds between 1972 and 1976 in Yugoslavia in which adenovirus infection was detected. They report increased shell deformation and oviduct atrophy with lowered hatchability and low resistance to disease in neonates. They do not, however, rule out the possibility of other factors being involved.

Berry (1971a) showed an egg production depressing effect of low virulence Avian Influenza A virus infection, with no comment on quality. Similarly, Johnson, Maxfield and Moulthrop (1977) described an outbreak of A/chicken/Alabama/75 (H4N2) which resulted in an acute and short duration fall in production in laying birds. Production was back to normal in 21 d with no record of abnormalities in egg quality.

Samadieh and Bankowski (1970) reported a similar finding in turkeys affected with two Influenza A virus serotypes in California, starting on the third day after challenge. Fertility was also affected. Conversely, Beard and Helfer (1972), although having a production drop from 30% to 60% in turkeys with Influenza A infection, found no effect on fertility or hatchability. The production drop lasted two weeks before returning to almost normal levels. Alexander and Spackman (1981) did have evidence of misshapes and depigmentation in 2% of the eggs produced by 40-week-old turkeys which were serologically positive to Influenza A during an outbreak in Norfolk in 1979. Virus was not isolated from this flock.

Hemsley (1964) described falls in production of 10% in broiler breeders infected with Infectious Avian Encephalomyelitis (Epidemic Tremors). This was accompanied by eggs rejected at grading, principally for small size, of 1–6%. Hatchability fell by an average of 5% and fertility fell in three flocks by 4–6%. There was an increase in cull chicks and in early mortality on the broiler farms. Only a few cases showed clinical signs of Epidemic Tremors in the chicks.

Effect of parasites on egg quality

DeVaney (1979, 1981) could find no effects of infestation by Northern fowl mite (*Ornithonyssus sylviarum*) on Haugh unit measurement or yolk colour, but detected an increase in shell thickness accompanying a fall in production of 5–15% in affected birds. Similarly, Red mite (*Dermanyssus gallinae*) infestations are associated with drops in egg production, but not in quality changes (Long, 1982).

Frazier (1973) suggests ascaridiasis and capillariosis as factors involved in changes in shell quality, and Husseini (1979) found that infection with *Ascaridia galli* or *Heterakis gallinarum* during rearing, but also treated at intervals, resulted in higher egg production and liveability, but lower shell weight and thickness and lower egg specific gravity than untreated controls.

Berg, Hamilton and Bearse (1951) and Vielitz (1976) mention coccidiosis as a cause of decreased shell quality in laying pullets. In the experiments of Berg, Hamilton and Bearse (1951) *Eimeria maxima* infection resulted in cessation of lay one week later, production being interrupted for about 7–10 d. Albumen quality was not altered but shell thickness declined until birds went out of lay. It was normal again on return to production.

Effect of toxic agents on egg quality

There are some 60000 distinct chemical compounds in commercial production in the world today, and some 1500 of these are sold as pesticides, fumigants, fungicides and related agricultural products. It is inevitable that some of these will find their way into the food chain, including eggs.

Many componds, particularly small and medium-sized organic molecules, are persistent and accumulative after very low levels of exposure in the atmosphere or diet (Kutz, Strassman and Sperling, 1979). Many of these compounds, notably organochlorine formulations, are preferentially excreted together with lipids into the yolk of the egg.

Several toxic products, both naturally occurring and resulting from chemical contamination, may result in lowered egg quality. Surveys have shown that in those areas where chlorinated hydrocarbons are used as pesticides, residues persist for years following application. Stadelman *et al.* (1965) found that exposure to the equivalent of 10–15 ppm of DDT resulted in levels of 4.6 ppm in egg yolks, these remaining for 26 weeks after pesticide withdrawal.

Wesley *et al.* (1966) showed, however, that by inducing moulting and restricting food intake to 20% of normal on a high protein diet, depletion rates of pesticide residues were increased compared with a low protein diet or not moulting. Conversely, Smith, Weber and Reid (1970), feeding 10 ppm DDT, found residue levels one month after induced moulting to be raised to 16.9 ppm in egg yolks from 5 ppm before moulting.

Lowering dietary calcium appeared to increase the accumulation of DDT residues in yolks in the work of Cecil *et al.* (1973). Eggs from birds fed a 3.5% calcium diet had residue levels equal to the level of pesticide in the food, but those fed only 1.5% calcium had 1.4 times the dietary level. Only birds on the higher calcium level suffered thinning of the egg shell as a result of feeding DDT. Davison and Sell (1972) could, however, find no effect of 20 or 200 ppm dieldrin or p,p'-DDT on egg shell thickness when a nutritionally balanced diet was fed.

Sauter and Steele (1972), feeding a variety of pesticides, could discover no effect on fertility, but all except malathion at 0.1 ppm resulted in lowered hatchability. This may in part have been due to the slightly thinner egg shells in the affected groups.

Cummings *et al.* (1966), using lindane, heptachlor epoxide, dieldrin, endrin and DDT, found that only lindane residues returned to background levels in egg yolks within one month of withdrawal of pesticide.

Using guide levels of 0.05 ppm for DDT, BHC, lindane and methoxychlor, Herrick *et al.* (1969) found varying levels of inclusion in dusting powders. A level of 200 ppm DDT in dusting powders applied to laying hens resulted in yolk residues above the guide levels within one week and remaining above this level for a further week. Up to 300 ppm BHC dust did not exceed the 0.05 ppm residue level, and 2000 ppm methoxychlor produced no detectable residues. When only the nests were dusted, no detectable levels of any of the pesticides were found in the eggs.

In the work of Scott *et al.* (1975) dietary polychlorinated biphenyls (PCBs), when fed at 0.5 ppm resulted in only 0.2 ppm residue levels in the yolk, and after eight weeks yolk residue level:fat residue level was 1:15. There was no effect on shell breaking strength, but hatchability was severely affected when 10 ppm PCBs were fed, although not at lower levels. Most embryo mortality was at the 21st day of incubation, often after pipping. Levels of DDT in the same experiment up to 200 ppm had little effect on egg production, shell breaking strength or hatchability, but both organic and inorganic forms of mercury had significant effects on hatchability. Methyl mercuric chloride at 10 ppm mercury content decreased deposition of albumen, as well as resulting in double ovulations, thin-sided and 'sandpaper' eggs and truncation of the shell with corrugations.

Levels of toxaphene up to 100 ppm were fed to White Leghorn females from one day of age by Bush *et al.* (1977). Toxaphene at 100 ppm gave 13.9 ppm residue levels in eggs with a half-life of 15 d after withdrawal. This was calculated to be faster than other chlorinated pesticides. Whitehead, Downie and Phillips (1972) found that feeding 100 mg gamma-BHC (lindane)/kg of diet to hens permanently reduced their egg production levels by 25% with no effect on shell thickness. Whitehead, Downing and Pettigrew (1972) confirmed these findings using up to 200 mg lindane/kg diet, and this is further supported by the work of Košutzký, Adamec and Bobáková (1976).

Karan *et al.* (1981), testing the ectoparasiticide fenitrothion for a six month period, showed that up to 300 ppm had no significant effects on egg quality parameters.

With the progressive lessening of use of chlorinated hydrocarbons the poultry industry has turned to the organic phosphates (such as malathion and coumaphos) and carbamates (such as carbaryl), these having less serious human implications. McCay and Arthur (1962) fed 200 ppm carbaryl for one week to laying hens and no residues above 0.01 ppm could be detected. Treatment of laying hens with 5% carbaryl dust on three occasions, four days apart, gave no egg residues, although the skin of the birds had residues of 19.3 ppm (Johnson, Critchfield and Arthur, 1963). Raun (1956) used 1% malathion spray or 4% malathion dust around a poultry house with birds in and found no residues in the tissues of the birds. Similarly, Harding and Quigley (1956) detected no residues in eggs of birds using nests treated with malathion. Knapp (1962) dusted birds with 0.5% coumaphos but found no residues in eggs, and Knapp and Krauss (1960) had similar results using 1% dust of fenchlorphos, where birds actually received 3–4 g of the compound.

Fogging a house with coumaphos resulted in 0.03 ppm in eggs (Shaw *et al.*, 1964). Treatment of poultry runs with 0.24 kg/m^2 (0.5 lb/100ft^2) of 5% fenchlorphos gave 0.004 ppm in egg yolks (Smith *et al.*, 1965). The fungicide arasan (TMTD) incorporated in a diet at 42 ppm (20% inclusion of soya treated with 210 ppm TMTD) resulted in lowered egg production and appearance of malformed and shell-less eggs (Riet-Alvariza *et al.*, 1978). This confirmed the work of Swanson *et al.* (1956) and it was shown also to produce teratogenic effects by Page (1975).

Kratzer *et al.* (1969) fed 2.7 ppm aflatoxin to laying hens without an effect on egg production or quality being detected, although a slight decrease in hatchability was noticed. No residues of aflatoxin could be discovered in eggs at this level of feeding. Conversely, Potts, Wyatt and Washburn (1976) found progressive decrease in strength of the shell with 2.5 and 5 ppm aflatoxin in the diet over three weeks. This was accompanied by a decrease in egg weight without change in food consumption. There were strain differences amongst the birds tested. As well as noting lowered egg production at 8 ppm, Nesheim and Ivy (1971) found an increase in fatty liver and haemorrhages in aflatoxin fed layers.

Lun, Young and Moran (1984) showed that levels of deoxynivalenol (vomitoxin) up to 82.8 mg/kg diet for 27 d had no effect on egg quality, but Hamilton, Thompson and Trenholm (1981) obtained thinning of the shell with increasing amounts of deoxynivalenol up to 0.7 ppm, although there was no effect on albumen or incidence of blood spots.

Effect of quality changes on hatchability

The correlation of depth of colour in brown eggs and hatchability has long been noted (Godfrey, 1947). No mention is made in that work of egg specific gravity relative to colour, but the link of low specific gravity with poor hatchability has also been made (Godfrey and Jaap, 1949; Coleman and McDaniel, 1975; Hanafi, 1978; McDaniel, Roland and Coleman 1979). Mussehl (1923), however, could find no linkage of specific gravity with either hatchability or viability of the neonate. Payne and McDaniel (1958) found significantly higher numbers of 'shuck-outs', eggs pipped but embryos then dying in shell, in turkey eggs of low specific gravity. The cause of the variation of specific gravity in all these reports is not clear. Disease processes cannot be ruled out, in view of the findings of Mussehl (1923).

Hall and Van Wagenen (1936), examining over 8000 eggs from 265 hens, found that embryo mortality was higher throughout incubation in eggs of hens having persistently poorer thick albumen quality, but particularly between 2 and 7 d of incubation, but again no mention was made of possible disease challenge in these birds.

Measures taken against disease and their effects on egg quality

Poultry farmers and veterinarians can take either preventive or curative action to combat the economic loss from disease and to ensure the highest state of health and bird welfare possible. Some of these measures, although achieving a reduction in mortality and morbidity, nevertheless have been shown to have adverse effects on egg quality.

Dean and Stephenson (1958) found that furazolidone increased egg production and had a slight improving effect on hatchability in breeding birds in cages or on litter. Penicillin, however, lowered egg production, while the addition of arsanilic acid to the furazolidone gave better results than either alone.

Tetracycline and chlortetracycline will give greenish-yellow discolouration of white-shelled eggs when fed at 1.117 g/tonne, whereas oxytetracycline does not give this change, even up to 0.5% of the diet (Bray and Ridlen, 1967). Even with identical intake and egg production patterns, individual bird variation in response is considerable.

The attempt to prevent the oxidative destruction of fats, vitamins A, D and E, carotene and xanthophylls in poultry diets involves the use of antioxidants. Amongst these Ethoxyquin when included in the diet of laying birds has been found to increase yolk colour in the eggs produced (Bartov and Bornstein, 1966).

Several anticoccidial drugs have been found to have effects on egg numbers and quality. Buquinolate at 0.011% of the diet had no effect on internal quality or fertility and hatchability, but resulted in thinner egg shells and a significantly lower egg production (Stephens, Barnett and Butters, 1967).

Food intake was depressed when amprolium was fed at 1000 mg/kg, but egg production was not affected until at least 4000 mg/kg was included. Less chicks were obtained from hens fed 2000 mg/kg and none at the 4000 mg/kg level (Polin et al., 1962). Those chicks which hatched were weaker and died even on the hatching tray at levels above 500 mg/kg. These authors also predicted that a 20% decrease in food intake from feeding 0.2% amprolium will result in a significant loss of egg weight the following week. If thiamine levels are low in the diet the adverse effects might be expected to occur at lower levels of amprolium. Stephens and Barnett (1970) found significantly lower Haugh unit scores in hens fed 0.0125% amprolium continuously. Monensin at 100 ppm was found to have no effect on production or quality (Ruff and Jensen, 1977).

The anti-coccidiosis drug nicarbazin has profound effects on egg quality. McClary (1955) was the first to point this out when he found that a level of 0.0125% in the diet depigmented the egg shells of White Rock hens within 3–4 d. Snyder (1956) reported that yolk mottling preceded egg shell depigmentation and became progressively worse with loss of pigment in the shell. McLoughlin, Wehr and Rubin (1957) further reported that egg production was also reduced by as much as 50% and returned to normal within two weeks of removal of the drug. Colour of shell also returned by between one and two weeks of the end of treatment with 0.0125% nicarbazin. No colour came back into the egg shells until two days after the end of medication. There were no significant differences in shell thickness or albumen quality, though yolk mottling was a feature. Polin, Ott and Siegmund (1957) found yolk mottling in control birds in their experiments and no significant rise in incidence until nicarbazin was incorporated in the food at more then 0.005%. All hens did not lay mottled yolked eggs when fed nicarbazin. Miller, Sunde and Elvehjem (1956) found 46% of yolks mottled when eggs were held for two days at room temperature when no nicarbazin was fed, so other factors may be involved. Polin, Ott and Zeissig (1958) noted a reduction in yolk size, and hence egg size, when birds were fed 0.007% nicarbazin. White Leghorns tended to be more sensitive to the drug than White Rock hens.

Sulphanilamide has been recommended both for treatment of blackhead in turkeys and coccidiosis in chickens. Hinshaw and McNeil (1943) found turkey hens produced soft-shelled eggs after a single dosing with the drug. There was no effect on fertility when males were dosed. White Leghorn hens also laid soft-shelled eggs following treatment with sulphanilamide, but normal eggs were produced when sulphaguanidine was used. After the soft-shelled eggs had appeared, production ceased for several days. Scott, Jungherr and Matterson (1944) showed that sulphanilamide exerts a specific inhibition on the secretory ability of the shell gland and not premature expulsion of a pre-calcification egg. This is brought about by more than 0.25% in the diet. Gutowska and Mitchell (1945) elaborated further on this by showing that injections of 0.16 g sulphanilamide/kg body weight affects the amount of carbonic anhydrase in the shell gland. Dalgaard-Mikkelsen, Langmack and Marthedal (1952) reported that sulphanilamide at 0.75% and 1% in the drinking water, and chloramine at 1% and 2%, caused thinning of the egg shell by blocking carbonic anhydrase activity, but that other sulpha drugs, such as sulphadimidine, sulphaguanidine, sulphaquinoxaline and sulphathiazole, do not and so have no unfavourable effects on the shell. However, 2% sulphadimidine in the drinking water lowers egg production. Sulphamerazine at 0.5% also reduces egg production (Riedel, 1950).

Blackshear, May and Noles (1968) examined causes of yolk mottling in commercial flocks in North Georgia where nicarbazin was not involved, and discovered that worming with piperazine or three-way wormer and treatment with insecticides within the previous six weeks had significant effects on yolk mottling. Worming treatment had no effects on albumen quality, but treatment with Sevin (carbaryl) or Sevin plus malathion significantly reduced Haugh unit scores below birds treated with malathion alone. Medication other than wormers also significantly reduced Haugh unit measurements. Beane, Siegel and Siegel (1965) also noted the effect of piperazine on yolk discolouration.

Supperer and Kutzer (1981) found febendazole to increase cracked eggs in Japanese quail and mebendazole to lower fertility and hatchability at 60 ppm within one week. Thiabendazole lowered egg production at 2000 ppm.

Prophylactic treatment must be given for viral infections, involving the use of live or inactivated vaccines or a combination of both. That these may have a profound effect can be seen from the summary of the first year in which ND vaccine was authorised for use in England and Wales (Loxam, 1964). Vaccinated flocks were out of production for an average of only 11 d following challenge compared with 17 d in unvaccinated flocks. Schubert and Gruhn (1975) have shown that in unprotected birds use of live ND vaccine can cause soft-shelled eggs to be produced, and Prier, Millen and Alberts (1950) showed the presence of live virus in the eggs of birds vaccinated with commercial vaccines. They also recovered live virus from an egg laid by a hen which was clinically affected by spread of vaccine virus from the inoculated birds maintained in the same room.

The danger in the field of poor vaccination technique or 'take' by the birds, leading to uneven protective antibody titres, is illustrated by the partial protection shown by McDougall's (1968) birds to challenge with IB.

Peters, Darbyshire and Cook (1979) showed that oviduct tissue is particularly susceptible to the H52 strain of IB vaccine. Crinion and Hofstad (1972) also demonstrated that the oviduct was susceptible to invasion by IB viruses of 7 and 55 egg passages, and both were pathogenic. The 55 egg passage virus was pathogenic in birds up to two weeks of age and the low passage strain up to 29 d of age. Koh and Loh (1978) reported considerable oviduct damage in birds exposed at one day of age to the H120 strain of IB vaccine, with frequent cystic tracts and appearance of non-layers later. McFerran et al. (1972) showed that white egg laying birds are more susceptible than brown egg layers to conjunctivitis following aerosol vaccination with live IB vaccine, while in both groups reaction was more severe when housed on the floor than in cages. H120 vaccine was shown to produce falls of 10% in egg production in birds exposed to the virus for the first time at peak lay and cycling of both high and low passage vaccines continued on multi-age sites, producing egg quality problems in flocks with low or reduced antibody titres. This is borne out by this author's own observations in the field, but the use of inactivated vaccine would appear to reduce this cycling effect and give a more even laying pattern and less quality problems if titres are high enough at point of lay. This is confirmed by other surveys carried out in the field (Gittings, personal communication), where flocks have been noted as moving from a mean egg specific gravity of 1.082 at point of lay and 1.072 at 72 weeks of age prior to use of inactivated vaccines on the site, to means of 1.088 and 1.082 respectively after one year's use of such vaccines. In terms of whole farm downgrading for cracks on these same units, figures have been reduced from 6.5% to 3.2% following the use of inactivated IB vaccine.

Conclusions

Though there are still considerable problems with long-standing and well-known disease, these are now many less than at the time of the last symposium on egg quality in 1967. New diseases have appeared in the interim, but preventative measures are now more sophisticated and only the ineffective use of otherwise adequate vaccines prevents an even better result in the downgrading of eggs due to the effects of disease. A 1% improvement on 30000 birds is worth £3500 at today's prices—double the cost of preventative medicine.

References

ALEXANDER, D.J. and SPACKMAN, D. (1981). Characterization of Influenza A viruses isolated from turkeys in England during March–May 1979. Avian Pathology, 10, 281–293
ALEXANDER, D.J., SPACKMAN, D., ALLAN, W.H. and BORLAND, L. (1979). Isolation of Newcastle Disease virus from a wild mallard duck (Anas platyrhyncos). Veterinary Record, 105, 328–329

ALEXANDER, D.J., WILSON, G.W.C., RUSSELL, P.H., LISTER, S.A. and PARSONS, G. (1985). Newcastle Disease outbreaks in fowls in Great Britain during 1984. *Veterinary Record,* **117**, 429–434

ALMQUIST, H.J. and BURMESTER, B.R. (1934). Characteristics of an abnormal type of egg shell. *Poultry Science,* **13**, 116–122

AMER, M.F. (1961). Incidence of meat and blood spots in eggs of Fayoumi and some standard breeds. *Poultry Science,* **40**, 1341–1344

ANDERSON, C.E. (1935). Investigation into the condition known as 'watery white' in eggs. *Journal of the Department of Agriculture of South Australia,* **39**, 662–680

ANON (1978). Guest editorial: Egg Drop syndrome—1976: A "New" disease of chickens. *Avian Pathology,* **7**, 189–191

BALL, R.A., SINGH, V.B. and POMEROY, B.S. (1969). The morphologic response of the turkey oviduct to certain pathogenic agents. *Avian Diseases,* **13**, 119–133

BALL, R.F., MACKIN, R.J., HILL, J.F. and WYATT, A.J. (1973). The nature and probable cause of rough shells laid by two lines of White Leghorns. *Poultry Science,* **52**, 500–506

BANKOWSKI, R.A., ALMQUIST, J. and DOMBRUCKI, J. (1981). Effect of paramyxovirus *Yucaipa* on fertility, hatchability and poult yield of turkeys. *Avian Diseases,* **25**, 517–520

BARNETT, B.D., RICHEY, D.J. and MORGAN, C.L. (1957). Effect of beta-aminopropionitrile on reproduction of chickens. *Proceedings of the Society for Experimental Biology and Medicine,* **95**, 101–104

BARTOV, I. and BORNSTEIN, S. (1966). Studies on egg yolk pigmentation. 2. Effects of Ethoxyquin on xanthophyll utilization. *Poultry Science,* **45**, 297–305

BAXENDALE, W. (1978). Egg Drop Syndrome. *Veterinary Record,* **102**, 450

BEANE, W.L., SIEGEL, P.B. and SIEGEL, H.S. (1965). Piperazine compounds and yolk discolouration. *Poultry Science,* **44**, 666–668

BEARD, C.W. and HELFER, D.H. (1972). Isolation of two turkey Influenza viruses in Oregon. *Avian Diseases,* **16**, 1133–1136

BERG, L.R., BEARSE, G.E. and HAMILTON, C.H. (1947). The effect of Newcastle disease on egg production and egg quality. *Poultry Science,* **26**, 614–622

BERG, L.R., HAMILTON, C.M. and BEARSE, G.E. (1951). The effect of coccidiosis (caused by *Eimeria maxima*) on egg quality. *Poultry Science,* **30**, 298–301

BERRY, D.M. (1971a). Egg production and disease: Avian Influenza A viruses. In *Proceedings of the 4th World Veterinary Poultry Association Congress,* pp. 323–327. Belgrade, World Veterinary Poultry Association

BERRY, D.M. (1971b). Egg production and disease: Adenovirus. In *Proceedings of the 4th World Veterinary Poultry Association Congress,* pp. 523–524. Belgrade, World Veterinary Poultry Association

BISGAARD, M. (1976). The influence of Infectious Bronchitis virus on egg production, fertility, hatchability and mortality rate in chickens. *Nordisk VeterinaerMedicin,* **28**, 368–376

BISWAL, G. and MORRILL, C.C. (1954). The pathology of the reproductive tract of laying pullets affected with Newcastle Disease. *Poultry Science,* **33**, 880–897

BLACKSHEAR, C.D., MAY, K.N. and NOLES, R.K. (1968). A survey of egg mottling and other quality attributes in North Georgia flocks. *Poultry Science,* **47**, 625–630

BOARD, R.G. (1966). Review Article—The course of microbial infection of the hen's egg. *Journal of Applied Bacteriology,* **29**, 319–341

BOX, P.G. (1964). Egg production of hens showing evidence of infection with Infectious Bronchitis virus. *Veterinary Record,* **76**, 1202–1206

BRANDLY, C.A. (1934). Some studies of Infectious Laryngotracheitis. *Journal of the American Veterinary Medical Association,* **84**, 588–595

BRAY, D.J. and RIDLEN, S.F. (1967). Discolouration of egg shells from feeding high levels of certain tetracyclines. *Poultry Science,* **46**, 258–259

BRITTON, W.M. (1977). Shell membranes of eggs differing in shell quality from young and old hens. *Poultry Science,* **56**, 647–653

BROADFOOT, D.I. and SMITH, W.M. JR (1954). Effects of Infectious Bronchitis in laying hens on egg production, percent unsettable eggs and hatchability. *Poultry Science,* **33**, 653–654

BROADFOOT, D.I., POMEROY, B.S. and SMITH, W.M. JR (1956). Effects of Infectious Bronchitis in baby chicks. *Poultry Science,* **35**, 757–762

BUCKLAND, R.B., ALLEN, A.B. and BJERRING, J.H. (1971). Survey on the relationships between environmental factors and egg quality in four geographic areas of British Columbia differing in population density of poultry. *Canadian Journal of Animal Science*, **51**, 333–339

BUNK, M.J. and BALLOUN, S.L. (1978). Ultrastructure of the mammillary region of low puncture strength avian eggshells. *Poultry Science*, **57**, 1892–1893

BUSH, P.B., KIKER, J.T., PAGE, R.K., BOOTH, N.H. and FLETCHER, O.J. (1977). Effects of graded levels of Toxaphene on poultry residue accumulation, egg production, shell quality and hatchability in White Leghorns. *Journal of Agriculture and Food Chemistry*, **25**, 928–932

CAIN, C.J. and HEYN, A.N.J. (1964). X-ray diffraction studies of the crystalline structure of the avian egg shell. *Biophysics Journal*, **4**, 23–39

CECIL, H.C., BITMAN, J., FRIES, G.F., HARRIS, S.J. and LILLIE, R.J. (1973). Changes in egg shell quality and pesticide content of laying hens or pullets fed DDT in high and low calcium diets. *Poultry Science*, **52**, 648–653

CLEGG, R.E. and MUELLER, C.D. (1951). Calcium metabolism during Newcastle Disease. *Poultry Science*, **30**, 157–158

COLEMAN, M.A. and McDANIEL, G.R. (1975). The effect of light and specific gravity on embryo weight and embryonic mortality. *Poultry Science*, **54**, 1415–1421

COLES, R.K. (1936). Egg quality: the influence of climate and soil. *Journal of the Ministry of Agriculture*, **43**, 317–332

COLES, R.K. (1938). Histology of the oviduct of the fowl in relation to variations in the condition of the firm egg albumen. *Anatomical Record*, **71**, 349–358

COOK, J.K.A. (1968). Duration of experimental Infectious Bronchitis in chickens. *Research in Veterinary Science*, **9**, 506–514

COOK, J.K.A. and DARBYSHIRE, J.H. (1981). Longitudinal studies on the Egg Drop syndrome 1976 (EDS-76) in the fowl following experimental infection at 1-day-old. *Avian Pathology*, **10**, 449–459

COOKE, A.S. (1970). Some observations on corrugated egg shells. *British Poultry Science*, **11**, 291–297

COWEN, B., CALNEK, B.W., MENENDEZ, N.A. and BALL, R.F. (1978). Avian adenoviruses: effect on egg production, shell quality and feed consumption. *Avian Diseases*, **22**, 459–470

CRINION, R.A.P. (1972). Egg quality and production following Infectious Bronchitis virus exposure at one day old. *Poultry Science*, **51**, 582–585

CRINION, R.A.P. and HOFSTAD, M.S. (1972). Pathogenicity of two embryo passage levels of avian Infectious Bronchitis virus for the oviduct of young chickens of various ages. *Avian Diseases*, **16**, 967–973

CRINION, R.A.P., BALL, R.A. and HOFSTAD, M.S. (1971a). Pathogenesis of oviduct lesions in immature chickens following exposure to Infectious Bronchitis virus at one day old. *Avian Diseases*, **15**, 32–41

CRINION, R.A.P., BALL, R.A. and HOFSTAD, M.S. (1971b). Abnormalities in laying chickens following exposure to Infectious Bronchitis at one day old. *Avian Diseases*, **15**, 42–48

CUMMING, R.B. (1970). Studies on Australian Infectious Bronchitis virus: IV. Apparent farm-to-farm airborne transmission of IB virus. *Avian Diseases*, **14**, 191–195

CUMMINGS, J.G., ZEE, K.T., TURNER, V. and QUINN, F. (1966). Residues in eggs from low level feeding of five chlorinated hydrocarbon insecticides to hens. *Journal of the Association of Official Analytical Chemists*, **49**, 354–364

CURTIS, M.R. (1916). Studies on the physiology of reproduction in the domestic fowl. XVI. Double eggs. *Biological Bulletin*, **XXXL**, 181–213

DALGAARD-MIKKELSEN, SV., LANGMACK, J.V. and MARTHEDAL, H.E. (1952). Effect of sulfonamides and chloramine on the egg production of hens. *Nordisk VeterinaerMedicin*, **4**, 481–493

DARBYSHIRE, J.H. and PETERS, R.W. (1980). Studies on EDS-76 virus infection in laying chickens. *Avian Pathology*, **9**, 277–290

DAVISON, K.L. and SELL, J.L. (1972). Dieldrin and p,p'-DDT effect on egg production and eggshell thickness of chickens. *Bulletin of Environmental Contamination and Toxicology*, **7**, 9–18

DEAN, W.F. and STEPHENSON, E.L. (1958). The influence of dietary furazolidone on egg production, hatchability, fertility and feed efficiency of laying and breeding hens. *Poultry Science*, **37**, 124–128

DELAY, P.D. (1947). Isolation of Avian Pneumoencephalitis (Newcastle Disease) virus from the yolk sac of four-day-old chicks, embryos and infertile eggs. *Science*, **106**, 545–546

DENTON, C.A. (1947). Observations on the incidence and characteristics of blood and meat spots in hen's eggs. *Poultry Science*, **26**, 272–276

DEVANEY, J.A. (1979). The effects of the Northern fowl mite (*Ornithonyssus sylviarum*) on egg production and bodyweight of caged White Leghorn hens. *Poultry Science*, **58**, 191–194

DEVANEY, J.A. (1981). Effects of the Northern fowl mite (*Ornithonyssus sylviarum*) on egg quality of White Leghorn hens. *Poultry Science*, **60**, 2200–2202

DOMERMUTH, C.H., GROSS, W.B. and DUBOSE, R.T. (1967). Mycoplasmal salpingitis of chickens and turkeys. *Avian Diseases*, **11**, 393–398

FABRICANT, J. and LEVINE, P.P. (1951). The persistence of Infectious Bronchitis virus in eggs and tracheal exudates of infected chickens. *Cornell Veterinarian*, **41**, 240–246

FISHER, H., GRIMINGER, P., WEISS, H.S. and HUDSON, C.B. (1961). Observations on water deprivation and blue-comb disease. *Poultry Science*, **40**, 813–814

FOWLER, N.G. (1982). How to carry out a field investigation. In *Poultry Diseases*, (Gordon, R.F. and Jordan, F.T.W., eds), pp. 307–327. London, Baillière Tindall

FRANK, F.R. and BURGER, R.E. (1965). The effect of carbon dioxide inhalation and sodium bicarbonate ingestion on egg shell deposition. *Poultry Science*, **44**, 1604–1606

FRAZIER, M. (1972). Diseases affecting egg shell quality. *Poultry Digest*, **31**, 332–333

FRAZIER, M. (1973). Diseases affecting egg shell quality. *Poultry International*, **12**, 54–56

GALE, C., McCARTNEY, M.G. and SANGER, V.L. (1961). Newcastle disease in turkeys. *Journal of the American Veterinary Medical Association*, **139**, 462–465

GARSIDE, J.S. (1967). Avian Infectious Bronchitis. *Veterinary Record*, **80**, Clinical Supplement No. 7

GENTRY, R.F. (1978). Immunization for avian MG improves egg production among multiple-age hens. *Pennsylvania Science in Agriculture*, **25**, 13

GODFREY, G.F. (1947). The relationship of egg shell colour to hatchability in some brown egg laying breeds. *Poultry Science*, **26**, 381–388

GODFREY, G.F. (1949). Shell colour as a measure of egg shell quality. *Poultry Science*, **28**, 150–151

GODFREY, G.F. and JAAP, R.G. (1949). The relationship of specific gravity, 14-day incubation weight-loss and egg shell colour to hatchability and egg shell quality. *Poultry Science*, **28**, 874–889

GORDEUK, S. JR and BRESSLER, G.O. (1950). Infectious Bronchitis—Its effect on rate of egg production and egg quality. *Pennsylvania State College Progress Report*, No. 36

GORDON, R.F. (1977). Introduction. In *Poultry Diseases*, (Gordon, R.F., ed.), pp. 1–9. London, Butterworths

GREWAL, G.S., KUMAR, R., SINGH, B. and SODHI, S.S. (1977). Role of *Escherichia coli* (*E. coli*) in lowering egg production. *Poultry Guide*, **14**, 30–33

GUTOWSKA, M.S. and MITCHELL, C.A. (1945). Carbonic anhydrase in the calcification of the egg shell. *Poultry Science*, **24**, 159–167

HALL, G.O. and VAN WAGENEN, A. (1936). The association of certain measures of interior quality with hatchability. *Poultry Science*, **15**, 501–506

HAMILTON, R.M.G., THOMPSON, B.F. and TRENHOLM, H.L. (1981). Feed intake, egg production and shell quality of hens given diets that contained vomitoxin contaminated wheat. *Poultry Science*, **60**, 1666

HAMILTON, R.M.G., HOLLANDS, K.G., VOISEY, P.W. and GRUNDER, A.A. (1979). Relationship between egg shell quality and shell breakage and factors that affect shell breakage in the field—a review. *World's Poultry Science Journal*, **35**, 177–190

HANAFI, M.S. (1978). Egg characteristics as affected by egg weight in New Hampshires and White Leghorns. 1. Relationship to traits of egg shell quality and their role in hatchability. *Mesopotamia Journal of Agriculture*, **13**, 45–57

HANSON, B.S. (1968). Disease and egg quality. In *Egg Quality. A Study of the Hen's Egg*, (Carter, T.C., ed.), pp. 171–180. Edinburgh, Oliver and Boyd

HARDING, W.C. JR and QUIGLEY, G.D. (1956). Litter treatment with malathion to control the chicken body louse. *Journal of Economic Entomology*, **49**, 806

HELBACKA, N.V.L. and SWANSON, M.H. (1958). Studies on blood and meat spots in the hen's egg. 1. The fluorescent properties of meat spots. *Poultry Science*, **37**, 869–876

HELBACKA, N.V.L., CASTERLINE, J.L. and SMITH, C.J. (1963). The effect of high CO_2 atmospheres on the laying hen. *Poultry Science*, **42**, 1082–1084

HEMSLEY, L.A. (1964). The incidence of Infectious Avian Encephalomyelitis (Epidemic Tremors) in broiler breeding flocks and its economic effect. *Veterinarian*, **2**, 193–201

HERRICK, G.M., FRY, J.L., FONG, W.G. and GOLDEN, D.C. (1969). Pesticide residues in eggs resulting from the dusting and short-time feeding of low levels of chlorinated hydrocarbon insecticides to hens. *Journal of Agricultural and Food Chemistry*, **17**, 291–295

HILL, R.W. and LORENZ, F.W. (1956). Studies on egg changes following avian respiratory diseases: 1. Diseases associated with egg changes. *Poultry Science*, **35**, 409–417

HINSHAW, W.R. and McNEIL, E. (1943). Experiments with sulfanilimide for turkeys. *Poultry Science*, **22**, 291–294

HINSHAW, W.R., JONES, E.E. and GRAYBILL, H.W. (1931). A study of mortality and egg production in flocks affected with infectious laryngotracheitis. *Poultry Science*, **10**, 375–382

HIRAKATA, V., HETSUKA, K.Ō. and OHASHI, T. (1977). Egg shell quality and carbonic anhydrase activity of the shell gland in the domestic fowl. *Bulletin of Faculty of Agriculture. Miyazaki University*, **24**, 1–4

HOFSTAD, M.S. and KENZY, S.G. (1950). Susceptibility of chicks hatched from recovered hens to Infectious Bronchitis. *Cornell Veterinarian*, **40**, 87–89

HOLDER, D.P. and BRADFORD, M.V. (1979). Relationship of specific gravity of chicken eggs to number of cracked eggs observed and percent shell. *Poultry Science*, **58**, 250–251

HUGHES, B.L. and PARKER, J.E. (1971). Time of oviposition of shell-less eggs. *Poultry Science*, **50**, 1509–1511

HUNTER, J.A., VAN WAGENEN, A. and HALL, G.O. (1936). Seasonal changes in interior egg quality of single comb White Leghorn hens. *Poultry Science*, **15**, 115–118

HUSSEINI, M.D. (1979). Effect of calcium levels, appetite enhancers and endoparasites on egg shell quality and performance of laying hens. *Dissertation Abstracts*, **39B**, 5157-B

ITOH, H. and HATANO, T. (1964). Variation of magnesium and phosphorus deposition rates during egg shell formation. *Poultry Science*, **43**, 77–80

JAAP, R.G. and MUIR, F.V. (1968). Erratic oviposition and egg defects in the broiler-type pullet. *Poultry Science*, **47**, 417–423

JEFFREY, F.P. (1945). Blood and meat spots in chicken eggs. *Poultry Science*, **24**, 363–374

JOHNSON, D.C., MAXFIELD, B.G. and MOULTHROP, J.T. (1977). Epidemiologic studies of the 1975 avian Influenza outbreak in chickens in Alabama. *Avian Diseases*, **21**, 167–176

JOHNSON, D.P., CRITCHFIELD, F.E. and ARTHUR, B.W. (1963). Determination of Sevin insecticide and its metabolites in poultry tissues and eggs. *Journal of Agricultural and Food Chemistry*, **11**, 77

JONES, R.C. and JORDAN, F.T.W. (1970). The exposure of day-old chicks to Infectious Bronchitis and the subsequent development of the oviduct. *Veterinary Record*, **87**, 504–505

KARAN, C.M., SINGH, B., SINHA, S.K. and MUKHERJEE, S.K. (1981). Effect of feeding of "Sumithion" on egg quality in White Leghorn laying birds. *Agricultural Science Digest*, **2**, 51–53

KING, N.R. and ROBINSON, D.S. (1972). The use of the scanning electron microscope for comparing the structure of weak and strong egg shells. *Journal of Microscopy*, **95**, 437–443

KNAPP, F.W. (1962). Poultry tolerance to excessive amounts of Co-Ral dust. *Journal of Economic Entomology*, **55**, 560

KNAPP, F.W. and KRAUSS, G.F. (1960). Control of the northern fowl mite, *Ornithonyssus sylviarum* (C & F) with ronnel, Bayer L 13/59 and Bayer 21/199. *Journal of Economic Entomology*, **53**, 4

KNOX, C.W. (1950). The effect of Newcastle disease on egg production, egg weight and mortality rate. *Poultry Science*, **29**, 907–911

KNOX, C.W. and GODFREY, A.B. (1934). Variability of thick albumen in fresh laid eggs. *Poultry Science*, **13**, 18–22

KOH, J.G.W. and LOH, H. (1978). Effects of vaccinating day-old chicks with a mild Infectious Bronchitis vaccine on subsequent egg production and oviduct development. *Kajian Veterinar*, **10**, 35–40

KOŠUTZKÝ, J., ADAMEC, O. and BOBÁKOVÁ, E. (1976). The effect of lindane on sexual maturity, egg production and shell quality in chickens. *Proceedings 5th European Poultry Conference*, **2**, 1302–1312. Malta, World's Poultry Science Association

KRALJ, M. and MAZIJA, F. (1978). The influence of adenovirus on egg production of laying hens. *Fortschritte der Veterinarmedizin*, **28**, 137–143

KRASSELT, M.M. (1981). Serotypes of IB virus that are different from the H-strain. One of the main causes of the present IB problem in the Netherlands. Notes prepared by Laboratoria dr. de Zeeuw bv.

KRATZER, F.H., BANDY, D., WILEY, M. and BOOTH, A.N. (1969). Aflatoxin effects in poultry. *Proceedings of Society for Experimental Biology and Medicine*, **131**, 1281–1284

KUTZ, F.W., STRASSMAN, S.C. and SPERLING, J.F. (1979). Survey of selected organochlorine pesticides in the general population of the U.S.: fiscal years 1970–1975. In *Health Effects of Halogenated Aromatic Hydrocarbons*, (Nicholson, W.J. and Moore, J.A., eds), *Annals of New York Academy of Sciences*, **320**, 60–68

LERNER, I.M., TAYLOR, L.W. and BEACH, J.R. (1950). Evidence for genetic variation in resistance to a respiratory infection in chickens. *Poultry Science*, **29**, 862–869

LERNER, M., TAYLOR, L.W. and LOWRY, D.C. (1951). Selection for increased incidence of blood spots in White Leghorns. *Poultry Science*, **30**, 748–757

LONG, P.L. (1982). Parasitic diseases. In *Poultry Diseases, 2nd Edition*, (Gordon, R.F. and Jordan, F.T.W., eds), p.166–197. London, Baillière Tindall

LORENZ, F.W. and NEWLON, W.E. (1944). Influence of avian pneumoencephalitis on subsequent egg quality. *Poultry Science*, **23**, 193–198

LORENZ, F.W., TAYLOR, L.W. and ALMQUIST, H.J. (1934). Firmness of albumen as an inherited characteristic. *Poultry Science*, **13**, 14–17

LOTT, B.D., DROTT, J.H., VARDAMAN, T.H. and REECE, F.N. (1978). Effect of *Mycoplasma synoviae* on egg quality and egg production of broiler breeds. *Poultry Science*, **57**, 309–311

LOWRY, D.C., DOBBS, J.C. and ABPLANALP, H. (1979). Yolk deposition in eggs of a line selected for simultaneous multiple ovulations. *Poultry Science*, **58**, 498–501

LOXAM, J.G. (1964). Newcastle Disease in England and Wales. Control by vaccination—the first year. *State Veterinary Journal*, **19**, 197–211

LUN, A.K., YOUNG, L.G. and MORAN, E.T. (1984). Effect of feeding vomitoxin deoxynivalenol contaminated corn diet on performance and distribution of the toxin in laying hens. *Poultry Science*, **63**(Supplement 1), 141

MADDISON, A.E. (1970). The incidence of downgrading at the present time. In *Factors Affecting Egg Grading*, (Freeman, B.M. and Gordon, R.F., eds), pp. 17–26. Edinburgh, Oliver and Boyd

McCALLION, D.J. (1953). A cytological and cytochemical study of the shell gland of the domestic hen. *Canadian Journal of Zoology*, **31**, 577–589

McCAY, C.F. and ARTHUR, B.W. (1962). Sevin residues in poultry products. *Journal of Economic Entomology*, **55**, 936

McCLARY, C.F. (1955). The restriction of oöporphyrin deposition on egg shells by drug feeding. *Poultry Science*, **34**, 1164–1165

McCRACKEN, R.M. and McFERRAN, J.B. (1978). Experimental reproduction of the egg drop syndrome 1976 with a haemagglutinating adenovirus. *Avian Pathology*, **7**, 483–490

McDANIEL, G.R., ROLAND, D.A. and COLEMAN, M.A. (1979). The effect of egg shell quality on hatchability and embryonic mortality. *Poultry Science*, **58**, 10–13

McDOUGALL, J.S. (1968). Infectious Bronchitis in laying fowls. *Veterinary Record*, **83**, 84–86

McFERRAN, J.B., ROWLEY, H.M., McNULTY, M.S. and MONTGOMERY, L.J. (1977). Serological studies on flocks showing depressed egg production. *Avian Pathology*, **6**, 405–413

McFERRAN, J.B., YOUNG, J.A., CLARKE, J.K. and WRIGHT, C.L. (1972). Observations concerning the use of living Infectious Bronchitis vaccine under field conditions. *Veterinary Record*, **90**, 527–530

McKERLEY, R.G., NEWELL, G.W., BERRY, J.G., ODELL, G.V. and MORRISON, R.D. (1967). The effects of some acidic and alkaline atmospheres on the changes in pH and Haugh Units in chicken eggs. *Poultry Science*, **46**, 118–132

McLOUGHLIN, D.K., WEHR, E.E. and RUBIN, R. (1957). Egg shell colour and egg production in New Hampshire laying hens as affected by Nicarbazin medication. *Poultry Science*, **36**, 880–884

McMARTIN, D.A. (1968). The pathogenicity of an infectious bronchitis virus for laying hens, with observations on pathogenesis. *British Veterinary Journal*, **124**, 576–581

McMARTIN, D.A. and MACLEOD, H. (1972). Abnormal oviducts in laying hens following natural infection with infectious bronchitis at an early age. *British Veterinary Journal*, **128**, xix–xxi

MEURIER, C. (1972). Economic consequences of disease in egg production. *Bulletin Technique d'Information*, **275**, 1259–1268

MILLER, E.C., SUNDE, M.L. and ELVEHJEM, C.A. (1956). Minimum protein requirements of laying pullets at different energy levels. *Poultry Science*, **35**, 1159

MILLER, P.C. and SUNDE, M.L. (1975). The effects of precise constant and cyclic environments on shell quality and other lay performance factors with Leghorn pullets. *Poultry Science*, **54**, 36–46

MUSSEHL, F.E. (1923). Influence of the specific gravity of hen's eggs on fertility, hatching power and growth of chicks. *Journal of Agricultural Research*, **23**, 717–720

NALBANDOV, A.V. and CARD, L.E. (1944). The problems of blood clots and meat spots in chicken eggs. *Poultry Science*, **23**, 170–180

NALBANDOV, A.V. and CARD, L.E. (1947). The problems of blood and meat spots in chicken eggs. *Poultry Science*, **26**, 400–409

NESHEIM, M.C. and IVY, C.A. (1971). Effect of aflatoxins on egg production and liver fat in laying hens. *Proceedings of Cornell Nutrition Conference*, pp. 126–129. Ithaca, Cornell University

PAGE, R.N. (1975). Teratogenic activity of Arasan fed to broiler breeder hens. *Avian Diseases*, **19**, 463–472

PARNELL, E.D. (1950). The keeping quality of shell eggs in storage as affected by Newcastle disease. *Poultry Science*, **29**, 153–155

PAYNE, L.F. and McDANIEL, G.R. (1958). Shell thickness as related to "shuck-outs" in turkey eggs. *Poultry Science*, **37**, 825–828

PETERS, R.W., DARBYSHIRE, J.H. and COOK, J.K.A. (1979). The susceptibility of chicken kidney and oviduct organ culture to a vaccine strain of avian Infectious Bronchitis virus. *Research in Veterinary Science*, **26**, 38–40

PLATT, A.E. (1936). Investigations into the nature of the condition known as 'floating yolk' in eggs. *Australian Journal of Experimental Biology and Medical Science*, **14**, 107–116

POLIN, D., OTT, W.H. and SIEGMUND, O.H. (1957). The incidence and degree of yolk mottling in eggs from hens fed diets with and without Nicarbazin. *Poultry Science*, **36**, 524–528

POLIN, D., OTT, W.H. and ZEISSIG, A. (1958). Field studies on the effect of Nicarbazin on egg quality. *Poultry Science*, **37**, 898–909

POLIN, D., PORTER, C.C., WYNOSKY, E.R. and COBB, W.R. (1962). Amprolium. 4. The effect of amprolium on reproduction in chickens. *Poultry Science*, **41**, 370–380

POTTS, P.L., WYATT, R.D. and WASHBURN, K.W. (1976). The effect of aflatoxin on shell strength of six commercial laying strains. *Poultry Science*, **55**, 1603

PRADHAN, H.K. (1979). Role of Infectious Bronchitis virus on egg production. *Poultry Guide*, **16**, 79–81

PRIER, J.E., MILLEN, T.W. and ALBERTS, J.O. (1950). Studies on Newcastle Disease. IV. The presence of Newcastle Disease virus in eggs of hens vaccinated with live virus. *Journal of the American Veterinary Medical Association*, **116**, 54–55

QUINN, J.P. (1950). Effect of Newcastle disease on egg quality. *Poultry Science*, **29**, 776

QUINN, J.P., BRANT, A.W. and THOMPSON, C.H. JR (1956). Effect of a naturally occurring outbreak of Newcastle Disease on egg quality and production. *Poultry Science*, **35**, 3–10

RAGGI, L.G., BROWNELL, J.R. and STEWART, G.F. (1961). Effects of Infectious Laryngotracheitis virus on egg production and quality. *Poultry Science*, **40**, 134–140

RAUN, E.S. (1956). Chicken louse and mite control with malathion formulations. *Journal of Economic Entomology*, **49**, 628

REID, W.H., MAAG, T.A., BOYD, F.M., KLECKNER, A.L. and SCHMITTLE, S.C. (1961). Embryo and baby chick mortality and morbidity induced by a strain of *Escherichia coli*. *Poultry Science*, **40**, 1497–1502

RIEDEL, B.B. (1950). The effect of sulfamerizine upon egg production and hatchability. *Poultry Science*, **29**, 621–622

RIET-ALVARIZA, F., CAPANO, F., CORBO, M., TALBO, M. and McCOSKER, P. (1978). Toxic effects of TMTD on number and quality of eggs. *Veterinaria Uruquay*, **14**(67), 85–91

ROLAND, D.A. (1976). The extent of uncollected eggs due to inadequate shell. *Poultry Science*, **55**, 2085

ROLAND, D.A. (1979). Factors influencing shell quality of aging hens. *Poultry Science*, **58**, 774–777

ROLAND, D.A. SNR, HOLCOMBE, D.J. and HARMS, R.H. (1977). Further studies with hens producing a high incidence of non-calcified or partially calcified egg shells. *Poultry Science*, **56**, 1232–1236

ROSENWALD, A.S., RAGGI, L.G., ROONEY, W.F., OGASAWARA, F.X., FEREBEE, D.C. and LORENZ, F.W. (1966). The effect of Newcastle disease virus on adult turkey hens. *Journal of the American Veterinary Medical Association*, **148**, 1353

RUFF, M.D. and JENSEN, L.S. (1977). Production, quality and hatchability of eggs from hens fed monensin. *Poultry Science*, **56**, 1956–1959

SAMADIEH, B. and BANKOWSKI, R.A. (1970). Effect of Avian Influenza-A viruses upon egg production and fertility of turkeys. *Avian Diseases*, **14**, 715–727

SAPRA, K.L. and CHABRA, A.D. (1972). Poultry disease and egg quality. *Indian Farming*, **21**(10), 45–46

SAUTER, E.A. and PETERSEN, C.F. (1974). The effect of egg shell quality on penetration by various *Salmonellae*. *Poultry Science*, **53**, 2159–2162

SAUTER, E.A. and STEELE, E.E. (1972). The effect of low level pesticide feeding on the fertility and hatchability of chicken eggs. *Poultry Science*, **51**, 71–76

SCHAIBLE, P.J., MOORE, J.M. and DAVIDSON, J.A. (1935). A note on the structure of egg white. *US Egg and Poultry Magazine*, **41**, 38–39

SCHUBERT, R. and GRUHN, K. (1975). Mineral mixes for laying hens and some aspects of the shell quality. *Monatshefte für Veterinärmedizin*, **30**, 63–68

SCOTT, H.M. and WAI-LAN HUANG (1941). Histological observations on the formation of the chalaza in the hen's egg. *Poultry Science*, **20**, 402–405

SCOTT, H.M., JUNGHERR, E. and MATTERSON, L.D. (1944). The effect of feeding sulfanilamide to the laying fowl. *Poultry Science*, **23**, 446–453

SCOTT, M.L., ZIMMERMANN, J.R., MARINSKY, S., MULLENHOFF, P.A., RUMSEY, G.L. and RICE, R.W. (1975). Effects of PCBs, DDT and mercury compounds upon egg production, hatchability and shell quality in chickens and Japanese quail. *Poultry Science*, **54**, 350–368

SEVOIAN, M. and LEVINE, P.P. (1957). Effects of Infectious Bronchitis on the reproductive traits, egg production and egg quality of laying chickens. *Avian Diseases*, **1**, 136–164

SHAW, F.R., SMITH, C.T., ANDERSON, D.L., FISCHANG, W.J., ZIENER, W.H. and HURNY, J. (1964). The effects of coumaphos on poultry and its residues in tissue and eggs. *Journal of Economic Entomology*, **57**, 516

SHERWOOD, D.H. (1958). Factors affecting egg quality—a review. *Poultry Science*, **37**, 924–932

SMITH, A.H., BOND, G.H., RAMSEY, K.W., RECK, D.G. and SPOON, J.E. (1957a). Size and rate of involution of the hen's reproductive organs. *Poultry Science*, **36**, 346–353

SMITH, A.H., HOOVER, G.N., NORDSTROM, J.O. and WINGET, C.M. (1957b). Quantitative changes in the hen's oviduct associated with egg formation. *Poultry Science*, **36**, 353–357

SMITH, C.T., SHAW, F.R., ANDERSON, D.L., CALLAHAN, R.A. and ZIENER, W.H. (1965). Ronnel residues in eggs of poultry. *Journal of Economic Entomology*, **58**, 1160

SMITH, S.I., WEBER, C.W. and REID, B.L. (1970). Dietary pesticides and contamination of yolks and abdominal fat of laying hens. *Poultry Science*, **49**, 233–237

SNYDER, E.S. (1956). Affects egg quality. Nicarbazin excellent for growers but not for layers. *Canadian Poultry Review*, **80**, 13

SPACKMAN, D. and CAMERON, I. (1983). Isolation of Infectious Bronchitis virus from pheasants. *Veterinary Record*, **113**, 354–355

SPENCER, J.L., GAVORA, J.S. and GOWE, R.S. (1979). Effect of selection for high egg production in chickens on shedding of lymphoid leukosis virus and gs antigen into eggs. *Poultry Science*, **58**, 279–284

STADELMAN, W.J. and LISKA, B.J. (1963). Pesticides in eggs, broilers and turkeys. *American Poultry and Hatchery News*, **38**, 5

STADELMAN, W.J., LISKA, B.J., LONGLOIS, B.E., MOSTERT, G.C. and STEMP, A.R. (1965). Persistence of chlorinated hydrocarbon insecticide residues in chicken tissues and eggs. *Poultry Science*, **44**, 435–437

STEGGERDA, M. and HOLLANDER, W.F. (1944). Observations on certain shell variations of hen's eggs. *Poultry Science*, **23**, 458–463

STEPHENS, J.F. and BARNETT, B.D. (1970). Effects of continuous feeding of Amprolium on performance of laying hens. *Poultry Science*, **49**, 205–207

STEPHENS, J.F., BARNETT, B.D. and BUTTERS, H.E. (1967). Effect of Buquinolate on growth and egg production of White Leghorn pullets. *Poultry Science*, **46**, 203–206

STOUT, J.T. and BUSS, E.G. (1980). Influence of the interval of shell deposition on eggshell quality. *Poultry Science*, **59**, 168–171

SUPPERER, R. and KUTZER, E. (1981). Tolerance of Mebendazole, Febendazole, Thiabendazole, Cambendazole and Fenbantel regarding egg laying capacity, egg quality, fertility and hatch rate of quails. *Berliner und Münchener Tierärztliche Wochenschrift*, **94**, 211–215

SWANSON, M.H., WAIBEL, P.E., HELBACKA, N.V. and JOHNSON, E.L. (1956). Shell egg quality as affected by Arasan in the diet. *Poultry Science*, **35**, 92–95

TAYLOR, L.W., GUNNS, C.A., GRAU, C.R. and LEPKOVSKY, S. (1953). Effect of a respiratory disease on reproduction. *Poultry Science*, **32**, 129–137

TIMMS, L. (1972). The effects of Infectious Bronchitis superimposed on latent *Mycoplasma gallisepticum* infection in adult chickens. *Veterinary Record,* **91**, 185–190

TULLETT, S.G., BOARD, R.G., LOVE, G., PERROTT, H.R. and SCOTT, V.D. (1976). Vaterite deposition during eggshell formation in the cormorant, gannet and shag, and in 'shell-less'' eggs of the domestic fowl. *Acta Zoologica (Stockholm),* **57**, 79–87

VAN ECK, J.H.H., DAVELAAR, F.G., VAN DEN HEUVEL-PLESMAN, T.A.M., VAN ROL, N., KOUWENHOVEN, B. and GULDIE, F.H.M. (1976). Dropped egg production, soft-shelled and shell-less eggs associated with the appearance of precipitins to adenovirus in flocks of laying fowls. *Avian Pathology,* **5**, 261–271

VAN WAGENEN, A. and WILGUS, H.S. (1934). Observations on the relation of the percentage of the different layers of egg albumen to observed interior egg quality. *US Egg and Poultry Magazine,* **40**, 37

VIELITZ, E. (1976). Poultry diseases and egg quality. *Poultry International,* **15**, 50–56

WESLEY, R.L., STEMP, A.R., LISKA, B.J. and STADELMAN, W.J. (1966). Depletion of DDT from commercial layers. *Poultry Science,* **45**, 321–324

WHITEHEAD, C.C., DOWNIE, J.N. and PHILLIPS, J.A. (1972). BHC not found to reduce the shell quality of hen's eggs. *Nature,* **239**, 411–412

WHITEHEAD, C.C., DOWNING, A.G. and PETTIGREW, R. (1972). The effect of lindane on laying hens. *British Poultry Science,* **13**, 293–299

WILHELM, L.A. (1940). Some factors affecting variation in egg shell quality. *Poultry Science,* **19**, 246–253

WINTERFIELD, R.W., FADLY, A.M. and GALLINA, A.M. (1973). Adenovirus infection and disease. I. Some characteristics of an isolate from chickens in Indiana. *Avian Diseases,* **17**, 334–353

WYBURN, G.M., JOHNSTON, H.S., DRAPER, M.H. and DAVIDSON, M.F. (1970). The fine structure of the infundibulum and magnum of the oviduct of *Gallus domesticus. Quarterly Journal of Experimental Physiology,* **55**, 213–232

Chapter 17

Effect of egg handling on egg quality

A. Oosterwoud

Introduction

Egg handling is the total treatment eggs must endure on the way from the laying unit to the consumer. Without giving a definition of quality, eggs have to meet certain quality standards. It is generally accepted in the egg business that the shell should be intact and clean. Consumers will generally ask for fresh eggs. In terms of quality this means that the egg contents must be very much like those of a newly laid egg. It would be a mistake however to suppose that newly laid eggs necessarily have the best interior quality. Peelability, for instance, is a problem with new laid eggs and consumers who have never eaten a real fresh egg will complain about the structure of the white when it has been boiled. Nevertheless, the egg contents have to meet certain quality standards.

When an egg is being laid it is intact and clean. Only environmental insults can cause damage to the shell. It is only after oviposition that the shell can get soiled. Problems of egg shell damage and soilage are well known to egg producers. Research on these problems will be discussed.

Once eggs enter atmospheric conditions, changes occur to the shell contents. The air cell forms due to a decrease in temperature and it enlarges by the evaporation of water through the pores in the shell. Carbon dioxide escapes from the albumen causing an increase in pH. At the same time the quantity of firm albumen decreases and there is an increase in thin albumen. Storage conditions can affect the changes described here and will be discussed. Long-term storage may cause special problems, like mould growth and changes in flavour. Indications will be given of how to reduce these effects.

Though oiling eggs is not forbidden in EEC countries, it is not useful since washing is not allowed. Egg washing is concerned with sanitation of the egg shell; oiling has an effect on the maintenance of certain characteristics of the egg contents. Attention will be paid to this subject.

Egg handling may obviously cause changes in egg characteristics. Part of this chapter will cover the relationship between egg characteristics and consumer attitudes.

Egg shell damage

Two fundamental reasons are obvious for the occurrence of egg shell damage:

(1) the egg shell strength is insufficient;
(2) eggs are exposed to impacts that even damage strong shells.

This gives two possibilities for reducing egg damage:

(1) improving the egg shell strength;
(2) decreasing the number and/or the force of the impacts.

Several egg shell strength characteristics have proved to be inheritable, so by selection on these criteria egg shell strength might be improved. A limitation to this selection is caused by the negative genetic correlation between egg shell strength and productivity. There is another reason why genetic selection on laboratory assessments of egg shell strength will be less successful than might be expected. Correlation coefficients between certain laboratory assessments of egg shell strength and the occurrence of cracked eggs are low. Wells (1967) found correlations between egg specific gravity and egg shell deformation versus percentage cracks varying from 0.32 to 0.53. This means that of the variation in percentage cracks only between 10.2% and 28.1% can be explained by the variation in the egg shell strength parameter. A similar conclusion was drawn by Shrimpton and Hann (1968) for the predictive value of shell deformation. Nevertheless, a certain amount of selection on egg shell strength will remain necessary in order to prevent an unacceptable increase in variability. Suggestions have been made to select on shell strength criteria based on egg shell structure but no such criteria are available at present.

Positive effects of nutrition and lighting regimens on shell quality measurements have been demonstrated recently, but it is not to be expected that the solution of the egg shell damage problem will come from this area.

The egg shell damage problem has become more apparent since hens were kept in battery cages. In the traditional deep litter houses a number of cracked eggs disappeared in the litter or they were eaten by the hens. An investigation on crack incidence was undertaken by Anderson, Carter and Morley Jones (1970a) at a time of expansion in the use of battery cages. The investigation was carried out during the period 1960–1968. In this period, the proportion of eggs produced in the cage husbandry system increased from 17.1% to 82.1%, while the incidence of downgraded eggs delivered to packing stations rose from 4.66% to 6.12%. The authors concluded that the rise in crack incidence was not due primarily to a deterioration of shell strength, but to an increase in environmental insults. The figures were obtained from packing stations' candling results. It would have been interesting to have the corresponding data on cracked eggs removed at the production unit. Another important conclusion from this paper is that cage type and not egg production affect crack incidence. The conclusion on increased environmental insults was further supported by the fact that neither shell thickness, egg weight nor shell curvature seemed to affect crack incidence in battery cages. Leech and Knowles (1969) had already found that the proportion of defective eggs was unrelated to egg shell deformation.

These papers and others should have indicated to battery cage manufacturers that their products were a major cause of egg shell damage. Battery cages are the first stage in egg handling. Enquires in Holland have shown that battery cages last between 10 and 15 years, or even longer in areas with a less humid climate. Once fitted in a poultry house it is difficult and expensive to change them. When new cages are to be bought the price is a very important factor. Though cage manufacturers are generally aware of the results of research on battery cages, they have to put more emphasis on keeping the price of their cages within the acceptable range than on reducing egg shell damage by changing the construction according to the latest findings.

Research on the relationship between cage construction and egg shell damage will reveal which construction factors affect egg shell damage. There is no good reason to expect that only single factor effects will be found. In the case of interactions of several factors, an optimising process will be necessary. In the ideal situation, when all effects of construction variables are known, it should be possible to predict the incidence of cracked eggs at the design stage.

A classical paper on battery cage research was that by Blount (1951). High percentages of cracked eggs were attributed to the thickness of the wire floors, which would not 'give' under the weight of the birds using them. A possible relationship between egg shell damage and laying behaviour (facing inwards or facing outwards) which caused a variation in the dropping distance to the floor was noted. A comparison between two types of battery cage floors was made by Elson (1968). Use of a rectangular welded wire floor resulted in 6.3% eggs with cracks and haircracks. For a wire netting floor the figure was 3.6%.

A very fundamental approach to the problem of egg shell cracking on the battery cage floor was taken by Anderson, Carter and Morley Jones (1970b). They introduced the concept of the 'effective mass' of the cage floor. This seems to be the most important factor affecting egg shell damage in the battery cage. Besides the floor's effective mass, 10 other variables were investigated and their effects were described. The paper gives much information and some advice that can be helpful in designing cage floors. The size of today's egg shell damage problem makes it evident that too little of this information has been used by cage designers.

A lot of work on the relationship between cage floor design and egg shell breakage has been reported in the annual reports of the Gleadthorpe Experimental Husbandry Farm in England*. Several combinations of welded wire and wire netting with different slopes were investigated. Suggestions from these investigations form the basis of recommendations by Elson (1980) for a cage floor which provides optimal conditions in the prevention of cracked and dirty eggs. Such a cage floor:

(1) is flexible in the area where the eggs are laid—to minimise shell damage on impact;
(2) allows eggs to pass rapidly from the cage to the collection cradle—to minimise damage and soiling by the birds;
(3) slows down eggs before they collide with each other in the collecting cradle—to reduce impact damage.

He also noted that such an ideal combination is hard to achieve in practice.

The actual situation concerning egg shell damage in Holland was studied by Aerts (1979). On 54 farms eggs from 67 flocks of hens were sampled. Each sample containing 600 to 900 eggs, depending on the number of cage tiers, was hand candled. It was found that egg shell damage ranged from 4.9–29.2%/flock, with an average of 13%. Part of this variation must be attributed to differences in age of the

*Meden Vale, Mansfield, Nottinghamshire.

flocks, but the high total variability indicates the necessity for further research on cage construction.

A completely factorial experiment on the effect of wire thickness, slope and mesh size in welded wire battery cage floors was reported by Oosterwoud (1981). A commercial three-tier stair-step battery system was used in the experiment. It was concluded that: (i) thin wire (2.05 mm) is preferable to thick wire (2.45 mm); (ii) a floor slope of 7° is preferable to one of 9° or 11°; and (iii) an increasing mesh size is compatible with a decreasing incidence of cracked eggs. A number of the combinations, however, proved to be unfit for practical use. The combination of the 2.05 mm thick wire with a 25 × 75 mm mesh size suffered from an unacceptable number of wire breaks, although the percentage of cracked eggs in this combination was the lowest found in the experiment. Other variables investigated in this experiment were: (i) wire coating; (ii) partitions between the cages made of welded wire mesh or galvanized plate; (iii) the number of hens per cage (5 vs 6); and (iv) the type of hen (SC White Leghorn vs medium-heavy brown layers). The experimental design was such that the effects of these variables could be calculated but tests for statistical significance could not be made.

An epoxy coating on the floor wires increased cracked eggs from 9.25% to 12.77%, as would be expected on the basis of effective floor mass. Welded wire partitions gave a reduction from 8.77% to 7.29% in cracked eggs. Six hens/cage instead of five reduced the cracks from 8.16% to 7.89%. The brown layers produced 6.28% cracked eggs compared to 8.16% produced by the SC White Leghorn. The lower incidence of cracks in the case of the welded wire partitions can be explained by the different methods of cage floor suspension. With the solid partitions, the floors were hanging on two plastic clips. All the vertical wires of the welded wire partitions were bent upwards so the back-to-front wire under each partition was supported eight times. This may have given a better distribution of forces causing fewer areas with a high effective floor mass.

A subsequent experiment has been partly reported by Oosterwoud (1985). In this experiment seven variables were included:

(1) type of battery (manure belt vs stair-step);
(2) slope of floor (7° vs 9°);
(3) mesh size of the floor (25 × 38 mm vs 25 × 50 mm);
(4) wire thickness (2.05 mm vs 2.45 mm);
(5) stocking density (4 vs 5 hens/cage);
(6) wire coating on the 2.05 mm wire within the manure belt system only (galvinised vs plastic);
(7) floor suspension (2 plastic clips vs 8 metal clips).

The experimental design permitted a test for significance of all main effects and interaction effects up to the three factor interactions. Results for a six-month laying period after forced moulting have been reported. Conclusions of the previous experiment were confirmed and it is notable that within the set of variables investigated in this experiment relative reductions in egg shell damage of up to 18.5% were achieved. This shows that there is great potential for reducing egg shell damage in cages. Further investigations will be necessary to find the optimal combination of factors and it may prove to be desirable to include other construction variables.

From literature cited already, it is known that a lot of damage occurs in the egg collection 'cradle' (Anderson, Carter and Morley Jones, 1970a). Elson (1975) states that on welded wire floors two-thirds of the cracks occur in the collecting area. Reducing the slope of the cage floor and placing a strip of foam plastic across the egg stop have been found to be effective in reducing egg shell damagae. Cage designers have chosen for solutions such measures as rounding the corner between the collecting area and the egg stop, and covering the edge of the egg stop with a plastic strip having a soft ridge to cushion the impact of the egg. No more recent data on the occurrence of damage in the cradle are available.

It is hard to find figures on damage caused by egg collection and farm packing. However, these aspects of egg handling should not normally cause serious problems since the equipment is permanently accessible for adjustment and repair. Raising the frequency of egg collection will undoubtedly be helpful to reduce egg cracking on the conveyor belt in the egg cradle. Elevators need frequent attention; if they are not well adjusted they can cause many cracked shells. Good control of the 'egg stream' to the packer is necessary in order to prevent the eggs piling up, especially where two conveyor belts meet or when the eggs have to pass through a narrow gate.

Egg transport on trays or in retail packs is not considered by the author to be an important source of egg shell damage. Unpublished data from research sponsored by manufacturers of egg packing materials have shown that with proper packaging less than 1% of the eggs will suffer some minor damage, like a haircrack or a star crack.

Dirty shells

Under EEC marketing regulations Class A eggs should have a clean shell and should not have been cleaned. Therefore, soiled and washed eggs have to be downgraded.

Very little research has been reported on the avoidance of dirty shells. In the two investigations by Oosterwoud (1981, 1985) the incidence of egg soiling was the other criterion investigated besides egg shell cracking. In the second experiment, the main effects of floor slope and stocking density were significant. The least dirty eggs were produced on the floors with the steepest slope (9°). The proportion of dirty eggs was reduced at the lower stocking density.

The effects of slope on egg soilage are opposite to those on egg breakage, so increasing the slope to avoid egg soilage will not provide a satisfactory solution. Decreasing the density from five to four hens/cage has unacceptable economic consequences.

Welded wire floors of larger mesh tended to give less shell soilage in these experiments and in other as yet unreported investigations with force-moulted birds. This factor might be used to diminish the soiled egg problem since it affects egg breakage in the same direction. Limits to increasing mesh size are set by material strength and animal welfare considerations.

General measures to avoid unnecessary dirt on the eggs are to: (i) keep the house free from dust; (ii) remove 'cracks' and 'leakers' before the eggs enter elevators to bring them on one level; (iii) clean collecting mechanisms immediately after an egg has broken. These measures, however, have to do with management rather than with egg handling.

Depending on economic considerations, it might be worthwhile to consider the introduction of egg washing in EEC countries as a solution to a major part of the dirty shell problem.

Egg storage

Egg storage is an essential aspect of egg handling. The main goal is to preserve important egg quality characteristics. Since there is now year-round egg production, long-term storage, to keep egg quality at a level acceptable for table eggs, is no longer as essential as it was. Hinton (1968) states 'an egg deteriorates from the moment it is laid'. This statement assumes that all aspects of quality are optimal at the moment of oviposition. This is true from the shelf-life stand-point, but with respect to a generally accepted definition of quality the statement has to be rejected. The definition of quality by Amarine, Pangborn and Roessler (1965) is: 'The composite of the characteristics that differentiate among individual units of the product and have significance in determining the degree of acceptability of that unit by the user'. It is generally known that the peelability of new laid eggs is a problem. Much research is done nowadays to overcome the problem of hard peeling of fresh eggs. For the industrial production of hard-boiled and peeled eggs the quality is improving from the moment they are laid and it reaches its optimal level within a few days.

An egg is clearly subject to changes from the moment it is laid. Some changes have a positive effect, others are considered to be negative. The changes in eggs during storage have been described fully by Hinton (1968). They will be summarised briefly.

Eggs lose weight due to water evaporation from the albumen. As long as the relative humidity (RH) in the atmosphere around the eggs is less than 99.6% water evaporates through the shell pores. The rate of evaporation increases linearly with the difference in RH inside and outside of the egg. It can be described in the equation:

$$L = P\,(1 - R)$$

where L is the loss in weight, P the permeability of the shell and R is the atmospheric RH. This formula holds for a single egg fully surrounded by an atmosphere with a certain RH. In a pile of packed eggs other conditions occur depending on the rate of ventilation through the pile. Piles of eggs usually are not well ventilated in the centre. This is the reason why in the centre the RH reaches equilibrium with the interior of the egg. At that point an atmosphere has arisen with a RH of about 99% and weight loss has been reduced to zero. Under these conditions mould growth often occurs, as described by Hinton (1968). When eggs have to be stored for periods longer than one week care should be taken that nowhere in the pile does the local RH exceed 85%. This can be achieved by proper stacking and proper ventilation. A rule of thumb is that under correct conditions eggs lose about 1% of their weight each week. Proper storage means that some loss in weight must be allowed. Weight losses can be restricted by oiling the shell, which decreases the permeability of the shell by closing the pores.

Due to the loss in weight the air cell size increases. Air cell size is often interpreted as an indicator of the age of the egg. This is only valid when the ambient RH and temperature are known.

In the first stage of storage eggs lose carbon dioxide. Carbon dioxide has dissolved in the albumen during shell calcification. Dissolved carbon dioxide causes 'cloudy white' which is a characteristic of a newly laid egg. Due to the low content of carbon dioxide in the atmosphere eggs lose it in a few days. This phenomenon gives rise to an increase in pH of the white.

Aging of eggs causes a reduction in the amount of thick albumen with its conversion into thin albumen. Since this is a chemical process its progress depends on temperature. The lower the temperature the slower the conversion of thick albumen proceeds. Storage temperatures should not be lower than $-2\,°C$ in order to prevent freezing of the albumen which will crack the egg shell. EEC regulations prohibit storage below $8\,°C$ in artificially refrigerated rooms for Class A eggs.

Storage temperature should be adjusted carefully to the ambient temperature and RH. Immediately the surface temperature of an egg is below the dewpoint of the air around it, water vapour will condense on the shell. This phenomenon of water condensation on the shell is called 'sweating' and should be prevented as it is very harmful. Since an egg is never sterile microorganisms will start to develop in the moist environment. They will gain access through the pores and continue to grow on the membranes. When microbial growth reaches the yolk the egg will spoil.

The yolk absorbs water due to osmotic activity during storage. At the same time the strength of the vitelline membrane decreases. These factors are responsible for the difference in appearance between yolks from fresh and those from stored eggs. When eggs that have been stored for a long period are hard-boiled the surface of the yolk will have a greenish colour. This is caused by the chemical interaction between iron present in the yolk and sulphur coming from decomposition in the albumen.

Hinton (1968) advised against storing washed eggs because of the removal of the cuticle. This is undoubtedly true for eggs that have been dry cleaned with abrasive material. However, Simons and Wiertz (1966) have shown that proper wet cleaning does not remove the cuticle. It is the author's opinion that wet cleaning and proper sanition of the eggs might improve their shelf-life when stored. Remembering the difficulty of the control of RH in a pile of egg cartons, the removal of dirt and reduction in the number of microorganisms might be an alternative measure against mould growth. Particularly for eggs which are to be transported over long distances, sometimes experiencing unexpectedly long storage times, washing and sanitising should be allowed. In these circumstances oiling could be useful as well. Cooling eggs as soon as possible from the temperature at oviposition to the storage temperature is advantageous for the maintenance of the firmness of the white (Van Tijen, 1965).

Most eggs nowadays are subjected to short-term storage only. They are usually in the retail stores within a week of being laid. Eggs can, however, lose many of their original characteristics in a week. Proper handling, storage included, is necessary to keep the consumers satisfied.

Consumer attitudes towards eggs

The definition of quality by Amarine, Pangborn and Roessler (1965) has been quoted already. In this definition the user of a product decides which characteristics of that product have significance in determining the degree of acceptability.

Doubts have arisen concerning quality characteristics of eggs, particularly whether those used relate to egg consumers' opinions. Wells (1968) with respect to internal quality states: 'It is generally assumed that consumers prefer for table use, especially for frying and poaching, an egg in which the albumen holds together well'. It is an assumption. In the same paper Wells also states: 'This in principle is a commendable feature of Haugh units as Van Wagenen and Wilgus when preparing their chart attempted to record the internal quality of the egg as it appeared to the consumer. However, it should be noted that there is no evidence that the photographs of the Van Wagenen chart were chosen as the result of reliable consumer research. It appears that they merely represent the opinions of scientists on the matter'.

It has been a standard procedure in marketing technology to establish quality characteristics without asking consumers for their opinions. In many cases consumers have accepted the criteria set for them. Many of the quality regulations have the goal of preventing the practice of false competition by food traders, or in other words, promoting honest trading. In this way consumers have some benefit from the regulations.

In the modern world every food has its own place and function (or functions) amongst all the foods available. That place and function has been given it by the consumers because they have buying habits based on opinions. If a goal of the egg industry is to expand egg consumption, it must be interested in consumer opinions about eggs.

It is well known that different consumers can have different attitudes towards quality criteria. Eggs of class A quality are supposed to be clean. Nevertheless, there is a tendency in Holland for people to buy their eggs on the poultry farm. Many of these people do not object to eggs with dirty shells. When filling cartons with free range eggs farmers often add some dirt (straw, feathers) purposely!

Reasons for buying eggs can differ on many grounds. Unfortunately, the egg industry appears to lack information on consumer attitudes towards eggs that could be helpful in attempts to increase egg consumption. More research in this field is needed and it may lead to new egg quality criteria.

References

AERTS, F.P.W. (1979). Eischaalbeschadigingen bij kippen op batterijen. Report No. 3279, Spelderholt Institute for Poultry Research, Beekbergen, The Netherlands
AMARINE, A.M., PANGBORN, R.M. and ROESSLER, E.B. (1965). *Principles of Sensory Evaluation of Food.* New York and London, Academic Press
ANDERSON, G.B., CARTER, T.C. and MORLEY JONES, R. (1970a). Some factors affecting the incidence of cracks in hen's egg shells. *British Poultry Science,* **11**, 103–116
ANDERSON, G.B., CARTER, T.C. and MORLEY JONES, R. (1970b). Some factors affecting dynamic fracture of egg shells in battery cages. In *Factors Affecting Egg Grading,* (Freeman, B.M. and Gordon, R.F., eds), pp. 53–69. Edinburgh, Oliver and Boyd
BLOUNT, W.P. (1951). *Hen Batteries.* London, Baillière Tindall and Cox
ELSON, H.A. (1968). Management factors affecting shell quality. *Agriculture, London,* **75**, 22–26
ELSON, H.A. (1975). Is your cage-floor raising seconds? *Poultry Industry,* **39** (October), 16
ELSON, H.A. (1980). Egg shell damage in cages. *Gleadthorpe Experimental Husbandry Farm Poultry Booklet,* No. 7, 41–45
HINTON, H.R. (1968). Storage of eggs. In *Egg Quality. A Study of the Hen's Egg,* (Carter, T.C., ed.), pp. 251–261. Edinburgh, Oliver and Boyd
LEECH, F.B. and KNOWLES, N.R. (1969). An investigation on commercial farms of factors thought to contribute to egg cracking. *British Poultry Science,* **10**, 139–147

OOSTERWOUD, A. (1981). Onderzoek naar de brewk van eieren op batterijkooien. Report No. 340. Spelderholt Institute for Poultry Research, Beekbergen, The Netherlands

OOSTERWOUD, A. (1985). Egg shell damage and battery cage construction. *Poultry (Misset)*, **1** (January), 30–33

SHRIMPTON, D.H. and HANN, C.M. (1968). An investigation into the value of measurements of egg shell deformation in predicting breakage due to transport and handling. *Experimental Husbandry*, **17**, 29–35

SIMONS, P.C.M. and WIERTZ, G. (1966). The ultrastructure of the surface of the cuticle of the hen's egg in relation to egg cleaning. *Poultry Science*, **45**, 1153–1162

VAN TIJEN, W.F. (1965). Het afkoelen van eieren op keyes en in draadmanden in verband met het behoud van de inwendige kwaliteit. *Veetelt- en Zuivelberichten*, **8**, 81–85

WELLS, R.G. (1967). Egg shell strength 2. The relationship between egg specific gravity and egg shell deformation and their reliability as indicators of shell strength. *British Poultry Science*, **8**, 193–199

WELLS, R.G. (1968). The measurement of certain egg quality characteristics: a review. In *Egg Quality. A study of the hen's egg*, (Carter, T.C., ed.), pp. 207–250. Edinburgh, Oliver and Boyd

Chapter 18

Poster papers

The following papers were presented by poster at the 20th Poultry Science Symposium.

How does dietary fat increase egg size?
A. Bowman, H. Griffin, C. Whitehead, and Margaret Perry
AFRC Poultry Research Centre, Roslin, Midlothian, Scotland.

Modeling the relationship of egg weight, specific gravity, shell weight, shell calcium and shell thickness
H.M. Edwards, Jr. and S. Sooncharernying
Department of Poultry Science, University of Georgia, Athens, Georgia 30602, USA.

Abnormal superficial coatings of eggs and their relationship to stress and disturbance in laying hens
A.B. Gilbert and B.O. Hughes
AFRC Poultry Research Centre, Roslin, Midlothian, Scotland.

Hygiene and egg quality
S. Matthes
Institute of Poultry and Small Animals, Section Hygiene and Diseases, D 3100 Celle, Dornbergstr. 25/27, Federal Republic of Germany.

The relationship between age, shell quality and individual rate and duration of shell formation in domestic hens
Y. Nys
INRA, Nouzilly 37380, France.

The relationship between laboratory measurements of egg shell quality and the percentage of cracked eggs; and breakage from farm to egg packing stations during transport
Lisbeth Ott-Ebbesen
National Institute of Animal Science, Rolighedsvez 25, DK-1958 Frederiksberg C, Denmark.

Influence of the cage floor on the frequency of cracked eggs

Susanne Therkildsen

National Institute of Animal Science, Rolighedsvez 25, DK-1958 Frederiksberg C, Denmark.

Index